D1161490

The Working Class in American History

Editorial Advisors
David Brody
Alice Kessler-Harris
David Montgomery
Sean Wilentz

*A list of books in the series
appears at the end of this volume.*

The Spirit of 1848

The Spirit of 1848

German Immigrants, Labor Conflict, and the Coming of the Civil War

Bruce Levine

University of Illinois Press

Urbana and Chicago

Publication of this book was supported in part by grants from the University of Cincinnati's Charles Phelps Taft Memorial Fund, the Division of Graduate Studies and Research, and the McMicken College of Arts and Sciences.

© 1992 by the Board of Trustees of the University of Illinois
Manufactured in the United States of America
C 5 4 3 2 1

This book is printed on acid-free paper.

Library of Congress Cataloging-in-Publication Data

Levine, Bruce C., 1949–
    The spirit of 1848: German immigrants, labor conflict, and the coming of the Civil War/Bruce Levine.
        p.   cm. — (The Working class in American history)
    Includes bibliographical references and index.
    ISBN 0-252-01873-7
    1. German Americans—History—19th century. 2. Working class—
United States—History—19th century. 3. United States—
History—1849–1877. 4. United States—History—Civil War,
1861–1865—Social aspects. 5. United States—History—Civil War,
1861–1865—German Americans. I. Title. II. Series.
E184.G3L5   1992
973'.0431—dc20   91-31512
                                                                         CIP

LIBRARY
ALMA COLLEGE
ALMA, MICHIGAN

To Seymour and Harriet Levine
with love and gratitude

Contents

Preface   xi

Introduction: "Either Social or Political Refugees"   1

PART I   FLEEING THE OLD WORLD

1. "So Deeply Interwoven": General Crisis and
   Emigration   15

2. "Social Freedom and Independent Existence": Labor
   and Revolution   35

PART II   ADJUSTING TO THE NEW

3. "Where Nobody Need Be Poor": Immigrants and
   Industry in America   53

4. "The Love of Liberty Is Almost a Religion": Political
   Unity and Dissension   83

5. "It Is Time to Fight Again": The Organizations of
   Labor   111

PART III   SLAVERY AND THE PEOPLE'S LAND

Introduction: The Challenge of Kansas-Nebraska   149

6. The Response in the East   159

7. The Response in the West   181

PART IV "THE SECOND FIGHT FOR FREEDOM"

8. "The Content of Freedom": Germans, Republicans, and Democrats   213

9. "The Spirit of 1848": Nationality, Class, and the Fight for Votes   233

10. "When Poor Men's Sons Must Sacrifice": The War and Beyond   257

Appendix   273

Notes   277

Selected Bibliography: Primary Sources   349

Index   357

Preface

This study of immigration, class formation, and politics in the Civil War era reflects three general interests that have engaged me since my undergraduate and graduate studies in the late 1960s and early 1970s—the transition from precapitalist to capitalist forms of social organization; the multiclass democratic revolutions that have often accompanied this transition; and the relationship between class and ethnicity. I have thus lived with this subject for quite a while, so any acknowledgment of the debts accumulated along the way tends to shade into autobiography.

I first grappled with many of the historical issues involved in industrialization in an undergraduate honors course at the University of Michigan led by Frederick D. Marquardt. About ten years later I was fortunate to reestablish contact with Fred (now at Syracuse University), and he has since then generously shared with me his knowledge and insight regarding pre-1848 ("*Vormärz*") German social history. In graduate school at the University of Rochester, an extremely intensive and intellectually exhilarating seminar on "The Rise and Development of World Capitalism" led by Eugene D. Genovese, Harry Harootunian, and the late Sanford Elwitt deeply influenced the way I have come to view many of the large themes broached in the present work.

These themes inspired my doctoral work, which was supervised by the late Herbert G. Gutman. When Herb moved to the City University of New York, Professor Stanley Engerman supervised the dissertation's completion; Marvin Becker and Mary Young prodded me to make a number of signal improvements. Stan Engerman is in many ways a model of what we all aspire to be—a learned, hard-working, committed, scrupulously honest scholar who generously aids colleagues regardless of his intellectual differences with them. Over the course of many years he has meticulously scrutinized successive drafts of this manuscript, guided me to valuable data, gently pointed out errors of commission and omission, and shrewdly counseled me about how best to present views that often diverged from his own.

In 1981 Herb Gutman brought me onto the American Social History Project as its director of research and writing. Then based at the Graduate Center of CUNY, the project set itself a major task—resynthesizing the history of American working people and presenting it in a popularly accessible form. One fruit of that effort is *Who Built America?: Working People in the Nation's Politics, Economy, Culture and Society*, the first volume of which appeared in 1990. My long and intensive involvement with that project and book necessarily protracted preparation of the present work. But it also substantially broadened my knowledge of the monographic and journal literature in American social history generally and deepened my understanding of the specific era in which the present study is set. At the same time, it put me into a close, day-to-day working relationship with a wonderful team of colleagues and friends. Especially supportive were Joshua Brown, Stephen Brier, Kate Pfordresher, and Michael Hyman, who encouraged me to find time for my own research and patiently read and criticized numberless drafts of research papers, articles, and manuscript chapters. Of course, working closely with Herb Gutman again between 1981 until his premature death four years later was the greatest gift of all. He was my teacher, collaborator, friend, and godfather. I owe him so much, and I still miss him terribly.

Since the fall of 1986 I have been teaching at the University of Cincinnati. Members and successive heads of the history department have been unfailingly supportive of my research and writing, as has the college administration. I have also been fortunate in working with a group of bright and talented German-born graduate students (Sigrid Adickes, Nina Mijagkij, Mathias Dreissig, Thomas Winter, and Michael Blum) who checked—and often corrected—my translations of nineteenth-century German-language materials. In 1988 a grant from the University Research Council supported a summer spent commuting back and forth from word processor to library. Subventions from the university's Charles Phelps Taft Memorial Fund, the McMicken College of Arts and Sciences, and the Division of Graduate Studies and Research facilitated publication of the final manuscript.

In addition to those already mentioned, a number of colleagues have generously read all or part of the present manuscript: David Montgomery, Sean Wilentz, Eric Foner, Fernando Fasce, Matteo Sanfilippo, Geoffrey Eley, Jean Quataert, Frederick C. Luebke, James M. Bergquist, Walter Kamphoefner, Roger Daniels, Jonathan Sperber, Nora Faires, Ira Katznelson, Jörg Nagler, Michael F. Holt, and Roger Ransom. Each has offered thoughtful suggestions for improvement. I have incorporated as many of them as I could without turning this book into even more of a life's work than it has already become. Still others (such as Horst Groschopp, Dieter Langewiesche, Hans-Arthur Marsiske, and Dieter Plehwe) have helped me obtain materials from Germany or (such as Hartmut Keil, Iver Bernstein, John Jentz, David W. Galenson, Jörg Nagler, and Nora Faires) allowed me to read their unpublished article and book manuscripts. Wolfgang Köllmann, Peter Marschalck, and Harvard University's Charles Warren Center for Studies in American History graciously granted permission to reproduce a map that originally appeared in the 1973 issue of *Perspectives in American History*.

The staffs of numerous libraries have contributed greatly to this book, including the New York Public Library (both the research branch at Fifth Avenue and Forty-second Street and the Annex), the Tamiment Institute, the Columbia University Library, the library at the CUNY Graduate Center, the Newark Public Library, the State Library of Pennsylvania, the Historical Society of Pennsylvania, the Historical Society of Western Pennsylvania, the National Archives (Legislative Division), the University of Chicago Library, the Chicago Historical Society, the Illinois State Archives, the State Historical Society of Wisconsin, the Iowa State Historical Department, the State Library of Ohio, the Ohio Historical Society, the Cincinnati Historical Society, and the Cincinnati Public Library. I have incurred my greatest such debts at the University of Cincinnati library system—notably to its superb and endlessly helpful bibliographer Sally Moffitt; to the German-American collection and its organizer and curator Don Heinrich Tolzmann (a historian in his own right); and especially to the good-humored, tireless, indefatigable, but too often anonymous staff of its interlibrary loan department—department head Dan Gottlieb as well as Michael Bramel, Christine Brunkala, Linda Gromen, Elizabeth Hamilton, Carole Mosher, Iqbal Nahwaz, Kathy Scardina, Diana Schmidt, and Tom White. I have wondered more than once whether their names belonged on the title page of this book rather than in the acknowledgments.

My relationship with the University of Illinois Press has been a pleasure. Over the many years since we first signed our contract, Richard Wentworth, director of the press and my editor, has managed to remain both patient and encouraging. Karen Hewitt and Theresa L. Sears have cheerfully and deftly piloted both manuscript and author through many twists and turns in the publication procedure and past numerous potential hazards that lurked along the way. The diligence, patience, and good humor of my copy editor, Beth Bower, has been a blessing.

This book is dedicated to my parents, Seymour and Harriet Levine, in partial compensation for so many years of moral and material support.

Though none of the individuals named above bears any responsibility for what follows, all deserve a share of the credit for whatever is of value here. To them—and to the many other friends and colleagues whose names I have failed to mention here—my deepest thanks.

Introduction

"Either Social or Political Refugees"

The present work explores relationships among international migration and class formation during a crucial phase in the economic and political development of Europe and North America. It integrates historical themes that have commonly been treated in relative isolation from one another. Studies of immigration or ethnicity, for example, have tended to focus rather tightly on the special problems and achievements of subgroups within society—or on those moving from one society to another. That preoccupation is both understandable and useful; it directs our attention toward a significant aspect of historical experience, one that is especially important in the United States. Oscar Handlin told us forty years ago, indeed, that "the immigrants *were* American history." And British historian M. A. Jones added almost a decade later that "immigration, which was America's historic *raison d'être*, has been the most persistent and the most pervasive influence in her development."[1]

But a focus on the immigrants alone is too narrow. It obscures the larger historical processes that uprooted them and helped decide their destination, that shaped the ways in which they affected, and were affected by, life in their new homeland. Broadening the inquiry to include these processes helps clarify the nature and significance of the immigrants' experience. Thus Jones emphasized "that immigrants were an integral part of an organic whole. Nothing they did in America had any meaning save in the larger context of the life of the nation." John Higham, too, urged us to reexamine immigration in the context of the evolving "structure of American society," specifying the need "to work out . . . the interrelationships between classes and ethnic groups."[2]

These strictures are particularly relevant to the study of immigrants in the antebellum United States. National development reached a decisive turning point during the two decades between 1840 and 1860 in economic, demographic, and political terms.

First, commercial and industrial development accelerated sharply. This was a pivotal period in the processes of industrialization and working-class formation. According to one rough estimate, fewer than a fifth of the nation's free labor force in Thomas Jefferson's day worked for wages, but by the time of Abraham Lincoln's election in 1860, more than one-half did.[3]

Second, immigration rose to unprecedented levels. Between 1840 and 1860, more than four million people entered the United States. This official statistic (which likely understates the reality) was equal to about 30 percent of the total free population of the nation in 1840. In proportional terms, this influx of immigrants was the largest in the nation's entire history. Almost three-quarters of the newcomers came from Ireland or the German states, and most settled in the nation's towns and cities. By 1860 the foreign-born accounted for upwards of half the population of Chicago, St. Louis, Milwaukee, and San Francisco; at least 40 percent of the residents of New York, Cincinnati, Buffalo, Cleveland, and Detroit; and imposing minorities in nearly all other major population centers. (These calculations, moreover, still exclude native Americans born of immigrant parents.)[4]

Third, the antebellum period's mounting struggle over the future of slavery was central to the reorganization of political life that destroyed the Whigs, split the Democrats, and spawned the Republicans. This struggle ultimately exploded in a civil war widely considered then, and later, to be a second American Revolution.

These three developments have often been examined individually, but their interconnections have received less attention. As a result, the momentous political issues of the Civil War era have often appeared unrelated to the most important economic and social changes that were reshaping antebellum society, and with it the lives of America's common people, native-born and immigrant alike. In fact, however, these processes—industrialization, urbanization, and the formation of a class of industrial wage earners; growing and changing immigration; and the deepening conflict over the slave labor system—were tightly interwoven.

The great transatlantic migrations of the nineteenth and early twentieth centuries were in no small measure the result of commercial and industrial changes in Europe and North America. Together (as Rowland Berthoff notes) these phenomena set the "radically altered context of the nineteenth-century economic revolution." They also gave rise to a new class structure characterized by "enormously greater distinctions between rich and poor than the aristocratic society of colonial America had ever known." This, in turn, formed the economic setting in which migration and its attendant social and cultural changes occurred.[5]

Immigration provided much of the human material with which the classes of industrializing America were built. Some new arrivals entered the ranks of the nation's economic elite, and many more found positions in the professions. Most impressive of all, however, was the central place that immigrants came to occupy within the nation's developing working class. This became especially pronounced during the economic expansion following the crisis years of 1837–43. A report to the British Parliament in 1854 on the state of American manufactures noted that "German workmen are largely employed in many departments of industry." Indeed, they already composed a significant part of the work force here in some of the occupations most affected by early industrialization. Uprooted Irish cotters, meanwhile, streamed disproportionately into the swelling ranks of unskilled labor. By the end of the next decade a British consular official here was reaching more sweeping conclusions about immigration and work in North America. Mr. Francis Clay Ford noticed a "decided disinclination" among the native-born "to share in the rough toil of purely muscular labor in which the newly arrived foreigner is readier to engage." The effect on the composition of the country's labor force was already striking, and not only in the unskilled occupations. "Foreign is every day replacing native skilled labor," too, Ford reported. The U.S. affiliates of the First International returned to this pattern repeatedly, and Protestant minister Samuel Lane Loomis observed late in the 1880s that while "not every foreigner is a workingman," still, "in the cities at least, it may almost be said that every workingman is a foreigner." The international recruitment of the American wage labor force had thus reinforced class divisions with ethnic ones. Rev. Loomis worried that "our own working people are even more widely separated from the rest of society than those in England, France, and Germany, because the differences in occupation and wealth which are becoming nearly as great here as there are emphasized here as they are not there, by still greater differences in race, language, and religion."[6]

Recent scholarship confirms some of these impressions. Poring over manuscript census returns, Herbert Gutman and Ira Berlin discovered a "radical alteration [in] the composition of the American working class between 1840 and 1880." "In fact," they reported, "with a few important exceptions, after 1840 most American workers were immigrants or the children of immigrants. In every American city and in almost every American craft, the disproportionate and generally the overwhelming majority of workers had been born outside the United States or were the children of men and women who were." The implications of these facts are profound: plainly, "it is impossible to examine American working-class development between 1840 and 1880 by focusing on native white male laborers and factory workers, as so many historians have tried to do." The same strictures apply to the study of working-class ideals and values. The "roots and traditions" of immigrant-stock wage earners "did not reach back in time to John Winthrop and his Puritan City on a Hill," Gutman and Berlin noted. They led, instead, back "to the peasant and commercial farms and especially to [the] capitalist labor gangs, workshops, and factories of Europe."[7]

What specific effects did this ethnic recomposition have on the organizational and ideological development of the nation's growing wage labor force? What impact, moreover, did it have on the nation's other social classes? "What did it mean to live in new and rapidly growing urban settings in which the vast majority of wage earners were not products of the [old] mainstream culture?"[8] This book offers some answers to these important questions.

Advent of the Germans

Germans were the largest single group to enter nineteenth-century America. During the 1850s, when the antebellum German immigration reached its peak, nine out of every ten continental European immigrants hailed from the states of the later German Empire.[9] The influence and impact of German workers went far beyond their numbers as they took the initiative in the economic and political activities of the working class.

Testimony to this effect was abundant. Reporting in 1850 that "the organization of the Trades into Protective Associations proceeds unabated," Horace Greeley's *New York Daily Tribune* added, "No class of our population goes more effectively to work than our German artizans, who have held meetings nearly every evening during the past week, and have succeeded in uniting many of these trades into Unions." "In general," summed up the German-American socialist Friedrich

Sorge, secretary of the First International and a man who could wax eloquent about his fellow immigrants' shortcomings, "the Germans were the driving and progressive element in the large and small unions."[10]

Others agreed on the facts without echoing Sorge's enthusiasm. "Skilled, educated, and intellectual," reported Isabella Lucy Bird in 1856 after a visit to the Midwest, the German immigrants "constitute an influence of which the Americans themselves are afraid," not least because "the creeds which they profess are 'Socialism' and 'Universalism.'" New York City congressman Thomas R. Whitney bluntly denounced the "Red Republicans, agrarians, and infidels" pouring into the country from the Continent. "Generally workingmen and tradesmen," they were "the malcontents of the Old World, who hate monarchy, not because it is monarchy, but because it is restraint. They are such men as stood by the side of Robespierre."[11]

The Democratic Revolution

This invocation of the specter of the French Revolution was neither fortuitous nor unique. The series of revolutionary conflicts that repeatedly shook societies on both sides of the North Atlantic in this era constituted the political crucible in which the outlook of many handicraft workers was forged. Many of these revolutions shared a number of characteristics. They were based upon a broad and diverse popular coalition. They were infused with what R. R. Palmer called "a new feeling for a kind of equality, or at least a discomfort with older forms of social stratification and formal rank." And much of the force of these revolutions was directed "against the possession of government, or any public power, by any established, privileged, closed, or self-recruiting groups of men."[12]

The kinship among these various revolutions was recognized at the time by those directly involved. The heritage of seventeenth-century English revolutionaries was invoked in eighteenth-century North America. The English and, even more, the American precedents inspired writers and fighters in France. The Great French Revolution, in turn, exercised a powerful influence on the Continental events of 1830 and 1848. Carl Schurz, a youthful participant in the latter conflict, recalled that "the history of the French Revolution furnished us models in plenty that mightily excited our imagination."[13]

Scholars have often grouped these revolutions under common adjectives and labels—liberal, democratic, modernizing, middle-class, bourgeois—depending on their particular standpoints.[14] Helpful in emphasizing the revolutions' official programs or leaders, principal beneficiaries, or long-term structural impact, the use of such labels should not obscure the highly complex and contradictory internal dynamics of these revolutions. The broad popular coalitions that supported them were frequently divided by important differences concerning ultimate goals and intended results. Among those with little or no property, some of the most active and enthusiastic champions of change displayed as little love for the forces of capitalist development (or "modernism") as for the despised ancien régime. To both of these they counterposed a variety of outlooks and programs all derived, as Eric J. Hobsbawm has perceptively noted, from "a vaguely defined and contradictory social ideal, combining respect for (small) property with hostility to the rich . . . a universal and important political trend which sought to express the interests of the great mass of 'little men' who existed between the poles of the 'bourgeois' and the 'proletarian,' often perhaps nearer the latter than the former because they were, after all, mostly poor." As E. P. Thompson has shown, that ideal was undermined, transmuted, and reinvigorated by the effects of economic development. This broad sociopolitical current—which I refer to as radical democracy—played important roles in 1848 in Germany and was carried abroad by many who joined the massive German emigration of these years.[15]

The view that 1848 was a "revolution of the intellectuals" continues to influence students of that emigration, many of whom are prepared to recognize as genuine "political exiles" only those from the intelligentsia. Other emigrants are presumed to have left Germany solely for (narrowly defined) "economic" motives and so to be innocent of radical views. Marcus Lee Hansen's seminal article of 1930, "The Revolution of 1848 and the German Emigration," gave classic formulation to this perspective. Professor Hansen simply dismissed the idea "that the large German emigration of the decade of the 'fifties was in some way associated with the course and outcome of the revolutions of 1848." Observers who "saw the crowds of stolid and slow-moving peasants, labourers with calloused hands, and worried and sober artisans," he asserted, "realized that their thoughts were not dwelling on politics or revolution." Making Hansen's assumptions even more explicit, Hildegard Binder Johnson described the certifiedly "political" forty-eighter as follows: "He affected student costume or imitated the style of the romantic hero of the Revolution, Friedrich Hecker, by wearing a broad-brimmed hat, a shirt open at the neck, and a loosely tied scarf. . . . He was set off from the mass of immigrants, the peasants and the craftsmen, by delicate hands that showed no signs of physical labor."[16]

This view of the revolution, who made it, and whom it touched obscured the dramatic broadening of the social base of popular dissent and protest that had taken place in Germany since the 1830s. A general social-economic and political crisis steadily undermined the position of German small producers and wage earners, urban and rural. In this context, attempting to make a sharp distinction between political and social-economic problems (or grievances) would be a thankless task. "We are all either social or political refugees," Friedrich Kapp pointed out in 1856. "Dissatisfaction with the political or social relations of Europe led us hither [and] . . . we came here with a firm determination to hold on to our principles and to our contentions of right."[17]

That the 1848 Revolution had sprung from a combination of grievances and had mobilized broad layers of the population was once widely acknowledged, as was its significance for the immigration. At the turn of the nineteenth century, one German-American historian thus recalled that "the revolutionists . . . defeated and forced to flee from Germany" in 1849 embraced not only "hundreds of professors, poets, musicians, artists, editors and professional men" but also the "thousands [who] were simple artisans." A contemporaneous work, though preoccupied with "successful German-Americans and their descendants," noted that "while prior to 1848 . . . the liberal movement was practically confined to the educated classes, it had now spread, especially in Baden, the Palatinate and Rhenish Prussia, to the body of the people. Consequently the [political] refugees were no longer almost without exception men of high attainments and superior abilities, as had been the case before. These classes still found a large percentage, but with them came small shopkeepers, artisans, farmers, and even laborers." Decades later, Carl Wittke acknowledged again that while "no estimate of the number of workers among the forty-eighters can be made with any reasonable accuracy," it was clear that "more of the revolutionary forces were drawn from the rank and file than from the intellectual or upper social classes. Among the German-Americans of whose part in the Revolution we can be certain there were carpenters, cabinetmakers, tanners, weavers, bakers, cigarmakers, butchers, bookbinders, gardners, foundrymen, millers, coopers, coppersmiths and blacksmiths, tailors and representatives of other crafts as well as men who belonged to the unskilled working class."[18]

The present study focuses on these less attended people. Specifically, it explores the migration to the United States of the many German craftworkers who were influenced by the social and political cri-

sis in Germany. It seeks to clarify the ways in which they and their
memories and values influenced—and were influenced by—life, work,
and politics in antebellum America.

The Civil War Era

The epochal struggle in the United States that culminated in the Civil
War and Reconstruction belonged to the family of democratic revolutions discussed above, as Charles and Mary R. Beard stressed more
than a half-century ago and as both James M. McPherson and Eric
Foner have more recently reminded us.[19] Many active in the antebellum antislavery movement proudly identified with this international tradition, not least of all with the popular upsurges of 1848.
Concerning such events, John Brown wished "only to say in regard
to those things [that] I rejoice in them, from the full belief that God
is carrying out his eternal purpose in them all." Frederick Douglass
urged a Boston audience to be ready to "hail with equal pleasure the
tidings from the South that the slaves had risen, and achieved for
themselves, against the iron-hearted slaveholder, what the republicans
of France achieved against the royalists of France." Wendell Phillips
told a mass meeting the next year that "the cause of tyrants is one the
world over, and the cause of resistance to tyranny is one also. Whoever,
anywhere, loves truth and hates error, frowns on injustice and holds
out his hand to the oppressed, that man lightens the chains of Carolina; and an infamous vote in the United States Senate adds darkness
to the dungeon where German patriots lie entombed." Republican
moderates, too, were sensitive to the international significance of their
cause. Abraham Lincoln presented the American Civil War in 1861
as "a people's contest. On the side of the Union it is a struggle for
maintaining in the world that form and substance of government whose
leading object is to elevate the condition of men—to lift artificial
weights from all shoulders; to clear the paths of laudable pursuits for
all; to afford all an unfettered start, and a fair chance in the race of
life." The outcome of this contest, Lincoln subsequently added, would
decide "whether that nation, *or any nation* so conceived and so dedicated, can long endure."[20]

The issues and conflicts of the Civil War era deeply influenced the
early development of the American industrial working class, its institutions, and ideas. In *Beyond Equality*, David Montgomery discussed
the impact of the war upon the craft and incipient political organizations of northern wage earners during the late wartime and postwar

years. "The political debates of that conflict," he observed, "provided the basic elements of the workingmen's ideology, the alignments of political and social groups effectuated by the war created the framework within which their movement unfolded, and the economic pressures the great struggle engendered spurred them into action."[21] Since the appearance of Montgomery's study, however, little close attention has been paid to the ways in which antislavery sentiments or actions related to other major aspects of northern working-class life in the antebellum era.[22]

A considerable body of literature has accumulated, on the other hand, that evaluates the way that German-Americans generally (as well as other ethnic components of the electorate) responded to partisan reorganization during the 1850s. In 1859 Frederick Douglass expressed the view that "a German has only to be a German to be utterly opposed to slavery. In feeling, as well as in conviction and principle, they are antislavery." Douglass proceeded to qualify this generalization, but such circumspection became less common over time. In 1910 William E. Dodd sweepingly credited "the idealism of the foreigners" with delivering the Midwest for Lincoln. A generation later, Donnal V. Smith reiterated that "the naturalized voter" had sided with the Republican party as a reincarnation of familiar European causes.[23]

Others, however, pressed the opposite view with equal vigor. Joseph Schafer asserted half a century ago that most Germans had been hostile to the Republicans because of their innate conservatism and religiosity. "On the whole," John A. Hawgood agreed, "the Germans and other immigrants tended to blame the North, and the Abolitionists above all, for the secession of the South which precipitated a war." A prolific student of pro-Confederate sentiment in the Midwest placed that region's foreign-born population squarely in the Copperhead camp, specifying "the rank and file German immigrant," "those who labored for a living." Another historian asserted still more recently that "the German masses continued determinedly to vote Democratic because they disliked black people and could not abide the Yankees who led the Republican party."[24]

This debate has lately revived with electoral studies that correlate nativity and religious affinities with voting patterns. The results have led many to conclude that "ethnicity" rather than "class or economic differences between groups" shaped the political perception and conduct of Americans, foreign and native-born alike.[25] I consider this stark counterposition to be analytically barren. It commonly rests upon the unexamined treatment of ethnicity as a superhistorical "given" and an independent variable; it glosses over the actual social construction of ethnic identity, culture, and values over time, just as it tends to brush past social cleavages within the ethnic population.

The present study employs a distinct approach. I have sought to demonstrate that ethnic (religious and national) cultures were heavily freighted with both socioeconomic and political significance. In the United States, for example, the most insistent advocates of making ethnicity the touchstone of political life were the so-called nativists. But the "American" values that nativists upheld were as deeply marked by socioeconomic origins and concerns as the "foreign" values they found so repellent. Issues bearing on ethnic and religious identity, conversely, also loomed large for German-Americans. But that fact never nullified "class or economic differences" among the immigrants. In both Germany and the United States, thus, Catholic and Protestant church leaders championed definite codes of temporal thought and conduct among their followers. In interpreting, evaluating, and responding to such clerical injunctions, German-American craftworkers could not help being influenced by the specific socioeconomic circumstances in which they lived and labored. The same was true, *mutatis mutandis,* of other sections of the German-American population. The German-American response to a range of ethno-political stimuli—from European news through nativist, temperance, and sabbatarian agitation in the United States—was also mediated by socioeconomic realities, including class identity.

The present work, in short, rejects the "either/or" approach to studying ethnicity and class. It aims, instead, to lay bare the manner in which cultural, economic, and political influences interacted to shape the experience of German-American craftworkers. Only in this way, I argue, can we understand how these people perceived and responded to antebellum partisanship and mounting conflicts over slavery.

In chapters 1 and 2 of this book, I examine economic, political, and cultural changes in *Vormärz* Germany, as well as the Revolution of 1848–49 itself. That in-depth discussion aims to clarify the causes of the German emigration as well as the emigrants' background. I then survey their social and economic conditions in the United States in chapter 3, paying closest attention to the skilled crafts they most commonly resumed in the areas where they settled most heavily. In chapter 4, I probe politics and political divisions within the growing German-American population, highlighting contrasts among adherents of conservatism, liberalism, Marxism, and various strands of what I call radical democracy. In chapter 5, I examine the distinctive role played by German-born craftworkers in the antebellum labor movement.

Against this general background I introduce the issue of chattel slavery in chapters 6 and 7 and the immigrants' reactions to it. In chapters 8 and 9, I study the reaction of immigrant craftworkers and others to the appeals of the Democratic and Republican parties during the second half of the decade, situating that subject within its larger class, ethnic, and religious contexts. A concluding chapter surveys the immigrant experience during the Civil War itself. It also traces the manner in which diverse German-Americans (and others) grappled in later years with the radical democratic legacy of the Civil War era. That account once more reveals human beings struggling to reconcile memories and traditions with a continually evolving reality. And it reminds us yet again of the contingent, contested, and historically evolving nature of (German-American) ethnicity and of the economic, cultural, and political characteristics associated with it.

PART I

Fleeing the Old World

1

"So Deeply Interwoven": General Crisis and Emigration

The arrival of Germans in North America was not news in the 1840s. That migration had begun almost two centuries earlier. In the 1840s and 1850s, however, its dimensions increased dramatically (see table 1). During the 1820s, an average of fewer than 600 German immigrants arrived. The 1830s brought a sharp increase—over 12,000 immigrants annually—and by the early 1840s over 20,000 were arriving. High as this level was, it would still be dwarfed in the years ahead. Almost 60,000 Germans arrived per year during the latter half of the 1840s, an annual rate that more than doubled once again in the early 1850s, when it surpassed 130,000. The average number of arrivals declined in the later 1850s, but the figures still topped even those of the late 1840s.

All together, at least one and a half million Germans emigrated to the United States between 1840 and 1860, comprising almost nine out of every ten continental European immigrants by the 1850s. The number of German-born residents in this country grew 123 percent during that decade, more than triple the growth rate of the entire U.S. population. Moreover, the official figures behind these calculations do not take into account those illegal immigrants whose arrival went unrecorded. By the end of the nineteenth century more Germans had landed on the shores of the United States than any other immigrant group.[1]

The evidence concerning the regional origins of the emigrants is very incomplete (as the fragmentary data summarized in table 2 indicate), but contemporary accounts and historians agree that the center of the emigration lay in Germany's western, and especially south-western, regions supplemented later in the period by emigrants from

Table 1
German Emigration and Immigration to the United States, 1820–60

	Overseas Emigration	Immigration to the U.S.
1820	3,000	968
1821	2,800	383
1822	1,100	148
1823	1,300	183
1824	1,600	230
1825	3,200	450
1826	1,400	511
1827	1,200	432
1828	5,200	1,851
1829	1,700	597
1830	5,500	1,976
1831	7,200	2,413
1832	11,213	10,194
1833	7,687	6,988
1834	19,455	17,686
1835	9,142	8,311
1836	22,778	20,707
1837	26,114	23,740
1838	12,851	11,683
1839	23,131	21,028
1840	32,674	29,704
1841	16,820	15,291
1842	22,407	20,370
1843	15,885	14,441
1844	22,804	20,731
1845	37,791	34,355
1846	63,317	57,561
1847	80,250	74,281
1848	62,611	58,465
1849	64,238	60,235
1850	83,169	78,896
1851	78,815	72,482
1852	176,402	145,918
1853	150,663	141,946
1854	239,246	215,009
1855	83,773	71,918
1856	80,927	71,028
1857	103,111	91,781
1858	56,834	45,310
1859	47,354	41,784
1860	57,876	54,491

Sources: Peter Marschalck, *Deutsche Überseewanderung im 19. Jahrhundert: Ein Beitrag zur soziologischen Theorie der Bevölkerung* (Stuttgart: Ernst Klett Verlag, 1973), pp. 35–36, 101; F. Burgdörfer, "Migration across the Frontiers of Germany," in *International Migrations,* ed. Walter F. Willcox (New York: National Bureau of Economic Research, 1931), vol. 2, p. 333; U.S. Bureau of the Census, *Historical Statistics of the United States: Colonial Times to 1970* (Washington, D.C.: Government Printing Office, 1975), vol. 1, p. 106.

Table 2
Regional Origins of the German Emigration, 1840–60

	Percent of All German Emigrants[a]
Southwest Germany[b]	27.0
West Germany[c]	8.5
Hesse	3.5[f]
Saxony	1.0[g]
Bavaria (east of the Rhine)	8.0
East Germany[d]	5.0
Mecklenburg	3.0
Northeast Germany[e]	0.5

[a]Rounded off to the nearest half-percent.   [e]Brandenburg, Pomerania, Silesia.
[b]Württemberg, Baden, Bavarian Palatinate.   [f]1841–58.
[c]Westphalia and Prussian Rhineland.   [g]1853–61.
[d]E. Prussia, W. Prussia, Posen.
Sources: Marschalck, *Deutsche Überseewanderung*, p. 38; Wilhelm Mönckmeier, *Die Deutsche überseeische Auswanderung: Ein Beitrag zur Deutschen Wanderungsgeschichte* (Jena: Verlag von Gustav Fischer, 1912), pp. 16, 75; Hildegard Rosenthal, *Die Auswanderung aus Sachsen im 19. Jahrhundert (1815–1871)* (Stuttgart: Ausland und Heimat Verlags-Aktiengesellschaft, 1931), p. 87.

Brunswick, Hanover, and Mecklenburg. The rest of the East Elbian lands, in contrast, still accounted for only a small proportion of the emigration.[2]

Regional and Occupational Backgrounds

All German social strata took part in this massive population movement. Scholars have traditionally focused on emigrating professionals, merchants, and large landowners. But these well-to-do strata, who had always constituted a minority of the emigrants, made up a still smaller proportion during the post-1845 era. Small cultivators, handicraft workers, and laborers comprised the overwhelming bulk of Germany's emigrants. For example, peasant families accounted for about 50 percent, and artisan families about 25 to 30 percent, of all those leaving Baden between 1840 and 1855. During the next four years (1856–60), of those emigrants departing from Württemburg who declared their occupations, up to 44 percent labored in agriculture, and 52 percent in manufacturing; only 4 percent were merchants and professionals. Table 3 presents the occupational makeup of those leaving through Hamburg, the chief port of departure from northern and

Germany in the Nineteenth Century
Scale 1: 6,000,000

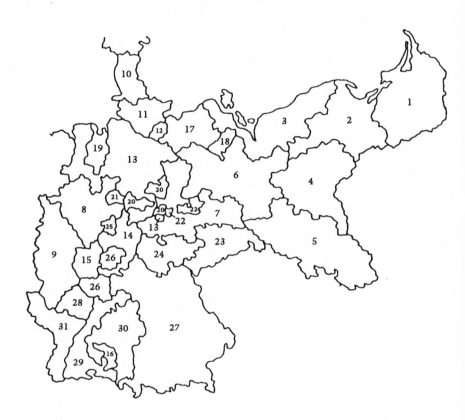

1. East Prussia	12. Lauenburg	22. Anhalt
2. West Prussia	13. Hanover	23. Saxony (Kingdom)
3. Pomerania	14. Hesse (Electorate)	24. Thuringian States
4. Posen	15. Nassau	25. Waldeck
5. Silesia	16. Hohenzollern	26. Hesse (Grand
6. Brandenburg	17. Mecklenburg-	Duchy)
7. Prussian Saxony	Schwerin	27. Bavaria
8. Westphalia	18. Mecklenburg-	28. Palatinate
9. Rhineland	Strelitz	29. Baden
10. Schleswig	19. Oldenburg	30. Württemberg
11. Holstein	20. Brunswick	31. Alsace-Lorraine
	21. Lippe	

Table 3
Occupations of Emigrants Departing from the Port of Hamburg,
1846–52

	Craftworkers and Tradesmen[a]	Peasants and Day Laborers[a]
1846	69%	31%
1847	67	33
1848	54	46
1849	60	40
1850	50	50
1851	48	52
1852	71	29

[a]Percent of total number of emigrants.
Source: Mönckmeier, *Deutsche überseeische Auswanderung,* p. 154.

central Germany. By the late 1850s growing numbers of landless laborers (notably from East Elbian Prussia) were also making their way overseas.

The economically depressed position of these people is suggested by data on the amount of money carried abroad by the average emigrant. At this time the liberal German journalist and political theorist Karl von Rotteck estimated the minimum working capital necessary for genuine personal independence at 400 gulden (or some 225 thaler), the equivalent of approximately $150. (The gulden was valued at about 38 cents, the thaler at 68 cents.) But throughout 1840–60, the average German headed abroad evidently carried considerably less than that estimated minimum (see table 4).[3]

Stagnation and Change

What was transpiring in Germany to drive all these plebeians abroad? Contemporaries and subsequent writers have given us a variety of seemingly contradictory explanations. Some emphasize chronic economic stagnation, others the disruptive effects of rapid industrialization. In fact, both explanations capture aspects of the reality.

If industrializing Britain in the early nineteenth century symbolized all that was new and growing in the western European economy, Germany seemed to be mired in backwardness. William Howitt expressed the typical view when he dwelt on the Germans' "long stationary condition in arts and husbandry, in domestic arrangements and manners, in their dreamy life in their colleges and houses, and their firm and

Table 4
Amount of Money Carried Abroad by the Average German Emigrant,
1840–60

Bavaria (in gulden)	Prussia (in thaler)	Baden (in gulden)	Hesse-Kassel (in thaler)
1840–45 303	1845 187		
	1846 164		
	1847 191	1840–47 241	
	1848 309	1848 285	
	1849 284	1849 252	
1845–50 259	1850 297	1850 236	
	1851 428	1851 137	
	1852 201	1852 137	1852 67
	1853 210	1853 149	1853 111
	1854 158	1854 140	1854 77
1850–55 235	1855 309	1855 174	1855 88
	1856 249		1856 103
	1857 319		1857 77
	1858 341		1858 153
			1859 145
1855–60 304			1860 112

Sources: Mönckmeier, *Deutsche überseeische Auswanderung,* pp. 159–60; Mack Walker, *Germany and the Emigration, 1816–1885* (Cambridge, Mass.: Harvard University Press, 1964), p. 160.

pertinacious adherence to old habits in everything, in spite of the progress of the rest of Europe." Indeed, he concluded, "The Germans are almost as unchangeable in their habits as the Eastern nations."[4]

Statistical proofs abounded. Only about 7 percent of Prussia's people lived in cities of ten thousand or more in 1800—half the concentration found in Belgium, one-third of that in England, and one-fourth of that in the Netherlands. More than three-fifths of Britain's labor force had left agriculture by then, while the same large majority of Germany's economically active population continued to till the soil. Only about one-fifth of Germany's total labor force—some 2.2 million individuals—was reportedly employed in nonagricultural production in that year. Of this fraction, the vast majority worked in small units, either in the old handicraft trades or in the market-oriented but decentralized putting-out (*Verlag*) sector.[5]

Germany's backward agrarian and small-scale manufacturing economy existed within a framework of social and political institutions that seemed at least as archaic. The agrarian population still labored under various types and degrees of feudal or semifeudal compulsions or obligations. Craft guilds survived in many places down through the 1860s. Much of German society retained an estate system of organization (*ständische Gesellschaft*) dominated by landed aristocrats and the higher clergy of established churches. Political power resided in an authoritarian state apparatus (*Obrigkeitsstaat*) despite gestures toward constitutional reform.[6]

These medieval vestiges reflected and reinforced a high degree of parochialism and national fragmentation. The French Revolution found Germany still divided into more than three hundred independent territories. As a Prussian privy councillor recalled of that era, "There was no nation in the state, not even provinces in the proper sense of the term; there were just separate estates in the various provinces, each with its own special interests, with no common ground between them." Innumerable tolls, tariffs, monopolies, and other barriers hobbled internal commerce. Even thirty years later, when the number of separate political units was substantially less, a British visitor was appalled to find

> no less than twenty-two tolls on the Weser betwixt Münden and Bremen, seven of which belong to the sovereign of Hanover. . . . At every toll every vessel is stopped and her whole cargo examined. On an average, more than one hour is employed at each toll to examine each vessel; so that every one loses one whole day in passing between these two towns. This is mere waste, a loss of time to all parties, more injurious probably than the duties which the merchants have also to pay. . . . It is merely to enrich them [the sovereigns], or rather to employ and pay a certain set of dependants.

"Similar tolls and impediments are known to exist on every river of Germany," he noted. Germany's overland transportation facilities remained quite primitive as well. In 1836, when France contained 140 kilometers of railroad track and Great Britain 650, there were only six kilometers of track to be found throughout Germany.[7]

That a society organized in this way could not hope to compete economically seemed obvious. Although Germany contained twice as many people as England, as late as 1830 it produced only 15 percent as much woolen yarn and only 10 percent as much pig iron while consuming only 7 percent as much coal. A decade later Germans were still turning out only 5 percent as much cotton yarn as the British; in 1834 only 626,000 cotton spindles were identified in all the states of the future German Empire. Even France, which was no industrial giant, had 2.5 million spindles that year, while Britain boasted 10 million.[8]

Beneath this appearance of utter stagnation, however, powerful forces had begun to transform the lives of Germany's agricultural and industrial producers. Slowly, unevenly, and very painfully, an old and familiar world—in which petty commodity production, merchants' capital, and seigneurialism had long if uneasily coexisted—was breaking down. One result was the rise of a new social stratum composed of increasingly prosperous merchants, contractors, and profit-oriented employers. Another result was the extensive expropriation of small producers in both town and country and the creation of a growing stratum of propertyless and nearly propertyless peasants and artisans, some of whom reentered the economy as agricultural or industrial wage earners. Many more simply sank into abject misery, stimulating mounting public anxiety about *Pauperismus.* Still others fended off that fate by accepting labor arrangements that fused aspects of the old economic system (small-scale production, primitive techniques, formal self-employment qualified by various degrees of patriarchal dependence) with elements of the new (increased emphasis on profitability, specialization, and ready-made production serving larger and more distant markets).[9]

Demographic developments contributed to all these changes. In the middle of the eighteenth century the population of Germany began to expand rapidly and had more than doubled by 1850 (from 15 to 35 million). This explosive population growth soon outstripped the economy's capacity to absorb it, most obviously in the countryside (see table 5). By 1800, only a minority of the rural population was able to support itself exclusively through agriculture. In this year, between one-fourth and one-third of rural dwellers owned plots too small to sustain themselves, and another fourth were totally landless. In southwestern Germany, a tax canvass in 1844 placed three-fifths of the agrarian population among the poor or propertyless.[10] Various inheritance and land tenure systems influenced and sometimes aggravated the problem.[11]

Landless and land-poor peasants (*Kleinlandwirte*) were forced to work for others, whether doing road maintenance or providing agricultural day labor for lords and wealthier peasants or via handicraft production. Rural cottage industry (particularly common in the weaving trade and later in the production of ready-made clothing) absorbed the efforts of men and women alike. At least some of these rural outworkers initially retained a substantial degree of independence—owning their own land, tools, and materials, selling their products rather than their time and effort, and dealing with a number

Table 5
Social Structure of Germany, 1800–1845

Social Stratum	Percent of Total Population	
	1800	1845
Elite	4	3
Self-employed urban middle stratum	11	11
Urban lower class	12	14
Substantial peasants	20	15
Poor peasants and rural craftworkers	29	26
Rural poor and propertyless (agrarian lower class)	23	31

Source: Diedrich Saalfeld, "Lebensverhältnisse der Unterschichten Deutschlands im Neunzehnten Jahrhundert," *International Review of Social History* 29 (1984): 220.

of different merchants. They depended upon the income only to supplement their agricultural efforts. Indeed, many marginal cultivators turned to *Verlag* work as a way to resist dispossession, destitution, and abject dependence.

In the end, however, rural cottage industry often served simply to prolong and complicate the process of impoverishment. Over time, the decline of farms and handicraft prices magnified the relative power of the middlemen. Direct producers fell into dependence upon individual merchants, who now increasingly provided not only orders but also raw materials and tools, and perhaps shelter as well. This pattern may already have prevailed in the Southwest by the early eighteenth century. In Germany as a whole, some 860,000 people reportedly labored as outworkers in 1780, or about 8.5 percent of Germany's total labor force. In another generation an additional 100,000 were so employed, raising the proportion to 9 percent. Once again, outwork's real extent was undoubtedly much larger, involving a great many people officially classified in other occupational categories.[12]

Parallel developments altered the nature of traditional handicraft production. At the turn of the century *Handwerk* involved some 1.12 million individuals, just over one-tenth of Germany's total labor force and just over half of all those producing nonagricultural goods. Here could be found large numbers of proud and reasonably prosperous masters well rooted in the broad middle class of Germany's towns and cities. Working with them, and still commonly living with them, were helpers—journeymen and apprentices—who anticipated one day becoming masters in their own right. In the meantime, these helpers' lives were regulated by customary practice, guild regulations, and governmental edict.[13]

This picture of corporatist stability, however, captured only part of the craftworker reality. Already at the turn of the nineteenth century, about half of all German masters—and at least three-quarters of those in Baden—employed only themselves, and perhaps other members of their own nuclear families. These *Alleinmeister* were particularly common in the largest of the mass-consumption trades: weaving, tailoring, and shoemaking. Crafting in their own shops, using their own tools and ancient techniques, they retained the outward forms of self-employment. More and more, however, they found themselves growing dependent upon merchants for orders and, in some cases, raw materials as well. While still a few notches above wage laborers, individuals working in this *Verlagssystem* found their positions gradually undermined by the growth of rural cottage industry and becoming less and less distinguishable from that of the cottage workers.[14]

During the next half-century, urban and rural lower classes came under still heavier burdens. The Napoleonic Wars and their aftermath helped to accelerate changes already underway in the political, social, and economic life of the country. Both Prussia's defeat by France (1806) and, a decade later, the pressure of increased economic competition from industrializing England strengthened the hand of those in the German (and especially Prussian) state bureaucracies seeking to achieve an administrative "revolution from above." Designed to streamline the *ständische Gemeinschaft* and amplify the economic resources at the disposal of the *Obrigkeitsstaat,* measures concerning land reform, occupational mobility (*Gewerbefreiheit*—trade freedom), taxation, industrial education, internal and international commerce, and certain industrial enterprises also aimed to limit the threat posed by economic change to the survival and supremacy of the existing German elite.[15]

Reforms of the Napoleonic and *Vormärz* (1815–48) eras thus liberated the serfs (*Fröner*), but often at high cost to rural smallholders. This was most obviously true east of the Elbe River. During the first third of the nineteenth century, administrative action relieved peasants of servile status while also relieving many of their land. Other edicts divided common lands, consolidated dispersed holdings, and eliminated collective methods of cultivation. All these measures encouraged the development of large-scale, rationalized, and market-oriented agriculture, partly by presenting a small class of aristocratic magnates (the *Junker*) with a mass of propertyless people and impoverished smallholders available for agricultural wage labor. The Junkerdom retained extra-economic power over this dependent work force, moreover, and remained a key social, economic, and political pillar of autocracy in Prussia and—as the pattern of counterrevolution would confirm in 1849—in Germany as a whole.[16]

In much of western Germany, where manorial cultivation was insignificant, the nobility lived on tribute from small cultivators. In the 1840s perhaps one-third of Baden's peasantry tilled land owned by members of the aristocracy. These titled landlords continued to exercise political privilege as well as economic power and strongly resisted attempts to cancel peasant obligations. Laws governing the mortgage and sale of peasant lands were liberalized. Given the depressed condition of southwestern agriculture, however, this liberalization often served to abet dispossession. Outside East Elbia, the practice of dividing the common lands made greatest and earliest progress in the Northwest, benefiting the already well-to-do while further undermining the position of the rural poor. The survival of obligations imposed by landlord upon cultivator in the Northwest attracted the attention of William Jacob, a British visitor to the Westphalia-Hanover border region in 1819: "The rent to the lord of the manor is paid, under various titles, sometimes in the produce of the soil, sometimes in a fixed number of days'-labour of the tenant, occasionally of his horse, and sometimes, though but rarely, in money. It however, very commonly, consists of a mixture of each of these different modes. The occupiers are generally a kind of copy-holders, under the proprietor, to whom they are bound as their feudal lord, and are called his subjects." Other burdens imposed by economic change on the agrarian lower classes included increased mercantile speculation in land and attempts by some west and central German aristocrats to mimic their East Elbian counterparts and transform themselves into large capitalist farmers at the expense of neighboring smallholders.[17]

In all of this, demographic growth continued to play its role. Between 1800 and 1850 the total German population expanded by more than half, the rural population alone by almost ten million. Land hunger drove up land prices and fed speculative fever. For those trapped on shrinking plots of land, survival required squeezing ever more out of the soil by reducing fallow, waste, meadow, and pasture land and depending more and more for sustenance on a few root vegetables, particularly potatoes and turnips. (Root vegetables composed only about 3 percent of the total Prussian harvest in 1800, but constituted nearly 25 percent by 1840.) "The increase of population," William Jacob noted, "would be an unsupportable burden on their families, if the general introduction of potatoes for subsistence did not keep them from the extreme of want." Want did exist, however, and those experiencing it grew more numerous. The rural lower class expanded during 1800–45 from about 30 to about 40 percent of the countryside's population, doubling in absolute terms.[18]

Already sizable at the turn of the century, the labor surplus in western Germany grew further during the *Vormärz*. The supersaturation of agriculture increased the importance of nonagricultural labor. By 1830 an estimated 1.4 million people (or 10 percent of the national labor force) worked in cottage industry, further blurring the already hazy distinction between town and country. Competition from more efficient foreign and native factories, however, stunted the further growth of rural outwork; migration abroad, and into middling and large German urban centers, accelerated. The population of towns and cities now grew 50 percent faster than that of the countryside. Some of the new urban dwellers entered the ranks of unskilled labor; others became sweated craftworkers.[19]

Facilitating these developments was a veritable revolution in Germany's transportation systems. Between 1816 and 1852 the length of the road system in Prussia more than quadrupled, and by 1850 Germany boasted canals totaling some 1,200 kilometers in length. In the late 1830s, moreover, workers laid some 550 kilometers of railway track in Germany, and by 1850 nearly 6,000 kilometers of track had been laid. Rail transportation alone reduced the cost of moving bulk goods more than 80 percent. In addition, the federal customs union (*Zollverein*) reduced the legal barriers to the movement of goods through Germany.[20]

During this second half of the *Vormärz* era—that is, beginning in the mid-1830s—the pace of industrial development quickened. The nonagricultural share of total investment in Prussia almost tripled. And while much of this increase went into buildings and improved transportation, some of it paid for technological innovation in production. The number of steam engines in the *Zollverein* more than tripled between 1834 and 1850. Mining output more than doubled in the two decades following 1830, and the production of hard coal increased even more quickly.[21] In textiles, the value of woolen goods rose more than 50 percent between 1830 and 1846–47, and that of cotton goods, almost 80 percent. Mechanization advanced, particularly in the cloth-printing and spinning sectors, both of which had already expanded appreciably by 1840. More important in the long run, during this period engineering and machine-building firms arose, most of which employed steam-driven equipment by 1848.[22]

The Scale and Mechanization of Production

The increase in scale and mechanization in some industrial enterprises altered the experience, composition, and character of the nation's labor force. The number of laborers reportedly employed in larger enterprises (including mines, unmechanized manufactories, and factories with machinery) doubled their proportional weight in the labor force.[23]

These changes proceeded unevenly. In the 1840s the Kingdom of Saxony was still without challenge the most densely populated, urbanized, and highly industrialized region in Germany. By the time of the 1848 Revolution, some 70 percent of all Saxon families held little or no land, and fully one-third of the kingdom's total population resided in towns and cities. As early as 1800 only about one in five members of the Saxon work force still labored exclusively in agriculture, and by the late 1840s more than 40 percent were engaged in manufacturing. This precocity helped produce a large stratum of hereditary wage earners as early as 1830 in Leipzig. Between 900 and 1,100 Leipzigers, or about 10 percent of the gainfully employed labor force, worked for factories or large enterprises by 1850, including machine builders and mechanics and growing numbers of spinners, weavers, cloth printers, wagonmakers, typesetters, and printers.[24]

In the Rhenish city of Cologne a comparable proportion of the labor force worked for larger enterprises by 1849. British and Saxon competition had enforced a radical concentration of production upon the city's textile industry. As late as 1835 the average woolen goods workshop had employed no more than 4 people; by 1845 that figure had risen to 17. In cotton weaving, where the first mechanical loom appeared in the late 1830s, the number working for the average enterprise more than doubled between 1836 to 1844, from 21 to 50. Although the city's old spinning industry was on the decline, surviving enterprises tended to be large; a few employed some 200 people apiece.

Nor was concentration restricted to the textile industry. Cologne's largest iron foundry employed 350 workers by the 1840s. Mechanization was also advancing in the production of locks and machinery, furniture, wooden and iron products, jewelry, wire and cable, rope, and baked and confectionery goods.[25] Germany's largest city, Berlin, also boasted some of its bigger industrial units. Here the number of people attached to factories, manufactories, and other large concerns reached 15,000 to 16,000 by the mid-1840s. In general, larger enterprises strove to make employees conform to the new behavioral demands of large-scale production, whether mechanized or not.[26]

Although this *Vormärz* industrial development was an important harbinger of the massive industrialization to come that would eventually transform all of German society, the fact is that in the 1850s mechanization remained quite atypical throughout German industry. Just as atypical were centralization, major economies of scale, and even substantial division of labor. Productivity therefore increased slowly. Net social product per capita, which rose 29 percent in just twenty years after the Revolution of 1848–49, grew only 7 percent over the entire first half of the nineteenth century. Even in the Rhineland, where steam power was most widely used, Thomas C. Banfield could still marvel in the 1840s at the prevalence of small-scale hand production. Compared to Britain, Germany's mechanized textile industry grew at a snail's pace. Until the 1840s most spinning was still done with hand mules and other equipment of a roughly 1780 British vintage. Even in 1849 the average German spinning mill contained only 7 percent as many spindles as its British counterpart. Only 2 to 3 percent of all woolen and cotton looms in Germany were mechanized by the time of the revolution; the rest were driven by hand. Indeed, it was precisely this technical backwardness that prevented textiles from playing the central role in Germany's industrialization that they had in Britain's.[27]

Nor did the existence of a relative handful of large factories and workshops significantly increase the scale of German production generally. Large enterprises, which by the end of the nineteenth century would employ one of five members of the German labor force, employed no more than one in twenty-five in 1850. Like similar statistics cited earlier, even these figures seriously exaggerate the actual scale of production in mid-nineteenth-century Germany. They include not only those actually employed *in* large enterprises but also those merely employed *by* them even if those producers worked in their own garrets or basement apartments. Nor, indeed, were such "large" enterprises necessarily bigger than any other. For the purpose of compiling these statistics, a "factory or large enterprise" was distinguished from a mere workshop not by the size of its work force but by the enterprise's relationship to the market. Craftworkers producing ready-made goods were often counted among the "factory" population even if they actually labored in small shops. This manner of counting heads obscures at least as much as it reveals about the actual concentration of production.[28]

A clearer picture emerges from other data. The average manufacturing enterprise in Prussia in 1849 absorbed the efforts of only 1.8 people, including the proprietor. The average work force was higher in construction (5 hands per firm) but actually smaller in the textile, food preparation, woodworking, and metal trades. The boom in Ruhr heavy industry lay ahead. To the south, those who worked the Siegen iron mines, as Banfield reported in 1846, were still "nearly all householders, who unite mining with their other occupations." He also found that in the cutlery center of Solingen, near Düsseldorf, "every artisan lives in his own house or rooms, and undertakes work by the dozen." With the single exception of a "cast-steel factory" at Burg, "no large establishments are anywhere found there," and the cutlery crafts were divided into a multitude of separate guilds "so jealous of their occupations, that no strange workman, nor any who has not regularly served his time, is allowed to work with them."[29]

Small-scale hand production prevailed in the great cities as well as in rural areas. The great majority of Leipzig's wage-earning craftworkers in the 1840s—including tailors, cigarmakers, bookbinders, hatters, clockmakers, and leatherworkers—continued to work in such conditions. The picture was similar in Cologne and Berlin. Few major changes had occurred in the size of craft shops in these cities by mid-century or in the production techniques they employed. The typical artisan still labored without machinery in a small establishment with the assistance of one or two helpers at most.[30]

Thus large-scale, centralized, and mechanized industrial production employed few Germans in the first half of the nineteenth century. The overwhelming majority of agricultural and industrial producers (including those who would join the emigration) continued to labor with tools and techniques—and in small-scale and decentralized conditions—inherited from the past. Even the distorted official statistics discussed above still located more than five times as many mid-century Germans (and more than eight times as many Badenese) in the handicraft and *Verlag* sectors as in the problematically defined "large enterprises." The accelerating collapse of the traditional economy and the stunted development of a new one had consigned these "*Proletaroiden*" to a painfully protracted transition "between *Mittelstand* and *Proletariat*" (in Pierre Aycoberry's phrase). Ultimately, simple wage labor and significantly altered methods of production would hold sway, but in the short run it was the transition process itself that conditioned the experiences and responses of most laborers, including most emigrants.[31]

Table 6
Growth of Principal Handicrafts in Baden, 1810–44

	Masters		Helpers	
	(N)[a]	(% increase)[b]	(N)[a]	(% increase)[b]
Linen weaver	12,369	51	3,417	92
Shoemaker	8,957	37	3,691	104
Mason	4,658	68	4,657	210
Tailor	5,734	17	2,324	70
Cabinetmaker	3,482	86	1,959	206
Carpenter	3,105	36	2,263	48

[a]Absolute number in 1844.
[b]Since 1810 (rounded off).
Source: Wolfram Fischer, *Der Staat und die Anfänge der Industrialisierung in Baden, 1800–1850* (Berlin: Duncker and Humboldt, 1962), pp. 290, 303. Note that in Fischer's table on p. 290, the data for tailors (*Schneider*) are erroneously entered under the first of two headings for blacksmiths (*Schmiede*).

Small Masters and Helpers

Within the handicrafts, two sources supplied much of the expanding dependent work force—journeymen and declining small masters. In *Vormärz* Germany journeymen and apprentices increased in number about twice as fast as the masters, faster still in some centers of sweated production (see tables 6 and 7). Most of these helpers would never attain even the title of master. Their employers included masters who avoided ruin precisely by squeezing their journeymen and apprentices, demanding up to fourteen hours of work per day from their helpers in return for a meager subsistence.[32]

Everywhere the number of helpers expanded at a faster rate than the number of masters, especially in the urban handicrafts, as the data for the Hessian city of Mainz illustrate (see table 8). Between 1816 and 1842–43, the number of masters in Mainz increased by only 0.5 percent, while the number of helpers increased by 52 percent. By the end of the 1840s most helpers in Cologne and Leipzig effectively worked for wages. In the Berlin handicrafts, the number of journeymen per 100 masters rose steadily from 78 to 180 between 1729 and 1846. As the size of the market increased and shops switched from

Table 7
Growth of Principal Handicrafts in Württemberg, 1835–52

	Masters		Helpers	
	(N)[a]	(% increase)[b]	(N)[a]	(% increase)[b]
Shoemaker	13,053	10	5,473	49
Mason	5,776	23	6,721	317
Tailor	7,139	4	2,818	28
Baker	6,613	−11	2,145	54
Cabinetmaker	5,304	25	2,128	29
Carpenter	3,591	−32	3,803	118

[a]Absolute number in 1852.
[b]Since 1835 (rounded off).
Source: Gustav Schmoller, *Zur Geschichte der deutschen Kleingewerbe im 19. Jahrhundert. Statistische und nationalökonomische Untersuchungen* (Halle: Verlag von Buchhandlung des Waisenhauses, 1870), pp. 110–11.

producing a wide variety of custom-made items to specializing in a few ready-made goods, the strain and social distance between masters and journeymen increased. An older type of patriarchal relationship gave way to one conditioned by the masters' mounting preoccupation with competition, profit, and loss. Once treated as members of the masters' households, journeymen increasingly lived separately from them or became simple cash tenants of their employers. Other results included the rise of piece-rate forms of payment, longer working hours, a sharp reduction in the term of employment, and increased liability to dismissal without warning.[33]

The gulf, then, between substantial employers of labor and wage-earning craftworkers widened. But this division never neatly coincided

Table 8
Growth of Crafts in Mainz, 1816–43

	Masters	Helpers	Total Population
1816	1,738	1,712	25,000
1842–43	1,748	2,598	33,826
Increase[a]	0.5%	52%	35.5%

[a]Percentages rounded off to nearest half-percent.
Source: Anne J. MacLachlan, "Übergang vom Handwerker zum Unternehmer in Mainz, 1830–1860," in *Handwerker in der Industrialisierung: Lage, Kultur und Politik vom späten 18. bis frühen 20. Jahrhundert,* ed. Ulrich Engelhardt (Stuttgart: Klett-Cotta, 1984), p. 154.

with the formal distinction between masters and helpers. As the size of the handicraft work force increased, so did the number of nominal masters—those who bore the formal title of master without actually enjoying the degree of independence traditionally associated with it.

The presence of this large intermediate stratum helped to blur class boundaries in Germany. Journeyman printer Stephan Born of Berlin headed one of the most militant labor organizations in the country in 1848 and led a nationwide strike against boss printers that year. It was his judgment that "there are still in our fatherland in no sense two sharply separated classes of people; there are capitalists and workers, but in [between] these groups still other elements are significant—elements that belong neither to the one nor the other of these two classes and which continue to maintain a significant independence."[34]

In Cologne and Berlin only somewhere between one-fifth and one-third of all nominal masters of craftwork owned enough working capital to be subject even to the regressive Prussian occupation tax. In Berlin the percentage of nominal masters rose rapidly during the *Vormärz*, especially among weavers, shoemakers, and tailors, who by themselves accounted for about half of all Berlin masters in 1846. Many fell increasingly under the domination of larger masters or merchants and had incomes worse than those of the better-placed journeymen. Official statistics actually listed some of these nominal masters as journeymen, and common usage placed them within the broad category of *Arbeiter*.[35]

Impoverished small masters were even more common outside the big cities and especially in the regions of Germany that experienced mass emigration. In 1835 Württemberg already contained nearly one master craftworker for every fourteen residents, a ratio far too high to permit a decent standard of living to masters, most of whom had little or no working capital. Baden reached the same point about a decade later. The ranks of the masters there swelled by more than 20 percent during the 1830s and 1840s, approximately twice the growth rate of the general population. By 1844 Baden had one master for every thirteen people. Nine in ten masters had no working capital at all, and that proportion rose still higher in the most populous trades (see table 9). Only about two percent of Baden's masters could claim a working capital valued above one thousand florins—less than $400.[36]

Poverty led to dependence. Badly in need of customers, more and more small masters became reliant upon orders from merchants and contractors linked to more distant markets. The same revolution in transportation and commerce that encouraged the expansion of the

Table 9
Masters without Working Capital in Baden, 1844

	Total Masters	Percent without Working Capital
Linen weaver	12,369	99+
Shoemaker	8,957	93
Mason	4,658	99
Tailor	5,734	99
Cabinetmaker	3,482	96
Carpenter	3,105	98

Source: Helmut Sedatis, *Liberalismus und Handwerk in Süwestdeutschland: Wirtschafts- und Gesellschaftskonzeptionen des Liberalismus und die Krise des Handwerks im 19. Jahrhundert* (Stuttgart: Klett-Cotta, 1979), pp. 131–32.

Verlag system soon subjected those dependent upon it to unequal competition from British and even nascent German factory production. Meeting this competition imposed increased expenses. To obtain the needed funds, declining masters obtained loans with interest rates of 10 to 20 percent, which only increased their burdens. Regressive tax policies added to financial pressures. Striving desperately to retain vestiges of independent proprietorship, these nominal masters slid toward pauperism or wage labor dependence.[37]

These changes in the status of masters and helpers occurred through the weakening of the guilds or with their complicity, occasionally both. In some cases, entrepreneurial-minded masters tightened requirements for full guild membership and turned the guilds into instruments of labor discipline—sometimes with government assistance. Elsewhere, government enforcement of *Gewerbefreiheit* simultaneously helped broaden access to master status and accentuate the vulnerability of those who attained it.[38]

Marginal producers, such as the nominal masters, lived at the edge of calamity, and any significant tremor in the domestic or international economy could plunge them over that precipice. The great economic shocks of the late 1840s and early 1850s meant full-scale disaster for them. The potato blight that struck Europe in 1845 devastated already impoverished German peasants and rural laborers. Reduced grain harvests aggravated the food shortage, and an international financial panic in 1847–48 delivered the coup de grace. Food prices shot upward as income from craft production continued to drop. As hard-pressed peasants reduced their purchases, the market for handicraft goods narrowed further. The soaring bankruptcy statistics for the Southwest only hinted at the impact of the panic on the region's small masters.[39]

The economic disasters of the 1840s made German society's general economic crisis acute, and the same desperation that now propelled thousands abroad also increased conflict at home, raising the stakes as well. German emigrants passing through the north European port city of Amsterdam explained to the U.S. consul there in the fall of 1847 that "the present crisis is so deeply interwoven in the events of the present period that 'it' is but the commencement of the great Revolution which they consider sooner or later is to dissolve the present constitution of things."[40] The prediction proved prescient—and sooner rather than later.

2

"Social Freedom and Independent Existence": Labor and Revolution

The popular response to Germany's deepening societal crisis in the 1840s reflected the complex, contradictory, and uneven character of the nation's social and political development. Plebeian protest in these years targeted both old and new demons. Rural crowds attacked wagons owned by landlords and merchants who were attempting to transport harvests from starvation-ridden regions in order to sell them more profitably elsewhere. The raiders thrashed the drivers and distributed the confiscated foodstuffs among the hungry. Impoverished cultivators in the Southwest vented their rage on merchants and creditors as well as the aristocratic beneficiaries of feudal dues and obligations, tax exemptions, and political and economic privileges. In Weinsberg, Württemberg, nearly one thousand peasants besieged the castle seeking "to burn the documents that reduce us to beggars." Similar riots took place in Baden, Hesse, and Bavaria. In Adelsheim a crowd set fire to all books and records in the baronial library suspected of documenting peasant obligations. Others demanded the restoration of access rights to hunting and forest lands. German towns and cities erupted in hunger riots in 1847. Anti-Semitic outbursts became common. Unemployed craftworkers repeatedly clashed with government troops. In some places workers attacked factories and destroyed machines.[1]

The collapse of the French monarchy and its replacement by a republic in late February of 1848 sent a thrill of fear through the German aristocracy, and petty princes scrambled to mollify prominent liberal critics. Within weeks, longtime opponents of aristocratic power found themselves appointed to government ministries throughout much of the country. On March 13, Prince Klemens von Metternich, *echtes* symbol of the *Vormärz*, resigned as Austria's chancellor. Five days later barricades appeared in the streets of Berlin, whose citizens fought pitched battles with soldiers loyal to the Prussian king, Friedrich Wilhelm IV.

The occupations of the revolutionaries who died on the barricades (the *Märzgefallenen*) reveal the popular movement's social breadth as well as its specific center of gravity. Of those identified, about 5 percent came from the urban upper strata, and 13 percent held minor occupations ranging from postman to groom. Nearly one in five belonged to the city's factory or other wage-earning work force (including both laborers and machine builders). Skilled craftworkers were by far the largest single group, constituting fully two-thirds of the total. Of these, 8 percent were apprentices, 18 percent masters, and 73 percent journeymen (notably, in descending order of incidence, cabinetmakers, tailors, shoemakers, locksmiths, blacksmiths, silk weavers, bookbinders, carpenters, and masons).[2]

On the day following the bloody street fighting in Berlin, the king capitulated and withdrew his troops from the capital. When he and his wife next appeared before a crowd of their subjects, it was to sheepishly pay their respects to those killed by the defenders of monarchical authority. Though Friedrich Wilhelm had by now donned the national colors of black, red, and gold, the crowd gathered in the palace courtyard that day remained unappeased. And when schoolteacher Theodor Hielscher roared the command, "Remove your hat before these dead!" the king could only comply. By the end of the month a new cabinet sat in Berlin containing such well-known liberal businessmen as Ludolf Camphausen and David Hansemann.[3]

The ancien régime's apparent failure of nerve emboldened all discontented social strata, encouraging each to present its own catalogue of grievances and demands. One effect was to illuminate the conflicting values and aspirations cherished in different quarters, a clash that had been partly obscured and muffled during the repressive *Vormärz* decades.

The wishes of poor peasants and agricultural laborers proved simple and straightforward. They wanted the great estates divided, mortgages on smallholdings canceled, taxes reduced, feudal dues and related obligations abolished, and the aristocracy's special powers and privileges eliminated.[4] In Germany's larger urban centers, liberal businessmen and their allies in the intelligentsia demanded increased civil liberties and an increase in their own political power. They sought to use their new offical positions "to assure for the middle class a preponderant influence over the state," in the words of Hesse-Darmstadt's Heinrich von Gagern, president of the national parliamentary assembly in Frankfurt. That influence would then lead to a more progressive government economic policy and an end to that anachronistic fragmentation of the German nation that had persisted even under the *Zollverein*. The liberals who dominated the Frankfurt Assembly found the appropriate political formula for their project in a constitutional monarchy based on a limited suffrage. "The bulk of the liberal element," Carl Schurz later recalled, "did not desire anything beyond the establishment of national unity and a constitutional monarchy 'on a broad democratic basis.' "[5]

Although wary of the social and political consequences of a truly free market economy, these men evinced little enthusiasm for attempts at social leveling. Condemning the "aristocracy of birth" as neither "natural" nor "necessary," Vienna's Joseph Schneider nevertheless explained to the National Assembly that "we will always have an aristocracy of wealth and . . . an aristocracy of intellect, human nature unfortunately being what it is." David Hansemann, similarly, had long opposed the rise of what he called a "hospital spirit" in politics, arguing that "when the state, or when societies and organizations undertake to support them, the poor come to assume that they have a legal right to help. This undermines morality which from the point of view of civil life consists in diligence, orderliness, thrift, a sensible ambition to increase one's wealth, respect for family ties, and fulfillment of family obligations."[6]

As the composition of the *Märzgefallenen* indicates, craftworkers played active roles in the revolution, often serving as its shock troops. "You are right when you maintain that it was essentially the workers who decided the revolution," a Berlin physician wrote to his father. And that fact, the doctor added discerningly, affected not only the fortunes but also the very character of the struggle, making "this revolution . . . not simply political but fundamentally social." In big cities and smaller towns alike, members of all trades gathered to discuss their interests and needs and how these might best be served. These meetings produced organizations throughout the country, including many in the southwestern centers of the era's emigration: the Rhineland, Baden, Württemberg, Hesse, Bavaria, and the Palatinate. The Cologne Workers Association quickly attracted six to seven thousand members. By mid-1849 twenty-four workers' clubs in Bavaria claimed a combined membership in excess of five thousand. In Hesse the Frankfurt workers' club became a major regional center of the new movement, helping to initiate and support other organizations throughout the Southwest. Their words and deeds offer a glimpse of attitudes current among those popular strata from which most of the emigrants of the 1840s and 1850s sprang.[7]

We have seen that the changing situation of German working people in the 1840s reflected the impact of both old and new historical influences. The interaction of the old and the new also influenced their social outlook, aims, and initiatives. Elements of traditionalism, parochialism, and corporatism mingled with (and were partially transformed by) democratic, libertarian, mutualist, nationalist, and internationalist currents and even hesitant hopes of sharing in the benefits of economic growth.

This process of intellectual ferment had begun decades earlier. Even under the police repression of the *Vormärz* era, a range of organizations existed in which some journeymen and small masters could regularly exchange views and impressions with one another and with sympathetic individuals from the professions and other social strata. These organizations included mutual benefit societies as well as educational and cultural groups like the Berlin Artisans' Association, the Hamburg Educational Society for the Improvement of the Working Class, and various singing societies and gymnastic associations (*Turnvereine*). Paris, Geneva, Brussels, London, and other European cities, meanwhile, played host to a variety of German associations composed of traveling journeymen and other workers, sundry expatriates, and emigré intellectuals. These groups provided recruits and conduits into Germany for liberal, radical democratic, socialist, and communist movements—the precise demarcations among which commonly remained rather hazy in these decades.[8]

As historians of the German working class and labor movement have emphasized, the revolutionary years saw conflict escalate between substantial employers and journeymen. This period also constituted an important stage in the development of social cohesion and independent economic organization among wage earners. Localized strikes proliferated in the spring and again during the summer of 1848. Journeymen in three trades (cigar making, tailoring, and printing) strove to knit together national organizations. When employers refused to accept the demands of the journeymen printers, the latter called the first nationwide strike in German history.

This division between labor and capital, however, appeared neither sufficiently sharp, universal, nor basic to fundamentally define politics or political alliances in 1848–49. The *Communist Manifesto*, which appeared in February 1848, proclaimed the doctrine of class struggle between bourgeois and proletarian, and the Communist League attracted a few hundred members, some of whom played important roles in labor and democratic movements in 1848–49. But proletarian consciousness as the Marxists defined it was not widespread in mid-century Germany. "The bourgeoisie and the proletariat," Stephan Born wrote at the time, "capital and labor, do not yet oppose each other so sharply as in France and England." Elaborating the point in his memoirs, Born explained, "The phrase 'class antagonism' at that time had, judged by the real conditions in Germany, barely any warrant. Aside from a few trades—the machine builders, the book printers, and perhaps one or two others—the master was generally only a former journeyman himself."[9]

Differing with Born on questions of strategy and tactics, Karl Marx and Friedrich Engels nonetheless reached similar conclusions concerning the overall state of industrial and class development in Germany. "At that time," Engels remembered decades later, "one had to seek out one by one the workers who had an understanding of their position as workers and their historico-economic antagonism to capital, because this antagonism itself was only just beginning to develop." Even the early Communist League, Engels added, reflected the economy's still-early stage of development. "The members, in so far as they were workers at all, were almost exclusively artisans," he observed. They were "not yet full proletarians but only an appendage of the petty bourgeoisie, an appendage which was passing into the modern proletariat and which did not yet stand in direct opposition to the bourgeoisie, that is, to big capital." It appeared natural to Engels that such people should gravitate to ideas appropriate to a preproletarian or semiproletarian existence, "that their old handicraft prejudices should be a stumbling block to them at every moment," and that general democratic slogans should seem to them adequate to "surmount every theoretical obstacle."[10]

But if Marxian communism exerted limited appeal for the mass of craftworker activists, the doctrines of free-trade capitalism found little support, either. One of the period's most representative craftworker gatherings, accordingly, concluded "that the adherents of free trade as well as the communists are on the wrong road." Struggling against ongoing degradation and impoverishment, handicraft workers in Reuss, Frankfurt, and Hamm, Westphalia, denounced the domination of small producers by the "money power" and complained bitterly that "capital has gobbled up the small but beneficent industry." Journeymen who acknowledged their status as wage laborers and organized on that basis often focused on immediate issues of wages and hours. They, too, rejected the supremacy of Adam Smith's "invisible hand." Strikes by journeymen printers and others asserted the collective right to limit the supply of labor and even the scale of production. Unbridled economic competition seemed as dangerous as oppressive autocracy and privileged aristocracy, especially when these two seeming opposites found ways to cooperate at the expense of the urban and rural poor.[11]

Most craftworkers who mobilized in 1848 evidently aspired to a more humane, stable, and cooperative society governed in the interests of actual producers, a society whose ordered and regulated economy would safeguard (in Born's words) the "social freedom and independent existence" (*"die soziale Freiheit, die unabhängige Existenz"*) of each and a just and amicable coexistence among all. "So unite, you German workers, journeymen, helpers or whatever you call yourselves," exhorted the Hamburg *Bildungsverein für Arbeiter*. "Cast your lots together to aid your education and training and thereby . . . become a golden middle estate [*Mittelstand*] and open a golden new age." The goal was not to dissolve all social classes but to create a mutually satisfactory relationship among them. "We do not want to abolish the difference between rich and poor," explained a typical artisan petition from the Grand Duchy of Hesse, "but we also do not want money to rule over the work of head and hand."[12]

Attempts to organize production and consumption on a voluntary, small-scale, cooperative basis flowed directly out of ambitions like these and out of the working and living conditions of many German (and other European) working people, rural and urban alike. Cooperative associations constituted the theoretical and practical pillars of the philosophies and programs formulated by Pierre-Joseph Proudhon and the wandering journeyman tailor Wilhelm Weitling. As late as December 1847, Engels was still gnashing his teeth over the tenacious attachment to their ideas displayed by artisan members of the Communist League itself. "Weitlingism and Proudhonism are truly the exact expression of these jackasses' way of life," he wrote Marx from Paris, "and hence nothing can be done." In 1848–49 diverse groups of rural cottage workers and urban craftworkers endorsed the cooperative principle. The fledgling national German workers' organization led by Stephan Born incorporated cooperativism into its platform, and cooperative enterprises in various locales were soon employing teams of weavers, cigarmakers, shoemakers, clothing workers (male and female), bakers, carpenters, and others.[13]

Goals like these, Born saw, addressed the needs and aspirations of far broader layers than those found in the wage-earning working class alone. "We count in our number," he asserted, "the greater part of the nation, not only the wage workers and the journeymen, but also the great number of small masters who are oppressed by the competition of large-scale capital, the agriculturalists whose parcel of land is no longer enough, the teacher who educates our children, the girl who sits at the embroidery frame or the machine are ours." His newspaper, *Das Volk* ("The People"), therefore spoke to, and in the name of, "manufacturers, small masters and workers" alike.[14]

Political themes repeatedly surfaced in the deliberations and petitions of working people in 1848. For journeymen and small masters, indeed, as for liberal merchants and industrialists, social-economic and political issues had become tightly interwoven. Under plebeian hands, however, the weave assumed a distinctive pattern. Few could muster much enthusiasm about winning "a preponderant influence over the state" for a new "aristocracy of wealth and intellect." Craftworkers came rather to champion broad democratic rights through an appreciation of the right to organize (and all the other liberties that this one implied) and through an ardent desire to redirect state intervention in economic life. Mainz's plebeian *demokratische Verein* (in Hesse-Darmstadt) as well as Esslingen's *Arbeiterverein* and Stuttgart's *Bildungsverein für Arbeiter* (both in Württemberg) strove "to bring the workers with all legal means into the full enjoyment of all civil rights," singling out "the realization of . . . popular sovereignty."[15]

This broader democratic perspective clashed openly and repeatedly with the narrower liberal project throughout the revolutionary period. On the afternoon of March 3—prior to the popular storm but with its warning flashes already on the horizon—municipal officials in Cologne drafted a resolution requesting an end to censorship, the immediate convocation of a United Prussian Diet, and the creation of a German National Assembly based on an expanded male suffrage. The city council asked the prosperous financier and merchant Ludolf Camphausen to submit this resolution to Friedrich Wilhelm IV.

At this point a large crowd composed primarily of workers interrupted the city council's deliberations. Led by three local members of the Communist League (former military officers Fritz Anneke and August Willich and the physician Andreas Gottschalk), the plebeians presented a petition of their own. It demanded a legislature and executive elected on the basis of universal manhood suffrage and eligibility for office at the state and local levels; unconditional freedom of speech, press, and association; guarantees of work and decent living standards for all; universal free education; and the replacement of the aristocratic standing army by a civil guard led by publicly elected officers. Ordered to withdraw, the workers refused. Only when the council brought in troops, who opened fire, did the workers finally disperse. Gottschalk and Willich were later jailed, while Friedrich Wilhelm appointed Camphausen prime minister. But similar demands continued to be raised throughout Germany.[16]

By summer both general and trade-specific labor organizations were striving to link up with one another to amplify their voice and increase their power. These efforts further clarified and specified the aims and assumptions of those involved. The first attempt at an all-German congress of craftworkers, the *Deutsche Handwerker- und Gewerbekongress,* met in Frankfurt-am-Main in July and August of 1848. Known as the Artisans' Congress, it championed a number of measures that would find ample plebeian support during the revolution, including graduated income and property taxes; legal restrictions on the length of the working day; government aid to the jobless, disabled, and widowed; the improvement of education and its extension to all free of charge. The delegates also requested protective tariffs, government banks to provide cheap credit to artisans, the elimination of capital punishment, a legally guaranteed right to work, and a ministry of labor.[17]

From the standpoint of building an ongoing movement of craftworkers, however, the Artisans' Congress proved a false start. It was dominated by guild masters who sought to reach a conflict-free, corporate society by regenerating the guilds and by banning outright all rural, household, public, and large-scale production of manufactures and once again preventing free entry into the trades. The traditional hierachy of masters, journeymen, and apprentices would remain, as would its paternalist trappings, including strict articles of apprenticeship, the work-book system through which masters and police kept tabs on wandering journeymen, a mandatory three-year period of travel for all journeymen, a renewed prohibition against all journeyman marriages, and the general denial of master status to anyone under twenty-five years of age. The same exclusionary spirit guided the election and certification of congress delegates. Out of more than one hundred present, only ten were journeymen. The masters at first planned to exclude even this small company from its deliberations. Only after a heated and lengthy argument were the journeymen permitted to stay—and even then they were denied a vote.[18]

Neither the program nor the self-conception of the Artisans' Congress offered much to the great mass of Germany's craftworkers. Harboring less affection for the past or for traditional state and guild hierarchies, as Jürgen Kocka has noted, journeymen suffered "from both the gradual destruction and protracted resistance of the old order." While "they were no admirers of the emerging system of capitalism," therefore, "they were no staunch defenders of the old order as it existed, either."[19] Much the same could be said about many hard-pressed (and especially sweated) nominal masters.

Far more representative of these constituencies were two other congresses that convened that season. The local organizations that participated subsequently fused into a single nationwide federation commonly known as "the Brotherhood" (formally called the *Allgemeine Arbeiterverbrüderung*). The *Verbrüderung* was led from Leipzig by Stephan Born and Christian Nees von Esenbeck.

Of particular relevance to the present study is the first of these two gatherings, since it drew its strength largely from the southwestern heartland of the mid-century *Auswanderung*. Originating in opposition to the Artisans' Congress, this gathering initially styled itself as the Journeymen's Congress. As it broadened its self-conception and constituency, it changed its name to the more inclusive *Allgemeiner deutscher Arbeiterkongress* (ADA—General German Workers' Congress).[20]

Some of the ADA's conclusions echoed resolutions already adopted by the Artisans' Congress. Unregulated economic activity was anathema to both, and both refused to trust the free play of market forces to regulate the economy. Both groups, moreover, sought to extend the boundaries of political rights. Nevertheless the two bodies interpreted these principles in markedly distinct ways. The ADA clung less tenaciously to the economic past and expressly supported the economic integration and development of the German nation, demanding the complete abolition of both internal tariffs and restrictions on the free movement of individuals and proposing nationalization and additional state construction of railroads, canals, and mines.

Concerning the nature and operation of government, the ADA called more consistently and insistently for democratic rights, specifically demanding the promulgation of universal manhood suffrage. Its delegates agreed that the state ought to impose a progressive tax system, establish credit institutions to serve small producers, provide tariff protection against foreign manufactures, enforce minimum wage and maximum hours laws, and furnish social insurance for the sick, widowed, and unemployed. To these state responsibilities, however, they added others, including the defense of employee rights and the obligation to mediate in disputes between masters and journeymen. And with its eye on the emigration, the ADA also called for state organization of and assistance to *Auswanderer,* including financial help in purchasing land in North America—a demand already raised in the New World by native-born Americans and immigrants alike.[21]

The distinctions must not be overdrawn, of course. The journeymen, small masters, and other working people represented at the ADA had not completely abandoned the language, traditions, or framework of guild organization. But when delegates there invoked the heritage and symbolism of the guilds, they did so in order to project a considerably less nostalgic, more libertarian and egalitarian vision than the one the Artisans' Congress upheld. At the ADA the old guild system came in for direct attack for its exclusive, hierarchical, and monopolistic nature. For journeymen, the delegates demanded the right to seek employment anywhere in Germany (including in factories) and rejected the work-book system and any obligation to travel. The stipulated length of apprenticeship would similarly be reduced. In place of the old guild framework, finally, the ADA called for one that would embrace all producers, including those employed in factories, and over which all producers would exercise joint control. This would constitute, it explained, a new "organization of labor" based on "a new guild system, completely different from the old, suiting our highly complex industrial conditions, acknowledging the equal rights of all producers and encompassing all social occupations [and] made possible only by freedom of movement and abolition of privilege."[22]

The Democratic Movement

The specific conditions and outlooks of hard-pressed urban and rural Germans profoundly influenced southwestern Germany's political and social history. All those hoping to lead or rule this population found themselves compelled, in one way or another, to adjust their programs accordingly. German liberalism proved no exception. Dreams of an electorate defined by property ownership and an economy regulated only by supply and demand simply could not be implemented. Popular insistence eventually compelled the Frankfurt Assembly, if not to declare a republic, at least to endorse universal manhood suffrage. Widespread fear of unregulated commerce and production forced reconsideration of Manchester-type economic precepts. To avoid even more severe a social-economic and political polarization, many politicians still respectful of laissez-faire principles retreated from their practical application.[23]

Other individuals—especially certain members of the democratic intelligentsia of western and southern Germany such as Gustav Struve, Karl Heinzen, Friedrich Hecker, Hermann Kriege, Julius Fröbel, and Gottfried Kinkel—went further in attempting to reconcile their ideals of personal liberty with the region's particular economic reality. Linking social justice and self-government with the preservation (or regeneration) of a large and viable *Mittelstand,* the most consistent of these individuals called for a republic that would offer some kind of positive state support to small handicraft and agricultural producers.

Professor Gottfried Kinkel argued for such support in his influential pamphlet of 1848 entitled, *Artisanry, Save Yourself! Or What Should the German Artisan Demand and Do to Better His Situation? (Handwerk, errette Dich! oder Was soll der deutsche Handwerker fordern und thun, um seinen Stand zu bessern?)* Asserting that "true well-being is fundamental to every democracy," Baden democrat Gustav Struve called for a "*soziale Republik,*" in which those who live by their own toil can obtain "a share in the profits of labor" and thereby partake of their natural birthright of "prosperity, education, and freedom for all." Only if this promise were realized, he admonished, could society guarantee the "security of property." "I do not wish to destroy individual property rights," Struve's fellow democrat and sometime collaborator Karl Heinzen explained in a similar vein. "I only wish to see that they are safeguarded for all."[24]

Although most democratic leaders proved more interested in political than economic rights, their social rhetoric and political republicanism deeply antagonized liberal political and business figures striving to curb the demands and mobilization of social groups below them. Its speakers and proposals spurned or ignored, the Left bolted the Frankfurt Assembly in frustration. The unresponsive and repressive policies of successive liberal governments produced deeper and more widespread popular disillusion and disaffection, an important factor in the counterrevolution's eventual triumph.

While a clear and comprehensive social profile of the democratic rank and file of 1848–49 remains unavailable, fragmentary evidence indicates that handicraft and other workers made up an important part of it. The democratic Frankfurt Assembly delegate Julius Fröbel presided over the convention at which the southwestern craft organizations joined the *Verbrüderung.* One of the Brotherhood's leaders, Stephan Born, convinced that the fortunes of German workers were "closely and firmly" linked to those of the democrats, participated in the second national Democratic Congress, as did Nees von Esenbeck and representatives of various local *Arbeitervereine.* In Württemberg in 1849, statewide elections that enfranchised broad layers of marginal producers yielded twice as many votes for radical left-wing as for liberal candidates. And about half of those identified as democrats by the police in Dresden and Leipzig worked in the handicrafts, including masters, journeymen, and apprentices. In the spring of 1848, workers also played a prominent role in Baden, where as many as six thousand people joined a republican uprising initiated by Struve and Hecker. The organized contingents included an *Arbeiter-Bataillon* from Mannheim (set near the junction of Baden, the Palatinate, and Hesse-Darmstadt) and a five-hundred-strong Turner unit from Hanau, a transportation and manufacturing town in Hesse-Kassel. Among the Turner soldiers identified, the ten most heavily represented occupations were (in descending order) goldsmiths, carpenters and cabinetmakers, shoemakers, tailors, cigarmakers, carvers, day laborers, students, merchants, and locksmiths/machinists.[25]

Democracy and Religion

The popular unrest that finally erupted in political and social revolution expressed itself in religious terms as well. This was not unusual. Because of the intimate linkages between ecclesiastical and temporal power in Europe over so many centuries, many political and theological controversies had become intertwined. The division of Germany into Roman Catholic and Protestant (Lutheran and Calvinist) states—according to the principle *cuius regio, eius religio*—complicated but hardly unraveled the pattern. And the bond joining the temporal and spiritual spheres asserted itself the more forcefully as the general crisis of society sharpened in the 1840s. Thus it was that a highly placed journalist asserted at the time, "Church ground is beginning to tremble. Religion now forms the axis around which everything, including politics, revolves, and this will become even truer in the near future."[26]

Catholicism was strongest in the southern and western states and in Austria. As in Europe generally, the Roman Catholic church and hierarchy constituted a bulwark of political, as well as religious, reaction in Germany, committed to defending the remnants of autocratic and aristocratic power against the threatening forces of "modernism." Pope Gregory VI, whose patriarchate lasted until 1846, starkly revealed the depth of his commitment to the status quo when he refused to support the 1830–31 revolt of Roman Catholic Poland against its domination by the despised Russian (Orthodox) Empire. In fact,

Gregory went further, specifically denouncing Polish artisans who had justified resistance to the Russian authorities on Christian grounds. He stigmatized those who, "under cover of religion, defy the legitimate power of princes, break all the ties of submission imposed by duty and plunge their country into misfortune and mourning." Rather than follow those insubordinates, the Pope admonished, Poles must obey their "mighty emperor who would show them every kindness." In his encyclical of 1832, *Mirari vos,* the pope generalized the point, denouncing the separation of church and state and "the senseless and erroneous idea, better still, absurdity, that freedom of conscience is to be claimed and defended for all men." He condemned the "complete and unrestrained freedom of opinion which is spreading everywhere to the harm of both the Church and the State," as well as freedom of the press, and all forms of rebellion against "our dearest sons in Jesus Christ, the princes."[27]

The accession of Pius IX raised initial hopes of liberalization. And early in 1848 some Catholic clerics in German states ruled by Protestant princes hoped that the revolution might enhance their own church's status and prospects. The degree of social discontent and scarcely concealed anticlericalism unleashed in 1848–49, however, stampeded both Rome and leaders of the national churches into the counterrevolutionary camp. Pius himself proved loyal to Gregory's principles and eventually summarized his reaction to the age of revolutions in his encyclical *Syllabus Errorum.* There he denounced the "error" of believing that "the Roman Pontiff can and should reconcile himself to and agree with progress, liberalism, and modern civilization."[28]

Lutheranism and Calvinism, of course, were born in revolt against the Catholic church. In the late eighteenth century, Enlightenment rationalism influenced a number of Protestant theologians in Germany. Here, too, however, liberal theological views became discredited by their political association. The shocks of the French Revolution and the Napoleonic Wars reinforced the alliance between the Protestant hierarchies and the Prussian monarchy and Junkerdom. This led, among other things, to the union of the Lutheran and Reformed (Calvinist) confessions in 1817.[29]

During the 1840s Friedrich Wilhelm IV of Prussia moved to bolster the forces of religious conservatism and homogenization by championing the reactionary pietists gathered around E. W. Hengstenberg. Sharing the papacy's hostility to the Enlightnment and all its offspring and works, Hengstenberg particularly emphasized the church's obligation to strengthen "the eternal foundation of all states" by "instilling obedience and respect for worldly authorities." The insistence by arch-conservative General Joseph Maria von Radowitz on the eve of the 1848 Revolution that "Protestantism is the principle of the Prussian state" said at least as much about that church as he did about the state. Rallying the forces of the right against those of revolution, Ludwig von Gerlach once more invoked the close connection between official religion and autocratic politics, pledging that counterrevolution would "give our consciousness of God a political form."[30]

Germany's Christian clergy, Protestant as well as Catholic, had long worried about the advance of popular religious disaffection—by which they meant less a growth of outright atheism than a perceptible and growing drift away from the churches, the clergy, and their specific doctrines and sacraments. William Howitt was struck in 1843 by the "vast amount of indifferentism and disbelief" he encountered in his German travels. Against this background, and particularly during the so-called hungry forties, the conservatives' emphatic identification of the official churches with the temporal status quo could only aggravate the religious doubts of those Germans nursing social and political grievances. The influence of the Enlightenment, economic development, and political ferment also left an indelible mark on Germany's (disproportionately urbanized) Jewish minority.[31]

Symptomatic of this pervasive if diffuse mood of spiritual dissidence, skepticism, and disaffection was the rise of two Christian rationalist movements during the mid-1840s: the so-called *Deutschkatholiken* (German Catholics) and the Protestant *Lichtfreunde* (Friends of Light). The *Lichtfreunde*'s suppression, in turn, spurred the growth of independent *freien Gemeinden* (free congregations). As early as 1846, 25,000 people adhered to 100 of these congregations. Seventy congregations formed in 1848–49 alone, even as the *Deutschkatholiken* claimed an organized following of 70,000 to 80,000. By 1851 more than 300 free congregations reportedly embraced about 150,000 members. In each case, the congregation attracted an unorganized periphery of sympathizers that was many times larger than the formal membership.[32]

These two movements attracted supporters of various social backgrounds, "from university professors to the lowliest artisans" (according to a contemporary description). Rationalists argued for greater rights for women, and the level of women's participation in their public meetings—including not only women married to professionals but also workers such as embroiderers and dressmakers—further scandalized opponents. Protests against the 1845 suspension of *Lichtfreunde* leader G. A. Wislicenus testified to the breadth of the movement's support. Drafted in Breslau and then circulated in fifty-two neighboring cities and towns, one petition defending the pastor acquired thousands of signatures. Clergymen, teachers, and students accounted for about 650 names; physicians, apothecaries, jurists, and provincial legislators, 350; landowners, including proprietors of knightly estates, 480; government employees, 700; merchants, 600. The largest single group of signatures—some 2,000—came from those engaged in industry, including both factory owners and artisans. The handicraft *Bildungsverein* of Magdeburg presented *Lichtfreunde* organizer Leberecht Uhlich with a set of silver candlesticks inscribed, "You wish for the good and love the true; therefore, accept our love." When that city's *Lichtfreunde* constituted themselves as a congregation, independent of the Protestant church and pledged to "Freedom, Truth, and Fraternity," an observer recorded that "the first hundred men who went before the court to indicate their secession from the state church were artisans. Among the hundred which immediately followed, there was a very large proportion of workers: stevedores, warehouse workers, railroad workers, and factory workers. After a few more weeks came several from the upper classes, then indeed many more, who followed the same course." Descriptions of some German-Catholic congregations in East Elbia as well as the Southwest also stress the participation of "the serving class" or the "proletariat."[33]

Much remains to be learned about the *Deutschkatholiken, Lichtfreunde,* and *freien Gemeinden,* but it appears that in the religious sphere, as in the political, those from different social backgrounds often brought distinct concerns to the same movements. More prosperous and educated adherents—the liberal-minded merchants, landowners, minor officials, assorted members of the intelligentsia, and well-to-do master craftsmen who usually led the congregations—generally emphasized issues of theological rationalism, intellectual freedom, and separation of church and state. For those of humbler status, who were less preoccupied with doctrinal subtleties, religious dissent or disaffection tended to combine a smoldering anticlericalism with some modern materialism and an older longing to make Christianity once more into the faith and vindication of the poor. Johann Hinrich Wichern, a permanent councillor in the Prussian Interior Ministry who specialized in identifying and quelling social unrest among the laboring classes, warned in the 1840s against the currency among traveling journeymen of such dangerous religio-political ideas. Wichern believed that the kind of materialism propagated in educated circles by radical Young Hegelians like Ludwig Feuerbach and David Strauss was circulating in simplified form among urban working people as well. In the late

1830s and early 1840, journeyman tailor Wilhelm Weitling (the premier leader and spokesman for some of Germany's most hard-pressed
craftworkers) successfully tapped underground currents of plebeian
Christian millenialism.[34]

Opponents of the *Lichtfreunde* and *Deutschkatholiken* therefore worried about the popular appeal of those rationalists. The arch-conservative *Evangelische Kirchen-Zeitung* raged against the Friends for organizing "mass meetings of all sorts of discontented elements" who
had "raised the banner of revolt against authority." Among those
gatherings was the outdoor meeting organized for Leberecht Uhlich
in March 1845 by the Berlin artisan association, whose membership
was top-heavy with Enlightenment-influenced journeymen. As the
Kirchen-Zeitung understood, the popularity of the dissident priests and
pastors reflected the already deep-seated dissatisfaction of those who
came to listen. Uhlich was especially dangerous, the editor warned
perspicaciously, because he "knows exactly what the people want" and
insists on voicing the "ideas, opinions, aspirations, and hopes of the
masses."[35]

Leaders and supporters of both rationalist currents did, indeed, figure prominently in the events of 1848. Many of them—including leaders
like Uhlich—identified with the mainstream liberal movement. Others stood to its left. In 1848 the co-chair of the Berlin Workers' Congress was the prominent German-Catholic Nees von Esenbeck, and
the "Ten Commandments of the Workers" published by the *Verbrüderung* included the injunction, "Thou shalt shut thy ears to priests."
Other *Lichtfreunde, Deutschkatholik,* or *freie Gemeinde* activists associated with the labor organizations and democratic associations of 1848
included Wislicenus himself, Robert Blum, Gottfried Kinkel, Johannes Ronge, Karl Theodor Bayrhoffer, Gustav Struve, and Friedrich
Hecker.[36] Their more numerous if less well-known plebeian constituents also left their mark, not only on the revolution but on the emigration as well. The poorest mid-century *Auswanderer* found the
cheapest passage to the United States via the port at Liverpool, England. Passing among such people, the German pastor in that city was
shocked by the tremendous "religious indifference, yea mockery and
enmity toward God" he found there.[37]

PART II

Adjusting to the New

3

"Where Nobody Need Be Poor": Immigrants and Industry in America

One of Carl Schurz's most vivid memories of village life in south-western Germany featured one family's departure for the United States and the neighbors' reaction. "I heard many a man say," Schurz later recalled, "how happy he would be if he could go with them to that great and free country, where a man could be himself." The youthful Schurz was fascinated by talk of a land "where nobody need be poor, because everybody was free."[1]

The story captures an important fact. Many German plebeians con-templating emigration in the first half of the nineteenth century en-visioned U.S. society as a near paradise. The availability of both land and jobs appeared far greater than in the *Auswanderer* regions of Ger-many, and living standards were correspondingly higher. Where would a small farmer or craftworker find a better chance to retain or regain personal independence—to escape *Pauperismus* and proletarianiza-tion? And where would one find greater equality of opportunity or greater relief from governmental abuses than in the freest and most democratic republic of the age? This message had been brought home to Germans since at least the 1830s in numerous and avidly read trav-eler's accounts. Still more powerful and widely circulated were en-thusiastic letters from friends or relatives already settled in the United States.[2]

By the late 1840s and 1850s this image had grown only more vivid and widely attractive. Throughout Germany, noted a well-traveled pastor, "the name of America has now become as familiar to every peasant and laborer, yea to every child in the street, as that of the nearest neighboring country, whilst to thousands and hundreds of thousands, it is a goal of their warmest wishes and boldest hopes."

"He who in Germany has to suffer from want and misery, or must expect these in the near future," concluded a contemporary German commentary on the emigration, is commonly led abroad by the news "that in North America there are far greater productive natural resources and that work has a greater value than in Germany." This was the vision that animated seventy-five departing natives of Baden, who determined, "since Capital so commands Labor in the Fatherland, to find a new home . . . where the reverse relationship prevails." An emigrant Württemberg shoemaker lamented that in Germany "reliance on the honest working man has declined; the capitalist and the rich have little or no heart for the destitute . . . their hearts beat only for Mammon. Therefore I preferred to go to a land where . . . a worker is worth his wage." Johann Caspar, in his first letter home to his German-Swiss wife, exulted: "Poverty is not shameful in America, and purses are not worshipped in political life. Civic virtue is not bought with money and not lost with the loss of property. Crimes are severely punished, but not being able to pay does not lead to [becoming] the criminal in prison."[3]

The massive emigration and the perceptions that encouraged it provoked a reaction; books appeared that strove to reduce the emigration fever. These typically argued that "many" of the "advantages" of life in America "are only apparent or are fully outweighed by evils intimately associated with the good points." But even these critics usually conceded the basic economic contrasts. "As compared with the increasing poverty in Europe, the uncertainty of political conditions, the increasing pressure of expenses, and the difficulty of earning a modest living even with great industry," Karl Büchele acknowledged, "the possibility of emigration to the United States exercises an extraordinary attraction," especially in light of "the ease with which land can be earned there, the absence of restrictions on commerce, trade, and traffic; low cost of living, political and religious freedom, absence of a standing army, and, at the same time, the undisputed internal as well as external peace."[4]

"North America," Gottfried Menzel agreed, "as a country with fertile land still partly unoccupied, a country thinly populated with flourishing trade and general freedom of trade, offers far greater and more abundant means of livelihood than Germany." He praised the United States' relatively low tax rate and the "complete freedom in the trades and professions," delighting that "there is no difference in rank," and "the public official has no advantage not shared by the farmer, the merchant, or the teamster." He added that "labor there has a high, and cost of living a lower, value" than in Germany. All this meant

Table 10
Changing Distribution of the U.S. Labor Force, 1800–1860

	Agricultural		Nonagricultural	
	Number of Individuals (in millions)	Percent of Total Labor Force	Number of Individuals (in millions)	Percent of Total Labor Force
1800	1.26	76.8%	0.40	23.2%
1840	3.52	70.6	2.17	29.4
1850	4.39	53.6	3.81	46.4
1860	5.82	52.6	5.24	47.4

Note: The figures in this table include all self-employed, wage-earning, salaried, or enslaved "economically active" individuals ten years of age or older, including unpaid family members.
Source: Thomas Weiss, "Revised Estimates of the United States Workforce, 1800–1860," *Long-Term Factors in American Economic Growth,* ed. Stanley L. Engerman and Robert E. Gallman (Chicago: University of Chicago Press, 1986), pp. 646–48.

that "on the whole the people are far less oppressed by want and need and the tormenting anxiety for one's daily bread." "That it is easier to make a living in America," he therefore concluded, "cannot be denied."[5]

The comparative dynamism of the North American economy in that period is striking, indeed. Between 1800 and the outbreak of the Civil War, the United States more than tripled its territory while its population grew sixfold, from 5.3 to 31.4 million. The rapid construction of an extensive transportation network steadily pulled distant locales into regional and eventually national markets. As University of Berlin historian Frederick von Raumer found during his visit in the 1840s, "The canals, steamboats, and railroads clasp it [the United States] together in their embrace; they have abridged both time and distance; have immeasurably augmented intercourse, as well as the imports, exports, and means of sale; have given value to the worthless timber; and have suddenly brought into the thinly peopled, uncultivated country, the most powerful means of effecting a rapid improvement."[6]

Growth crowned all sectors, and its pace quickened during the 1840s. Agriculture absorbed the energies of more than half the nation's work force in 1860, and the absolute size of the farm population continued to expand as pioneers moved westward (see table 10). Fewer than one in seven inhabitants of the United States had resided in the West in 1800; by 1860 the proportion had risen well above one in three,

Table 11
Growth of U.S. Manufacturing, 1840–60

	Value Added (in billions of dollars)[a]	Mfg. Work Force (millions employed)	Value Added per Worker[a]	Mfg. as % of Total Commodity Output[b]
1840	0.19	0.5	$380	17
1850	0.49	1.2	$408	30
1860	0.86	1.53	$562	32

[a]In 1879 dollars.
[b]For the years 1839, 1849, and 1859.
Sources: U.S. Bureau of the Census, *Historical Statistics of the United States, Colonial Times to 1970,* vol. 1, pp. 139, 239; Robert E. Gallman, "Commodity Output, 1839–1899," *Trends in the American Economy in the Nineteenth Century* (Princeton, N.J.: Princeton University Press, 1960), p. 26.

surpassing the proportion resident in the Northeast. And still the density of population in the United States remained far below that in the German states.[7]

Even more explosive was the growth of manufacturing, which accounted for fewer than 3 percent of the country's work force in 1800 but 14 percent in 1860—20 percent, if one adds mining and construction. During the 1840s and 1850s alone, the manufacturing work force nearly tripled in absolute size, and productivity (value added) per manufacturing worker increased by 50 percent (see table 11). As a result, these decades saw manufacturing's share of the nation's total output of commodities nearly double (to 32 percent), while agriculture's share declined from 72 to 56 percent. (The remainder in each year represents the share contributed by mining and construction.)[8] In the 1830s German immigrant Francis Grund was already proclaiming that "no other nation did at any time engage in such a variety of industrious pursuits and none can boast . . . a greater rapidity of progress." He likened the United States to "one gigantic workshop, over the entrance of which there is the blazing inscription, 'No admission here, except on business.'" Tocqueville noted admiringly that "no people in the world have made such rapid progress in trade and manufactures as the Americans." By 1860, at the latest, only Great Britain surpassed the United States as an industrial producer. Even earlier, astute British observers had predicted that the United States would soon "rear up a fabric of commercial greatness, such as the world has hitherto been a stranger to" and soon rival British manufacturers, "hitherto the chief manufacturers of the world."[9]

Table 12

Urban Population as a Percent of Total Population, 1800–1860

	1800	1840	1850	1860
United States	6.1	10.8	15.3	19.8
New England	8.2	19.4	28.8	36.6
Middle Atlantic	10.2	18.1	25.5	35.4
East North Central	0.0	3.9	9.0	14.1
West North Central	—	3.9	10.3	13.4
South Atlantic	3.4	7.7	9.8	11.5
East South Central	0.0	2.1	4.2	5.9

Source: U.S. Bureau of the Census, *Sixteenth Census of the United States,* vol. 1, *Population* (Washington, D.C.: Government Printing Office, 1942), p. 20. By definition, urban centers contained at least 2,500 inhabitants.

Towns and cities thrived on such vigorous economic development. In 1840 the nation contained some 130 urban centers, and about one in ten Americans lived in them. Just a generation later, in 1860, the country boasted more than 400 towns and cities, which contained one of every five U.S. residents. Regional data are still more arresting. In New England and the Middle Atlantic states, where the industrial revolution had proceeded furthest, the urban population already embraced more than one-third of all residents by 1860 (see table 12). But even in the overwhelmingly agricultural upper Midwest (the East and West North Central regions in table 12), the proportion dwelling in urban centers rose between 1840 and 1860 from only about 1 in 25 to greater than 1 in 7. "Towns spring up in the course of a few weeks or months," marveled one observer, "not to speak of years; and extensive tracts of country which, till lately, were all but unexplored, yearly add to the industrial resources of the nation."[10]

The German "Place" in the United States

This was the booming society that attracted such huge numbers of European emigrants at mid-century. As M. A. Jones observes, "in proportion to the total population, [this was] the largest influx the United States has ever known." As a result of the massive *Auswanderung,* the German-American population was increasing three and a half times as swiftly as that of the native-born by the 1850s.[11]

Impressive as this rate of increase was, however, the German immigrants still numbered only some 1.3 million in 1860, or about 4 percent of the total U.S. population. Had the newcomers spread evenly across the country and through its various occupations and social classes, their subsequent conduct would have attracted much less attention. Instead they concentrated both geographically and occupationally in some of the principal centers of the expanding commercial and manufacturing economy. In 1860 more than three-quarters lived in the nine mid-Atlantic and Midwestern states—New York, New Jersey, Pennsylvania, Ohio, Illinois, Wisconsin, Indiana, Michigan, and Iowa. Their visibility and impact in this region grew further because of what census officials called a "preference of the city to the country in the selection of their places of occupation and residence."[12]

Some of the immigrants did, of course, enter agriculture, particularly in the western states. But in 1860 only about a third of all German-born males over twenty years of age in this country tilled the soil. By 1870 the proportion had slipped to just over one-fourth. Moreover, in that year (the first for which we have such data) one-fourth of these immigrant farmers worked for others as hired farm laborers. Another subgroup of unknown dimensions rented the land they cultivated. While "the majority of the Germans emigrating to America wish to seek their fortunes in agriculture," Gottfried Menzel advised his readers, "the purchase of land has its dangers and difficulties. The price of land is, in proportion to its productivity, not so low as is generally believed. To establish a farm on new and uncultivated land is for the newcomer an almost impossible task." A would-be farmer arriving in the port of New York City needed fairly substantial assets (between $750 and $1,500 by one conservative estimate) to purchase transportation west and obtain land, implements, housing and fencing materials, livestock, and sustenance during the first unremunerative year of clearing and planting. As noted in chapter 1, however, assets of those proportions were uncommon among immigrant German newcomers in these years. Thus restricted, the immigrants tended at least initially to congregate disproportionately in the nation's growing urban centers (see table 13). In 1860 the average German immigrant was almost three and a half times as likely as the average U.S. citizen to live in one of the country's major cities.[13]

This relative concentration in urban areas gave the Germans a disproportionate weight in many important centers of population and industry (see table 14). Entire sections of these towns and cities became German enclaves—New York's *Kleindeutschland*, Philadelphia's Spring Garden and Kensington districts, Cincinnati's "Over-the-Rhine" neighborhood, Newark's "Hill" district, parts of Chicago's North Side, and Milwaukee's east- and westside "German Town" neighborhoods.

Table 13
Residential Concentration of the German-born in Urban Settlements, 1860

	Total Population	German-born	German-born in Total Population
New York State			
Seven cities[a]	1,311,788	177,402	13.5%
Rest of state[b]	2,568,947	78,850	3.1%
Pennsylvania			
Four cities[c]	642,296	55,616	8.7
Rest of state	2,263,919	82,628	3.6
New Jersey			
Two cities[d]	99,545	12,200	12.3
Rest of state	572,472	21,572	3.8
Ohio			
Three cities[e]	219,707	56,602	25.8
Rest of state	1,119,804	111,608	10.0
Illinois			
Chicago	108,305	22,230	20.5
Rest of state	1,596,018	108,574	6.8
Wisconsin			
Milwaukee	45,140	15,981	35.4
Rest of state	729,570	123,879	17.0
Michigan			
Detroit	44,216	7,220	16.3
Rest of state	698,098	38,787	5.6

[a]Albany, Brooklyn, Buffalo, New York City, Rochester, Syracuse, and Troy.
[b]Includes smaller cities and towns. Thus this category probably overstates the proportion of immigrants in rural settings.
[c]Allegheny, Philadelphia, Pittsburgh, and Reading.
[d]Newark and Jersey City.
[e]Cleveland, Cincinnati, and Dayton.
Source: Secretary of the Interior, *Statistics of the United States in 1860* (Washington, D.C.: Government Printing Office, 1866), pp. lvii–lviii.

Teetotaling Anglo-Americans usually fixated upon the ubiquitous German taverns and beer and wine gardens that sprang up there in such quantity and variety—from tiny to cavernous, from the basement saloon catering to restive single men to the quite respectable street-level *Lokal* serving entire families, children included. In truth, these places served important community functions. Besides offering sanctuary, relaxation, and companionship, they also provided meeting rooms for the plethora of *Vereine* (associations)—benevolent, musical, literary, theatrical, sporting, militia, craft, political, and others—through

Table 14
Share of the German-born in Some Major U.S. Population and
Manufacturing Centers, 1840–60

	Total Population			Percent German-born	
	1840	1850	1860	1850	1860
United States	17,069,453	23,191,876	31,443,321	2.5	4.1
Baltimore (8)ª	102,313	169,054	212,418	11.5	15.4
Buffalo (23)	18,213	42,261	81,129	—	22.5
Chicago (16)	4,470	29,963	109,260	16.9	20.4
Cincinnati (3)	46,338	115,435	161,044	29.0	27.2
Cleveland (34)	6,071	17,034	43,417	—	20.9
Louisville (12)	21,210	43,194	68,033	17.4	19.7
Milwaukee (27)	1,712	20,061	45,246	36.2	35.3
Newark (6)	17,290	38,894	71,941	9.8	14.7
New York (1)	312,710	515,547	813,669	10.9	14.8
Philadelphia (2)	220,423	340,045	565,529	6.8	7.7
Pittsburgh (14)	21,115	46,601	49,217	—	23.0
St. Louis (7)	16,469	77,860	160,773	29.0	31.4
Brooklyn (5)	—	—	81,129	—	22.5

ªThe parenthetical numeral following each city indicates its rank among the nation's leading manufacturing centers in 1860.
Sources: J. D. B. DeBow, *Statistical View of the United States, Compendium of the Seventh Census* (Washington, D.C.: Beverley Tucker, 1854), appendix, p. 399; Secretary of the Interior, *Statistics of the United States in 1860*, p. xviii; *Twelfth Census of the United States, Taken in the Year 1900* (Washington, D.C.: United States Census Office, 1902), pp. 430–33; Joseph C. G. Kennedy, *Population of the United States in 1860; Compiled from the Original Returns of the Eighth Census* (Washington, D.C.: Government Printing Office, 1864), pp. xxviii, 599, 603–5. The raw population figures for Philadelphia contained in the twelfth census are obviously erroneous and have been replaced by figures from the eighth.

which so much social life flowed, in German America as it had in Germany. German churches, schools, theaters, and restaurants flourished too; German-language newspapers multiplied; and in fair weather large throngs enjoyed open-air concerts, gymnastic competitions, parades, and picnics.[14]

Immigrant Social Structure

The social structure of German America reflected this heavy urban concentration. Probably twice as many of them made their living in

Table 15
Distribution of Major Ethnic Groups by Occupational Category, 1870

	All U.S.	Native	Irish	German
Agriculture	47%	54%	15%	27%
Personal and professional service[a]	21	19	45	23
Trade and transportation	10	9	13	13
Manufactures, mechanical, and mining industries	22	18	28	37

[a]Includes large numbers of unskilled workers.
Source: Francis A. Walker, *Statistics of the Population of the United States in 1870* (Washington, D.C.: Government Printing Office, 1872), pp. 698–99.

manufacturing and commerce as in agriculture (see table 15). In 1870, the first year in which the U.S. Census Bureau reported such data, gainfully employed Germans concentrated only half as heavily in agriculture as did the native-born but twice as heavily as the latter in "Manufacturing, Mechanical, and Mining" industries. The German immigrants then fall into subgroups defined by differences in wealth and power. The relative size and internal structure of each stratum varied from city to city, reflecting differences in the specific locale's size, location, age, and stage of industrial development, the particular ethnic mix of its population and work force, and the era in which each group arrived.[15]

At the top of the social pyramid was a group of very wealthy, well-connected, and influential (and especially transatlantic-oriented) merchants, financiers, and manufacturing employers. "Already," *Hunt's Merchant's Magazine* observed in the late 1840s, "the class of German merchants, resident here, and maintaining constant business communication with the land of their birth, is very large." The Whig *North American Review* agreed that "the German merchants who are found in our cities accumulate fortunes with rapidity." In the seaports of New York, Philadelphia, Baltimore, and New Orleans, this upper class traced its lineage at least to the turn of the nineteenth century and often earlier. After a few decades their counterparts could also be found in a number of other cities as well. New infusions from abroad regularly reinforced their ranks, as did the financial success here of immigrants with humbler European antecedents. Taken together, Karl Büchele reported in 1855, these "big businessman of the principal cities" constituted "the aristocracy of German immigrants." Below this elite lay a much more broadly based stratum of medium- to large-scale entrepreneurs (merchants, manufacturers, and proprietors of the bigger hotels and restaurants), associated professionals (clergy, physicians, attorneys, and journalists), and local politicians.[16]

But the great majority of German-born urban dwellers entered the ranks of the United States' mushrooming working class. They formed an important contingent in what George Rogers Taylor referred to as "that great body of industrial wage earners now regarded as typical of capitalistic economy." The growth of this class paralleled the dynamic expansion of the nation's economy.[17]

Unable in the short run to obtain farms in the New World, many uprooted German peasants sustained themselves through unskilled work. Draymen, hackmen, and teamsters, longshoremen and porters, domestic servants, and a wide variety of laborers employed in construction, transportation, and manufacturing combined to make up the bottom tier of the German-American working class. Across the country unskilled jobs like these sustained perhaps one-fifth of the economically active German-born population.

It was such people with whom charitable and other relief societies became familiar. Much of the unskilled work available to men was very heavy and dangerous. Employment commonly lasted only a few days or weeks at a stretch and was poorly paid. Moreover, the arbitrary withholding of all or part of a laborer's wage was a popular form of cost-cutting. In 1852 the New York Association for Improving the Condition of the Poor reported that "more than half the needy are Irish and German" and that "the foreigners relieved . . . are mostly persons who have been trained to no trade or regular employment, and having little skill in any, are forced to accept of such as is offered." Although this report focused on "our Atlantic cities," the profile was similar elsewhere. Although women could find unskilled work in domestic service, it paid little, especially for recently landed immigrants, and such work was available almost exclusively to girls and unwed young women. Language barriers posed another hurdle. "It was always very hard to send the little one out in the streets to make a living," a single German-born mother in *Kleindeutschland* said of her twelve-year-old daughter in 1852. "But I couldn't help it; I must pay the rent some way."[18]

Throughout the region of heavy German settlement, both previous training and current opportunity led especially large numbers of Germans back into the traditional handicrafts—principally into the garment, shoemaking, food preparation, woodworking, ironworking, and leatherworking trades. Federal census marshals in 1870 found Germans working in disproportionate numbers in clothes production, carpentry, and furniture making, and as boot and shoemakers, black-smiths, butchers and bakers, masons and plasterers, cigarmakers, and coopers. The proportion of Germans in these trades was well above their share of the population at large. At the time of the ninth census (1870), only 1 in 23 U.S. residents had been born in Germany, but the German-born accounted for 1 in 8 tanners, curriers, leather fin-ishers, saddle and harness makers, and masons; 1 in 6 boot and shoe-makers; 1 in 5 clothing workers generally; more than 1 in 4 cabi-netmakers; almost 1 in 3 butchers; and nearly 40 percent of all bakers.[19]

These figures on the German place in American manufacturing only confirmed a trend that had become obvious decades earlier in some of the country's major cities. Reporting on the state of American in-dustry in the 1850s, British investigator George Wallis found that "German workmen are largely employed in many departments of in-dustry, and being generally an intelligent and orderly class of men, are highly esteemed." In 1860 the New York Association for Im-proving the Condition of the Poor noted that "German mechanics and tradesmen" were "settl[ing] in our large towns, where they almost monopolize certain branches of trade and industry." Sprinkled through their ranks were members of the immigrant intelligentsia unable to support themselves here in their original professions. Some tried their hands at small proprietorship, notably as restaurant or tavern owners. Others became craftworkers, obtaining employment as cigarmakers, painters, tailors, furniture workers, or in other occupations.[20]

In the 1850s, for example, the largest German-American settlement was New York City, the nation's principal population and manufac-turing center, which at that time still included only Manhattan Island. In 1860 some 120,000 Germans—or nearly one out of every ten Ger-mans in the country—lived there. More *Auswanderer* lived there than in the next two largest centers of German-American residence (St. Louis and Cincinnati) combined. The only other cities in the world with larger concentrations of Germans than New York were Berlin and Vienna.

The occupational concentration of New York's Germans was strik-ing. Accounting for some 15 percent of the city's total population in 1855, Germans already composed 22 percent of its work force. More than half of those gainfully employed immigrants were craftworkers, and 3 out of 5 of those craftworkers were concentrated in the garment industry (tailors, dressmakers, and seamstresses); shoe manufacture; and furniture making (cabinetmakers, turners, carvers, gilders, and upholsterers). In absolute numbers, German workers were in the ma-jority among New York's more than 12,000 tailors, 6,700 shoemakers, 4,600 furniture makers, and 3,700 bakers and confection-ers—some of the city's most populous trades.[21] Comparable patterns prevailed in Philadelphia, Pittsburgh, Newark, Buffalo, Cincinnati, Milwaukee, St. Louis, and Chicago.[22] The trades toward which these German immigrants gravitated were central components of the American manufacturing economy at mid-century (see appendix tables A and B).

Economic Opportunity

Business success beckoned to enterprising immigrant craftworkers with the right skills, contacts, commercial experience, and liquid assets. Many local histories bristle with the names of those who responded to the call. In the context of so swiftly expanding an economy, hard work, thrift, and shrewd calculations permitted many to become proprietors of thriving firms. Some carved out niches for themselves in less competitive markets. Highly skilled artisans did very well furnishing quality goods—high-fashion jewelry, clothing, boots and shoes, furniture, ornamental ironwork, coaches and carriages—in limited quantity on a made-to-order basis.[23]

There were also good craft jobs to be had outside the luxury markets—in geographic regions (especially the West) or occupations as yet less affected by the transportation revolution, job competition, division of labor, and mechanization (notably the construction trades, butchering, and brewing). House carpenters, for example, who composed a large and relatively well-paid segment of the nation's work force, normally commanded between $1.50 and $2.00 per day in most parts of the country during the 1850s. Though their work was seasonal, these rates permitted a living standard higher than was typical of most other traditional crafts. The native-born usually monopolized these choice craft occupations in long-settled areas of the East; immigrants found it easier to break into them farther west.[24] Small-scale, self-employed butchers serving local customers (as distinct from the nascent meat-packing industry, which was oriented to more far-flung regional markets) required above-average amounts of operating capital but also realized substantial profits. Working conditions in these butcher shops suggest little degradation, and the employees received daily wages of about $1.50. As noted, German butchers were numerous by the mid-1850s in many northern cities.[25]

Other business-minded immigrant craftworkers prospered by employing their own *Landsleute* (and occasionally others) precisely in the more densely populated regions and especially competitive branches of industry (including ready-made clothing, shoes, and furniture). The experience of the Puchta family in Cincinnati is a good example. Arriving in the Queen City in 1856, twenty-three-year-old Lorenz Puchta began his career as a shoemaker's apprentice. Within a decade he owned his own shop and shoe store. As his business expanded, his role began to change. Although Lorenz continued to measure and cut the leather and fit up the lasts while his wife, Barbara Katharina, helped run the establishment, he now assigned other production tasks to outworking employees. Lorenz's achievements, in turn, made possible the even greater commercial success of his son, George, whose business prominence ultimately helped elect him mayor of the city.[26]

The blossoming of entrepreneurial opportunity in the 1840s and 1850s was made possible in large part by the huge immigration of impoverished European working people. Their arrival finally began to ease the notorious dearth of wage laborers in the North—and consequently the high price of labor and workers' intractability. The New York Association for Improving the Condition of the Poor declared that "the Germans constitute the best portion of our immigrant population," noting, inter alia, that Germans "can work for less wages than Americans, and live where an Irishman would starve." Similarly, the *New York Daily Times* found Germans "industrious, sober, and economical, and above all, fitted to do the cheap and ingenious [i.e., skilled] labor of the country," adding that "the Germans will live as cheaply and work infinitely more intelligently than the negro." In the West, the *Chicago Daily Tribune*—which was "without any strong predilections in favor of foreigners of any kind"—nonetheless repeated the *New York Times*' favorable appraisal of German craftworkers nearly verbatim. Indeed, the availability of so much skilled but low-wage labor roused in the boosterish Chicago editor "a much more cordial feeling toward our German population than to any other class of citizens who are not 'native and to the manor born.' "[27]

Initially tempering such praise was concern about the immigrants' accustomed work pace. Nineteenth-century European visitors unfailingly noted the greater speed with which labor was performed in America; German tourists were no exception. " 'Always in haste!' is the motto of these active, restless people," the middle-class liberal traveler Moritz Busch wrote approvingly in the early 1850s. The Americans he encountered "live fast. . . . They sing fast. . . . They love to make money fast—for that is the intention with which anyone here who has the stuff devotes himself to business. They do everything fast, so why shouldn't they work at the same rate?"[28]

Not all immigrants adapted easily to this pace. The *New York Daily Tribune* noted of German craftworkers that upon "arriving on our shores they do not *drive business,* as is a distinguishing characteristic of our native mechanics." But most newcomers did adjust. The more entrepreneurial-minded made the transition willingly, even enthusiastically, speeding their labors the more quickly to ascend the ladder of success. Recalcitrants required prodding—as by the fact that incomes were based on very low piece rates. Work pace, working hours, and material living standards thus became variables in a single equation; immigrant craftworkers learned the hard way that the price of even subsistence living was unprecedentedly intense and protracted effort. "After they have been some time among us," the *New York Daily Tribune* thus observed with satisfaction, "a decided improvement in this respect can be plainly observed," adding that "there is not perhaps a more industrious working class in our city than the Germans," who "rise early and retire late." Moritz Busch encountered and applauded the same accommodation in the Midwest, as a result of which "even a German boot artist moves awl and hammer at least twice as quickly" as he did in Germany. "The 'mason's tinder' that costs our workers so much time in the lighting of pipes," he cracked, "doesn't grow on American soil, and just as little thrive here the coziness and deliberateness with which they apply themselves in Germany to every miserable repair job."[29]

The satisfaction expressed in these quarters was not universally shared. Native-born youth fled low-paid and hard-driven jobs in search of higher incomes and more congenial conditions. Immigrant craftworkers with fewer alternatives often found their life in the United States considerably harder than expected. Like German-born journeyman coppersmith Nikolaus Schwenck, they discovered that "in all branches of business" in the New World "everything has to work under high steam." "He who has not from his youth up been performing continuously the most severe labor," Gottfried Menzel cautioned, "so much more will he lack, in America . . . the necessary strength and ability," since there "labor is much more severe and much more work is required for the higher wages he receives than is usual in Germany."[30]

That not even protracted and concentrated effort guaranteed comfortable incomes came as an even greater shock. "Many," affirmed Chicago's *Illinois Staats-Zeitung,* "were bitterly disappointed" by economic conditions in the United States, and "many among us fought a severe fight for a material existence." "It would be an exaggeration to claim that the poor in this country are already as badly off as in Europe," German shoemakers in St. Louis acknowledged in the mid-

1840s. But, they quickly added, "the passage of time brings us ever closer to that point." A group of Milwaukee German tailors posed the issue more sharply a few years later, warning that "the social position of the great mass of the people—the workers—in our present political organization is such that the future will bring us poverty for ever increasing numbers through more widespread lower pay." As a result of an increasing division of labor, a German Cincinnati tailor reported, "every year another skilled craft ceases to exist." For that reason, as well as periodic wage cuts, inflation, and seasonal bouts of unemployment, "the condition of the workers continues steadily to deteriorate."[31]

Economic Development and Craftwork

The discovery in the New World of certain social-economic conditions associated with the Old reflected some basic similarities in the form that economic development took in the United States and Europe. As in Europe, improvements in the nation's transportation systems and the resulting integration of local markets, along with the growth of light manufacturing, introduced important changes into the economy. These included increasing wholesale production, the intensification and division of labor, stepped-up competition, and declining skill requirements. But these developments coexisted with—and were often mediated by—significant vestiges of the more traditional, small-scale, artisanal economy. Much craftwork in the United States continued to occur on a decentralized basis in small shops and private dwellings, using skills and tools characteristic of the trades for centuries.

What was true of productive methods and techniques applied as well to the social status of the producers. The ubiquitous independent artisan, who was lionized in Jefferson's day, was giving way to the wage laborer. For many caught up in this process of change, the transition was neither sudden nor clear in all its implications. It usually unfolded in a protracted and uneven manner, with producers passing through intermediate degrees of semidependence upon merchants and subcontractors.

The persistence of the old and familiar amid the new and strange was striking even in some sectors of the economy that began to mechanize during the antebellum era. By the 1850s, for example, growing numbers of cabinetmakers (especially in the Midwest) found themselves employed in major factories equipped with steam-driven equipment. Great numbers of small cabinetmaking shops, however, continued to exist alongside these factories. Even within the latter, moreover, numerous aspects of production retained a nonmechanized, semi-artisanal character. This was still truer in the production of shoes and men's clothing, where extensive outwork and subcontrating arrangements survived even the first appearance of sewing machines.

The complex nature of economic development deeply affected the way that craftworkers viewed themselves, their employers, and their interests. For a time, both the nature and full extent of the transformations under way were obscured, as were some of their causes. In short, both the direction of industrial change and its uneven and protracted nature helped convince many that perceptions of the world and plans for its improvement that they had first encountered in Europe retained value in the industrializing United States.

The Boot and Shoe Industry

Since the 1830s Lynn, Massachusetts, had been the national center of the thriving boot and shoe industry. By 1850 the biggest and most efficient firms there each employed between three and five hundred hands. During the next decade Massachusetts further tightened its grip on the national market; according to the manufacturing census for 1860, every second shoe worker in the nation lived in the Bay State. In the mid-Atlantic and midwestern states, where German cordwainers were most numerous, the pressure of competition from the Massachusetts shoe firms was keenly felt. Already in 1845 the *New York Daily Tribune* reported that most of the made-to-order footwear worn in New York City had been imported from "the Eastern States [New England], where the workmen can live for almost less than half the sum it costs our city mechanics." Since, moreover, "transportation from those places [to] here amounts to a mere song," Lynn shoes could be priced low, "and the laborer on this branch of Industry in our city is compelled to submit to the grinding competition engendered, and give all his labor, his time, and his health to earn food and clothes."[32]

The small number of New York shoemakers who performed more highly skilled work, especially luxury work, largely escaped this pressure. The rest usually found themselves driven downward into repair work and the production of cheap, rough wear for military, western, and southern markets. In this large sector of the industry, frequent spells of unemployment during the 1850s alternated with periods of hard-driven and protracted labor at long hours (commonly twelve to sixteen hours per day) for low wages (between five and eight dollars per week). "No class of mechanics in New York," the *Tribune* reported, "average so great an amount of work for so little money as the journeymen shoemakers."[33]

Even in Lynn, production often appeared to be more centralized than it really was. The biggest firms based there continued to employ large numbers on an outwork basis. Alan Dawley has described this arrangement as "a transitional mode of organization that combined both artisan and factory techniques." This description applies even more aptly to working conditions in the mid-Atlantic cities. New York's biggest shoe firms were substantially smaller than Lynn's, and the great mass of New York shoemakers worked in small shops, as the *Tribune* reported in 1845. The dozen largest New York firms employed twenty to thirty hands apiece. Even five years later, little more than one-fifth of the city's boot and shoe labor force worked in factories, none of which had yet mechanized significantly. About the same number worked for subcontractors, many of them former journeymen, in small garret sweatshops. Twice as many still worked on their own premises, commonly supplementing meager piece-rate incomes with occasional repair jobs. "Pretty much all the capital one requires," noted the *Tribune,* was "a bench and tools, a side of leather, a ball of thread, a little wax, and a glass showcase, stuck out by the door containing a specimen of work."[34]

Heavy immigration, low overhead costs, and the small scale of production all encouraged rapid overcrowding of the industry's labor market, and by the mid-1850s straitened German and Irish immigrants dominated New York's shoemaking work force. Germans alone constituted half of all cordwainers in the city. Moreover, as the *Tribune* had previously noted, "the manner in which the different classes of the Shoe-makers live varies according to the nation." The city's comparatively few native- and English-born journeymen clustered in the more desirable positions while the Germans and Irish found themselves relegated to the bottom rungs of the industry's ladder. "The Germans," discovered the *Tribune,* were "generally found occupying basements and cellars," and a description of such a combination dwelling-and-workshop followed a few days later:

> The floor is made of rough planks laid loosely down, and the ceiling is not quite so high as a tall man. The walls are dark and damp, and a wide, desolate fireplace yawns in the center to the right of the entrance. . . . In one corner is a squalid bed, and the room elsewhere is occupied by a work bench, a cradle made from a dry goods box, two or three broken and scattered chairs, a stewpan, and a kettle. . . . The

miserable room is lighted only by a shallow sash [window], partly pro-
jecting above the surface of the ground, and by the light that struggles
down the steep and rotting stairs.

Into such quarters three generations might crowd—husband and wife,
five or six children, and one or more grandparents. Conditions such
as these embittered relations between poor shoemakers and the industry's larger employers.[35]

In Philadelphia one in five shoemakers was German-born. Here,
too, decentralization remained typical. Even among that half of the
industry's work force producing for larger manufactories in 1850, only
a small minority actually worked on the employer's premises. The rest,
former census official Edward Young reported, were employed on an
outwork basis, in which "the work is cut in the establishment, and
given out to the men who work at their homes." Another third or so
of those Philadelphia shoemakers listed in the 1850 manufacturing
census worked for garret bosses, who then sold the finished product
to jobbers or retailers. As in New York, the fastest and most dexterous
sweated workers could earn from eight to ten dollars a week—and
some as high as twelve. But even for those employed by "the best
houses," the average male wage hovered around a dollar per day, and
some workers took in only five dollars per week. The average female
employee working outside a family unit reportedly earned only one-
third as much annually as her male counterpart. Similar conditions
prevailed in Newark, where Germans nearly doubled their share of
the shoemaking work force during the 1850s. A newspaper report
described a shoe firm there in 1854 "employing 400 hands and whose
system of doing business we consider the most perfect we are ac-
quainted with." The firm's five-story building, however, was devoted
primarily to storage, cutting the leather, and "giving out and receiving
the work when made."[36]

Few immigrant cordwainers in the West worked in qualitatively
different settings. In Milwaukee and Chicago, hard-pressed shoemakers worked on a small-scale basis and received nominal wages
equivalent to those paid in the East. Until late in the 1840s, Cincinnati's modest shoe industry concentrated on serving a local market in
custom wear, while New England imports satisfied most of the demand for lower-priced, off-the-shelf shoes. At last, however, Cincinnati's swift growth and development and the arrival of so many foreign-born (especially German) craftworkers encouraged a number of
local firms to challenge eastern manufacturers for a share of the area's
own ready-made market. From some 650 shoemakers in 1840, the

work force had reached nearly 1,800 by 1851 and had absorbed nearly another thousand by 1859.[37]

Although the Cincinnati shoe industry grew quickly and ownership fast became concentrated, the work process itself changed more slowly. The largest manufactory in the city in 1851, owned by the firm of Filley and Chapin, occupied eight rooms in the upper stories of a large building and boasted a work force totaling two hundred, including both male journeymen and female stitchers and binders. Many of its employees, however, evidently worked at home and received wages comparable to those paid in New York, Philadelphia, and Newark. Cincinnati booster Charles Cist proudly related the examples of "a woman with three boys [who] earned in this business, three dollars a week, and each of the boys, three more" and of "an elderly man, who was out of employment when he came to Cincinnati" but who was by the early 1850s "now earning, with [the aid of] three or four children, twenty dollars per week."[38]

Men's Clothing Production

The production of ready-made men's clothing first became a thriving business in the United States during the 1820s. By 1850 it was booming, most notably in New York and Cincinnati, and absorbing large numbers of German immigrants. Across the country, indeed, one in five tailors was German-born by the end of the 1860s.

Even more than in the shoe industry, expansion in men's clothing production signified decline for many self-employed small craftworkers, a fact that census officials attributed to a "natural tendency of capital to reduce the number of small tailoring establishments, and to build up, in the principal business centers, extensive ready-made clothing houses." No more than in boot and shoe production, however, did concentration of ownership necessarily centralize production. Large clothing manufacturers remained heavily dependent on subcontracting and putting out work to poor native-born females and immigrants. In most places tailoring paid less than shoe work. Even when the growing use of sewing machines began to drive some workers into centralized shops late in the 1850s, most clothing production remained decentralized.[39]

The country's leading garment center by mid-century was New York City, which turned out about one-third of all the men's clothing produced nationwide and a still bigger share of the coarse men's garments worn by small farmers, poorer urban dwellers, and slaves. The city's clothing firms employed more than one of every seven economically active German immigrants in New York in the 1850s. These thousands of German tailors dominated the industry and constituted the city's largest single block of foreign-born craftworkers in any trade.[40]

The overwhelming majority of German tailors in New York City worked in the industry's wholesale branch for firms employing upwards of fifty people each. The average firm employed more than one hundred; the largest, five thousand. In this case, too, however, it was easy to erroneously link the concentration of capital with modern factory methods. For example, the sheer scale and efficiency of the Lewis and Hanford Company's operation clearly impressed a writer for *Hunt's Merchant's Magazine,* who found that firm occupying four storefronts and thirteen large rooms on downtown Pearl Street. He described the firm's division of labor in loving detail.[41] But of the thousands of New York tailors employed by Lewis and Hanford, only a small fraction actually worked on the Pearl Street premises—including the male, generally native-born, highly skilled, and better paid cloth cutters. In contrast, the 3,600 operatives who sewed the precut cloth pieces into garments worked in their own homes, where they were "employed 'from early dawn to latest eve' in plying the needle." Other "outsiders" worked in small garret workshops maintained by jobbers and other small entrepreneurs.[42]

As this description suggests, hours were long and wages low. This was particularly true for immigrant tailors. A weekly income of five dollars was not unusual in 1853, for which German tailors (and other members of their families) commonly worked fourteen to eighteen hours per day. Women working outside the family unit generally received between half and two-thirds as much as the men did. Even these rates could dazzle the most impoverished, job-hungry German immigrants, though, and some found ways to profit from the need of others. "Some of the poor tailors in New York," reported one observer, "rent a room, occupy a spot themselves, and rent out the rest of the room to others at the same kind of work, charging fifty cents for seat room for a man and a girl to assist him; thirty-seven cents for a man alone."[43]

New York City's garment firms were unable to dominate the national market in men's ready-made clothing in the way that Lynn dominated the shoe industry. The production of cheap men's garments flourished throughout the mid-Atlantic and midwestern states. In Newark, Philadelphia, Cincinnati, Milwaukee, and even Chicago, clothing manufactories of varying sizes depended upon outside labor—especially that of German and female sewers—to produce most garments; garret sweatshops picked up much of the slack. Both working conditions and incomes proved remarkably uniform nationally. Freedley's description of a major Philadelphia clothing firm, indeed, reads as though it had been lifted directly from the description of New York's Lewis and Hanford establishment in *Hunt's*. As late as 1859, most of Cincinnati's seamstresses continued to ply their needles by hand.[44]

Hat and Cap Production

Germans employed in wholesale hat and cap production confronted similar conditions. Large manufactories centered in Newark and uptown Manhattan employed steam-driven equipment for certain tasks. Similar operations appeared in growing numbers in Philadelphia and Cincinnati as well. But much of the hand work in the 1850s continued to be sent outside—to urban women, immigrants of both sexes, and small-town and rural residents. Employer access to so large a labor supply kept wages falling, working days long, and the incidence of unemployment high. The average male hatter in New York reportedly earned only eight to twelve dollars per week in 1845, and most female cap stitchers received only fourteen to twenty-five cents per day. Thereafter conditions appear to have deteriorated further. By 1853 hatmakers were working twelve-hour to sixteen-hour days and receiving only five to seven dollars per week. The workers' bitter resentment was hard to miss. "The separation in feeling and interest between employer and employee," the *New York Daily Tribune* regretted, "is perhaps more strictly kept up in the business of Hat-making than in most other branches of mechanics."[45]

Furniture Making

The history of furniture production offers a partial contrast with that of shoemaking and men's clothing. In 1850 most immigrant German cabinetmakers still worked in relatively small settings. Only about two-fifths of all male cabinetmakers listed in the population census of 1850 were evidently employed by the industry's larger firms (those with an annual product in excess of five hundred dollars). Even these more substantial firms employed on average fewer than six workers. During the following decade, however, some furniture manufacturers pointed the way toward a more mechanized and centralized system of production.[46]

Commanding an ample share of the national market since the 1830s, New York City's furniture industry at this time depended upon a nearly all-male labor force. More than 80 percent of this work force was foreign-born, and Germans alone made up more than 60 percent of the city's 3,500 cabinetmakers and upholsterers and 50 percent of its 1,200 wood turners (lathe operators), carvers, and gilders. The scale of production varied substantially from shop to shop. Half of all cabinetmakers in the city worked for a relative handful of furniture bosses who employed more than twenty workers each. One of the better-known big entrepreneurs was Charles A. Boudine, whose plant on the corner of Broadway and Anthony (now Worth) streets employed 70 cabinetmakers and nearly 130 carvers, varnishers, and upholsterers. The other half of the city's furniture work force crafted in smaller shops. A few of the latter catered to the luxury trade. But most clustered in or around *Kleindeutschland* and operated on a wholesale basis, each typically supplying contractors with a single type of furniture—beds, sofas, chests, bookcases, chairs, tables, or desks.[47]

No matter where German journeymen were employed or what markets they served (local customers or far-flung markets in the West, the South, and the Caribbean), they typically used their own hand tools. In smaller shops they were even expected to supply their own workbenches. Steam-powered machinery was rarely seen; heavy sawing, molding, or turning was done elsewhere, in specialized mills. Steam heat was absent, too; wood-burning stoves offered the only defense against winter's cold.

These craftworkers commonly earned about a dollar—perhaps a dollar and a quarter—per day, about twenty-five dollars per month, a wage that represented a steep decline since the mid-1830s. Others were still worse off; some of the smallest shops paid as little as ten to fifteen dollars a month in the 1850s. Small employers frequently survived only by squeezing themselves as well as their employees, as Ernest Hagen's experience testifies. Arriving from Hamburg with his family in 1844, the fourteen-year-old Hagen worked first as an apprentice and then as a journeyman cabinetmaker. In 1858 he and workmate J. Matthew Meier bought out their employer. Thereafter, Hagen recalled, "we worked ourselves at the bench with 2 or 3 hired men and could hardly make as much as our men, which was about one Dollar a day, after defraying shop expenses. We economised where we could and held on, hoping for a good time to come. We worked mostly for the trade, supplying the furniture stores, who paid very poorly; and we had to wait a long time to get [paid] and also lost some pretty large bills altogether by failures [of retail stores]." In Philadelphia, the German share of the industry's work force jumped from 32 to 42 percent in the 1850s. The firms there catered heavily to the southern market and organized their production much as their New York counterparts did and paid comparable wages.[48]

During the 1850s demand from the swelling inland rural population justified an appreciable increase in the scale, mechanization, and centralization of U.S. furniture manufacture. The absolute number of the more substantial firms remained stable (and may even have declined slightly), but these firms employed a rising share of the industry's total work force. As the scale of production increased, so did the division of labor. Coupled with a major increase in capital investment, this reorganization yielded nearly a 20 percent boost in productivity per worker nationwide.[49]

The pioneers of change were based not in New York or Philadelphia but in Cincinnati. During the 1830s and 1840s some enterprises there had begun shifting from the production of expensive, custom-made furniture to the high-volume production of less expensive, ready-made furniture to satisfy mounting demand in the South and West. By 1850 three out of five Cincinnati furniture workers were employed by firms with at least fifty employees each. Immigrants supplied much of the labor required by this booming industry.[50]

Charles Cist gloried in the changes taking place in Cincinnati. The new, six-floor factory built by Frederick Rammelsberg and Robert Mitchell, he noted, "directly and indirectly" employed some 250 workers, primarily native- and German-born. "As many as two hundred pieces of furniture, and the various parts in the same series, prepared and adjusted to fit . . . ," Cist enthused, "are taken from story to story, until on the upper floors, they receive their final dressing and finish, for market." Steam-driven circular saws and other machines performed the rough-cutting, planing, slitting, and boring, while skilled employees did the finishing work. The C. D. Johnson firm owned a seven-story factory and employed some 160 workers, primarily Germans, to turn out chairs for the wholesale market all along the Ohio and Mississippi river system. And Clawson and Mudge employed 130 workers at its five-story bedstead factory.[51]

These impressive factories achieved major advances in productivity by reorganizing the work process and introducing substantial amounts of steam-driven equipment, including lathes, saws, and drills, as well as planing, tapering, and tenoning machines. Although machines were generally used in the early, roughing-out stages of production, skilled cabinetmakers continued to perform the finishing operations completely by hand. Indeed, the demand for skilled labor increased as the industry expanded. Increased productivity, output, and profitability at the larger shops could support substantially higher wage rates—reportedly around $1.75 per day at Mitchell and Rammelsberg's factory—than those found at the smaller shops.

In other cities—including older furniture-making centers on the Atlantic coast—the competition of modernizing firms like Cincinnati's actually discouraged large-scale mechanization. New York City cabinetmakers began to retreat into luxury production. Other midwestern firms hesitated to challenge the already established larger outfits for command of regional markets and kept their operations modest. Milwaukee's largest furniture manufactories boasted only about forty workers each in 1850. Though some specialization began in Chicago during the 1840s, the typical workplace in 1850 was still a tiny shop whose proprietor toiled alone. A growing local market in Chicago encouraged some firms to expand and mechanize during the 1850s. These apparently remained at least as dependent as the considerably larger firms of Cincinnati upon the labor of skilled cabinetmakers.[52]

Blacksmithing

Other trades employing German immigrants in disproportionate numbers displayed, in varying degrees and combinations, the traits discussed in connection with the three industries surveyed above. One of these was blacksmithing. By mid-century, the nation's rapidly expanding and increasingly specialized demand for iron products was causing the local all-purpose blacksmith's shop to slip in prominence. During the 1850s, the number of sizable shops dropped, and the number of hands they employed shrank by more than a third. This did not mean, however, that blacksmiths themselves were disappearing. On the contrary, the population census recorded more than a 12 percent increase in their total number, which partly reflected the influx of German-born ironworkers. Some of these people worked (alone or with one or two others) in shops too small for inclusion in the manufacturing census. These small shops served local needs for horseshoeing, repair work, and the like. Other German immigrants found jobs in new (or newly expanded) ironworking industries. One of these was the production of coaches, wagons, and carriages.[53]

Coach and Wagonmaking

Interregional migration, the steady growth of agriculture, the expansion of the overland stagecoach and the urban omnibus systems, and a swiftly growing demand for stylish business wagons and private carriages all encouraged expansion and changes in the manufacture of horse-drawn wheeled vehicles of every type. The carriage-making industry's work force nearly doubled in the 1850s, and both the division of labor and steam-driven mechanization made great strides. In Cincinnati the average shop's work force increased by about half (from 9 to 14) during the 1850s, and the city's largest firm grew just as fast, augmenting its work force from 60 to between 90 and 100. Chicago, which was already serving regional midwestern markets by mid-decade, was not far behind. In 1854 three of its manufacturers employed at least 70 workers apiece; two years later a new shop employed 100. By the late 1850s one Philadelphia carriage firm had 125 male employees who plied nine distinct trades in its four-story factory. The city's largest wagon-building works employed 173, while another, newly built, was expected soon to employ 250.[54]

Cooperage

The rapid expansion of transportation and trade in the early nineteenth century multiplied the demand for commercial containers, notably barrels. By 1820 master coopers were already responding with production innovations, and additional tool improvements (especially the refinement of stave knives) during the late 1830s and early 1840s kept productivity rising. During the 1850s the nascent brewing industry raised barrel demand even higher, and the new Benson stave-bucker mechanized the shaping (or "dressing") of staves. Thus, while the average firm's capitalization nearly doubled and the value of product per worker increased 40 percent over the decade, the number of workers employed in the average firm rose but slightly, from four to five. Coopers continued to experience long spells of unemployment, and wages remained low by craftwork standards. These conditions evidently encouraged a major exodus from the trade by native-born workers.[55]

Leather Making

An outgrowth of the cattle-slaughtering industry—and key supplier for a range of others—leather making was a complicated process involving much dirty and strenuous labor performed by relatively large teams of skilled and unskilled workers in increasingly mechanized settings. This was true even during the first decades of the 1800s. Further mechanical and chemical improvements in hide splitting, tanning, and dressing introduced down through the Civil War saved time, boosted production, and increased the quality of finished leather.[56]

In the meantime, leather-making operations expanded. The average Cincinnati firm, which had employed 6 hands in 1840, doubled its size during the following decade. By 1854 two of Chicago's larger tanneries were employing upwards of 40 hands apiece. Milwaukee's largest tannery employed 35 hands in 1850, 60 hands just ten years later. By 1860 the nation's average leather-making enterprise was capitalized at $7,000—almost four times the sum invested in the average shoemaking establishment included in the manufacturing census and more than ten times the average investment required in blacksmithing.[57]

Along with growth and development went a greater division of labor and the employment of larger numbers of unskilled laborers. But, as in many other developing industries in this era, highly skilled craftworkers remained crucial to the manufacturing process. The animal hide had first to be separated from hair, epidermis, and fleshy substrate through a combination of soaking and scraping. Tanners then soaked the hides in a solution of tannic acid (obtained from oak, chestnut, or hemlock bark) and water or gelatine. One contemporary noted that because "the processes employed are so various, and the modifications occasioned by temperature, strength of the liquor, and quality and condition of the hides, are so numerous and so different," the tanning industry "depends almost wholly upon the skill and judgment with which its complicated manipulations are conducted." When tanning was completed, skilled curriers then resoftened the leather, beating it with a mallet, shaving its underside of irregularities with a two-handed knife, and—after another immersion in cold water—rubbing the other side with a stretching iron. After being "dubbed" with cod oil on both sides, the leather was dried and then once more rubbed with a "graining board," a grooved hardwood hand tool. Only then was it ready for sale and use.[58]

Saddle and Harness Making

Like shoemaking, saddle and harness making revolved around the sewing of leather (in this case, hogskin, because of its softness and ability to resist the elements). Although this industry, too, experienced a growing division of labor and increasing reliance upon the outwork system, until the 1850s it remained virtually untouched by mechanization. Nationally, the average saddle shop employed fewer than four workers in 1850. One of Cincinnati's larger firms, however, employed 25 early in the 1850s. The average shop in Newark—an important locus of the industry—employed more than 50 by 1860, and at least one employed 400 in 1870. As in shoemaking, male wages were generally low.[59]

Cigar Making

Workshop organization came slowly to the manufacture of cigars, and division of labor and mechanization proceeded more slowly still. Well into the nineteenth century, much of this industry remained organized on the domestic system and depended upon the efforts of farm women and children. The urban settlement of large numbers of experienced but low-wage European (male) cigarmakers helped shift the industry into the cities.

Cigar shops began to appear in New York City around mid-century. By 1860 Philadelphia was the country's largest cigar-producing center, with a total work force of about 4,000 that now included both "journeymen and girls." The scale of production and the size of the shops remained rather modest, however. Perhaps three-quarters of the cigar labor force worked for small entrepreneurs employing 5 or 6 workers apiece or less; the remainder worked for larger firms with upwards of 10 workers apiece and an average of 35 hands. The biggest firm in the city employed only 65. Though still considered a skilled craft, cigar making (like housepainting and sign painting) could be learned more quickly than many other trades. For that reason, it attracted more than a few declassed immigrant professionals unable to find work in their chosen fields. Once again, employer access to an ample work force kept wages very low indeed. In Philadelphia most cigar workers earned only about five to six dollars per week. The shift into shop production occurred somewhat earlier in St. Louis and Cincinnati, and by 1850 Cincinnati and its environs already boasted nearly thirty cigar manufacturers with an average of 40 employees each, including both adults and children. The largest boasted a work force five times as big.[60]

Baking

German-born bakers in America—like their native-born counterparts—were barely affected by outwork, subcontracting, growing mechanization, or expansion. Even in bigger cities like New York and Philadelphia, whose sizable local markets encouraged a larger scale of production, most bakers worked alongside only a handful of others.

Nonetheless, their working conditions were less than ideal: heavy labor around hot ovens and an unusually long workday. "They commence work at midnight," reported the *New York Daily Tribune* in 1850, "and often continue fourteen, sixteen, and eighteen hours," with "no respite on Sundays as a general thing." Especially in big cities, a large labor supply kept wages low, unemployment high, and living conditions miserable, and the poverty of the bakery workers dragged some down into virtual debt-peonage. Confectionary workers confronted similar conditions, which persisted even decades later, reflecting the especially protracted survival of an "old-fashioned," "antediluvian style" of production, as one German-American labor journalist put it. "While other industries have advanced and are carried on on a larger scale," he observed in the 1880s, "the bakers go on as they used to do in old times."[61]

The Business Cycle and Its Impact

Conditions common to the industrial economy as a whole added to the hardships imposed upon immigrant craftworkers. The 1843–54 period was one of substantial overall growth and rising total employment for the nation. But this growth brought with it high inflation, which accelerated following the discovery of gold in California in 1848. Throughout the industrial regions of the country the rising cost of living eroded wages and undermined living standards. "To make the wages of to-day equal to the wages of three years ago," declared the *New York Daily Times* in March of 1853, "twenty per cent should be added to them; for rents are vastly higher, and food is far dearer." One didn't have to be a bakery worker, sweated shoemaker, or seamstress to feel threatened by declining living standards.[62]

At the end of 1854 a period of more extreme economic fluctuations began. That winter witnessed a sharp financial panic and an attendant decline in commerce and production. A promising recovery in 1855–56 gave way to a new and even more stunning collapse in 1857. Sales, prices, credit, and manufacturing all plummeted. Encountering "universal prostration and panic," *Harper's Weekly* observed that "not for many years—not in the life time of most men who read this paper—has there been so much grave and deep apprehension." The Germans' old acquaintances—unemployment and extreme privation—reappeared. In Philadelphia between twenty and thirty thousand workers were reportedly turned out that season. Estimates of the number of newly jobless in New York ranged up to 100,000.[63]

The impact was less devastating in midwestern cities. Cincinnati fared better in 1857, its chamber of commerce believed, than "any of the other leading cities of the Union." The *Chicago Daily Press* boasted that "while city after city was falling beneath the plowshare of ruin," word "went forth to the world that Chicago stood firm and unshaken." But immigrant workers fleeing the ravages of depression in the East found no certain refuge in Cincinnati, St. Louis, or Chicago, either.[64]

One who learned this fact the hard way was journeyman coppersmith Nikolaus Schwenck of Württemberg. After arriving in Philadelphia in 1855, Schwenck "took all imaginable pains to possibly find a position," "but all in vain," since "business was very poor . . . with thousands out of work." Rather than stay put, he and his wife "decided instead to go further inland" and late that summer settled in Chicago. Over the next year and a half, as the nation's economy rebounded, Schwenck found journeyman's work in a small factory there and even "saved a respectable bit of capital." But since "work for others as a journeyman" was "not really what I want," Schwenck determined "to take a step which, if luck would have it, could lead to independence"—to take his savings and buy some "good farm land." The next year, however—1857—found him describing Chicago in virtually the same bleak terms he'd so recently applied to Philadelphia. The city, he reported to relatives that November, was suffering through "the worst of all bad times," and "thousands of workers are unemployed and look with fearful hearts towards the approaching winter." "What is worst, most criminal of all," he added, "what little they had put aside with the sweat of their brows and invested in savings banks— is gone! Most banks are bankrupt, or at least have suspended their payments." Schwenck was lucky enough to retain his factory job; sixteen of his twenty coworkers were laid off. Of such people, a Chicago German Society report noted: "Some honest, upright craftsmen and their families, who were reluctant to ask strangers for help, were forced to bring beds, clothes, and household goods to the pawnbroker. For many, the payment or foreclosure date is at the door, and most of them have neither work to earn the money nor friends from whom to borrow it."[65] A tepid recovery began in 1858 and continued through the end of the decade. But many wage cuts dating from the crisis months remained in effect, and relative employment levels stayed below those of the early 1850s.

The essence of America, it often appeared, was change. Different observers focused on different results of that dynamism. To some, the

United States' distinctive combination of rapid economic development and widespread civic freedom was pregnant with opportunity.
Individuals such as Carl Schurz, therefore, often did believe they had
found here a land "where nobody need be poor, because everybody
was free." Others found less to cheer about. "In Europe," Karl Büchele
warned, "people still adhere too much to the picture of the American
republic as it was conceived by its founders. But if they could only
glance a moment at the present reality there they would take scant
pleasure from the many new traits that have over time been acquired."
Ironically, perhaps, the very economic growth and social fluidity that
made the United States unusual sometimes created working and living
conditions that seemed to many immigrants disturbingly familiar. "We
have come to this country because our own country had oppressed
us," noted a German tailor in New York in 1850. "But what have we
gained by the exchange? In what are we bettered by our coming? We
have found here nothing but misery and hunger [and] oppression."
The first fruits of the American Revolution, he believed, had with-
ered, and "the working men were reduced to the same condition of
insufferable, incessant, and unrequited toil and labor as in Europe."[66]

4

"The Love of Liberty Is Almost a Religion": Political Unity and Dissension

Economic hardship reinforced other strong forces that pulled German-Americans together across bounds of social class. The sharing of a common language and innumerable customs and points of cultural reference over time proved a powerful source of unity, the more so in a new, strange, English-speaking, and increasingly xenophobic land. German America's churches, theaters, beer and music halls, mutual insurance societies, cultural *Vereine,* and other community institutions variously offered spiritual refuge, camaraderie, and material assistance. Problems of adjustment—exacerbated by unemployment, poverty, and ethnic discrimination—tended to strengthen community cohesion and ethnic identity. Paradoxically, perhaps, these conditions nourished the development of an all-German national self-identity among many emigrants previously accustomed to regarding themselves first and foremost as Palatines, Prussians, Hessians, or Bavarians. Formal or informal ties to well-to-do *Landsleute*—individuals at once wealthier, better educated, and better informed about and connected to the surrounding society—offered hard-pressed immigrants still other cherished sources of emotional and practical security.[1]

Joyous reaction to news of the 1848 Revolution strengthened these ethnic bonds. Everywhere the German-language press's circulation shot upward. "The kings by divine right are quaking in their boots," trumpeted the normally cautious *New Yorker Staats-Zeitung.* "Liberty's day is dawning throughout Europe." In New York great contingents of Germans—bolstered by French, Irish, Italian, Swiss, Polish, and native-born residents—paraded enthusiastically down Broadway for hours. Afterward Mayor William V. Brady presided over a huge outdoor rally featuring speakers and officers from a broad social and political spectrum. Jakob Uhl, publisher of the *New Yorker Staats-Zeitung,* and Jakob Windmüller, a leader of the German Society and the German wing of the Democratic party, found themselves celebrating beside radical activists such as Karl Heinzen, J. A. Försch, Hermann Kriege, and Heinrich Ahrens.[2]

Demonstrations in one city after another—Philadelphia, Newark, Boston, Buffalo, Pittsburgh, Cleveland, Cincinnati, Detroit, Chicago, Milwaukee, Baltimore, Louisville, Richmond, Charleston, St. Louis, New Orleans—drew upon similarly broad constituencies. There, too, mayors and other city officials eagerly accepted invitations to speak or preside; there, too, well-dressed and well-rooted *Dreissiger* (immigrants of the 1830s) mingled on reviewing stands with down-at-the-heels newcomers, big merchants and ethnic politicians mixed with workers and saloonkeepers. There, too, proponents of parliamentary democracy in Germany were flanked by champions of a "social" or "red" republic.

Despite their many differences, all these people looked forward to a new era in their native land. Each, after all, had been sufficiently dissatisfied with life in the old Germany to accept the multiple pains and indignities involved in relocating across the Atlantic. And particularly at the exuberant outset, individuals with the most diverse political, religious, and social-economic interests and views could hope that the revolution would evolve according to their own principles. In Columbia, South Carolina, *Dreissiger* liberal professor Francis Lieber dismissed his college class. Having learned just that day "that Germany too is rising," he told the students, "my heart is full to overflowing," leaving me "unfit for you this afternoon." Hundreds of miles away, fellow *Dreissiger* Gustav Körner (of Belleville, Illinois) experienced the moment in nearly identical terms. My "heart swelled with joy," he later recalled, because "the ideal of my youth for which I had sacrificed all, seemed in process of realization." Even three years later, visitor Moritz Busch observed that when the celebrated exile Gottfried Kinkel arrived in Belleville, he was "surrounded by a jubilant crowd." Indeed, "all Belleville seemed to be there, and all the dignitaries of the place . . . were there to pay their respects to the guest of honor."[3]

Amid this widespread enthusiasm, *Revolutions-Vereine* pledged to change in Germany formed in many big cities and scores of smaller towns. Some of these societies sought to help their members return home and join personally in the *Freiheitskampf.* Others succored the revolution's injured, martyred, and exiled partisans and their families. Still others emphasized educational and propaganda activities in the

United States, striving to persuade the American public and federal government to befriend Europe's nascent republics. In the early 1850s two competing networks of *Revolutions-Vereine* raised funds to finance a revival of the routed revolutionary movement.[4]

From the outset, German-American craftworkers and radical-democratic advocates played critical roles in sustaining these organizations. But like the mass meetings of 1848, most *Revolutions-Vereine* were oriented to a broader constituency. Since they aimed "to find means of terminating the desperate condition of the liberty-thirsting people of Europe," explained one convention straightforwardly, the partisans of German freedom sought "the cordial co-operation of all who seek it." In New York City officers of the solidarity organizations included the cotton exporter Leopold Bierwirth, the big tobacco merchant Maximilian Rader, and an editor of the *New Yorker Staats-Zeitung* named A. Kruer.[5]

This ecumenical approach shaped the *Revolutions-Vereine*'s political platform. Struggling to unite individuals and groups who subscribed to very different general outlooks, the January 1852 congress of the American Revolutionary League for Europe (the *Amerikanischer Revolutionsbund für Europa*) held in Philadelphia typically chose "to explore the middle ground upon which all parties could honorably and cheerfully unite their forces." The lowest common denominator proved to be consistent political republicanism: "the overthrow of monarchy and the establishment of the Republic. . . . Direct and universal suffrage and the recall of representatives by the majority of their constituents . . . [and] [t]he abolition of standing armies and inviolability of the right of the people to bear arms." Even this platform situated the revolution's organized supporters well to the left of the Frankfurt Parliament's constitutional-monarchist majority. But the Philadelphia congress's studied silence on the *sociale Frage* in Germany distinguished it even from the (often reticent) Frankfurt Left and drew criticism from the latter's emigrant sympathizers.[6]

Along with this exclusive emphasis on political republicanism went an apotheosis of the United States and its unqualified endorsement as a model for the new Germany. A mass meeting in Philadelphia characteristically appealed to the German common people to "chase away all princes and create a completely free republic" of the North American type. A manifesto drafted in New York urged the German people to "look across the ocean, see the size, the flower of our Republic" and "hopefully and confidently look to us" for inspiration. In the name of the immigrants of Belleville, Gustav Körner assured the Frankfurt Parliament that "we see accomplished here [in America] what we wish for you." Especially instructive, he believed, was the the co-existence of political liberty and economic accumulation. "Although we enjoy here the utmost liberty," Körner explained, "and everyone, whether capitalist or wage-worker, exercises the right of voting, property is nowhere better regarded, better protected."[7]

Two leaders of the American Revolutionary League for Europe expressed their own admiration for American society in terms nearly identical to Körner's, emphasizing that "private property is no where so secure, acquisition no where so easy, organization and combination no where so unrestricted, discussion and agitation no where so absolutely free." Indeed, attempts to link the European revolution with that of the United States became most concrete—and extreme—when the league as a whole reconvened in Wheeling, Virginia, nine months after the Philadelphia plenum. Now calling themselves the People's League for the Old and New World (*Volksbund für die alte und neue Welt*), the Wheeling delegates urged the American government to welcome all liberated nations into its own federal Union. "Every people, upon throwing off the yoke of its tyrants," the Wheeling convention resolved, "ought to demand admission into the league of states already free, that is, into the American Union; so that these states may become the nucleus of the political organization of the human family, and the starting-point of the World's Republic."[8]

At last, however, this organized alliance of the emigrant left and center sagged and then collapsed, and much of the initial enthusiasm of more conservative and well-to-do German-Americans gave way. The consolidation of reaction in Germany, foreclosing hopes for an imminent revolutionary revival, doubtless played a role. Also involved, however, was dismay at the social conflicts and political polarization that the 1848 overturns had unleashed. The editors and publishers of the *New Yorker Staats-Zeitung* thus began to stress that their hopes for German unity and liberty excluded support for "revolutionary quacks" and "fire-eating philosophy." The *Dreissiger* Columbus *Westbote* also denounced the "quacks and miracle men" of the 1848 Left. A Boston-based immigrant had "sanctioned and supported the revolution because it was an attempt of the people to strike for those rights and liberties of which they were deprived by a system of absolute monarchism and sham constitutionalism." But the revolution's results had changed his mind. "The army was insulted" and there was too much "talking about 'socialism and communism,' and a division of property." Now it was necessary to draw the lessons: "Having been an eye witness and an actor in the epoch of 1848 and 1849, I have learned enough to be here a *conservative,* whereas I was at that time a *revolutionist.*"[9]

Many others agreed. In Cincinnati Karl Reemelin came to believe that "the year 1848 brought mischief untold . . . because there was then a furor over the world, for liberty, whose real import was little understood. Men ceased to be leaders that should have been continued; and men became leaders that were inadequate to the situation." Gustav Körner denounced the "many" leaders of the 1848 Revolution who "belonged to the extreme and most radical wing of the Liberals." "Full of the most fantastic and utopian ideas," he declared, including "the socialistic and communistic ideas of Fourier, Proudhon and Cabet," they "had materially contributed to the failure of the Liberal cause." Körner's friend and neighbor, the Belleville patriarch Theodor Hilgard, referred to Friedrich Hecker as "the quintessence of all German rabble rousers." The Indianapolis *Volksblatt* similarly blamed "these world-reformers and the blind crowd which followed them . . . for the failure of all hopes which at that time were awakened in all Germans." Francis Lieber branded the "rabid democrats" active that year as "novices, and therefore fanatics in politics." Wheeling delegates Theodore Pösche and Charles Göpp agreed that "the European revolution failed, in great measure, from the phantom of socialism; a successful revolution requires . . . a guarantee to possessors against spoliations."[10]

As these recriminations mounted, activists and observers began to correlate political and social divisions. Their reports contrasted ongoing support for revolution among German-American workers with a growing caution and estrangement among their better-off *Landsleute.* German governments heard that while "demagogues and workers" were striving to help make Germany into a republic, the respectable immigrant mercantile element was growing suspicious of revolutionary agitation. Philadelphia's *Freie Presse* noted bitterly that "the workers have done vastly more than the rich and prosperous, who have done absolutely nothing" for the cause and that "the exceptions to this rule are not worth mentioning." Articles in the *New Yorker Staats-Zeitung* confirmed the pattern. In the Midwest, too, Moritz Busch traced Kinkel's failure to raise funds to the disinterest of the prosperous and the poverty of the more zealous.[11]

Pittsburgh's reception for the visiting Hungarian nationalist leader Lajos Kossuth in January 1852 captured these contrasts. As elsewhere, German residents made up a big and especially enthusiastic section of the greeters. In the manufacturing suburb of Birmingham, workers from a number of enterprises agreed to contribute a portion of their year's wages to the cause of Hungarian freedom. Christian Kaiser, an employee of the Bennet and Berry Alkali Works, greeted Kossuth before a large assembly of local wage earners. Speaking as "a working man" who had escaped "the oppression of oligarchy in Germany" and "as the representative of my fellow laborers," Kaiser assured Kossuth that, "in case of need, we in this factory *will yearly respond to your call.*" Kossuth, a well-to-do attorney, was neither a radical nor even a consistent liberal democrat, which makes his reaction on this occasion the more interesting. Thanking Kaiser and the assembled workers for an act of almost "too great a generosity," Kossuth added pointedly that "if that example should be imitated by the richer classess"—and even if "not to such an extent"—then "within a year the whole of Europe would be *free.*" But then, the Hungarian reflected, "the working classes—those who by their honest toil gain their daily bread . . . are animated more by a disinterested love of principle and of freedom, than [are] a great part of those who are not in your condition. . . . With you the love of liberty is almost a religion."[12]

The Plebeian-Democratic Milieu

Diverging attitudes toward revolution in Europe paralleled deepening differences about immigrant life in the United States. Having fled to North America in search of economic salvation, large numbers of immigrants were unprepared for the hardships imposed here precisely by industrial development. In the United States, asserted a German-born resident of Pittsburgh, "the laboring masses are treated in as shameful a manner as in Europe, with all its ancient prejudices," adding that "nowhere in the world is poverty a greater crime than in America. In the land which boasts of its humanity, which claims to be at the very top of civilization, society does far less for the poor than anywhere else." Responsibility for this state of affairs rested with an "arrogant cheese, fish, and cotton artistocracy"—whose "*evangelium* is rapacity and the hideous monster speculation"—and which was "ten times more presuming than the aristocracy of birth, for that can at least claim a prestige in its favor."[13] Denouncing "aristocrats, drones, and idlers," still another New York German tailor objected bitterly that "we provide all they enjoy by our labor, and we have to stand by and look on them revelling in every luxury, while we are driven to a bare mouthful of bread and that only to be got by hard toil and sweat. We build the houses and they, the idlers, step in and enjoy them, and we are driven out without house and home." "The whole business world is one big battle in the open marketplace, everyone for himself, and nobody on anyone else's side," wrote Chicago coppersmith Nikolaus Schwenck and his wife Marie later in the decade. Realizing a 20 percent rate of profit "is the primary goal of life," and aside from that "nobody gives a damn, or in plain English *Help yourself* is the only rule, and everybody has to accommodate himself to it." New York German shoemaker and labor journalist Peter Rödel told a receptive crowd in January 1855 that "in our country we have fought for liberty and many of us have lost, in battle, our fathers, brothers, or sons. Here we are free, but not free enough." In America, he declared to sustained applause, "you don't get bread nor wood," even though "there is plenty of them." "We want," he exclaimed, "the liberty of living."[14]

Nor did all realize their initial expectations of finding true civic equality in America. Evidence of political corruption and legal inequities seemed everywhere. Dubbing the United States "The Land of Contradictions," an article in the German-language press specified: "America is the land of equality, especially in the equality before the laws, and yet, we do not find in any part of the world a more shocking inequality before the laws, than that which exists in this very country! Distinguished individuals, family connections, and to the utmost degree the 'almighty dollar,' creates in this land of freedom an influence as widely extended, as even in some monarchies. . . . The rich and distinguished stand here higher above the law, than in any other country." A few years later, a congress of the *Allgemeinen Arbeiterbunde von Nordamerika* declared that the prevailing "disproportion between poverty and wealth . . . robs the great majority—in their political as well as their social existence—of their natural rights."[15]

In the meantime, state and local governments waged war on certain activities dearly cherished by the immigrants, especially by some of the poorest among them. Laws restricting the sale of alcoholic beverages and circumscribing public conduct on Sundays offended Germans (and Irish) of diverse economic standing. In principle these laws seemed to be an unconscionable interference in private concerns and a violation of personal liberty. Many of the laboring poor, though— for whom festive, even boisterous, Sundays and fraternizing in the nearby *Lokal* over a stein of *Lagerbier* were central to leisure and social life—took particular exception to such laws, regarding them as gratuitous pieces of class discrimination. Innumerable groups of craftworkers denounced "all laws, such as Sunday laws, temperance laws

and the like, that encroach on the workers' enjoyment of their liberty."
The *New Yorker Demokrat,* a forty-eighter newspaper in New York
City, agreed that prohibition laws simply added up to *"ein Attentat
gegen die Arbeiter."* Immigrant journalist and labor organizer Fritz
Anneke repeatedly scourged those "champions who, in the exclusion
of all spiritous drinks, in the church, bible, and Sabbath, hope to find
the safety of the world." Their piety, Anneke added, was hypocritical.
"This money aristocracy, which has the time and means to take care
of its body through the whole week, and which in spite of its hypocritical laws, knows how to serve all worldly desires on the holy Sabbath," nonetheless "strives zealously to deprive the working man of
every means of escape from his drudgery."[16]

Attempts to enforce prohibition laws occasionally laid bare something of the breadth and depth of such resentment. In 1855 new temperance laws and the jailing of *Lokal* owners who violated them led
to a violent melee between police and Germans of Chicago's North
Side; it kept the city in a virtual state of siege for four days. Rumors
that a policeman had stabbed an immigrant blacksmith during the
initial confrontations triggered further rioting, in the course of which
one German was killed and many others wounded, including a Chicago policeman attacked by a cigarmaker. The state government of
New York outlawed the Sunday sale of liquor and beer in that same
year. In July 1857, fears of an impending attempt to enforce that ban
sparked rioting in New York City's heavily German Seventeenth Ward.[17]

The German-American political leader Carl Schurz casually dismissed much immigrant disaffection with America as misguided. "The
newly arrived European democrat," he wrote, "having lived in a world
of theories and imaginings without having had any practical experience of a democracy at work, beholding it for the first time, ask[s]
himself: 'Is this really a people living in freedom? Is this the realization
of my ideal?'" Schurz himself, shielded from personal adversity by a
wealthy wife and a successful career, viewed most sources of such immigrant disappointment calmly. To him they were merely natural by-
products of "a democracy in full operation on a large scale." Less
comfortably situated, some of his countryfolk were also less Pangloss-
ian in their reactions. A feeling spread that reaching North America
had not ended their quest for independence, freedom, and dignity as
much as transplanted it. The journalist Christian Esselen, whose labor
organizing in 1848 had forced him abroad, made the same point in
another context. "We must not look upon ourselves as refugees in
America," he wrote. "Here one can fight as vigorously as in Europe

for our highest and most sacred ideals, and the battle for the realization of those ideals is rightly ours."[18]

A variety of organizations attempted to do just that—to bring American society into closer harmony with the ideals of forty-eighter democracy. Among the most important of these were the *Turnvereine*. Founded in Germany to develop the minds and bodies of patriotic German youth during the Napoleonic era, the Turner movement continued to grow and evolve during the following decades and infused its nationalism with an increasingly radical democratic content.[19]

Galvanized by a visit from the German democratic hero Friedrich Hecker, a handful of emigrés living in Cincinnati gathered in the rented rooms of housepainter J. A. Eiselen in October 1848 to found the United States' first *Turnverein*. Before long the group rented a lot and erected a hall, which became one of the central meeting places of German democrats. In 1852 a large rally there greeted the German forty-eighter Gottfried Kinkel and the Hungarian leader Lajos Kossuth, whose paths crossed in that city. By 1854 the chapter claimed some 330 paid-up members. A New York *Turngemeinde* appeared on the heels of Cincinnati's and was soon followed by others in Philadelphia, Brooklyn, Newark, Boston, Baltimore, Peoria, Indianapolis, Rochester, Cleveland, St. Louis, Louisville, Pittsburgh, Poughkeepsie, and Chicago. In 1850 a convention in Philadelphia created a national Turner association that, one year later, made still more explicit its identification with the left wing of the 1848 Revolution by adopting the name *Sozialistischer Turnerbund* (Socialist Gymnastics Union). The *Bund*'s founding documents called for "full participation in struggles for the complete independence of the individual" in order "to achieve freedom, prosperity, and education for all" (*Freiheit, Wohlstand, und Bildung für Alle*). The latter phrase, popularized by Gustav Struve and other leaders of the Frankfurt Left, appeared in the literature and on the marching banners of the *Turnerbund* and other groups claiming a forty-eighter lineage.[20]

Throughout the country, individuals prominent in liberal and radical circles in Germany became active in the new Turner movement— Struve himself, Franz Sigel, Sigismund Kauffmann, and Franz Arnold in New York; Wilhelm Rapp in Philadelphia; Karl Heinzen in Boston; Theodore Hielscher in Baltimore, Indianapolis, and Chicago; Fritz Anneke and August Willich in Milwaukee. As in Germany, the *Sozialistischer Turnerbund*'s explicit championing of radical doctrines led many individuals and whole chapters to turn away. The federation nevertheless grew impressively through the first half of the decade. In

Table 16
Occupations of Early Cincinnati Turners

Occupational Category	Number	Percent of Total
Skilled crafts	48	66
Merchants, shippers, financiers	9	12
Manufacturers	3	4
Restaurant- and innkeepers	5	7
Professionals	2	3
White-collar	3	4
Unskilled	3	4
Total	73	100

Source: Hugo Gollmer, *Namensliste der Pioniere des Nord-Amerik. Turnerbundes der Jahre 1848–1862* (St. Louis: Henry Rauth, 1885).

the fall of 1851 it claimed 22 clubs with more than 1,500 members. By early 1852 there were 30 clubs and 2,000 total members. By 1855 the national organization claimed to have doubled its size again, boasting 74 clubs with 4,500 members.[21]

What kind of people made up the rank and file? In 1854 *Turn-Zeitung* editor Wilhelm Rapp declared that "with few exceptions, the members of the Turner Union belong to the working class."[22] Decades later Hugo Gollmer (a Stuttgart-born lithographer and cofounder of the Cincinnati *Turngemeinde*) compiled occupational and other data for hundreds of early Turner members (1848–62). Though flawed and incomplete, his data suggest that Rapp had exaggerated the "working class" composition of the Turners—but also that his words contained an important kernel of truth (table 16 presents Gollmer's Cincinnati data). In New York, which early became and long re-

Table 17
Occupations of Early New York Turners

Occupational Category	Number	Percent of Total
Skilled crafts	93	68
Merchants, shippers, financiers	14	10
Manufacturers	6	4
Restaurant- and innkeepers	8	6
Professionals	8	6
White-collar	8	6
Total	137	100

Source: Gollmer, *Namensliste.*

mained the largest and most influential Turner center, the profile is remarkably similar (see table 17).

These two profiles reaveal two important characteristics of the Turner movement—and, for that matter, of the larger immigrant democratic milieu. First, craftworkers furnished its social-economic core, composing a large majority of the membership. Jewelers, for example, many of them veterans of the south German and Hanau *Turnerwehr* referred to in chapter 2, played a conspicuous role in founding the chapters in Newark and New York City. Indeed, the first Newark *Turnverein* occupied the rear of a saloon in the heart of the jeweler's district on Green Street. Other crafts strongly represented among the early American Turners included tailors, cigarmakers, printers, machinists, and housepainters. The second point is this: the activities, doctrines, and organizations that attracted these workers also appealed to other members of the community, particularly small and middling property owners. The Turner rank and file included physicians, architects, attorneys, teachers, journalists, and other professionals; hotel and restaurant owners, small merchants, and manufacturers; and clerks, bookkeepers, and others in white-collar occupations. Early Turner enthusiasts like Dr. Karl Beck considered this social diversity a signal asset, noting that the movement united "all the different classes of people who, for the most part, are widely separated by their different education and pursuits of life."[23]

But the Turners were no random cross-section of the immigrant population. Their worldview distinguished them. Turners tended to be *Freisinnigen*—"religious liberals," rationalists, "freethinkers"—who identified with the Enlightenment, denigrated supernaturalist doctrines, and harbored deep suspicion of organized churches and clerical hierarchies. The *Sozialistischer Turnerbund* thus counted among its enemies "tyranny, clergy, princes, prostitutes." Gustav Struve typically chided those "people [who] imagine that they can carry on revolution without interfering with the Popish faith. They might as well try to carry on war without cannon and swords. Religion (especially in Austria) is the basis of all political dogmatism. Republican principles are altogether at variance with that passive obedience which the priests inculcate [into] their flocks." Lutheran conservatism and "American Puritanism" received their share of criticism as well. American Turners commonly celebrated the birthday of Thomas Paine as a *Verein* holiday and esteemed his "heretical" *Age of Reason* as highly as his *Rights of Man*. The national *Turn-Zeitung* judged that while its members covered a spectrum ranging "from adherents of orthodox Christianity to atheists of the Hegelian school," still, "the greatest number subscribe to an independent naturalist philosophy." In that last category, agnostics mixed with various types of Christian liberals plus a sprinkling of nontraditionalist Jews.[24]

Naturally, conservative German-American clergymen reacted strongly against the spread of such views among their *Landsleute*. "Rationalism," declared the *Deutscher Kirchenfreund,* "is the greatest enemy of the church." After a decade in America, Protestant theologian Philip Schaff returned to Germany and complained about "the modern European heroes of liberty, or rather licentiousness—too many of whom have unfortunately been sent adrift upon us by the abortive revolutions of 1848." They included "the very worst forces of irreligion and infidelity, which, as far as their influence extends, cover the German name in the New World with shame and disgrace." Immigration thus threatened, as another clerical journal warned, to carry into America a contagion already afflicting Germany, where "behind the dazzling sign of liberty, equality, and the brotherhood of man the devil has designed to tear down through armed mobs the government by the grace of God and to set up by popular sovereignty a government which would shortly destroy all ecclesiastical order and restraint, would let fleshly equality and license in, meaning communism in women and property, and would turn Germany into one great robbers', murderers', and whorers' den." Among German Protestants, the powerful "Evangelical Lutheran Synod of Missouri, Ohio, and other States" (the Missouri Synod) took the lead in the fight against the rationalist horde, stressing the link between religious and secular conservatism. Its spiritual leader, C. F. W. Walther, bluntly declared that "every revolution is sinful, and that all governments and constitutions are of divine origin no matter how they originated." *Der Lutheraner* warned its readers to avoid all newspapers edited by forty-eighters as well as all activities and organizations inspired by them, for they aimed "to destroy religion, property, and the family."[25]

The hostility of German Catholicism was even more obvious and certainly better organized. The Catholic *Wahrheits-Freund* of Cincinnati warned that "Those fleeing from the various unsuccessful revolutions of Europe, who sought to unite the holy cause of freedom with enmity toward the Church," were "almost all without any religion and full of hatred toward Catholicism." From Milwaukee, Austrian missionary priest Anthony Urbanek in 1852 anxiously informed Vienna's Archbishop Milde of the "rotten elements [that] have stolen into this country in large numbers since 1848 with the crowd of troublesome fugitives, and caused annoyance to church and state, for to certain people even [George] Washington is a despot. So how can the

Catholic Church, with its Pope, find favor in their eyes?" New York's *Katholische Kirchenzeitung* warned that contact with the *Sozialistischer Turnverein* would contaminate the Catholic youth (it was "not good for Catholic blood") and "turn him out of the church."[26]

The German Catholic hierarchy offered alternatives to organizations such as the *Turnverein* and to secret fraternal bodies as well. It sponsored a network of mutual benefit societies that sought to aid parishioners materially while reinforcing loyalty to the church, its clergy, and its doctrines. Rev. George Rumpler, C.S.S.R., informed the pastor of Milwaukee's St. Mary's Church that "to prevent the Catholic men and young men, for the sake of earthly gain, from joining societies forbidden by the Church, I have organized in my congregation a Catholic benevolent society, and I advise you to do the same." By 1845 representatives of seventeen such associations were meeting to found a *Central Verein,* whose constitution provided "that only practical [practising] Catholics who fulfill their Easter duties, lead an honorable life, are dutiful children of the Church, and obedient to bishop and pastor can become and remain members."[27]

The politico-religious polarization evidenced here tended to pull or drive liberal- or radical-minded immigrants out of the Catholic church and the more conservative Protestant congregations. The clergy found this differentiation preferable to internal disunity and disloyalty. Milwaukee's Rev. Urbanek anticipated that dissident "ringleaders" might indeed join the Freemasons or some other "secret society"—"or become pilgrims of the Workingmen's Republik . . . of Weitling." In either case, their exodus "eliminates those alien members," so that "the time approaches even nearer when the fermenting elements will be sifted and clarified."[28]

In truth, freethinkers were theologically, politically, and socially diverse, just as they were in Germany. Moritz Busch noted in his travels that "people of intelligence here turn away from the church in general," while Philip Schaff anguished over the broader "swarms of emigrants" who "belonged to the lower and uneducated classes" and lived in a "sad state of spiritual decay." He guessed that "perhaps more than half the late emigrants are almost entire strangers to Christianity." Rationalist leaders included ministers serving regular congregations, such as *Dreissiger* August Kroll in Cincinnati and *Achtundvierziger* (forty-eighter) Friedrich August Lehlbach in Newark. Trained in theology at the University of Giessen, Rev. Kroll emigrated to the United States in his mid-twenties in 1833 and became pastor of a German Evangelical church in Louisville five years later. In 1841 he transferred to Cincinnati's Protestant Johannis Church, the oldest German parish in the city, and remained there for the last two decades of his life. With colleague Friedrich Bottcher, Rev. Kroll launched the *Protestantische Zeitblatter* in 1849; it was destined to become one of the most important organs of liberal German-American Protestantism. The younger Pastor Lehlbach received his training in the seminary at Halle, a rationalist center, and served as a deputy in Baden's revolutionary constituent assembly in 1848. Sentenced to fifteen years in solitary confinement by the counterrevolutionary authorities, Lehlbach fled Germany and settled in Newark, where he ministered for many years at the First German Reformed Church on Mulberry Street and became a fixture of the city's emigré democracy.[29]

Usually more heterodox than these pastors and their congregations were the independent "free congregations" (*freien Gemeinden*), which were not affiliated with any synod or denominational organization. The radical "German-Catholic" priest Eduard Ignaz Koch led a free congregation in New York City; so did Johan (John) A. Försch and Halle-trained pastor and labor educator Rudolf Dulon. Organized New York German book printers regularly sponsored Sunday morning freethought lectures. One meeting of the *Gemeinschaft freier Menschen* reportedly attracted one to two thousand New Yorkers in 1858. In Philadelphia a *freie Gemeinde* initiated by Nikolaus Schmitt, a liberal businessman and former member of the Frankfurt Parliament, soon established ties to the Sunday school run by the city's *Arbeiterbund*. Other free congregations arose across the Midwest—in Indiana, Ohio, Illinois, Kentucky, Michigan, Wisconsin, and Missouri. More than seventy free congregations sprang up in the Ohio Valley alone.[30]

But it was the *Freimännerverein* (commonly translated as either the League of German Freemen or, more simply, the Free Germans) that most consistently and militantly asserted the link between secular democratic and theologically rationalist doctrines. Like the *freien Gemeinden*, *Freimännervereine* flourished widely. Boston, New York, Philadelphia, St. Louis, and Baltimore all boasted such societies. The Cleveland body, founded in late 1851, grew from fifteen to two hundred members in its first year of existence.[31]

Larger and more famous was Cincinnati's *Verein für geistige Aufklärung und sociale Reform* (Society for Spiritual Enlightenment and Social Reform), founded in 1850, which abbreviated its name early in 1852 to the *Verein freier Männer*. With a membership somewhere between five hundred and one thousand and a sizable periphery of sympathizers, the Cincinnati *Freimännerverein* conducted public meetings in its hall each Sunday morning (in deliberate defiance of native-born Protestant sensibilities); organized its members and supporters into mutual insurance, reading, discussion, theater, gymnastic, and women's auxiliary groups; and sponsored a variety of public lectures and other cultural events. Its membership seems to have been heavily weighted with craftworkers but also included professionals, small manufacturers, and merchants. Among its leaders were blacksmith Michael Doberrer, tailor George Friedlien, and machinist J. P. Fisch, as well as teacher Edward Steffens and successful bookbinder and Turner cofounder Charles Meininger.[32]

The Cincinnati *Freimänner* found their most articulate and colorful representative in Friedrich Hassaurek, a young self-styled *Social Demokrat*. As a sixteen-year-old student at the University of Vienna, Hassaurek had participated actively in the Austrian revolution. The triumph of reaction then sent him to the United States, and toward the end of 1850 he began editing the weekly Cincinnati *Hochwächter* ("Guardian"). A journal by that name had been published in the late 1840s by Württemberger George Walker, a rationalist and polemically inclined seminarian. Under Hassaurek's direction, the new *Hochwächter* became the Freemen's voice in the city. Initially identifying itself as "an organ for religious enlightenment and social reform," the paper increasingly broadened its interests. In the fall of 1854 it began describing itself as "an organ of general progress." By that time the *Freimännerverein* had become an important political and cultural force in German Cincinnati, with Hassaurek supporting and exhorting the city's labor movement, repeatedly challenging editors of the liberal German *Volksblatt* to verbal duels, and actually engaging in public debate such prominent opponents as the German Methodist patriarch Wilhelm Nast. Before long even the Whiggish and wary *Daily Cincinnati Gazette* was acknowledging the Freemen's best-known leader to be "a young man of much intellectual ability and force as a writer"— and, more significantly, "one of the principal men of influence in this city." In 1855 the largely German Tenth Ward sent Hassaurek to the city council.[33]

To many later writers, European anticlericalism appeared alien, anachronistic, irrelevant in the United States, which had formally dispensed with its established church half a century earlier. But immigrants quickly discovered that Protestantism retained great power, including legislative influence, here. Much of America's native-born middle class regarded a Protestant asceticism essential to sustain a republican government and prevent its becoming a tool of a voracious and insatiable rabble. Tocqueville, thus, had noted of the United States during the 1830s that religion "must be regarded as the foremost of political institutions of that country" and was widely considered "indispensable to the maintenance of republican institutions" generally.[34]

The subsequent progress of industrial development, with its attendant shocks and grievances, made such a religiously grounded code of popular self-discipline seem even more necessary. "A nation of freemen," admonished the Committee on Foreign Affairs of the House of Representatives, "no matter how great or powerful, cannot long continue as such without religion and morality, industry and frugality; for these are indispensable supports of popular government." Clergymen regularly sermonized on "the necessity of Civil and Religious Restraints for the permanence and happiness of society"; newspapers repeatedly affirmed that "the observance of the Christian Sabbath" was "intimately associated with public virtue and with the permanence of the Commonwealth." The proliferation of statutes during the 1850s prohibiting the consumption of alcoholic beverages and strictly regulating public conduct on the Sabbath demonstrated the political power of this socioreligious outlook and the relevance of the immigrant secularists' preoccupation.[35]

The conduct of American Catholicism seemed no more reassuring. Hostile to Protestant evangelicalism, Catholic clergy and newspapers also denounced liberal and radical democratic emigrés and values. A meeting of Pittsburgh's German democrats pilloried "the conduct of the Catholic press of this country, which openly attacks and repudiates republican principles, and strives to uproot the love of liberty and self-government, so essential to be taught to suppress monarchical and aristocratic tendencies." Lajos Kossuth's American tour drew the church's anger like a lightning rod. No "good Catholic will wear out his shoes for Kossuth," that "Hungarian clown," promised one German priest. The archbishop of Pittsburgh amplified the point in a public letter, explaining that "the Catholics of the United States generally have shown little sympathy for Mr. Kossuth," who had earned their enmity by cooperating with "European Socialists and Red Republicans."[36]

Other church militants expressed themselves more strongly. The Catholic convert and editor Orestes Brownson raged at a public forum that Americans "import traitors from Europe and make heroes of them!" He received enthusiastic support from his "religious friends." On the home front a dispute over public education erupted at this time. Citing a pervasive Protestant influence in public school curricula, Catholic church leaders sought public funding for Catholic parochial schools (or exemption from the public school tax for families supporting the parochial system). German freethinkers bridled. As ardent champions of a secularized but strengthened system of public education, they regarded the church's initiatives as a reactionary assault on one of their most cherished republican institutions. In this atmosphere, therefore, German-born democrats saw scant reason to abandon the militantly secular and anticlerical aspects of their worldview. "I was a Freeman in Germany," reasoned Cincinnatian Lewis Dericus, "and why should I not be in this country?"[37]

Accused then and later of religious bigotry and even an ersatz Know-Nothingism, *Freimänner* replied that they held "the right of free expression of religious conscience untouchable, as we do the right of free expression of opinion in general; we therefore accord to the believer the same liberty to make known his convictions as we do the non-believer, as long as the rights of others are not violated thereby." But this emphasis on "liberty of conscience" left Freemen "decidedly opposed to all compulsion inflicted on dissenting persuasions by laws unconstitutionally restricting the liberty of expression." Freemen therefore "hold the Sabbath laws, Thanksgiving days, prayers in Congress and Legislatures, the oaths upon the Bible, introduction of the Bible into the free schools, the exclusion of 'atheists' from legal acts, etc., as an open violation of human rights as well as of the Constitution, and demand their removal." Pronouncements like these horrified much of the country's native-born population, but attacks upon sabbatarian and temperance laws did align the Freemen in practice with the great mass of the less radical immigrant population, both Irish and German.[38]

The Marxists

Like the Turners and Freemen, early German-American Marxists also commonly expressed themselves in language resonant of the Enlightenment. The statutes of the New York Communist Club "reject[ed] all religious faiths, in whatever shape or form they may be presented, as well as any point of view which is not based on immediate perception of the senses." They, too, asserted strongly egalitarian principles. "Equality of all human beings—irrespective of color or sex—is their belief." And the Communists even formulated their ultimate aims in terms familiar to other forty-eighters: "Our goal is nothing less than the reconciliation of all human interests, freedom and happiness for all mankind, and the realization and unification of a world republic."[39]

The first organized Marxist nucleus, the *Proletarierbund,* appeared in 1852. A small propaganda society evidently claiming fewer than twenty members, the *Bund* intervened effectively in the great strike movement of the following year, playing a role far out of proportion to its size. Four years later, in the fall of 1857, with unemployed demonstrations breaking out across the country, some thirty German-Americans regrouped in the New York Communist Club. Most of these immigrant Marxists had been members of the Communist League who had been hounded out of Germany like so many others in the late 1840s and 1850s. At one time or another their ranks included Joseph Weydemeyer, a former army officer, journalist, and engineer who had been active in Cologne's democratic and labor organizations; fellow engineer Adolphus Cluss; Abraham Jacobi, a Westphalian physician and pioneer pediatrician; Fritz Jacobi, an attorney who had participated in the Baden uprising; Rhineland businessman Albert Komp; Friedrich Kamm, former member of the Executive Committee of the Bonn Democratic Club; Sebastian Seiler, a journalist and former supporter of Wilhelm Weitling who had participated in the revolutionary movement in Baden and Westphalia; teacher and journalist Wilhelm Wolff; F. A. Sorge, the future secretary of the First International; and the prodigals Fritz Anneke and August Willich.[40]

Distinct from the rest of the 1848 Left, the Communists subscribed to a particular interpretation of history from which a particular political and economic program flowed. In their view, the ongoing transformation of work and social structure confirmed Marx's prediction that petty production was doomed and that those engaged in it would divide into proletarians and capitalists.

This prediction appeared to be as applicable to the United States as it was to Europe. "The American feeling of independence," Weydemeyer wrote in the *Turn-Zeitung,* "which imagines that Americans are less subject to the influence of industrialization than the peoples of old Europe, is now finished." He believed in the early 1850s that "the petty bourgeoisie is everywhere on the brink of bankruptcy," and "the disappearance of the petty bourgeoisie means the disappearance of the class which has up to now formed the bridge between bourgeoisie and proletariat and which, if it did not eliminate the contradictions between them, at least obscured them." This left only the proletariat capable of consistently championing democratic liberties, material progress, and "the entire legacy of the bourgeoisie." It was therefore "up to the proletariat" to replace the rule of capital with "the rule of its own class—the class that no longer has any other class below it," whose rule would initiate "the abolition of all class privileges" and, indeed, "an end [to] every political rule whatsoever."[41]

As these statements implied, the Communists welcomed the development of industry and repudiated what they regarded as nostalgic longings for the past. "We preach revolution in the interest of untrammeled progress," the Communist Club emphasized, and it scorned attempts to idealize—much less perpetuate—the artisanal system. Unfortunately, Weydemeyer sighed, "it is a well-established fact that no social class abandons hope of its own regeneration so long as its demise has not occurred—even if the ground under its feet is already giving way." Nor, he added, has there ever "been a lack of fools ready to systematize such ignorant hopes." But humanity's real salvation would come not "with the rebirth of the artisan crafts, the dissolution of big industry," not through a "return to the Middle Ages or a redivision of capital." On the contrary, once the proletariat obtained political supremacy, it must nationalize the means of production. Only by thus abolishing "so-called bourgeois property, whether inherited or acquired," the Communist Club subsequently declared, could all obtain "a reasonable share in the natural and spiritual riches of the earth."[42]

Some Marxists would play important roles in the labor and antislavery movements, but their general perspective attracted few of their emigrant countryfolk in the 1850s. Numerous immigrant democrats continued to refer to themselves as socialists, as they had done in Europe. But very few believed in an irreconcilable struggle between labor and capital, much less one destined to collectivize existing property and eventually dissolve classes altogether. For most, on the contrary, class conflict was caused—or at least made intolerable—only by special privilege and the abusive exercise of governmental power. Years of bitter experience with German state intervention in the economy on the side of traditional elites served to reinforce among the immigrant democrats a preoccupation with "monopoly" (and enthusiasm for its putative historic enemy, Andrew Jackson) that was already widespread in the United States. The equalization of political and economic rights, it was assumed, would go a long way toward resolving antagonism among the country's social classes to the mutual benefit of the contenders.

Many years later, the *Sozialistischer Turnerbund* explained that "the socialism of today, in which we Turners believe, aims to remove the pernicious antagonism between labor and capital. It endeavors to effect a reconciliation between these two and to try to establish a peace by which the rights of the former are fully protected against the encroachments of the latter." The counterposition in the United States between this vision and the Marxist one had become explicit considerably earlier. Even as Joseph Weydemeyer was paraphrasing the *Communist Manifesto* in the *Turn-Zeitung,* that paper was serializing a discussion of socialism that was doubtless more familiar and congenial to a Turner readership. Apparently written by Franz Arnold, a Frankfurt-born mechanic, labor organizer, and tireless advocate of cooperative production, this series of articles equated socialism with "a democratic-republican constitution that guarantees everyone prosperity, free quality education to maximize personal capabilities, and the elimination of all sources of hierarchical and privileged power." All the ingredients required for this recipe could, of course, be found in the motto of the German republicans of 1848. August Willich considered himself a militant proletarian communist. But he also expressed repeated reservations about the doctrine of relentless class struggle and emblazoned the masthead of his Cincinnati trade-union newspaper with slogans characteristic of smallholder values and protest: "Value in exchange for value!" (*Werth gegen Werth*) and "To each his own!" (*Einem Jeden das Seine*).[43]

In Louisville, Kentucky, in 1854 Karl Heinzen summarized the core outlook and demands of the German-American radical democrats at mid-century. This "Louisville platform," reprinted in some thirty German-language newspapers, inspired similar documents elsewhere in German America. Feuding and bickering were endemic among the German-born radical democrats. But while differences of substance existed, much of the polemical fury reflected petty rivalries and exaggerated sensitivities typical of other emigré milieus. The Louisville platform and the general (if often unacknowledged) endorsement it received indicated the extensive ideological and programmatic common ground on which most of the principals stood. Gatherings of Freemen, Turners, and other democratic organizations that convened in Indiana, Illinois, Wisconsin, Kentucky, and Ohio during the 1850s ratified similar general views, sometimes even the identical language.[44]

Regarding the U.S. Constitution as "the best now in existence . . . yet . . . neither perfect nor unimprovable," the Louisville platform sought a fuller democratization of government processes, structures, and policies. To that end, it advocated measures such as the direct election and subjection to recall of all public officials, a stricter separation of church and state (as noted above), the liberalization of naturalization laws, a general defense of immigrants against all manner of victimization, and an interventionist foreign policy serving international "liberty and democracy" rather than the principle of neutrality.

More boldly, the Louisville platform asserted that "women, too," held the inalienable rights invoked by the Declaration of Independence. As noted, the questioning atmosphere of the 1840s had begun to affect thinking about gender roles in Germany. The outstanding immigrant champion of women's rights was Mathilde Giesler Anneke, daughter of a wealthy Catholic landlord and mine owner in Westphalia. An unhappy marriage, divorce, and bitter fight in Germany over the custody of her daughter had helped reorient Giesler's life, estranging her from her religion and class and committing her above all to the social and intellectual emancipation of women. She soon came into contact with dissident circles that included Marx and Engels, Gottfried Kinkel, the revolutionary poet Ferdinand Freiligrath—and Fritz Anneke, whom she married in 1847 and whose journalistic and military duties and risks she shared in 1848. The couple settled in Newark, New Jersey, in 1852, and Mathilde promptly set out on a speaking tour in behalf of democracy and women's rights that carried her through New Jersey, New York, Maryland, Pennsylvania, Ohio, and Kentucky. The success of her tour reflected and reinforced support for women's rights elsewhere in German America. German Free Women's Societies published the weekly *Neue Zeit* for a few years later in the decade in support of female equality. The cause nonetheless remained highly controversial even within forty-eighter circles, and this section of the Louisville platform was rarely endorsed by its imitators.[45]

Far more popular was the platform's Enlightenment-inspired stress on reason and education as the keys to freedom and prosperity. "All, indiscriminately, must have the use of free schools for all branches of education," it held, adding a provision particularly dear to the hearts of its constituents—that "wherever a sufficient number of Germans live, a German teacher should be employed." The platform's discussion of "Prosperity," finally, reflected ideas circulating through the German labor movement of 1848–49 and the assumptions underlying the Turner concept of socialism noted above. "Labor has an incontestable claim to the value of its products," the platform declared, urging that "the laboring classes be made independent of the oppression of the capitalists." A strong democratic state was assigned an important role in this project. Where necessary, for example, the state "must . . . aid the [cooperative] associations of working men" by establishing special credit banks for that purpose and by awarding government contracts wherever possible "to associations of workmen, rather than to single contractors." Where workers remained in the employ of others, the state must "mediate between the claims of the laborer and the capitalist" by enforcing minimum wages equal to the "value of the labor" and limiting the working day to ten hours, in accordance with "the demands of humanity."[46]

But of all the demands in the radical democratic lexicon, few found a bigger or more receptive audience than the call for land reform. Since the beginning of European settlement of North America, the promise of land for homesteads had drawn millions across the Atlantic in search of alternatives to or rescue from one or another form of dependence. Industrial development and the growth of a wage-dependent population in North America itself added a new dimension to the problem, leading trade-union and workingmen's movements in the 1820s and thirties to press repeatedly for measures that would facilitate homesteading in the West. A number of factors intensified the interest in homesteading: the calamitous depression of 1839–43; the further expansion of immigration, wage labor, and agrarian tenancy during the business revival that followed; and, later, the wresting of great chunks of territory from Mexico and American Indians. Fears that railroad companies and land speculators would preempt and "monopolize" western lands stimulated popular protest.[47]

In 1844 former New York Working Men's party leader George Henry Evans convened a group of veteran craftworker and other activists and launched the National Reform Association to agitate around the land issue. The movement took as its central axiom the individual's right of independence and the freedom to obtain the material prerequisites thereof. "If any man has a right on the earth," Evans reasoned, "he has a right to land enough to raise a habitation on. If he has *a right to live,* he has a right to land enough for his subsistence. Deprive anyone of these rights, and you place him at the mercy of those who possess them." Support grew for the movement, especially in eastern cities. Some hoped personally to become farmers. Others wished only to reach the booming (and more labor-scarce) towns and cities of the West. Still others wished simply to allow their neighbors to move along and thereby reduce the local labor supply and job competition. By 1850 residents of the western states and territories were also taking up the call. Evans's message appealed to many who had left the Old World precisely to escape poverty and proletarianization. Difficult economic conditions encountered in New York, Philadelphia, and Newark sharpened interest in westward migration while strengthening the belief that government aid would be necessary to make relocation a reality. The National Reformers thus recruited exiled Chartists like Thomas Devyr of Ireland, John Cluer of Scotland, and James Pyne of England.[48]

Hermann Kriege brought the word to the German immigrants. This Young Hegelian "true socialist," student of Ludwig Feuerbach, friend of Robert Blum, and member of the old League of the Just had sailed for the United States promising to propagandize for communism but shortly forsaking that ideology in favor of a "democracy of the land." In New York City he first sought the aid of the German Society, since it pledged to help poor immigrants enter American society. Ignored, Kriege launched the *Association der Social-Reformer* (the Social Reform Association, or SRA) in the fall of 1845 with the aid of more sympathetic figures. One of these was Heinrich Ahrens (or Arends), a worker from Riga who had also belonged to the League of the Just and who in New York apparently found work as a cartman. At the end of October Ahrens chaired an amply attended meeting of the new organization in New York that "recognize[d] in the National Reformers our fellow laborers in the cause of progress, as pioneers of a better future, as the advocates of the cause of the oppressed children of Industry." Kriege and the SRA stressed that in America, just "as in Europe . . . lasting prosperity, peace, and freedom can exist nowhere until the division between work and pleasure, poverty and wealth, is actually abolished." This could be accomplished only (and here the SRA borrowed language from the English-speaking National Reform Association) by asserting the "inalienable right" to "the use of such a portion of the earth, and the other elements, as shall be sufficient to provide . . . the means of subsistence and comfort." Indeed, the SRA added, "the right of man to the soil" was "the first and most sacred of all rights." Sympathetic forty-eighter journalists agreed that for the poor of Germany, land reform in America constituted "the road . . . to peace, prosperity, and freedom."[49]

The SRA soon boasted between four and six hundred members in New York, and affiliates in Newark, Philadelphia, Boston, Milwaukee, Cincinnati, and St. Louis. In Chicago Dr. Karl Hellmuth—a physician and early editor of the *Illinois Staats-Zeitung*, where Hermann Kriege worked briefly in 1849—became a leader of the movement. The land reform theme also echoed through the broader network of immigrant reform *Vereine*, including labor associations (cooperative, mutual benefit, and protective alike), Turner groups, and Freemen societies. The 1854 Louisville platform thus reflected widespread sentiment when it called for the "free cession of public lands to all settlers" in place of "wasting them by speculation" and for state aid to poor settlers "lest said measures prove useless for these very persons who most need it." Virginia's Robert Dabney complained as early as 1849 that the Germans "are always *land-mad*," and the ardor with which these immigrants embraced the cause eventually led opponents of homestead legislation to deride such measures as the "offspring of the German school of socialism."[50]

Democracy and Americanism

Some immigrant democrats noted that the measures they advocated would, if instituted, bring about a qualititative change in American life. Most, however, held that the changes they desired would simply enforce principles promulgated in the founding documents of the American republic. The *Association der Social-Reformer* thus couched its demands in the language of the Declaration of Independence and announced, "We have no other interest than those of the American people, because America is the asylum of the oppressed everywhere, and because the interest of the American people is the interest of the whole human race." With some justice, forty-eighter democrats depicted themselves as upholding a venerable North American tradition. Free thought, rejection of sabbatarian and temperance edicts, and demands for greater political democracy and societal aid for the poor were certainly no strangers to the New World. Groups of hard-pressed American craftworkers and small farmers had defended kindred beliefs at least as early as the American Revolution and as recently as the 1830s.[51]

The cult of Thomas Paine aimed to emphasize claims that the democratic visions of 1776 and 1848 derived from a common source. In 1847 Kriege published a volume entitled *The Fathers of our Republic in their Life and Works (Die Väter unserer Republik in ihrem Leben und Wirken)*, lionizing the life and works of both Paine and Benjamin Franklin. In 1854 the Louisville platform appropriated the slogan, "Liberty, Welfare, and Education for All," calling it "the great principle of the [German] Revolution, which the Free Germans have brought, as a collective expression of their exertions, from the old Fatherland." But, it then added immediately, "with this they have not put up any new political theory; for we find the same principle expressed, in different words, in the Constitution of North America and in the Declaration of Independence of 1776." Or, inquired Theodor Hielscher's Indianapolis *Freie Presse,* had Americans already "forgotten that this great land began with a revolution, that Washington, the father of the fatherland, was also a revolutionary?"[52]

Anglo-American critics rejected such claims, asserting a distinctly foreign provenance for the forty-eighter radical democracy. The latter had nothing in common with—indeed, was fundamentally antithetical to—American principles of government and social organization. Newark's weekly *Sentinel of Freedom,* for example, warned against "the apparently increasing disposition among that portion of our population born in foreign lands, to band together in organized societies, both voluntary and political; some of them engaged boldly in disseminating the rankest infidelity, and others composed of men not sufficiently masters of the English language to read the laws of the land, endeavoring to effect the demolition of long-established customs and institutions." "Look at the ignorance and vice of the multitude that come among us," urged "A True American" in a letter to the *Newark Daily Advertiser.* Look at the "socialism and red-republicanism, the infidelity and aetheism of the old world, here finding lodgment."[53]

The consequences appeared dire. "American politics," declared the governor of Delaware, "have been stained with vices foreign to the American character." These recent arrivals urge upon us "the same type of democracy which has undone the cause of liberty in Europe," Tennessee Whig John Bell told his Senate colleagues in the spring of 1852, "and its mission in this country can never be accomplished but by the ruin of liberty in America." "Ignorant and presumptuous," a leading nativist writer fumed, radical Germans "are not satisfied to adopt American views or learn the tendency of American institutions; but they bring forward all the exploded European heresies, and endeavor to make them current here." "Theirs is a democracy eminently European," agreed another nativist author, John P. Sanderson. "No one can mistake its paternity. . . . It is not the republicanism of Washington, Adams, Jefferson, Hamilton, Jay, Madison, and their illustrious compeers." "Americans should rule America," insisted a widely circulated nativist tract. "To become an American citizen and a voter, a man should have been born and educated among us. . . . He will then have some chance of understanding the nature of our institutions, and the working of our system. He will have no foreign prejudices to get rid of. He will have no foreign preferences to forget. He will have no foreign ignorance to be enlightened."[54]

Commonly couched in broadly nationalist terms like these, such criticism actually reflected and championed specific social and political views—views neither peculiar to the United States nor endorsed by all its native-born citizens. Reciprocally, the doctrines advocated by these radical forty-eighters were objectionable less for their European origin than for their practical content.

Thus Know-Nothing congressman Thomas R. Whitney of New York City specifically regretted the arrival of those who "clamor for 'universal suffrage,' 'free farms,' and 'intervention' in European affairs." Their offense was not a too-close affinity with European ways in general; they were repulsive, in fact, precisely because of the way and degree in which they opposed the European status quo. They were "the malcontents of the Old World, who hate monarchy, not because it is monarchy, but because it is restraint. They are such men as stood by the side of Robespierre." Nativist writer Dr. Samuel C. Busey, scouting the Louisville platform as "antagonistic to the fundamental principles and established usages of the government" in this country, explained that investing "all powers . . . exclusively in the masses" would leave society dangerously "dependent upon the will of an uncontrollable and licentious majority." Theirs, wrote John P. Sanderson, "is the democracy of the leaders of the revolutionary movements in Europe, whose ultra, wild, and visionary schemes and theories have brought obloquy upon the very name of republicanism in Europe." "They preach for political doctrine," complained J. Wayne Laurens, "Fourierism, agrarianism, and that particular form of red republicanism, which consists in overturning the foundations of society, and dividing the property acquired by the industrious among the idle and dissolute."[55]

German-American opponents of radical democracy also buttressed their arguments with the rhetoric of American patriotism. Particularly fond of doing so were earlier immigrants who had successfully adapted to the new society and its dominant culture. Denouncing the "utopian ideas" advanced by these immigrant "world reformers," such people accused Heinzen, Hassaurek, Kriege, Struve, and others of prescribing social and political nostrums in America without a license. "There is a class among us," complained "An Old German" in a letter to a Newark daily, "who have arrived since 1848, who can scarcely understand the English language, and who are not yet entitled to citizenship, that endeavor without understanding the institutions of the country which has afforded them a refuge, to overthrow them and bring upon us the immorality and disorder of Europe."[56]

Was it therefore really so surprising, wondered Illinois's Gustav Körner, another old German, that many of the native-born responded angrily to "the ignorance, the arrogance, the insolence and charlatanism of these would-be reformers"? "The American Democracy," declared the *New Yorker Staats-Zeitung* with approval, "is certainly not

the same as what one understands by that term in Europe nowadays."
"The German radicals," agreed the editor of the *Pittsburg Republi-kaner,* "understand under liberty quite a different thing from what the
Americans do." In Newark the long-settled cutlery manufacturer Ro-
chus Heinisch and his neighbor Jacob Hundertpfund, a prospering
umbrella manufacturer, denounced recently arrived critics of the city's
sabbatarian-prohibitionist ordinances. These self-styled "American citizens of German birth" distanced themselves from *Landsleute* who were
"not yet citizens of the United States," insisting that they felt "at home
in the land of our choice; we love it and its institutions. We revere
and see the need of its laws and their enforcement."[57]

Much of this emphatic endorsement of "American" ways reflected
a waxing faith in economic individualism and in capitalist development unimpeded by tradition, state policy, or popular pressure. Stunted
in the Fatherland, that liberal faith blossomed among ambitious German immigrants on the soil of North America. "Every disturbance of
property is a proportional blow to industry," wrote Francis Lieber,
so that "no farther increase in capital" means "no increase in property,
no advance in civilization. . . . If it be true that overgrown fortunes
are dangerous and inexpedient, it is equally true . . . that one of the
great blessings of a people consists in a great number of substantial
private fortunes, and that values which collectively can be used pro-
ductively to the highest advantage for the laborer and the community
at large, melt away if slivered into small proportions." He concluded,
"Let *all* men, therefore, rejoice whenever they see that one of their
fellow-creatures has succeeded in honestly accumulating a substantial
fortune."[58]

If not every convert to liberalism was as ready to accept its full
implications, the ranks of yea-sayers nonetheless grew swiftly during
the 1850s. One recruit was the young Oswald Ottendorfer, who vowed
upon landing in New York City in 1850 that here "I don't stand
behind anyone, there is nothing for me that is too big or too high,
that I can't attain." These ambitions were not, to be sure, immediately
realized; an old acquaintance soon discovered Ottendorfer "peddling,
in utter want and sheer desperation, baskets of gorgeously-labeled
beverages of doubtful composition among houses of questionable re-
sort." Before long, however, fortune did smile. Ottendorfer joined
and came to dominate the *New Yorker Staats-Zeitung,* which hotly
denounced all attempts to redirect the course of U.S. social or political development, rejecting alike communism, socialism ("nothing but
communism's purgatory"), "red republicanism," and "other systems"—"because democracy is enough for us."[59]

Others also became strongly enamored of economic liberalism, and Carl Schurz became one of its earliest and most prominent advocates. Schurz had first attracted public attention as a protégé of Gottfried Kinkel, who urged shielding small masters against the high winds of free trade. But soon after Schurz reached the United States he announced that his "political views have undergone a kind of internal revolution." He had been deeply impressed by the discovery that "all the great educational establishments, the churches, the great means of transportation, etc., that are being organized here—almost all of these things owe their existence not to official authority but to the spontaneous co-operation of private individuals." To Schurz these achievements proved the superiority of the social "anarchy" that "exists here in full bloom" over the "lust for government" so characteristic of the European-born "hot-headed professional revolutionists." The goal of all reform, Schurz therefore concluded, should be "to break every authority which has its organization in the life of the state." Theodore Pösche and Charles Göpp specifically attacked the land-reform movement and its presumed desire to "relapse into the semi-culture of those sentimentally-idealistic times, when every man sits 'under his own vine and fig-tree,' and mankind are divided into innumerable little familistic societies of three or four individuals, separated by the width of a farm from the rest of the world, plodding and vegetating, without progress or development." On the contrary, they held, "large capital and large enterprise is as much needed in agriculture as in other pursuits and free business will as surely counteract all its dangers."[60]

The cultural commonalities and practical considerations that tended to unite German-Americans, thus, could not erase deep-going differences in actual condition and social-political outlook. On the contrary: immigrant advocates of conservative, liberal, and radical democratic doctrines clashed repeatedly, as they had in Germany. Nor did the issues and interests involved touch only an educated handful. Their wider resonance became apparent in bitter periodic struggles waged over economic rights and power.

5

"It Is Time to Fight Again":
The Organizations
of Labor

Immigrant liberals believed that in the society they extolled, working people would have few legitimate complaints. Like all other members of the community, workers would reap the full fruits of their labors. The Cincinnati *Volksblatt* enthused that "in America, the worker is sovereign." Neither princes nor guilds interfere with the worker's business. "Who is it who sets the price of labor?" it asked, replying, "It is the worker." Thus it was that "most millionaires have become such only by first being workers." The up-and-coming Chicago lawyer and politician Hermann Kreismann admonished fellow immigrants seeking government aid for the unemployed "that our government was not like the European despotisms which they had escaped; that here there was no obligation on the part of the governing power to secure to the laborer food and work, because it leaves him always free to follow what calling or pursuit he may choose."[1]

It followed that, in the eyes of *Dreissiger* liberals such as Cincinnati's Karl Reemelin, aggressive collective action in pursuit of higher wages was unjustified. Reemelin trusted the free market to judge and reward individual abilities and efforts. As he later recorded in his memoirs, "I had brought with me, from Germany," the belief that "those that get more wages than they merit, accumulate ill-will against themselves, while those who get less than they deserve, accumulate credit for merit." Francis Lieber bluntly branded trade unions "un-lawful combination[s]" that were "peculiarly serious because we know to what insufferable social tyranny, to what evil habits and fearful crimes they lead." And prosperous German-American boss cabinet-maker Frederick Rammelsberg, who helped lead employer resistance to union wage demands in Cincinnati, claimed that among the employees "no wrong, much less suffering, exists except when incapability or intemperance is the cause." Rammelsberg and his colleagues assured one and all that "the law of Supply and Demand will regulate the scale of prices, and fix it on an equitable basis." The Chicago German Society endorsed fundamentally the same view. Rev. Philip Schaff sniffed that "the modern European heroes of liberty, or rather licentiousness" had become "mere cyphers" in America without "influence or importance."[2]

Others were considerably less sanguine. Distasteful and alien as they found radical democratic doctrines, many observers unhappily acknowledged their attraction for hard-pressed *Achtundvierziger* plebeians. An article in the *North American Review* generally sympathetic to German immigrants expressed concern about freedom's ambiguous effect upon them. "The measure of liberty which has proved so congenial to the industry and enterprise of the Germans" in this country, it cautioned, "has also permitted the excessive development of some of the worst tendencies of their character" so that "the earnest and industrious mechanic of Nuremberg grows into the tumultuous haranguer and street-fighter of New York."[3]

Nativist congressman Thomas R. Whitney made the dichotomy sharper and more shrilly. German-American "men of business, capital, and respectability," he affirmed, were a "class of immigrants [that] is always desirable." But Whitney grew nearly apoplectic about "the red republicans, agrarians, and infidels," who were "generally workingmen and tradesmen." Numerous immigrants made similar observations. Gustav Körner despised Karl Heinzen and the kind of "socialistic and almost anarchistic agitation" distilled in the latter's Louisville platform. Körner gloated that a writing style "hard, dry, and scholastic and without the least bit of charm" had left Heinzen an unsuccessful journalist in the United States. The content and appeal of Heinzen's social and political beliefs, however, was not so easily dismissed. On the contrary, Körner acknowledged, they had "found many followers." Moritz Busch was similarly disconcerted to discover, during his 1851–52 "travels between the Hudson and the Mississippi," that a man with Heinzen's extreme views could find—"can one believe it?"—"a not insignificant following, especially among the younger people of the working class."[4]

One of the chief bastions of entrepreneurial liberalism in German America was the New York German Society. Founded to help immigrants adjust to their new environment four years before the U.S. Constitution was ratified, the society provided a model for many later emulators in other centers of heavy immigrant settlement. Dominated by well-to-do immigrants of an earlier era (John Jacob Astor served as president in the 1830s), it become increasingly estranged from its impoverished countryfolk. Surveying the desperate condition of immigrants who arrived during the 1840s and 1850s, German Society leaders stonily concluded that they simply "should not have emigrated." In 1845, when Hermann Kriege asked the society to endorse land reform laws to aid these people, the society's officers declined even to reply. They had their own ways, it appeared, of helping straitened immigrants adjust to America: the following spring, when five hundred Irish longshoremen on Brooklyn's Atlantic docks went on strike for higher wages, the German Society furnished employers there with four hundred freshly landed, work-hungry German replacements. Ordered to leave the premises, the Irish dockers resisted and, taking exception to this form of immigrant aid, attacked the German laborers, killing one and injuring many more before the state militia arrived.[5]

This well-publicized incident increased the general friction between Irish and German immigrants and also deepened some sociopolitical divisions within the city's German-American population. Fledgling German labor organizations hotly denounced the German Society's conduct. Similar organizations appeared across the nation, taking root earliest in New York City and Philadelphia, and then spreading during the late 1840s and early 1850s to lesser cities with sizable German-American work forces—notably Newark, Buffalo, Wheeling, Pittsburgh, Cleveland, Detroit, Chicago, Milwaukee, Davenport, Indianapolis, Cincinnati, Baltimore, Louisville, St. Louis, and New Orleans. Indeed, by the start of 1852, according to one estimate, immigrant labor societies of one kind or another already counted twenty thousand members nationwide. Men in their twenties and thirties evidently predominated.[6]

Diverse in purpose as well as composition, these early German-American labor groups shared members, leaders, meeting places, periodicals, and many principles and purposes with other organizations (such as *Turn-* and *Freimännervereine*) that sprang as well from the forty-eighter plebeian democracy. In an era when the state assumed few social welfare responsibilities, such *Vereine* commonly offered members insurance against the costs of sickness, injury, or death, and education and leisure activities ranging from sports, theater, and music to reading, discussion, and debate. Many labor *Vereine* took particular pride in their affiliated singing and dramatic groups.[7]

Craft-specific labor organizations divided into two main types: tradewide mutual benefit societies and the more combative journeymen's organizations known variously as "business organizations" (*Geschäftsvereine*) or "protective associations" (*Protektivunionen*). In both, the membership was composed overwhelmingly, and sometimes exclusively, of those practising a particular occupation. The more inclusive general *Arbeitervereine*, in contrast, embraced individuals of various occupations and even spanned social classes. Alongside large craftworker majorities were smaller numbers of day laborers, professionals, small proprietors, and in some cases even substantial businessmen. About seven in ten members of Cincinnati's *Arbeitereverein* in 1852 made their living in craft production, most commonly as tailors and cabinetmakers but also as shoemakers, carpenters, masons, bakers, locksmiths and machinists, coopers, and saddlers. But the *Verein* also contained handfuls of day laborers and merchants as well as a teacher and a surgeon. Arising later in the decade, Chicago's *Arbeiterverein* welcomed "men of different trades and professions, such as mechanics of all kinds, laborers, accountants, literary men, musicians, etc."[8]

This social diversity reflected and reinforced the widespread view that all but the wealthiest and most predatory idlers belonged in the extended family of "workingmen." Perhaps the most explicit and extreme statement of this view came from a member of the Chicago *Verein*, who seemed to echo Karl Beck's early praise for the Turners. Through the Chicago *Arbeiterverein*'s inclusiveness, he wrote, "it is to be hoped the dissents of our German Americans, such as misunderstandings between the less and more educated classes among us, will gradually be removed and smoothed away, all true friends of the independence of the people uniting in an undertaking which has no other object than the mutual interest and common benefit of all."[9]

These labor organizations threw up leaders of diverse backgrounds as well. Societies based in particular crafts usually selected officers with the same occupation. (The Chicago *Wagner-Verein* gave this tendency unintended emphasis when it made wagonmaker Jakob Wagner its president.) Skilled workers, particularly those whose trades were undergoing the most drastic transformations, also led many of the broader *Arbeitervereine*.

German-American tailors proved especially ubiquitous in the labor movement's leadership. Wilhelm Weitling of New York City was the most prominent, but many others were also active: Kaspar Gams, Johann Hempel, and Johann Blankenheim in Cincinnati; Carl Buschmann, Louis Frankoni, Jasper Bechmeier, J. Andrew Handschuh, and Victor Pelz in New York City; and Joachim Kersten, M. Schroder, A. Haas, A. Gudath, and H. Deph in Chicago. Boot and shoemakers were often leaders as well, such as Peter Rödel and Philip Stoppelbein in New York and C. Ludwig Mahlke and T. Conrad Liebrich in Philadelphia. Chairmaker Gottfried Lindauer helped organize Newark's *Arbeiterverein*, and cabinetmakers like John G. Braubach, Hermann Toaspern, George Vogel, Henry Klein, and F. Steffen helped lead New York City's immigrant labor organizations, along with gilder August Vecchioni and upholsterer Charles Crux. Cabinetmaker L. A. Maffey and Gottlieb F. Wiest (who was also a *Turnverein* cofounder and sometime *Freimänner* member) played the same roles in Cincinnati, as did A. Schultz in Chicago. Other significant leaders included machinist Heinrich Richter, who headed the New York City *Arbeiterverein*'s membership commission; and H. Höhn, H. Dürlam, and H. Kasperi, who led the machinists' union in St. Louis. Franz Arnold, the tireless mechanic from Frankfurt, helped found both general *Arbeitervereine* and individual trade societies in New York, Philadelphia, Baltimore, and Pittsburgh. Less often, leaders arose from the ranks of the coopers, turners, printers, and bakers; more rarely still, from the ranks of the unskilled, such as laborer-turned-cigarmaker Augustus Thum, carman Heinrich Ahrens, and laborer Frederick W. Knapp (who chaired Cincinnati's Working Men's Literary and Debating Society).[10]

Like other organizations of the broad forty-eighter democracy, immigrant labor bodies contained numerous professionals and middle-class intellectuals in their leading councils. Among them were Cincinnati's Johannes Peyer, a Swiss-born physician and a veteran of the revolutionary agitation at the University of Vienna, and New York's Abraham Jacobi, a pioneering pediatrician born in Westphalia. Chicago's Dr. Ernst Schmidt, another youthful veteran of 1848, was another physician who linked his fortunes with immigrant working people. Some religious rationalist leaders like Rev. Johan A. Försch and Gottlieb Kellner of New York, Wilhelm Rosenthal of Philadelphia, and Eduard Schläger of Boston and Chicago brought oratorical and journalistic skills to the labor movement as well. Architect John Kreitler headed the Newark *Arbeiterverein*'s membership committee. Engineers Joseph Weydemeyer and Adolphus Cluss helped lead the Marxist wing of the labor movement. In 1850 the immigrant journalist and attorney Louis Jonassohn seemed to be present everywhere in New York where German craftworkers were organizing and helped represent the wheelwrights at meetings of the New York City Industrial Congress. The journalist Christian Esselen, who had played an active role in the labor movement in Cologne in 1848, remained linked to *Arbeitervereine* in the United States. Teacher Theodor Hielscher, prominent in Berlin during the revolution, became successively a founding member of the Baltimore *Freimännerverein,* a leading Turner and editor of the *Freie Presse* in Indianapolis, and president of the *Chicagoer Arbeiterverein.*[11]

Certain types of small proprietors were also found in leadership positions. Grocer Caspar Butz helped direct the Detroit *Arbeiterverein* in the early 1850s. New York labor activist Erhard Richter, in addition to his personal abilities, could offer his colleagues a congenial meeting place, for he was also a saloon owner. So could Eugen Lievre, owner of New York's Shakespeare Hotel and an early ally of Wilhelm Weitling. Across the Hudson River lived Ludwig Albinger, a self-employed baker and brewer, one of a band of emigrés in Newark that tried to return to Germany in 1848. Perched above Newark's Market Street Post Office, Albinger's second-story *Lokal* hosted Thursday-night meetings of the city's *Arbeiterverein.*[12]

The Cooperative Vision

Both general-membership *Arbeitervereine* and craft-specific mutual insurance and protective societies sponsored producer cooperatives in trades undergoing transformation at mid-century. Viewed by their most zealous advocates as a way to restore wage earners and marginally self-employed producers to social independence and economic prosperity, these ventures drew upon the experience of two continents. Groups of native-, British-, and Irish-born Americans grappling with the effects of industrial change experimented with cooperative ventures during the 1840s. Carpenters, cabinetmakers, printers, tailors, bookbinders, stove molders, and foundrymen launched cooperative enterprises in New York, Boston, Philadelphia, Newark, Pittsburgh, Cincinnati, St. Louis, Louisville, and elsewhere. A committee of Boston's Mechanics' and Laborers' Association captured the prevailing spirit in an 1845 resolution affirming that "the direction and profits of industry must be kept in the hands of the producers" and that "laborers must own their own shops and factories, work their own stock, sell their own merchandise, and enjoy the fruits of their own toil. Our Lowells must be owned by the artisans who build them and the operatives who run the machinery and do all the work." "We don't think it right," explained New York carpenter Ben Price five years later, "for one man to have at his command 100 or 200 men, which he can discharge at any time, or cut down their pay."[13]

Seeking bulwarks against the pressures of the marketplace and the steady spread of wage-dependency, German-born craftworkers displayed even more enthusiasm for forming cooperatives than their native-born counterparts. In New York shoemakers and tailors took the lead in the spring of 1850. A great tailors' strike that summer spawned a large cooperative shop in August 1850 that employed more than forty workers by the fall. Franz Arnold soon reported that Philadelphia's German shoemakers and tailors were adopting the same cooperative constitution as their New York counterparts and putting its provisions into practice even more expeditiously. In Buffalo a cabinetmakers' cooperative employed ten German tradesmen, and a German tailors' cooperative employed eighty people. Immigrant tailors, carpenters, cabinetmakers, turners (lathe-operators), shoemakers, printers, watchmakers, metalworkers, bakers, button and fringe makers, and glassblowers also founded cooperatives in Newark, Baltimore, Pittsburgh, Cincinnati, Detroit, Cleveland, Milwaukee, Louisville, St. Louis, San Antonio, New Orleans, and many smaller population centers.[14]

The tailor Wilhelm Weitling was antebellum German America's leading, most persuasive, and most visionary apostle of cooperativism. His remarkable vision, in turn, captured a poignant and ambiguous moment in craftwork's transition from artisanship to factory-based production. To account for the poverty, degradation, and dependence of once-proud craftworkers, Weitling and those who subscribed to his thinking blamed a system of unequal exchange relationships foisted upon small producers by unscrupulous merchants and financiers ("capitalists"). These middlemen situated themselves between producers and consumers to exploit both and profit at their expense: consumers received less than they paid for, while those who actually produced society's necessities were paid below value for their efforts.[15]

If Weitling added little to centuries-old complaints about the lot of marginal proprietors in a crowded market, the solution he urged was more novel. A simple return to independent artisan status was abjured. Contemporary injustices could be righted only by reorganizing all economic relations—in production as well as exchange—along cooperative lines. The constitutions adopted by cooperatives of tailors, cabinetmakers, and shoemakers in New York and Philadelphia all sought to "guarantee to each member steady work and the full value" of the labor each worker performed by circumventing idle employers and merchants. Ultimately, Weitling believed, this could be accomplished only by firmly integrating cooperative shops into a far-flung network of affiliated shops, warehouses, and labor exchange banks.[16]

The German-Jewish mechanic and cooperative advocate Charles Schiff found a receptive audience for this analysis and program in August 1850, when he attended a session of the New York City Industrial Congress. At present, Schiff explained, there were simply too many "merchants, grocery dealers, rum sellers, agents, and other idle creatures, which the workingman has to support," a state of affairs that violated the original precepts of both the American republic and Christianity. (Schiff called himself "a Jew with Christian principles.") "Our great Constitution says that we are all born alike," Schiff reminded his listeners. But if so, and "if we are all the children of one Almighty God, how can it be that one child has to work to support two or three of his brethren in idleness?" Parasitical middlemen throve by underpaying real producers for their labor while overcharging them for life's necessities. Instead, Schiff urged, "give to that workingman the real worth of his work" and "let him have his necessaries for their real value"; he will then be able to save half his earnings. Once cooperative self-employment has abolished exploitation through unequal exchange, Schiff asserted, "our merchants will will no longer be our bosses"; they will become instead "our agents or servants." This would truly be "a Republic of Workingmen," "a Society where every man is rich," a place where "as Moses said to the Israelites, there shall be no poor among you." When "we are all masters, there will no longer be any difference between man and man." Then "we can be without the present expensive Government, and have no need of police, lawyers, ministers, poorhouses, and prisons." Here at last would be a society guided by "a few words which Christ said 1,800 years ago to his Apostles . . . 'Thou shalt love thy neighbor as thyself.'"[17]

For Weitling and his sympathizers, the voluntary establishment of cooperative enterprises was not just a goal, it was the chief means of liberation. Few other forms of economic or political action seemed worthwhile. A new and harmonious economic system would arise, develop, mature, and displace the existing order gradually, inexorably, and peacefully. "You must not believe that I am going to make a revolution," stressed Schiff. "Far be it from me." Similarly, although Weitling's New York newspaper, *Republik der Arbeiter,* reported sympathetically on work stoppages and the journeymen involved, its editor denied that these struggles could significantly improve conditions. Higher prices would wipe out whatever nominal wage gains were won. Weitling's hopes of restoring harmony within the crafts and his persistent tendency to locate capital and exploitation in the sphere of commerce rather than production only intensified his distaste for strike action.[18]

Though its appeal was real, the cooperative movement proved incapable of mobilizing or protecting large numbers of craftworkers against the deleterious aspects of economic change. Many more craftworkers strove to defend their interests and build mass organizations on the terrain of industrial capitalism itself, in the midst of its ongoing development. The avowed goals of these organizations and their struggles usually seem modest beside the grand cooperative vision. But their thrust—their trajectory—often propelled those involved into sharper conflicts with capital than did the steps Weitling and Schiff were proposing. Over time, indeed, a growing number of these trade-union confrontations raised issues and involved methods unanticipated and unexplored by most radical democratic theorists.

By the late 1840s labor struggles were already pitting German-American journeymen against their employers in one trade after another. These clashes gave rise to new protective associations and swelled the ranks of existing ones. As these disputes spread throughout the economy, both employers and employees reached out for allies. As local, shop-specific disputes began to fuse into broader and more generalized conflicts, labor organizations modified their form, goals, outlooks, and rhetoric. New York, as the nation's principal manufacturing city and home of the largest and most hard-pressed immigrant labor force, witnessed these trends earliest and in some of their most fully elaborated forms. But a similar escalation of conflict and organization could also be observed elsewhere during the 1850s—first of all in other eastern cities and then in the Midwest. This development laid the basis for ambitious attempts to unite workers across the country.[19]

Conditions in the economy at large and in its various sectors set the basic parameters of these labor struggles. Protests by unemployed workers took center stage during the economic panics of 1854–55 and 1857. The principal strike movements of the 1850s arose during peak periods of business expansion in 1850, 1853, and 1858–60. Strikers' demands focused most commonly on limiting the length of the working day and week in industries where the work process had become most centralized, with large numbers of employees in the same workplace under the direct supervision and discipline of their employers. The construction, textile, iron-making and ironworking, baking, and confectionary industries thus became centers of such disputes. Germans employed there joined these struggles, as did some working for larger firms producing furniture, barrels, wagons, and other commodities. Toward the end of the decade the introduction of the sewing machine spurred the growth of centralized clothing factories, and some groups of tailors began striking for shorter hours, too.[20]

The great majority of antebellum strikes arose out of disputes over wages ("prices"). But, as suggested earlier, for those who worked on a subcontracting or outwork basis, piece rates indirectly governed many other aspects of labor and living conditions, including the pace and intensity of work, the length of the working day and week, and the nature and amount of time available to spend with family members. Thus a dispute that nominally focused on piece rates could involve other grievances as well. In demanding a 25 percent increase in piece rates in 1850, for example, New York's multiethnic journeymen carvers' union sought to raise workers' incomes partly to reduce the number of hours they had to work in order to survive. The same consideration influenced New York City tailors in 1850.[21]

Wage disputes could also evoke or inflame still more general grievances about the state of the crafts and the lot of immigrant workers in American society as a whole. In 1848 German cabinetmakers in Milwaukee rejected low price lists that would mean "donating our labor free, thereby robbing our families of the necessary means to live." They reminded their employers that they were not "simply vassals" but rather "upright mechanics" who scorned a "submissive" demeanor. In 1850 the Pittsburgh *Arbeiterverein,* supporting local ironworkers locked in a fierce struggle of their own, asserted that "the earth and all the elements necessary for the happiness and well-being of the race belong alike to the whole of mankind; and there can be no just or natural right existing on the part of a select few to monopolize that which by right belongs equally to all for use." Looking back upon their wage strike the previous year, four hundred of New York's highly skilled German pianoforte makers in 1854 asserted their hostility to both "the piece system" and to "the encroachments of the 'day-work system' in our trade," and hoped others would not "glory in a system forced on them by their necessity, and in opposition to their feelings of independence and self-respect." Through various means—including street processions accompanied by the raucous *Katzenmusik* ("cat music") traditional in German charivaris—strikers alerted the rest of the community that their employers were greedily violating common (and assertedly traditional) standards of just behavior and thereby disrupting social harmony.[22]

Whatever the immediate grievance, all these struggles turned on the exercise of power, a fact that few antebellum employers overlooked. Demands for a collective wage increase or a reduction in hours challenged the employer's assumed right to govern the enterprise unilaterally. A German boss cabinetmaker of Brooklyn named Helmuth voiced the indignation of many proprietors when he "threatened to disperse the Cabinet Makers Association with Cannon balls" upon receiving the *Verein*'s wage demands in 1850. Only the threat of a strike induced Herr Helmuth later to "pay whatever was wanted" and reportedly promise "never [to] say such words again, which he had only uttered in a moment of excitement."[23]

The workers' increasing insistence on formal labor agreements measured their growing distrust of employers. Insisting in 1853 that boss painters agree to raise wages twenty-five cents per day, a leader of New York's journeymen painters put this motive plainly: "It is not for that sum we now hold out, but on principle." Without a written agreement, "there is nothing to prevent those persons reducing our wages still lower. They have broken their word before, and may again." Employers particularly bridled at demands that all employees be compensated at a uniform rate. Boss painters in New York thus agreed with their journeymen in 1853 that "the question has now become not one of wages merely, but one of right and principle." At issue, they asserted, was "whether employers shall surrender their privilege—a privilege ever conceded to employers in all branches of trade—of remunerating journeymen according to their capacities, or whether we shall be solely ruled in this matter, as well as in the choice of our workmen, by the dictates of a combination." To concede on this point, they insisted, would be "degrading and humiliating" and "bring our profession into disgrace and reduce us to the condition of menials."[24]

Further steps in the same direction followed. Some groups of journeymen tried to protect previous gains and resist anticipated attacks by solidifying the ad hoc structures thrown up during work stoppages. And during the 1850s various groups of cabinetmakers, printers, shoemakers, tailors, pianoforte makers, and other craftworkers sought union-shop agreements, according to which all employees would have to join the journeymen's association within a specified period. In 1859, for example, Cincinnati's multiethnic but predominantly German journeymen cabinetmakers' association coupled wage demands with calls for union-shop guarantees and employer recognition of a permanent union standing committee (*ein stehende Comité*) in each enterprise to speak for its work force on a day-to-day basis. The employers responded predictably. Frederick Rammelsberg and other major furniture manufacturers "firmly protest[ed] against any interference in the control or management of our factories" and vowed to "resist all action of any *union* assuming to dictate rules or regulations for adoption."[25]

Solidarity and Consciousness of Class

These economic conflicts reflected and spurred a powerful polarization within the trades that affected patterns of affinity and loyalty in German America. On one side, this process increased the social distance, friction, and antagonism between larger masters and their journeymen, substantial employers and their employees. Complementing this development was the reciprocally growing sense that, despite the many differences that distinguished them from one another, workers in different shops, trades, and even cities had many interests in common and must somehow band together in mutual support. Central to any definition of class consciousness, this belief led to the forging of stronger, more sustained, and more far-reaching bonds of solidarity with other wage workers. Ultimately it led to the dramatic multiplication of both protective associations and intercraft alliances at the citywide level and to some important attempts to form nationwide trade unions.

This feeling of solidarity—of identification and readiness to support other workers actively—extended farther and more readily in some directions than in others. The nation's industrial labor force was becoming increasingly diverse, and much that distinguished American workers from each other also inhibited united action among them. Wilhelm Weitling dolefully noted in the fall of 1850 that "here the proletariat is divided among various nationalities, languages, and religions and for that reason often divided against itself." The 1840s and 1850s witnessed repeated clashes pitting groups of German immigrants against groups of native-born and Irish workers. As in the case of the 1846 Brooklyn dock strike, employers recognized and took advantage of these frictions, thereby exacerbating them.[26]

Even among German-American workers themselves major obstacles often barred the way to united action. As they strove to fix the parameters of their class (and define the bounds of loyalty), the immigrants wrestled with contradictory principles and considerations that pushed now in the direction of broader solidarity, now toward greater exclusivity.

At its most extreme, a narrow definition of self-interest excluded almost any collective action at all, as when English-speaking New York patternmakers and millwrights who sought pay increases from their employers announced in 1853 that they "preferred individually to speak for themselves to signing any memorial" as a group. Such, they explained, was "the proper way to address employers—in a free republican manner." Among certain groups of German workers, guild traditions encouraged efforts to protect working and living standards by strictly demarcating skill levels and otherwise restricting entry to the labor market. Apprenticeship and its terms could raise related issues. Journeymen and small masters had long resisted abuses of the apprentice system as one way to combat debasement of the crafts. A majority of New York's organized German cigarmakers thus contended in 1850 "that bunglers had spoiled the trade" by "selling the worst kind of cigars, and badly manufactured, at a price limited only by their necessities of life." The association's solution was to require full three-year terms for all apprentices. A minority, however, heatedly objected that "the trade and the work must remain *free* and every emigrant arriving here must be placed at liberty to embrace whatever employ or work will suit him best." The dissenters warned that strict apprenticeship rules "would recall the time of German [guild] restrictions" and foster antagonism toward the *Verein* among the workers thereby denied employment.[27]

Apprenticeship rules, moreover, were often used specifically to bar the employment of women, and probably the most durable division within workers' ranks, immigrant and native-born alike, followed the gender line. As already noted, women had been entering traditional consumer goods crafts in rising numbers in both Europe and the United States. Attempting to address this development, fledgling German-American labor organizations found themselves wracked by conflicting impulses. At the center of the artisan's vision of "independence" was a male breadwinner whose income was sufficient to support the entire family and so sustain the gendered division of labor within it. (The first issues of Hermann Kriege's *Volks-Tribun* featured a masthead that captured this image perfectly. It depicted a rustic male, knife in hand, shielding a cowering female from an unseen attacker.) In both Europe and the United States, the entry of women into the paid work force represented an erosion of that vision. Most skilled male workers viewed women as unwarranted intruders into the job market, witting or unwitting tools of unscrupulous merchants and employers, degraders of skill levels, and wreckers of the trades generally. By taking work away from male family heads and allegedly performing it with less skill and for lower pay, moreover, females were seen as undermining both the conditions and status of journeymen and their families.

This perception encouraged stubborn rearguard battles to keep (or drive) women out of wage work. The feminist journalism of forty-eighter Mathilde Giesler Anneke ran afoul of these efforts in 1852. Hiring German women to set type, Giesler Anneke began publishing her monthly *Deutsche Frauenzeitung* in the printshop of Milwaukee's largest German-language daily. In May, however, the newly founded German printers' union denounced this use of "unauthorized interlopers," compelling Giesler Anneke to transfer operations to another shop.[28]

As the debate among the German cigar workers revealed, however, the labor movement's restrictive tendencies did not go unchallenged. Among some workers, at least, the dictates of egalitarian ideology militated against exclusionary policies. The United States, moreover, had little or no guild tradition of its own to which immigrants could appeal. On the practical level, the inclusion of women and less skilled males had already become a fait accompli in a number of the most hard-pressed trades by the 1850s. The survival of many craftworker households employed on an outwork basis already depended upon the efforts of female family members. In such industries, attempts to unite the existing work force against employers had to accommodate this fact. For example, although New York's (native-born) Journeymen's Cordwainers' Association stipulated that "no woman shall work in any shop which this Society has control over," the association permitted exceptions for the wives and daughters of its male members.[29]

Some male German-American labor leaders also bowed in the direction of sexual equality. Wilhelm Weitling's *Republik der Arbeiter* formally acknowledged women's rights, and a few women (usually widows) belonged to the labor societies that he led. But no one worked harder or more effectively to bolster support for women's rights in the immigrant labor movement than Mathilde Giesler Anneke. Her national speaking tour in the summer of 1852 hammered home the right of women to work and to vote, and receptive listeners included some men active in labor circles. After moving that fall from Milwaukee to Newark, Giesler Anneke resumed publication of the *Frauenzeitung* (now a weekly) and joined Weitling's organization, whose newspaper advertised and helped circulate her publication. Thereafter, she later recalled, Giesler Anneke regularly lectured before the *Arbeitervereine* of Newark, New York City, and Williamsburg on her view "that the social question could only be solved by the emancipation of women."

During the labor upsurge of 1853, Giesler Anneke joined Joseph Weydemeyer's new *Amerikanische Arbeiterbund*, which eclipsed Weitling's organization. Emphasizing that "all workers who live in the United States without distinction of occupation, language, color, or sex can become members," the *Bund* honored Giesler Anneke at a major public banquet, where she once again addressed the situation and needs of women before a large and apparently receptive audience of both male and female workers. Meanwhile, the Williamsburg *Arbeiterverein* (which was also affiliated with the *Amerikanische Arbeiterbund*) established a *Frauenverein*—in which "our sisters are warmly invited to take their places." In the later years of the 1850s the national leadership of the German-American labor movement changed hands yet again. But under the leadership of Gustav Struve, the new *Allgemeine Arbeiterbunde von Nordamerika* also emphasized its support for "equal rights for all, regardless of color, religion, nationality, or sex." August Willich's *Cincinnati Republikaner* defended a similar stance.[30]

None of this signified, of course, that the battle had been won. Many male craftworkers still cherished hopes of excluding women from the paid work force and seized upon opportunities to do so. When factory organization came to the clothing and shoemaking industries late in the 1850s, organized German tailors in Cincinnati insisted that female outworkers be replaced by male factory hands. This demand, noted the editor of the New York *Sociale Republik* with dismay, was "reminiscent of guild restriction."[31]

German labor organizations commonly proved readier to reach across barriers of language and ethnicity than across gender lines. In the late 1840s the Philadelphia *Arbeiterverein* voted to "act in concert" with the "American Laboring classes" represented in the city's new Trades Convention. Similar overtures followed in Pittsburgh, whose *Arbeiterverein* enthusiastically greeted and pledged full cooperation to the new English-speaking United Trade and Laborers' Organization of Allegheny County. German and native-born cabinetmaker organizations in Cincinnati successfully collaborated during the strike movement of 1853, and Chicago's *Arbeiterverein* a few years later also looked forward to "eventually cooperating with our Anglo-American fellow citizens who still hold fast to the great truths upon which our Republic is founded." When English-speaking shoemakers in New York went on strike for higher wages in April of 1850, the association of German cordwainers adopted the same price list and forbade members to work for struck employers. In 1853 the two unions resumed and deepened their collaboration. German bakers cooperated with their native-born counterparts in 1850, as did organized German journeymen upholsterers.[32]

The desire for interethnic unity produced some unified craft organizations. New York's German blacksmiths and wheelwrights reached out to their English-speaking counterparts, since "we all belong to one great family—the Workingmen's family." The city's German cabinetmaker society restructured itself in 1850 "for the accommodation of all nations." The German ironworkers in April 1850 solicited "the cooperation of their fellow workmen, without distinction of nation, at their future meetings." Unified organizations in that city also eventually enrolled varnishers, upholsterers, carvers, pianoforte makers, silversmiths, and cigarmakers. In 1853 German- and English-speaking Chicago tailors formed a single committee and presented a common bill of prices for both custom and shop work. In Cincinnati, English- and German-speaking cabinetmakers, who had been cooperating since 1853 while retaining separate organizations, formed a united association in March 1859. That initiative set an example soon followed by furniture workers in Louisville, Kentucky.[33]

This push toward interethnic unity, though more successful than attempts to unite across gender lines, suffered setbacks as well. The employment of English- and German-speaking workers in distinct enterprises or even different branches of a given trade could weaken recognition of common interests. Where unitary organization occurred, moreover, it necessitated either parallel meetings of different language-groups or the ongoing translation of proceedings within a common meeting. Both arrangements were clumsy and time-consuming.

Differences in political temperament also took their toll. Fresh from heady experiences in continental Europe, many Germans considered English-speaking workers (native-, British- and Irish-born alike) to be rather slow-witted, narrow-minded, and timid in asserting their rights. August Willich had concluded "after the first years of my stay here" that "in this republic a beginning is possible only through the German element," since "the American with his hasty action has less feeling for purposes which are less immediate and less quick to attain and bear fruits." For their part, many English-speaking workers looked with at least equal distaste and suspicion on the Germans, viewing them as visionary chatterboxes, impractical hotheads, and dangerous infidels.[34]

Strike Movements and Union Development: 1850

The first major strike movement involving German immigrants began early in 1850 in New York City, where wholesale prices had risen by more than 20 percent in four years. Beginning in the winter, inflation propelled journeymen, outworkers, and day laborers into unprecedentedly numerous and powerful organizations and strikes. That spring the *New York Daily Tribune* marveled that "the organization of the Trades into Protective Associations proceeds unabated." Organizing is "going on in every trade and every department of industry," a leader of the journeymen coopers could still cheer three months later, "to an extent never before dreamed of." Some of the better-paid journeymen—carpenters, masons, and painters as well as shipwrights, caulkers, and others employed in construction and shipbuilding—played key roles.[35]

Numerous observers noted that German-American craftworkers took a particularly active part. German carpenters, masons, and painters joined in the work stoppages initiated in their trades. But the craftworkers in the light consumer goods industries really led the mobilization of immigrant labor. "No class of our population," the *Tribune* held, "goes more effectively to work than our German artizans [*sic*], who have held meetings nearly every evening during the past week, and have succeeded in uniting many of the trades into Unions." All told, some twenty German trade unions or trade-union fractions organized themselves in New York that year.[36]

First to move were the journeymen cabinetmakers. Their shop delegates began meeting in early February 1850, and in March their *Schreinerverein* downed tools. This decisive act galvanized the work force: the *Verein* soon boasted eight hundred members, and before the end of May at least one thousand had been organized into eight geographical districts, making the *Schreinerverein* the largest trade union in the city. Other groups of German craftworkers followed the cabinetmakers' lead, including tailors, carvers, upholsterers, boot and shoemakers, button and fringe makers, bakers, confectioners, turners, watchmakers, capmakers, locksmiths, silversmiths, coopers, book printers, coach painters, and cigarmakers. Many of these organizations conducted their meetings at Hillenbrand's Mechanics' Hall on Hester Street. Others met in Eugen Lievre's Shakespeare Hotel on William near Duane Street, and still others in the *Lokal* run by Erhard Richter.[37]

The breadth and momentum of the strike wave strengthened the desire for firmer coordination across craft lines. Responding to a call initiated by Wilhelm Weitling and Franz Arnold early in the year, 2,400 German craftworkers from at least ten trades in the New York metropolitan area (Manhattan, Williamsburg, and Newark) sent delegates to form a *Centralkommission der vereinigten Gewerbe* (CVG—

Central Commission of the United Trades).[38] When a broad array of benevolent and protective associations constituted the New York City Industrial Congress that spring, the CVG welcomed and participated in the new body while continuing to provide German-American craftworkers with an independent voice. In six months' time, the CVG claimed a membership of 4,500 members in seventeen trades.[39]

This strike wave swept through other urban centers, including Newark, Philadelphia, Baltimore, Buffalo, Pittsburgh, Cleveland, Cincinnati, and St. Louis, in each case involving substantial numbers of German workers. By the summer of 1850 strikes in a score of Philadelphia trades had sparked the formation there of a *Centralkommission* representing German tailors, shoemakers, cabinetmakers, metalworkers, cigarmakers, weavers, bakers, and others. A similar body arose in Baltimore, and still another began to crystallize in St. Louis, where a tailor and a cooper presided over an ad hoc coordinating committee uniting fifteen trades.[40]

German Workers and the 1850 Tailors' Strike

One of the nation's largest, most explosive, and most illuminating labor conflicts at mid-century revolved around immigrant craftworkers. New York City's organized German tailors played a crucial and often determining role in their trade's strike movement in 1850 and in the strike support movement that this cause célèbre spawned. The enormous stresses generated by this strike revealed much about the tailors and about German-American workers in general, at the same time shedding light on interclass relations within German America and on efforts to rally workers of distinct cultural backgrounds around a common cause.

That New York's tailors would attract and merit so much attention was by no means obvious when the year began. In the winter of 1850 the trade's two main contingents—the Germans and the English-speakers, who were heavily Irish-born—remained isolated from and suspicious of one another. This fragmentation of the work force only aggravated widespread feelings of helplessness and hopelessness among the city's impoverished clothing workers, further undermining efforts at organization.

The German tailors' association (the *Vereinigte Protektivunion der Schneider*) began as a small body and grew slowly. It claimed only about 250 members by early spring, when the society of English-speaking tailors, acting on its own, formulated a new price list. A turning point came in May, when the *Protektivunion* decided to approach the Irish and propose collaboration. By June, German tailor leaders such as Jasper Bechmeier and J. Andrew Handschuh were regularly attending meetings of the English-speaking group. In mid-July a mass meeting of both organizations voted to present employers with a common scale of prices.[41]

At last kindling hopes of success, this display of interethnic unity encouraged optimism, militancy, and organizational growth among journeymen tailors at large. By the end of July more than two thousand Germans and a roughly equal number of English-speaking tailors had joined their respective associations, whose committees were by then meeting virtually round the clock. As they had in Europe, German workers marched through the city's streets, calling upon their employers to accept the terms submitted by their *Union*, which claimed three thousand members by August.[42]

The German workers' leadership initially depicted the strike as a struggle simultaneously to win justice for the journeymen and to harmonize relations within the industry. "Never was the demand for a rise of wages more moral, moderate, and just than in the present instance," argued the *Centralkommission*. But raising the living standards of the journeymen "secures the interest of the employer as well as the employed," it continued. "Even many of our most esteemed employers acknowledge this, and not only adhere to the new bill of prices, but also favor this movement in other ways." Indeed, the CVG explained, the journeymen tailors' overriding goal was "to unite together all the Journeymen Tailors as well as their Employers who adhere to this bill [of prices] into one great Protective Union, which should guard the rights and promote the interests of all." More than a few small employers did accept the terms proposed by the protective union, but prospects of any wider harmony soon faded. The same edition of the *New York Daily Tribune* that carried the CVG's conciliatory statement also reported that "the principal dealers in 'Southern work'" had already met to map out "the necessary steps for preventing the adoption of the list of prices proposed by the Journeymen Tailors."[43]

During the next two weeks the level and intensity of the conflict escalated dramatically as *Protektivunion* members and their allies clashed with employers, strikebreakers, and the city police. On July 22, approximately 300 strikers, more than nine in ten of them German, marched to the downtown Nassau Street premises of one of New York's largest clothing manufactories. Longstreet and Company employed some 1,500 tailors within the city and about another 1,000 in the surrounding countryside; many of the garments so produced were sold to southern customers. When the demonstrators arrived at Longstreet's and sought to speak to the heads of the firm, nonstriking employees barred their way, and a melee quickly ensued. Police arrived and arrested seven of the strikers, most of them German. When other strikers tried to free the prisoners by force, the police called in reinforcements, and the battle escalated. The constables intended to incarcerate their prisoners at the Tombs Jail but, upon learning that "a large number of the craft were collected" nearby, detoured to the office of the city's police chief. Word of their arrival there quickly spread, however, attracting another angry crowd. City authorities mobilized police reserves from four wards to guard the police chief's headquarters.[44]

This angry confrontation was only the heat lightning auguring an even more dramatic and violent storm yet to come. Tailors continued to demonstrate at the premises of Longstreet (now defended by police officers) as well as other large employers. Throughout the city teams of strikers accosted strikebreakers, sometimes forcefully marching the latter down to strike headquarters or simply confiscating their unfinished work on the spot. As such incidents multiplied, so did collisions with the police. On one occasion police who arrested a pair of strikers found themselves under assault from other unionists attempting to rescue the prisoners. The tailors got the best of it at first, but the arrival of police reinforcements turned the battle's tide. At day's end nine more prisoners sat in the Tombs, including *Protektivunion* and CVG leader Louis Frankoni. Police arrested another seven strikers at the end of July for allegedly assaulting a Catholic priest in *Kleindeutschland*'s Seventeenth Ward; strikers accused the priest of distributing two cartloads of scab work to members of his parish.[45]

Violence reached a crescendo on Sunday, August 4, when between one and two hundred strikers led by tailor George Short confronted Frederick Wartz in front of the latter's house on West Thirty-eighth Street in the garment manufactory district. Wartz, a subcontractor of coarse garments reportedly distributing work at prices below those demanded by the *Protektivunion*, refused to surrender more than one hundred unfinished coats in his possession. At this point, Wartz claimed, some of the strikers attacked him while others tried to break into his house in search of the garments in question. A squad of police arrived and arrested George Short, hauling him off to jail, once again with fellow strikers in hot pursuit and hurling rocks at the police.[46]

Fearing retribution, Wartz himself repaired to the station house. A few hours later a still larger crowd—apparently composed mostly of young, recently landed German tailors—set out again to challenge

Wartz and other strikebreakers. Informed of these plans by under-cover agents, however, the police intercepted the demonstrators a few blocks from Wartz's home. According to the strikers, the police then attacked them without warning, arresting about forty, clubbing many others to the ground, and shooting at least two.[47]

Those who assumed that violence and police crackdowns would demoralize New York's labor movement were soon disappointed. Instead the situation grew only more polarized. German tailors bitterly concluded that although they had "employed at the beginning of our strike all possible reasonable measures to bring the bosses to an understanding of . . . their own interest," subsequent events proved that "all this was of no use." Employers had revealed their kinship with familiar enemies—they were "despots and aristocrats" joined in an "unholy alliance of landlords, brokers, employers, and their purchasing mercenaries." Now convinced, moreover, that the smaller custom tailoring shops were aiding the targeted big "Southern" firms, both German- and English-speaking journeymen voted to shut down every clothing establishment in the city until it accepted the strikers' bill of prices.[48]

Meanwhile, the mass arrests and shootings of pickets also focused hostility upon government and police officials. Attempting to express their outrage, immigrant labor activists once more resorted to European parallels. "We did not expect to find in this free country a Russian police," the CVG spat. Repression also convinced other branches of the German-American labor movement that their own futures were at stake in the tailors' strike. "We must assist the tailors," urged a leader of the capmakers. "We must not let them be put down; it is the cause of each one of us; we are all deeply interested in their success whatever our trade may be." The CVG, fortified since the spring by the affiliation of an additional seven trade organizations and two thousand more rank-and-file supporters, declared it was "now absolutely necessary for the assembled workingmen to unite, if we will not permit one of our companies to be trampled under foot." Protective associations of German shoemakers, bakers, cabinetmakers, turners, and upholsterers, plus the Williamsburg *Arbeiterverein,* the *Sozialistischer Turnerbund* (represented by 1848 veteran Dr. Benjamin Maas), and *Kleindeutschland*'s ubiquitous rationalist and radical democratic leader, Rev. John A. Försch, all drove home this same basic message. German workers rallied to the tailors' support in boisterous meetings called at shop, craft, ward, and citywide levels. Meanwhile, German-language newspapers relayed news of the strike across the country, and *Schneiderevereine* in Newark, Philadelphia, Baltimore,

Cincinnati, St. Louis, and other cities extended both moral and material assistance to the strikers. These solidarity efforts actually unified Cincinnati's disparate craftworker groups into a single *Arbeiterverein* for the first time.[49]

In New York's *Kleindeutschland* talk of raising the level of confrontation now filled the air. Journeymen shoemakers offered to halt work in sympathy with the tailors should the latter deem that useful. Others urged caution. Convinced of the need for broad and active labor unity, a leader of the better-off German carpenters named Sauer nonetheless urged the trade societies to continue to "strike one at a time, and support each trade in its effort." They "must not all strike at once, and together, else we shall have nothing to eat at once and together!"[50]

But the struggle's growing intensity and scope were leading many to reappraise the conflict's stakes and significance. To them, Sauer's concerns had been overtaken by events. An attempt simply to raise one trade's labor prices, observed a German capmakers' committee, had grown into "a general and powerful attempt of all workingmen to ameliorate their condition." The CVG, having abandoned early talk of reconciling employees with the big employers, declared that nothing less was now involved than the "Emancipation of the Workingmen."[51]

Sentiments like these dominated the mass meeting of German workers that filled the park in front of City Hall on August 3. "It is now necessary for the millions to rise," tailor Frederick Klein exhorted, "to put down the despots and aristocrats who get the working men to work in droves for them like slaves and then laugh them to scorn." A capmaker named Dengler electrified the crowd by linking the New York tailors' strike to recent struggles in the Old World. "Many among us have before been engaged in fighting for liberty in [the] Fatherland. Now, brethren . . . it is time to fight again, and to fight boldly; we must not flinch; we must be resolute." From the crowd came cheers and shouts of "we will, we will." A tailor named Fries who belonged to the strike committee (the Committee of Thirteen) called upon his listeners to "assert and insist upon our own rights," adding that "we must fight for them if necessary." Indeed, he added, "if necessary we will have another revolution rather than go on to be trodden down any longer." Fries had to shout to be heard over the "loud and rapturous cheering" that greeted his militant language. After a German cabinetmaker leader also referred to those present as "revolutionists," a tailor named Bornhard (or Bomhart) tried to put teeth in such rhetoric. What in the experience of German craftworkers, he wanted to know, should incline them to trust the promises of the powerful? "If the aristocrats [of New York] give their words that they will submit," he warned, "Goddam them, it is not enough, they will not keep to it. We cannot trust them." Therefore let the trades "all strike together" and break the power of their enemies once and for all. "Let the butchers and bakers begin and cut off the supplies . . . and then the aristocrats will all starve."[52]

This call for a general strike, too, struck a responsive chord, and by the time the meeting's president (tailor leader Carl Buschmann) returned to the podium, the insurrectionary refrain had become virtually obligatory. "Think you," Buschmann asked, that "we can get our freedom by peaceful means, and gentle remedies? No, indeed! We must meet force with force; so, and only so, can we be free!" "My brethren," he urged, "my friends, my fellow citizens! Revolution is the word! We must have a revolution; we cannot go on and submit any longer." At this, a reporter noted, "one loud, unanimous, long continued shout of consentient applause burst simultaneously from the dense crowd, with prolonged shouts of bravo! bravo!"[53]

The rally outside City Hall captured something of the disillusion, desperation, and outrage then coming to a head among a section of *Kleindeutschland*'s workers. The mood it conveyed was considerably more militant than Charles Schiff's presentation to the New York Industrial Congress. But calls for a general strike and open threats of revolution did not address the problems immediately confronting the tailors and their supporters. First of all, as one Irish-American labor leader reminded them, "New York is not the United States"; even "if a revolutionary movement took place here it would not revolutionize the country." In New York itself, meanwhile, embattled strikers urgently needed the support of a united labor movement; CVG leaders resolved "to act in accordance with the Industrial Congress."[54]

This sober decision, however, pointed to another stubborn fact—that the subjective preconditions for revolution were far from ripe in New York City itself. The cautious carpenter Sauer had spoken for many workers in *Kleindeutschland* who supported the tailors but were unready to go much further. That stance was considerably more common among other sectors of the city's working class. Most of New York's English-speaking labor activists (among them advocates of cooperative production and land reform) displayed considerable discomfort with the combative language and conduct of their German allies. And while the Irish and German tailors had managed to collaborate since early summer despite differences in political disposition, some English-speaking journeymen continued to regret that alliance.[55]

Then, in August, on the eve of the Thirty-eighth Street bloodletting, a new difference arose to menace interethnic unity. The *Protektivunion*, convinced that "Southern work" employers were underpaying tailors even more severely than other boss tailors, demanded of them a correspondingly greater wage increase. At meetings of the English-speaking journeymen, Irish tailor leader Edward Mallon rejected the Germans' new demands as "so extravagant that it was impossible for the bosses to pay them" and further proof that "the Germans were not as practical as they ought to have been." A compromise was ultimately reached, but not before acrimonious exchanges led some English speakers once again to question the value of the German connection.[56]

Underlying frictions continued to surface. Henry Crate, a leader of the English-speaking printers' union and secretary of the Industrial Congress, strenuously objected to all talk of revolution, since "peaceable means"—especially the organization of cooperatives—"are ample for all purposes"; tailor Edward Mallon continued to denounce those who dreamt of "the gun or the chain" on "the barricades of Paris." John Lowe of the Journeymen Silversmiths' Protective and Beneficial Association was "with all the trades that strike for higher wages" but "want[ed] to see those strikes conducted with decency, and within the law." Like some others attending the Industrial Congress, Lowe refused to denounce police conduct in the Longstreet incident. It was not the police, he said, but the tailors themselves who had "acted rashly." Lowe had "seen their conduct and cannot approve of it."[57]

Fortunately for the strike, it was not these voices but those that spoke for continued labor solidarity that ultimately prevailed. "For my own part," one Irish tailor bluntly told Edward Mallon, "I would rather lose the strike than separate from the Germans." The Industrial Congress as a whole compared police conduct in 1850 to the notorious attempt in 1835 to crush the city's last major strike of journeymen tailors. In that spirit the congress orchestrated strike support efforts, declared a boycott of recalcitrant clothing manufacturers, and joined the CVG in sponsoring a huge solidarity rally on August 12 that mobilized more than fifty individual trade and general-membership workers' associations. Unable to break the strike in their industry and confronted by so aroused and massive a movement of labor citywide, garment firms began to concede, and the organized journeymen tailors claimed victory.[58]

The strengthened spirit of interethnic unity had thus proved decisive. But differences in sociopolitical temperament remained. Even those English-speaking labor leaders who spoke up for the Germans generally distanced themselves from the latter's rhetoric and conduct. "I beg you will see the necessity of going far to excuse the poor German," wrote tailor George Clancy to the hostile *New York Herald*, "it being notoriously a fact that unprincipled [business]men in this city have taken greater advantage of them than they could have done had the German spoke our language." Finally "unable longer to bear with it" and "hurried away by their feelings," the German tailors "mistake their interest by opposing the law" and "by such means give strength to their enemies."[59]

Irish-born shoemaker and land reformer William V. Barr also believed fervently in labor solidarity. "Tell the capitalists," he proclaimed at one open-air meeting, "that while the workingman has a shilling, the tailors on strike will never want a penny. And why? Because the blow aimed at the tailors is a blow aimed at every workingman in the city. If that blow succeeds, the next blow will be at some other branch of labor." Following the Wartz incident, Barr spearheaded efforts to mobilize the Industrial Congress and its affiliates behind the strikers. Even Barr blanched, however, when he heard the inflammatory views being "discussed too freely" by the Germans. "One class are discussing the propriety of an open revolutionary movement against the authorities of the city," he acknowledged unhappily. "For my part," he declared, "I am opposed to any such movement," agreeing with more cautious colleagues that "the peaceable means of the ballot box are sufficiently strong to overthrow the oppressor."[60]

The Program of the Solidarity Movement

The dramatic events of 1850 spurred a search for a general program of action that could unite and give direction to the New York City's diverse labor movement. Wilhelm Weitling and the CVG continued to emphasize plans for cooperative production and exchange. In the light of recent experience, however, the social content and significance of cooperation was altering. The big firms' implacable hostility led the German tailors' Commiteee of Thirteen to launch a cooperative shop open to journeymen and small producers alone. The September issue of Weitling's *Republik der Arbeiter* identified cooperationism as the proper basis for an "alliance of all workers and small employers against Capital, our mutual enemy." Far from blunting or circumventing class conflict (as Weitling had originally anticipated), the new tailors' cooperative would arise from and symbolize that conflict—a characteristic shared with a growing number of cooperatives in Milwaukee, Cincinnati, Cleveland, Buffalo, and elsewhere during the 1850s.[61]

Other aspects of the evolving action program revealed even more clearly the impact of the year's bitter clashes. New York's German labor movement now escalated its assault on employer prerogatives. It was no longer considered sufficient for employers individually to make concessions. As the tailor Bomhart had put it, "Goddamn them, that is not enough," because "we cannot trust them." It was necessary for the government to assure employer probity. Specifically, CVG leaders called for minimum-wage and maximum hours legislation and "severe penalties" for all violators. Some English-speaking unionists seconded such demands, as they did the call—championed by American workers at least since the 1820s—for an effective mechanics' lien law to enforce payment of wages owed.[62]

But the demands raised most persistently that season revolved around land reform. The prominence at strike support meetings of veteran land reformers George Henry Evans, John Commerford, Gilbert Vale, Lewis B. Ryckman, and John H. Keyser bespoke continuing support for this cause in labor circles. A multilingual meeting of workers in *Kleindeutschland*'s Seventeenth Ward typically ratified the program shared by English- and German-speaking land reformers.[63]

To implement their general social-economic agenda, finally, leaders of the movement stressed electoral action. The apparent need to parry police repression gave special urgency to this political initiative. Denouncing "the brutality and insolence with which many of our Policemen have conducted themselves in the numerous arrests which have been made," the CVG trusted that "the people" would refuse to "sustain these officials in their evident abuse of power." Repeatedly, German- and English-speaking labor orators agreed that "the only remedy for the evils we suffer is such political action as will secure to the Workingman fair representation" and government support "of the rights of the Toiler." This meant, in the first instance, "demand[ing] of our parties that they select men that are with us, and of us, and for us." But if the existing parties ignored such appeals, "we will do our own selecting of candidates and electing of them, too." Effective political action by workers, it was further held, required government protection of workers' liberty and freedom of action. Accordingly, mass meetings during the summer demanded "defense of the political rights of the journeymen" and the "prevention of all endeavors and influence of the Capitalists upon the workingmen at the time of the elections."[64]

These themes reverberated in Wilhelm Weitling's attempt that fall to organize German-American labor at the national level. During the last week of September, on the heels of the tailors' triumph, Weitling and his supporters in the New York and Philadelphia *Centralkomissionen* called for "the solemn confirmation and organization of the *Arbeiter-Verbrüderung* (Workers' Brotherhood) of the United States."[65]

A month later, on October 22, the founding convention of the *Allgemeine Arbeiterbund* (General Workers' League) met in a Philadelphia hall hung with banners proclaiming "Equal Rights and Duties." Delegates represented some 2,400 workers caught up in the year's labor upsurge. In addition to the sponsoring *Komissionen*, delegates spoke for local labor *Vereine* based in Pittsburgh, Buffalo, Cincinnati, Baltimore, Louisville, and St. Louis. The New York contingent included leaders of the German tailors (e.g., Louis Frankoni), cabinetmakers (F. Steffen), and turners (H. Seeman). Resolutions and discussion focused primarily upon Weitling's elaborate cooperative plans. But delegates also endorsed a battery of other demands close to the hearts of both German and American radical democrats. These included calls for easier naturalization procedures, direct election and recall of all government officeholders, repeal of all sabbatarian laws, and a major expansion of the public school and library systems. And again the principles of land reform received a ringing reaffirmation.[66]

The Strikes of 1853

Birth announcements of a German-American labor *Verbrüderung* aroused much enthusiasm in the country's *Arbeitervereine*. In fact, however, the *Allgemeine Arbeiterbund* was designed neither to lead nor to coordinate the economic struggles of its craftworker constituents against their employers. Although the 1850 strikes had to some extent compelled the New York CVG to play such a role, Weitling clearly felt job actions a distraction from his own priorities. It was to the latter, therefore, that he now returned. During the next two years organized craftworkers fighting over living standards and working conditions received little direction, guidance, or even attention from the *Allgemeine Arbeiterbund* or its newspaper. Thrown back upon their own resources, some local *Vereine* survived and even grew, but Weitling found it increasingly difficult to keep them in his national organization. Two years after its founding, the *Allgemeine Arbeiterbund* was in steep decline.[67]

Labor unrest, however, continued. In 1853 the economic expansion initiated about a decade earlier was cresting, and so was the inflation it caused. Meanwhile, the alliances and enmities manifested in

1850 had continued to mature. The type of interemployer alliance effected during the great New York City tailor strike, for example, became ever more commonplace in that city and elsewhere. Immigration, which was now reaching an antebellum peak, provided industry with a steady supply of labor power and potential strikebreakers.[68] Inflation and aggressive employer policies triggered a strike movement that lacked the stark drama and bloodshed of New York's 1850 clothing industry confrontation but spread farther and involved larger numbers of workers.[69]

These clashes failed to reinvigorate Weitling's *Arbeiterbund* significantly. At least part of the reason was programmatic: by 1853 bright hopes that cooperativism could solve the social problem had faded. Dependent upon the meager financial resources of wage earners and marginally independent producers, few cooperatives could compete successfully with large and well-financed enterprises that took advantage of an increasingly crowded labor market to pay low wages and push forward the division of labor. Some cooperating craftworkers sought to stave off ruin through stringent self-denial. The New York tailor cooperative enterprise launched in 1850, for example, required loans from other protective unions and well-wishers. Until those loans were paid off, the owner-employees pledged to take in return "for our work [only] so much as to pay our board and leave the remainder in the general stock." Other cooperative ventures survived competition by transmuting themselves into simple profit-oriented business partnerships.[70]

When in 1853, therefore, some again urged cooperative self-employment as an alternative to trade-union militancy, one shoemaker patiently but succinctly explained why "the working men . . . were not able to carry this substitute into effect." Most who tried, he said, had insufficient "capital" or "business talent," while "the good bookkeeper, salesman or cutter was not always a good handy-craftsman, and unless every man was all this, and that they had capital beside, this self-employment could not be carried into effect, for experience proved that co-operative stores seldom prospered—and if they did prosper it was only when they went from being the property of the general trade into the hands of the few."[71]

Against a backdrop of rising class antagonism and disappointment with the cooperative panacea, the drive to create more combative journeymen's associations grew stronger and broader, spreading farther geographically than it had in 1850. So did the tendency of protective associations based in distinct trades to assist and link up with one another. Towns and cities in much of industrializing America became embroiled in major organizing drives and strike waves in 1853. And in many of these locales, but especially in the principal strike centers, German workers once again played important roles.[72]

The spark was struck in Baltimore, where railroad shopmen on the Baltimore and Ohio line walked off work in February. Soon almost three thousand workers in various trades were calling work stoppages of their own throughout that city. By the time the movement peaked, nearly forty crafts had organized. Among German craftworkers the most active were the cigarmakers and bookprinters.[73]

The movement in Baltimore aroused sympathy and encouraged emulation among New York workers suffering from the ravages of inflation. Even the proper *New York Daily Times* acknowledged that, while "it would doubtless be desirable that employers should volunteer such an advance in wages," still, "experience shows that reliance upon their doing this is not [a method] by which wives and children can be fed and clothed." Between five and six thousand New York machinists, most of them native- or English-born, downed their tools in support of a demand for a 10 percent wage increase. Other groups of better-off, predominantly English-speaking workers (notably workers in skilled construction, shipbuilding, and related trades) also became embroiled in labor conflicts that year. Various groups of unskilled workers took action as well, including steamship firemen and coal passers, dockside coal hoisters, longshoremen, teamsters, carters, coachmen, hod carriers, and construction laborers. In May a union of six to seven hundred hotel waiters, primarily German- and Irish-born, went on strike as well.[74]

The core of the city's German labor force remained employed in the consumer-goods trades, at least twenty-five of which mobilized in 1853, led by bookprinters, hatters, bakers, confectioners, leatherworkers, saddle and harness makers, blacksmiths, cabinetmakers, upholsterers, cigarmakers, and pianoforte makers. Strikers commonly demanded wage boosts of between 10 and 25 percent, increases that were (as the *Times* noted) "in most cases . . . not excessive. They are not greater, and in most cases are not so great, as the increase in rent, provisions, and the cost of living." Among the Germans, shoemakers and tailors proved the best organized; by the end of April the latter boasted an elaborate structure of action committees rising from the shop level upward.[75]

Philadelphia's labor mobilization paralleled New York's. Here, too, some two dozen crafts mobilized, led by those employed in the construction, garment, furniture making, leather and metalworking, food, and printing industries. The strikes reached westward to Pittsburgh and Allegheny City, where workers in more than a score of trades held meetings, formed organizations, and frequently halted work. Down the Ohio River in Cincinnati, workers involved in the wage movement ranged from seamstresses through finishers, patternmakers, blacksmiths, and other workers in the metal trades. A meeting of craftworkers pressing for a 15 percent increase in wages that March "heartily approve[d] the conduct of our brother tradesmen in Baltimore and elsewhere" and laid the foundation for what became a powerful citywide General Trades Union. With the active encouragement of such forty-eighter radicals *Freimänner* leader Friedrich Hassaurek, German tailors, cigarmakers, bookprinters, and waiters organized for higher wages, and German cabinetmakers collaborated with native-born fellow tradesmen to the same end. German leatherworkers in Dayton, cabinetmakers in Cleveland, and tailors in Milwaukee all demanded price increases, too. And it was evidently in 1853 that groups of Chicago's German workers—most notably tailors, plasterers, and house carpenters—first organized and struck in appreciable numbers. This was all the more remarkable for the fact that industry in Chicago had only begun to burgeon the year before. "The call to independence sounded by the oppressed workers of the East," exulted immigrant Cincinnati tailor and labor leader Kaspar Gams, "has found a thousand-fold echo in the hearts of the western workers, who share their lot."[76]

This explosion of militant labor activity encouraged the creation of a new organization inspired by the "the recent workers' struggles in Baltimore and other American cities" and convinced that workers could "win our aims . . . only through a single, tightly knit movement." On March 21, 1853, eight hundred German-American workers from the New York metropolitan area met at Hillenbrand's Mechanics' Hall in *Kleindeutschland* and there founded a body that made militant labor solidarity its watchword. Pledging to resist wage cuts, extensions of the work week, and the decay of working conditions, this new organization eventually dubbed itself the *Amerikanische Arbeiterbund*. "United we stand," it declared, "divided we fall."[77]

Joseph Weydemeyer, Marx's friend and collaborator, played an active, leading role in this organization, and his views influenced the new *Arbeiterbund*'s words and actions at many points. The preamble to a programmatic document adopted later that year, for example, bore his stamp. It asserted that "societal relations are no longer the same as they were when the Republic was founded. The introduction and development of large-scale industry has brought on a new revolution, dissolved the old classes, and above all, brought into being our class, the class of propertyless workers."[78]

At Weydemeyer's behest, the *Amerikanische Arbeiterbund* pledged early to assert its "independence . . . from existing political parties" and later to "strive for the organization of the working class into a cohesive and independent political party" of its own in order "to obtain and guarantee the rights of the workers."[79] In the summer of 1850 the tailor solidarity movement had also urged political action to achieve labor's goals. In practice, however, this had turned out to mean more energetic lobbying among Whigs and especially Democrats. Weitling himself had regularly denounced the country's existing party organizations and urged working people to create a party of their own. When the state's Democratic gubernatorial candidate in 1852 promised to fight sabbatarianism and nativism, however, Weitling endorsed the campaign. In the same election, in contrast, Weydemeyer urged labor to remain strictly independent and called upon workers to present themselves before the nation with their own party based on their own plan of national transformation.[80]

In neither program nor purpose, however, did the *Amerikanische Arbeiterbund* simply reprise the Communist *Proletarierbund*. Through the *Arbeiterbund*, rather, Weydemeyer hoped to reach and collaborate with that growing number of workers who had not accepted the full Marxist worldview but did seem ready to proceed down the road of united and militant labor action. That experience, Weydemeyer hoped, would nurture their incipient class consciousness and strengthen support for a program of total social reorganization that required political action as well. The *Amerikanische Arbeiterbund's* brief program thus included calls for such now-familiar reforms as relaxed naturalization laws, an end to child labor, a ten-hour working day, a mechanics' lien law, a major expansion of public education, federal legislation to protect labor's rights, and the "abrogation of all laws that interfere with the workers' enjoyment of their freedom, such as Sunday laws, temperance laws, and the like." Regarding the disposal of the public lands, Weydemeyer initially resisted widespread calls to divide and sell it off. Instead, urged the program, let these lands remain publicly owned, to be cultivated collectively by teams of agricultural workers. (In this it also followed the lead of some non-Marxist German land reformers active even before Weydemeyer's arrival in the United States.)[81]

As labor confrontations mounted in 1853, the *Amerikanische Arbeiterbund* did succeed in attracting (and in other cases helped to establish) New York's most militant German protective associations, including those of the cabinetmakers, varnishers, shoemakers, tailors, cigarmakers, painters, printers, and machinists. By early summer local units of the *Bund* had been organized in eleven of New York's twenty wards plus Staten Island, Brooklyn, and Williamsburg. The *Sozialistischer Turnverein* affiliated, too, as did labor organizations in such other cities as Philadelphia, Newark, Cincinnati, Akron, Buffalo, and New Haven. Among the activists drawn to the new *Arbeiterbund* were many previously allied with Weitling.[82]

The *Amerikanische Arbeiterbund* was thus an organized coalition embracing individuals with a broad spectrum of social-political views; the handful of Marxists were overwhelmingly outnumbered by adherents of one or another variety of radical democratic "red republicanism." This diversity, unavoidable in a German-American organization seeking a mass labor base in the 1850s, complicated Weydemeyer's plans. His difficulties surfaced early at the level of doctrine. Beneath the *Arbeiterbund*'s complaint that "our position must inexorably deteriorate with each passing day so long as industry serves only capital," for example, lay the unstated assumption that capital and labor could—and might yet learn how to—share in industry's bounty. And the *Bund*'s aim "legally to halt competition among capitalists over the labor-force as well as competition among the workers themselves" echoed guild-spirit hopes current in 1848.[83]

More tangibly, Weydemeyer's cherished goal of achieving political independence for the working class—like his opposition to the division and alienation of public lands—became a dead letter in the *Arbeiterbund*. The great mass of its members evidently still hoped to influence the Democratic party. Others (and these, too, far outnumbered the Marxists) aspired to build not a multiethnic party of workers but a specifically German "party of progress" oriented toward a broad, multiclass immigrant constituency. Beneath these doctrinal and programmatic differences lay a still more telling problem—the *Arbeiterbund*'s inability even to sustain membership levels beyond a given round of wage confrontations. The organization's decline became marked by summer, advanced by fall, and alarming by year's end. All of which convinced a discouraged Weydemeyer that he had overestimated most German-American workers' appreciation of their actual social position and interests.[84]

From Protests of the Unemployed to Labor Revival

The *Amerikanische Arbeiterbund* lingered on for another year or so in this badly weakened form; the panic of 1854–55 finally laid it to rest.

That economic downturn and the more devastating and protracted crisis that broke out in 1857 wreaked havoc on the nation's labor organizations generally. Joblessness depleted their ranks while the slack labor market drained their bargaining power. Impelled by falling prices and profits and encouraged by crumbling resistance, employers slashed the pay scales of their workers. Some protective associations barely clung to life during the decade's middle years; many more simply disintegrated.

The locus of worker protest shifted from strikes to demonstrations of the unemployed, where calls for land reform (to reduce job competition in the cities) mingled with demands for food, housing, and public employment projects. Shoemaker Peter Rödel chaired one such meeting on Saturday evening, January 1, 1855. A large body of German workers crowded into Hillenbrand's in *Kleindeutschland* and ratified calls for laws "to secure . . . to such citizens as shall be otherwise landless, the right of free occupation of the public lands, in limited quantities, to actual settlers."[85]

Forty-eight hours later, in response to calls in both the English- and German-language press, some five thousand unemployed workers and sympathizers came to Hope Chapel, at Seventy-second Street and Broadway, and there endorsed resolutions asserting "the duty of the government" to "secure to us our right to labor, involving the right to the soil, the enjoyment of inalienable homes, and a representative currency based on labor." Rödel was present and visible again, reminding the crowd that "Louis Napoleon had given four millions [*sic*] and a half to build houses for the workingmen, [so] that they might be relieved from the extortions of the landlords." As noted, native- and foreign-born liberals scorned such measures as those peculiar to an unfree society. Rödel felt otherwise. "If Napoleon did this," he reasoned, it was "the duty of a republic to do still more." Apparently referring to the 1848 experience, Rödel noted that workers had won concessions in Europe then only because "we were 200,000 bayonets strong," adding, "Let us therefore remember that union is strength. I have nothing further to say than to advise you to put in practice the principles of the social republic." When J. A. Försch took the floor, he reiterated the demand for land reform and asserted, "We don't want excess but order; but if they do not listen to our wants we must restore order in this republic. Let us be united; let us show ourselves to be men; let us show our strength, and we will obtain liberty, and liberty in full."[86] Here, once again, was a variety of republicanism markedly distinct from that espoused by liberals, immigrant and native-born alike. The *New York Herald*, which usually prided itself on its sympathy for the working man, denounced such meetings, which "breathe vengeance and demand present relief, not as a favor, but as a right."[87]

Similar scenes unfolded on a still larger scale during 1857 in New York, Philadelphia, Boston, Chicago, Baltimore, Cincinnati, and elsewhere.[88] Once again speakers asserted "the *right* to live not as a mere charity, but as a right" and insisted accordingly that "governments, monarchical or republicans [*sic*] must find work for the people if individual exertions prove not sufficient." New York's city council wished that the jobless might behave "in a manner partaking less of the style of the disaffected population of European cities." In Newark two to three thousand workers gathered in November 1857 and resolved that "we do not wish alms, but the opportunity to earn our living by useful industry." Most in attendance were foreign-born, and many "came with shovels in their hands as if expecting to be set immediately to work," the *Mercury* reported. That evening forty-eighter editor and labor activist Fritz Anneke chaired a "very large" German meeting at the *Turnhalle*. The crowd disquieted native-born observers; it "enthusiastically applauded" angry speeches in which the crisis "was attributed to all conceivable means. The banks, the manufacturers, and the market-men came in for their fair share of condemnation."[89]

These unemployed workers' protests provided the initial impetus for the decade's third and last major attempt to rally and organize German-American labor. During the first week of December 1857, a new German labor federation—the *Allgemeine Arbeiter-Bund in den Vereinigten Staaten*—held its constituent assembly in New York City. But it was the economic recovery of 1858–60, hesitant though it was, that sustained the new *Bund* by encouraging employed workers' attempts to force wages back up to precrisis levels. Across the belt of German-American settlement—in New York, Brooklyn, Williamsburg, Philadelphia, Newark, Trenton, Baltimore, Cincinnati, Columbus, Cleveland, Louisville, Chicago, Milwaukee, and St. Louis—surviving trade organizations grew and new ones appeared. Strikes spread among German cabinetmakers, carvers, turners, upholsterers, tailors, capmakers, cigarmakers, coopers, printers, piano makers, shoemakers, and iron molders. At its midsummer peak the new *Arbeiterbund* boasted nine ward associations in New York City. Once again, the *Association der Social-Reformer* and the Williamsburg *Arbeiterverein* joined, too. So did immigrant labor bodies in eleven other cities.[90]

In some respects, thus, this latest German-American labor federation resembled its antecedents. The platform adopted at its January 1859 national convention contained many familiar planks advocating "equal rights for all regardless of color, religion, nationality, or sex"; simplification of the laws and legal system; land reform; a labor court system; and a democratic foreign policy. Opposed with equal firmness were nativism; "all laws that violate anyone's natural rights, like temperance, sabbath, or other prohibitionist laws"; church influence in politics and public education; and the freedom of church property from taxation. Once again, the new *Arbeiterbund* contained a variety of social-political tendencies; journalist Sebastian Seiler, a member of the newly formed Communist Club, served as the *Bund's* first organizational secretary.[91]

Compared to the situation in 1853, however, the group's political center of gravity had decisively shifted. Effective national leadership now rested with forty-eighter democrat Gustav Struve and his circle. The views that had so frustrated Joseph Weydemeyer in 1853 now bore official organizational imprimatur. As if to make this unmistakable, the *Arbeiterbund's* newspaper urged workers in 1859 to "confront oppressing capital not as workers but above all as human beings" and to unite politically in a vaguely defined German-American "Independent Party of Freedom" (*selbständigen Partei der Freiheit*).[92] It was with such intellectual-political equipment that immigrant craftworkers and their leaders confronted the political crisis that befell the United States during the 1850s.

PART III

Slavery and the People's Land

Introduction: The Challenge of Kansas-Nebraska

Measured against the principles of radical democracy, chattel slavery was an abomination, an ugly stain on the banner of the North American republic. The ownership of one human being by another clashed head-on with all the democratic ideals of 1848 and inevitably stirred bitter memories of the European aristocracy (whose culture southern planters enthusiastically attempted to mimic) and the system of unequal privilege and unfree labor upon which that class rested.[1]

To some, these aristocracies seemed to be linked not only symbolically but practically. "Opposition to the politics of slavery in America," Karl Heinzen believed, "is a battle against reaction in Europe. This republic cannot and will not be able to do anything for European freedom until it has shaken the yoke of slavery from its neck." When a society of free blacks in Cleveland expressed sympathy for and offered "material aid" to the cause of German freedom in 1851, grateful forty-eighter democrats in that city expressed their "conviction that the German people, as soon as they shall have obtained the Democratic republic in the coming struggle, [will] use all means which are adapted to abolish slavery, an institution which is so wholly repugnant to the principles of true democracy." The Louisville platform's preamble—after asserting that the forty-eighter motto of "Liberty, Welfare, and Education for All" was but a restatement of the promise of the American Revolution—inquired, "Have these solemnly proclaimed rights become truth in North American life? . . . Instead of ensuring *Liberty to all*, more than three millions [*sic*] of human beings have been condemned to slavery, and [the slaveholders] try to increase their numbers daily." Slavery was "a political and moral cancer, that will by and by undermine all republicanism." The platform's authors also objected to discrimination against free blacks in the North on the grounds that "the color of the skin cannot justify a difference of legal rights."[2]

Similar sentiments were heard in other quarters. The Cincinnati *Freimännerverein*'s *Hochwächter* demanded the repeal of the Fugitive Slave Law. The *Sozialistischer Turnerbund*'s 1855 national convention in Buffalo denounced slavery "as unworthy of a republic and directly opposed to the principles of freedom." Declarations such as these eventually led fugitive slave and abolitionist leader Frederick Douglass to proclaim that "a German has only to be a German to be utterly opposed to slavery. In feeling, as well as in conviction and principle, they are anti-slavery." Karl Büchele, on the other hand, fretted that "by treating black men with a certain familiarity and good nature," the plebeian immigrant "lowers himself even more in the estimation of the [social] circle to which he belongs." Sometimes, thus, "in answer to the question, 'Was he a white man?' one will hear, 'No, sir, he was a Dutchman.' "[3]

For some time, however, putting an end to slavery seemed to most German-Americans a matter of little personal urgency. The great majority of them settled in states in which slavery was already prohibited, and most immigrants were preoccupied with matters that appeared to affect them more immediately. As for slavery's persistence farther south, Germans could simply continue to settle in the free states; was there not plenty of room for them there?

The type of antislavery measures embraced by even ardent radical democrats reflected these assumptions and priorities. The authors of the Louisville platform did not champion immediate abolition. They called instead for prohibiting the extension of slavery to new regions, repealing the 1850 Fugitive Slave Law ("demoralizing and degrading and . . . contrary to human rights and to the Constitution"), and then proceeding to the "gradual extermination of slavery." Some German democrats threw their support to the Free Soil party, formed in 1848 to keep the West free of slavery. With the aid of German-born Chicago land reformers led by Dr. Karl Hellmuth, that party recorded some modest successes on the city's German North Side in 1848. Karl Heinzen, too, supported the Free Soil party in 1852, as did the pro-labor *Neu England Zeitung* and a handful of other small German-language newspapers. Already in 1851, the *Sozialistischer Turnerbund* endorsed "the principles underlying the radical Free-Soil Party and urges all members to support that party in every way possible."[4]

In the summer of 1851, the *Verein Social-Reformer* and the *Sozialistischer Turnverein* of New York called a public meeting in Eugen

Lievre's Shakespeare Hotel to form a local German Free Soil party. Prominent in the proceedings were leaders of journeyman protective unions (including cabinetmaker Hermann Toaspern, carpenter Charles Kaiser, and cigarmaker G. Feldner) as well as the cooperative advocate Franz Arnold, the rationalist democrat J. A. Försch, and pro-labor *Lokal* and restaurant owners Erhard Richter and Lievre himself. The party's platform endorsed a range of reform measures dear to the hearts of forty-eighter radicals. But particular stress was placed on hostility "to Slavery in whatever shape it might be seen" and a determination "to carry out land reform measures in the most radical manner." Platform planks demanded that the Fugitive Slave Law be abolished, that the Union refuse to admit any additional slave states, and universal manhood suffrage (that is, for blacks and whites alike) in New York State.[5]

Most German immigrants, however, remained loyal in these years to the regular Democratic party and, in 1852, to its presidential candidate, Franklin Pierce.[6] Northern Democrats attracted and retained this support by enthusiastically welcoming the immigrants, verbally endorsing the cause of European freedom, shunning strict sabbatarian and temperance laws, and in general presenting themselves as defenders of popular rights and welfare against "monopolistic" designs ascribed to the Whigs. The Northern Democrats' embrace of land reform—in the form of homestead bills—helped convince Hermann Kriege and a wing of the German-American land reform movement that its proper place was in the Democratic fold. Late in 1853, indeed, even some active partisans of Joseph Weydemeyer's *Amerikanische Arbeiterbund* continued to regard President Franklin Pierce as "the champion of the progressive Democracy."[7]

It took the Kansas-Nebraska Act of 1854 to transform widespread but generally passive antislavery sentiments in the North, and among German immigrants in particular, into overt, organized, and eventually partisan action. It accomplished this feat by fusing the issues of free soil and antislavery with those of land reform and free labor in the West.

This turn of events had not been easy to foresee. Hermann Kriege (like his American mentor, George Henry Evans) had earlier concluded that antislavery and land reform were conflicting priorities. Repugnant as chattel slavery was, Kriege would not support emancipation until the conditions of free labor had fundamentally improved. To act otherwise, he argued, would only worsen the already difficult position of the wage earner; the newly emancipated slaves would surely stream northward, drastically increasing job competition there. The New York *Volks-Tribun* had thus announced in 1846 "that we should declare ourselves in favor of the abolitionist movement" only "if we wished . . . to extend competition among 'free workmen' beyond all bounds, and to depress labor itself to the last extremity." The unfortunate truth, Kriege concluded, was that "under the conditions prevailing in modern society, we could not improve the lot of our 'black brothers' by abolition, but only make infinitely worse thereby the lot of our 'white brothers.' "[8]

As for the free-soil cause, the 1850 congressional compromise that brought California into the Union as a free state was widely advertised as a final and peaceful resolution of the issue of slavery's future. It led Martin Van Buren's dissident "Barnburner" faction of the New York Democratic party to return to the Democratic fold, which dealt a stunning blow to the Free Soil party. Lewis Cass, the Democratic presidential candidate in 1848 whose defeat owed much to the defection of free-soil voters, now declared with satisfaction, "I do not believe any party could now be built in relation to this question of slavery. I think the question is settled in the public mind." For his part, Illinois's Stephen Douglas expected "never to make another speech upon the slavery question in the Houses of Congress." German immigrant leaders (including both Charles Reemelin and Gustav Körner) and newspapers (notably the *New Yorker Staats-Zeitung*) endorsed the Compromise of 1850 in the same spirit. Some, it is true, such as fortyeighter journalist and Newark labor activist Fritz Anneke, remained "convinced that the old parties are on the verge of dissolution." But among most antislavery activists, hopes of attracting mass support reached a nadir in the early 1850s, especially in light of the poor showing by the Free Soil (Free Democratic) party in the 1852 elections. President Franklin Pierce assured Congress in December 1853 that "this repose is to suffer no shock during my official term, if I have the power to avert it." As Pittsburgh's leading Whig editor noted just a few months later, "If any opponent of slavery, during the last presidential campaign, had predicted that the first specific measure of General Pierce's administration would be the repeal of the Missouri Compromise, he would have been denounced as an anti-slavery fanatic of so extravagant a character as to be only fit for a lunatic asylum!"[9]

The Kansas-Nebraska Act

On January 4, 1854, Stephen Douglas introduced a bill into the Senate designed to facilitate the political organization, settlement, and economic development of the Nebraska Territory—a vast region that included all the lands obtained half a century earlier in the Louisiana Purchase but not yet politically organized. This proposed legislation was necessary, Douglas explained, so that "the Indian barrier" could be "removed" and "the tide of emigration and civilization" permitted to "roll onward until it rushes through the passes of mountains, and spreads over the plains, and mingles with the waters of the Pacific."[10]

Concerning the legal status of slavery there, the bill took a leaf from the Compromise of 1850 and left it to the legislatures of the territory's future states to decide the issue. This "popular sovereignty" formula implicitly superseded the strict geographic limits placed on the northward expansion of slavery by the 1820 Missouri Compromise. This represented a concession to southern congressmen, without whose support the Senate would never have passed a Nebraska bill at all. But the South's Senate leadership wanted more. To assure the right of slaveowners to enter the territory with their slaves—and to finally annul an agreement that had rankled for decades—southern leaders demanded an explicit revocation of the Missouri Compromise. Douglas acquiesced, and on Monday morning, January 23, he introduced a new "Kansas-Nebraska" bill, drafted in his Committee on the Territories and already privately endorsed by President Pierce, that finally satisfied all the South's requirements. The Senate passed this bill on March 3. After a long and heated debate, the House added its assent by a narrow margin on May 22. President Pierce signed the bill into law a week later on May 30, 1854.[11]

The reaction to Douglas's bill was swift. On January 24 the District of Columbia's abolitionist periodical, the *National Era*, carried an impassioned "Appeal of the Independent Democrats in Congress to the People of the United States." Its authors were Salmon Chase, Joshua Giddings, and Edward Wade of Ohio; Charles Sumner and Alexander DeWitt of Massachusetts; and Gerritt Smith of New York.[12] Douglas's bill, the appeal declared, was no less than "a gross violation of a sacred pledge," a "criminal betrayal of precious rights." Previously the West had been considered a haven for "freedom loving emigrants from Europe and energetic and intelligent laborers from our own land." The Kansas-Nebraska bill, however, would turn this huge territory "into a dreary region of despotism, inhabited by masters and slaves." That alone would "exclude . . . immigrants from the old world and free laborers from our own states," since "freemen, unless pressed by a hard and cruel necessity, will not, and should not work beside slaves. Labor cannot be respected where any class of laborers is held in abject bondage." Specifically, the appeal called for unleashing a torrent of "protest, earnestly and emphatically, by correspondence, through the press, by memorials, by resolutions of public meetings and legislative bodies." Finally, the authors "earnestly" requested "the enlightened conductors of newspapers printed in the German and other foreign languages to direct the attention of their readers to this important matter." This appeal was widely reprinted and even more widely paraphrased, and the response deeply gratified the authors. By mid-March, opponents of the bill had already convened between two and three hundred large protest meetings. Only a handful could be organized in its support, and some of these (in Boston, New York, and Chicago) were taken over by anti-Nebraska forces. By September, major anti-Nebraska rallies—most of which boasted hundreds and often enough thousands in attendance—had occurred in Massachusetts, Connecticut, Maine, Vermont, Rhode Island, New Hampshire, New York, New Jersey, Pennsylvania, Ohio, Illinois, Indiana, Iowa, Michigan, and Wisconsin.[13]

Among German-Americans, hostility to the Kansas-Nebraska bill proved even more broad-based and vociferous than the authors of the appeal had dared hope. German immigrants flocked to meetings of their own in New York, Newark, Philadelphia, Pittsburgh, Cleveland, Cincinnati, Canton, Indianapolis, Chicago, and elsewhere.[14] Forty-eighter editors in Pittsburgh called a public meeting for February 9 that declared, "We are enemies of slavery, and consider all extension of it a treason to mankind; adverse to the humanity of the age; adverse to the doctrines of the Declaration of Independence, which taught to all the world that the American people were enlightened and progressive on the subject of human rights." The organizers of this meeting characteristically grounded their antislavery sentiments in their particular transatlantic experience. They had "left their Fatherland for the love of freedom, to find it here, and to aid in fortifying the temple of liberty." Slavery had always seemed to them a grievous flaw in that edifice. But in the past, at least, "we have been of the opinion that our most prominent statesmen, of the largest and most liberal principles, have borne with the hateful 'peculiar institution' for the sake of the peace of the country, and from a regard to the unfortunate condition of the slaveholders, trusting that the ideas and principles of the patriots of the Revolution, in relation to human rights and the abolition of slavery, would lay the foundation for gradual emancipation." "The late proceedings of the Senate," however, had now "deeply shaken this opinion."[15] Far from encouraging gradual emancipation, the Douglas bill held out before German-American opponents of slavery the prospect that the coveted soil of the West would be preempted by a homegrown aristocracy that cordially despised free labor. Immigrant farmers and workers who tried to live there would see their living standards and social status driven down to levels prevailing in the Old World.

On March 2, two months after Douglas first reported his bill out of committee,a majority of his allies in the Senate took a step that further inflamed anti-Nebraska sentiments in German America. Repelled by the social and political radicalism (and antislavery sentiments) with which so many of the recent immigrants seemed tainted, Delaware's Whig senator John M. Clayton offered an amendment to the Nebraska bill that would deny to resident aliens the right to vote or to hold public office anywhere in the new territories. They would thus be barred from participating in the "popular sovereignty" process provided for in the Nebraska bill. This was a serious and by no means routine restriction in the context of the times. It took five years to shed one's alien status, and in much of the Midwest immigrants wishing to participate in territorial political life had faced far less stringent requirements than those Clayton was now trying to impose.[16]

Delaware's Democratic senator, James A. Bayard, presented the thinking behind his Whig colleague's proposal: "Sir, when a foreigner comes here, I am ready to receive him, if he comes to be Americanized. If he comes here to un-Americanize us (if I may use such an expression), and to introduce his theoretic notions of government, his wild and impractible ideas of a liberty inconsistent alike with social order and organized government among men, then I wish such foreigners would remain in their own country." Unfortunately, however, such people were entering the United States in record numbers and were now attempting to propagate their noxious views. "It is the display of this feeling, which we have seen some increase of late," Bayard concluded frankly, "that teaches me the necessity of more strongly holding to the rule that none but citizens of the United States should be authorized to impress the first laws upon the Territories of the United States." Parallel sentiments were voiced by Senator Richard Brodhead of Pennsylvania. "I confess I have witnessed some recent demonstrations that do not please me," he told his colleagues. For example, he recalled, "the movements of Kossuth in this country did him no credit." And now, in the political crisis surrounding the Kansas-Nebraska bill, Brodhead detected "a quailing before the spirit of Abolitionism and a foreign influence."[17]

The Senate approved Clayton's amendment in a vote that starkly correlated nativist and pro-slavery politics. Of those who supported Clayton's measure, all but one (Brodhead) came from slave states; all who opposed it hailed from free states. Only the action of the House of Representatives—where the bill's embarrassed and alarmed Democratic supporters refused to accept the inflammatory Clayton rider—killed that measure. But not before anti-Nebraska speakers and writers throughout the North and West publicized the Senate's action to demonstrate further that slavery and the rights and welfare of immigrants were fundamentally incompatible.[18]

Anti-Nebraska newspaper editors naturally greeted the eruption of German-American hostility to the Douglas bill joyously. "One of the most gratifying signs of the times is the noble stand taken by our German fellow citizens on this question," cheered a Pittsburgh editor. "The Democratic German population is fully aroused to the iniquity of the Nebraska outrage and cannot be wheedled or coaxed into its support." Chicago's antislavery weekly, *The Free West,* held that "no class of citizens have manifested more indignation . . . than our immigrant and native Germans." "We understand," reported the *Daily Cincinnati Gazette,* "that our German population are almost to a man opposed to the bill," an observation that the *New York Evening Post* seconded, even deleting the *Gazette*'s qualifying "almost." A Buffalo editor found it "gratifying to perceive that our German fellow citizens . . . are true to their principles of freedom when acting in regard to the pending Nebraska scheme," while the *Newark Daily Mercury* applauded "the unanimity with which the German mind grasps this great and exciting question." Horace Greeley's *New York Daily Tribune* summarized, "The Germans are moving all over the North and West. They feel even more deeply than the native citizens." The American and Foreign Antislavery Society, meanwhile, meeting in New York in May, "rejoice[d] in the great unanimity manifested by the German presses, and our German fellow-citizens throughout the country, in opposition to the Nebraska scheme." Decades later, George Schneider (who was editor of the *Illinois Staats-Zeitung* during the Kansas-Nebraska conflict) still recalled with evident ethnic pride how in New York, Philadelphia, Chicago, Cincinnati, and St. Louis, "all the principal [German] papers in those cities opposed at once the extension of slavery in the new territories, and, in fact, slavery itself." William Vocke (an officer of the *Chicagoer Arbeiterverein* during the late 1850s) similarly remembered that "German-American citizens, acting independently everywhere, planted themselves firmly on the side of freedom."[19]

While capturing something of the ardor of the anti-Nebraska feeling that existed among the Germans, accounts like these ascribed a unanimity of sentiment to the immigrant population that did not in fact exist. The most obvious division ran along sectional lines. Among the small minority of Germans who resided in the Deep South, few challenged the peculiar institution. The antislavery resolutions ratified by the national Turner convention in 1855 precipitated a split by chapters based in Charleston, Mobile, Augusta, Savannah, Houston, and eventually New Orleans (although others in the Upper South cities of St. Louis, Wheeling, Baltimore, Louisville, Covington, and Newport remained).[20] But even in the mid-Atlantic and midwestern states, the Douglas bill divided German America into three broad political currents, each of which drew support from a particular constellation of social groups.

Many leaders of the the small but influential German mercantile elite and their allied newspapers joined with politically conservative immigrant clerics and immigrant Democratic officeholders to defend the Nebraska Act and denounce free-soil forces, English- and German-speaking alike, as instruments of nativists and sabbatarians. The most active, prominent, and powerful single German-born Democrat in this period was financier August Belmont of New York City, representative of the Rothschild interests and a major businessman in his own right. An enthusiastic booster of southern Democratic plans to annex Cuba, Belmont saw his filibustering dreams dissolve in 1854 when opposition to the Kansas-Nebraska bill produced major Democratic losses during the congressional elections.[21]

The *New Yorker Staats-Zeitung* set the tone for German America's "pro-Nebraska" tendency and found echoes in papers like Davenport, Iowa's *Demokrat,* Peoria's *Illinois Banner,* the Columbus, Ohio, *Westbote,* and the Cincinnati *Demokratisches Tageblatt.* It defended the position taken by most mainstream northern Democrats. Asserting its own distaste for slavery, the paper had nonetheless opposed both the 1846 Wilmot Proviso (an attempt to exclude slavery from all lands acquired during the Mexican War) and the Free Soil party. Federal restrictions on the spread of slavery it held unconstitutional, undemocratic, and unnecessary. Climate and soil in the West would by themselves discourage the settlement there of slaveowners and their chattel while attracting migrants from the Northeast and Europe. The latter could then vote to ban slavery outright when the territories became states. In the interim, German immigrants could manage perfectly well in the presence of slave-based agriculture. "The states of Maryland and Louisiana are the first destinations of many of our brethren," the *Staats-Zeitung* averred in 1848. "Thousands of them are gone to slave countries and do well and do not complain." As for the slaves themselves, the editors coolly observed, they were but another form of private property; they could not be taken from their owners without violating the fundamental law of the land. In any case, the editors were disposed to waste little sympathy upon people who were little more than "apes" when compared to "the white race" and whose inferiority made all talk about interracial equality "unnatural." The *Staats-Zeitung*'s attempt to stir up racial hostilities during the 1850 tailors' strike was thus consistent with its overall record.[22]

Different groups opposed the Nebraska bill for different reasons and in different ways. The most militant and aggressive opponents commonly arose from within the plebeian radical democratic milieu and the intellectuals associated with it. Anchoring their opposition to slavery's expansion in an assertive hostility to slavery as such, their meetings usually scorned attempts to conciliate the slaveowners and declared their sympathies for the slaves. Not infrequently, their attacks on the Nebraska bill were linked to calls to repeal the Fugitive Slave Law and strike down legal discrimination against northern free blacks. They were also among the first to demand a break with pro-Nebraska politicians and to call for a new political party.

Flanked by Douglas's partisans on one side and antislavery radical democrats on the other, a third, middle-of-the-road current emerged from the ranks of German-American liberalism. Stronger in the Midwest than in the East and usually led by older, established community leaders who had immigrated in the 1830s and earlier, this current did oppose the Nebraska bill, but did so primarily to restore the sectional peace of the status quo ante. They had hoped that the entire subject of slavery had been safely disposed of by earlier compromises, and they feared that the new bill, by reopening that issue, could detonate a bigger political explosion than the nation had yet seen. These "moderates" strove to limit the focus of the protest to the bill itself, usually expressed their objections to it in conciliatory language, and earnestly sought to convince southern planters that the bill endangered their own interests. Initially they resisted calls to abandon the Democratic party in favor of a new one. As partisan politics polarized further, however, this current divided. Some returned to the Democratic fold, while others joined the Republicans.

In the interest of political expediency, liberal and radical democratic opponents of the Nebraska bill commonly collaborated in 1854, jointly sponsoring, organizing, and addressing many of the mass meetings that unified opposition to the Douglas measure. In many cases, such alliances continued on into the period of the Republican party's formation. That the partners in this alliance subscribed to different views and represented different constituencies, however, remained evident, both in 1854 and afterward.

6

The Response in the East

In threatening to preempt western soil for slavery, the Kansas-Nebraska Act seemed to many a direct attack upon hopes of escaping permanent wage dependency in the crowded cities of the East. Reflecting such hopes, half a dozen members of the House and Senate had declared their intentions in December 1853 to bring homestead bills onto the floor.[1]

On January 3, just one day before Stephen Douglas brought his bill into the Senate, the New York State convention of the cooperativist Mechanics' Mutual Protectives appointed a committee to report on the subject of land reform. Committee members included J. A. Handschuh, veteran of the New York Tailors' *Protektivunion,* and John Commerford, former Working Men's party leader and longtime land reform advocate. The report they produced urged passage of a homestead law. The massive immigration then underway, the cooperativists specified, made it all the more imperative to ease the eastern workers' access to western lands:

> As it is admitted that over half a million is about the annual average who come to the United States, we must perceive that at least three-fourths of this number reach their destination without any adequate means of subsistence, or distinct arrangements as to their immediate employment. This being the case, we must readily conjecture that such places as the Atlantic cities will be always liable to an over supply in the labor market . . . [which allows] the capitalist . . . full scope in affixing the prices for which the operative shall labor . . . [resulting in] a depreciation of the rate of wages.

The same oversupply of workers, moreover, had led to "an exorbitant increase in rents, with corresponding advance upon the articles of subsistence." This state of affairs was abetted "by the contrivance or stupidity of our Government," which allowed "the choicest and largest amount" of the public lands to be "seized upon as largesse by partisan capitalists, and held by them until such time as the need of the pioneer or settler obliged him to pay whatever the rapacity of these men shall demand." Was it "not enough that the laborers of Europe are obliged to leave the homes and graves of their ancestors and flee from the dreadful consequences of the poverty which has overtaken them, from the effects of being deprived of the land by the monopolizerers of it?" Must they then reach the New World only to find some there seeking "to reestablish a system which is now depopulating the countries wherein it has been practiced"?[2] Here was precisely the kind of sentiment that the so-called Independent Democrats sought to tap by linking the issues of free soil and free land.

New York City: "To Start the Cry, 'Revolution!'"

In New York City, German America had by far its biggest and most economically and politically heterogeneous center. The various political currents in German America tended to find their clearest and most forceful expressions here. This was true partly because of the cosmopolitan character of the nation's premier port city; new human and intellectual arrivals kept the mixture churning. Partly, too, it reflected the fact that great extremes of wealth and poverty, luxury and misery, coexisted among the city's German population. Some of the poorest immigrants tended to collect here, unable to pay their way further west. But the same commercial tides that cast these people up onto New York's shores and left them stranded there also buoyed the wealthiest and most powerful representatives of the German-American elite. During the first half of the nineteenth century, these included the fur king and investor John Jacob Astor; the financiers August Belmont, Eugene S. Ballin, and the Seligman brothers; the shippers and import-export merchants Caspar Meier, Gustav Schwab, Frederick Gebhard, Leopold Bierwirth, and Charles Hallgarten; and sugar refiner William F. Havemeyer, rubber manufacturer Carl Poppenhausen, pencil manufacturer Eberhard Faber, piano manufacturer Henry Steinway and his sons, builder Marc Gidlitz, and prosperous boss cabinetmaker Henry Weil.[3]

The economic elite exercised great political power in New York City's German community because of its sheer wealth and its ties to the New York German Society, the Democratic party apparatus, and the widely read *New Yorker Staats-Zeitung*. Owned and edited by liberal emigrants of the 1830s and 1840s, the *Staats-Zeitung* over the years kept a vigilant watch over excesses of word and deed on the part of its more radical-minded *Landsleute*.[4]

The *Staats-Zeitung*'s influence, however, did not go unchallenged. In 1846 the *New Yorker Demokrat* began publication. Over the next fifteen years its editors included a range of prominent forty-eighter firebrands—August Becker (whose journalistic efforts won him the sobriquet *"der rote Becker"* as he worked on the *Demokrat,* the Baltimore *Wecker,* and the Cincinnati *Hochwächter*), Adolph Douai (imprisoned in Germany for revolutionary activities and a longtime sympathizer of Karl Heinzen's before Douai moved toward Marxian socialism in the 1860s), and Gustav Struve. Wilhelm Weitling published his *Republik der Arbeiter* throughout the first half of the 1850s. From 1851 to 1853 the *Sozialistischer Turnerbund* published the *Turn-Zeitung* in New York before transfering it successively to Philadelphia, Cincinnati, and Baltimore. The *Criminal Zeitung und Belletristisches Journal* appeared in 1852. Edited by cousins Rudolf and Friedrich Lexow (both forty-eighters, Friedrich having spent eight years in a German prison), the journal soon became the *Staats-Zeitung*'s chief competitor. In 1853–54, Joseph Weydemeyer and forty-eighter democrat Dr. Gottlieb Kellner jointly published *Die Reform,* which initially served as the organ of the *Amerikanische Arbeiterbund.* The *Abendzeitung,* organized on a cooperative basis by a group of journeymen typesetters, was for a time edited by forty-eighter Friedrich Kapp.[5]

From the first, the Kansas-Nebraska dispute aggravated the political warfare already endemic to New York's *Kleindeutschland*. To launch their public campaign in support of the Kansas-Nebraska bill, pro-Douglas Germans led by *Staats-Zeitung* editor and Customs House officer Gustav Neumann and the Democratic party's United German Democratic Central Committee called a public meeting for February 23, 1854. The published call strove to identify Douglas's "popular sovereignty" formula with German democratic ideals while linking anti-Nebraska forces with the disunionism and evangelical fanaticism ascribed to native-born abolitionists. "Vindication of the Constitutional Rights of All Citizens!," it urged, "Maintenance of the Union!—Democracy vs. Abolitionism!—Self-government vs. Guardianship! No Maine Law!" The *New York Daily Tribune* wondered "whether the Germans of this City will allow themselves to be swindled by these poor tools of Slavery in the way contemplated."[6]

The answer came that night, and it revealed the depth and intensity of feeling that animated both sides of the Nebraska dispute in *Kleindeutschland*.[7] Between one and two thousand German-Americans arrived at Washington Hall, a meeting place for German Democrats located near the corner of Grand and Elizabeth streets. The Douglas Democrats controlled the podium. To retain that control, alleged the *New Yorker Demokrat,* they had enlisted a body of paid strong-arm men. The *Demokrat* subsequently reported that "the *Staats-Zeitung* clique, in the consciousness of their moral weakness, took refuge, as we prognosticated, in brute force. Feeling convinced that the lackeys of the administration would be in a minority at the meeting, they have been enrolling loafers for the last two days. No money was spared for this purpose. In no state or charter election have such large sums been laid out by a clique as on this occasion." The *Demokrat* was apparently correct about at least one point. Most of those gathering that evening at Washington Hall opposed the purpose of the meeting's sponsors.

Shortly after 7:30 P.M., Mr. Jakob Windmüller, president of the city's German Democratic Central Committee and a leader of the German Society, convened the meeting and called for the election of a presiding officer. Several voices promptly sang out, nominating Windmüller himself. Anti-Nebraska Germans nominated a Turner leader and *New Yorker Demokrat* editor named Joseph Hartmann.

When mounting noise and confusion frustrated an attempt to determine the majority's will by voice vote, someone proposed to divide the house physically; soon, the two camps faced each other from opposite ends of the hall. The anti-Nebraska forces insisted that their number was clearly larger, but the pro-Nebraska group rejected that claim with equal vehemence, demanding that the opinions only of naturalized citizens be considered. It remained a stalemate.

Both Hartmann and Windmüller now mounted a table in order to address the assembly, but the tumult was too great for either voice to be heard. When the roar momentarily subsided, Hartmann declined his nomination in favor of Erhard Richter, the well-known radical *Lokal* owner. Loud shouts of approval greeted Richter's nomination, but the pro-Douglas faction was hardly mollified by this substitution. Pandemonium erupted anew, and for the next two hours the two parties fought for control of the hall. At times, three or four speakers tried simultaneously to address the crowd, standing atop tables and chairs in an effort to be heard. As tempers rose, fistfights broke out around the floor. At one point, J. A. Försch managed to begin an anti-Nebraska speech, but the regular Democrats cut him off with howls and catcalls as soon as they caught the thrust of his remarks. Attempting to quell the fighting, the band struck up "Hail Columbia." For a moment, the tactic succeeded. Both sides were anxious to present themselves as authentic defenders of the national tradition and interest. The entire assemblage therefore joined in the singing. When the music stopped, however, the struggle resumed.

On one side of the room, a body of anti-Nebraska Germans now gathered around a table atop which stood its leaders, headed by Richter. Suddenly, a body of pro-Nebraska Germans rushed this table, overturned it, toppled Richter and company to the floor, and broke the table itself into splinters. With this, the level of violence increased sharply. "Men were tossed over heads, trampled under foot, and pulled and pummeled in every quarter," reported the pro-Douglas *Herald*. "In the midst of the battle a broom handle was elevated upon which was a placard, reading in German, 'No Slaves.' The fight then became terrific; some seized pieces of a broken table, knocked men over the head and brought blood from several."

At about 9:00 P.M., Richter, Försch, Hartmann, and their supporters—deprived of their tabletop platform—seized control of the hall's elevated music gallery and from there tried again to impose order on the meeting. By now the evident anti-Nebraska majority in the hall was making its weight felt, and only a hard core of pro-administration Democrats refused to acknowledge their defeat. As the insurgent majority began reading aloud resolutions opposed to the Douglas bill, diehards began once more to hoot, jeer, whistle, stamp their feet, and pound the floor, walls, and tables with clubs and canes. Firm measures were evidently required if the meeting was to proceed; members of the *Sozialistischer Turnverein* were on hand to apply them.

As the *Tribune* reported: "A few notes from a small horn near us penetrated the entire hall. There was a call to such members of the *Turnverein* as chanced to be present. Some 15 or 20 collected in an open space, and the leader gave them instructions. Again the horn sounded, and their numbers increased to some forty, who quietly turned and marched to the rear of the company which at this time was making the disturbance. These fellows were now commanded, besought, entreated to desist and come to order." When earnest pleas accomplished nothing, the Turners resorted to more direct forms of persuasion. One of their leaders shouted, "Out with the slaveholders!" Then "the Turners in an instant rushed upon the rowdies, and in spite of their clubs and their extemporaneous weapons, obtained by breaking the stools and benches to pieces, in three minutes the hall was cleared of them."

The ejected hecklers were followed by the rest of the pro-Douglas forces. When the meeting then reconvened, two-thirds of the original assembly remained in attendance. This body adopted by acclamation a resolution denouncing the Nebraska bill, after which it addressed the subject of Douglas's German allies, singling out the *New Yorker Staats-Zeitung* for special attention. One man rose from his seat to berate that paper's editors for "kissing the feet of the slaveholders" and introduced a resolution pledging "that those present will never take that sheet into their hands." The crowd expressed its approval with loud shouts and laughter and passed this resolution, too. The meeting then quietly adjourned.

The *Demokrat* reported proudly that "the clique who imagined that they could rule the German citizens of New York has been defeated, and have received the wholesome lesson, that the Germans are not afraid of the fists of hired ruffians." That paper and its allies now initiated a citywide German anti-Nebraska meeting to be held a week later at the same location. The published call urged "the friends of liberty, opposed to the hunker clique of the *Staats-Zeitung*," to "attend in mass, as free and independent men, to maintain the liberty of speech against brutality and paid rowdies." Germans must "come in mass, and show that you are not slaves, but men who stand on the side of right and humanity." A postscript "earnestly requested that there will be no disturbances."[8]

Before this gathering could take place, however, the leaders of the *Amerikanische Arbeiterbund* called a meeting of their own to stake out the *Bund*'s position on the Nebraska issue. On the last day of February, thus, residents of *Kleindeutschland* awoke to find their streets posted with copies of the *Arbeiterbund*'s call. Despite the short notice, five hundred people met the following evening at Erhard Richter's Forsyth Street tavern in the German section of the Tenth Ward. Speakers included such leaders and friends of the *Arbeiterbund* as Joseph Weydemeyer, Augustus Thum, Wilhelm Meyerhofer, Gottlieb Kellner, J. A. Försch, and Erhard Richter himself.

The meeting took as its theme the interests of free working people in the disposition of western lands. As Försch subsequently recalled, his own remarks that evening emphasized "how the land monopoly in the West tends likewise to the enslaving of the white laborer in the East" and thus "tend[ed] to destroy the liberty of the poor emigrant laborer." Resolutions approved pointedly blamed both slaveowners and northern businessmen for the Nebraska bill's assault on the rights of labor. "This bill authorizes the further extension of slavery," the resolution said, "but we have, do now, and shall continue to protest most emphatically against both white and black slavery." The forces of "capitalism and land speculation" were responsible for a bill that "withdraws from or makes unavailable in a future homestead bill vast tracts of land." "Lawmakers, wire-pullers, and the hireling masses" were now endeavoring to mobilize support for that proposed legislation. The *Arbeiterbund* resolved to "solemnly protest against this bill," to "brand as a traitor against the people and their welfare everyone who shall lend it his support," to attempt to organize "a general organization of working men" to oppose the Nebraska bill, and to participate as a body in the broad German anti-Nebraska meeting already scheduled for that Friday, March 3, at Washington Hall.[9]

The March 3 meeting attracted an audience whose size and animation were impossible to deny. The *New York Daily Times* carried the most conservative crowd estimate of two thousand, most of whom seemed to be "working men." Both the anti-Nebraska *New York Evening Post* and the pro-Nebraska *New York Herald* counted three thousand in attendance. The *Staats-Zeitung* tersely acknowledged that the gathering was "unusually numerous" (*ausserordentlich zahlreiche*). "The capacious ballroom of the Hall was literally jammed" by 8 P.M., according to the hostile *Herald*. "Ten minutes after the doors were thrown open not a foot of space was to be had; the stairs and passages were crowded to suffocation, and a considerable space on either side of the entrance was filled." The rooms located on the floor below the ballroom were also packed.[10]

Throughout the meeting itself, memories of 1848 and the kinship between the European democratic revolutions and the antislavery struggle were invoked. From the speakers' stand the Stars and Stripes hung alongside the black-red-gold banner and the red flag, the nineteenth-century symbol of European democracy; the first order of business was the singing of the *Marseillaise*. According to a reporter, "The whole throng joined with a chorus, repeated cheers, and a tremendous stamping of feet beating time to the music." Transparencies ceremoniously carried into the hall and placed on both sides of the balcony demanded, "No slavery" as well as "No Maine Liquor Law." A third depicted the relationship among Windmüller, *Staats-Zeitung* publisher Anna Uhl, and Stephen Douglas as a corrupt and indecent one.

Several delegations then marched into the ballroom in parade formation accompanied by their own marching bands. Prominent among them were the *Arbeiterbund* and the *Turnverein*, which (noted even the *Herald*) "were received with a tremendous outburst of enthusiasm; hats were thrown in the air, segars were tossed frantically after them, and such shouts arose from every red republican present that the crowd below caught the inspiring sound in all its volume and responded with great goodwill."

Presently the crowd began calling on the convenors to speak. Voices demanding "Richter! Richter!" brought that man to the fore. Expressing his satisfaction at the size of the meeting, Richter ridiculed attempts by Douglas and associates to depict all German-Americans as supporters of the Kansas-Nebraska bill. On the contrary, he asserted, this meeting showed that Germans would ever be ready to ward off any such "traitorous blow" aimed at the nation's freedom. He concluded these brief introductory remarks to the accompaniment of loud cheers and a roll of drums. The body then elected him president of the meeting.

Now the assemblage moved to pay for the damages the hall had suffered during the turbulent meeting of February 23, agreeing to collect thirty-six dollars, as proposed by Wilhelm Schlüter, chief editor of the *Demokrat*. Next Hartmann presented the main resolution, which denounced the Nebraska bill "as a glaring violation of the rights of the free North and as a direct attack on the principles of liberty and humanity, and also on the Declaration of Independence of the United States." The resolution followed those endorsed by the *Arbeiterbund* in stressing the bill's implications for immigrant German plebeians: "We hold this Nebraska bill to be in direct opposition to the principles of land reform and of the Free Homestead Bill, since it opens up an immense territory now belonging to a non-slaveholding people to land monopoly and Slavery, and renders it inaccessible to free labourers and free possession."

The resolution went on to threaten electoral opposition to any politician who supported the bill: "We oppose by all rightful means allowed by the institutions of the United States the execution of the principles contained in the Nebraska bill, and we will not give our votes in a national election or a Congressional election to any man who is in favor of this bill or to its maintenance; and we declare a traitor to the people's cause every advocate of this bill or its principles." The last phrase came almost verbatim from the *Arbeiterbund* meeting two days earlier.

Finally, the resolution linked Pierce's neglect of his electoral promise to support the rights of foreign-born Americans traveling abroad with his decision to "make common cause with the defenders of the unhallowed extension of Slavery, and those who would steal away the rights of the free North."

Applause and cheers greeted the reading of the resolution. There followed a series of of speeches presenting views that ranged across the anti-Nebraska spectrum. But the crowd reacted most positively to those expressing the strongest, most uncompromising sentiments, suggesting a spirit of antislavery fervor even greater than that contained in the formal resolution.

George Dietz, an anti-Nebraska member of the *Staats-Zeitung* staff, followed Försch to the rostrum. Forbidden to express his opposition to the Douglas bill in the pages of the *New Yorker Staats-Zeitung,* Dietz had attempted to do so at the earlier meeting at Washington Hall. But there, he noted, the Nebraska bill's supporters had made it impossible for him to gain the floor. Nevertheless, as Dietz was at pains to explain, he was no antislavery zealot. Like others at the *Staats-Zeitung,* he had opposed the Wilmot Proviso in 1846; in 1850 he had acquiesced, though unhappily, in the Compromise of 1850 in hopes that it would finally put the whole issue of slavery to rest. Dietz, for one, had no desire to revive it. Responsibility for "the storm that now shakes the very foundation of this Union" lay not with the Nebraska bill's critics, he held, but with its sponsors.

Another German liberal, a Mr. Rosenstein, followed Dietz. He was "no greenhorn, not at all"; he had lived in the United States for seventeen years. And having supported the Democratic party for "so long a time," it was "rather a hard thing for me to speak here tonight." The audience cheered when he equated German nativity with the love of freedom. "There never was a German," he swore, "who dared call himself by that name, who wished to enslave a fellow man. He, who himself would be free, must acknowledge the freedom of others." This sweeping rhetorical formula did not, however, signify a determination to uproot chattel slavery where it already existed. "None of us," Rosenstein felt sure, "want to take away their slaves from the South." To the speaker's evident chagrin, however, these words evoked not cheers but challenges. "Oh, yes! Oh, yes!" members of the crowd retorted: they did indeed want to carry freedom southward. Taken aback, Rosenstein snapped, "Well, if you do, I don't. I am not an abolitionist." The speaker summarized his own stand as follows: "You, gentlemen of the South . . . keep your slavery, but keep it to yourselves."

Gottlieb Kellner of *Die Reform* got a better reception by focusing on the particular stake of "the laboring classes" in the struggle against slavery's westward expansion and by asserting that slavery was inherently volatile: "As long as there are slaves, so long will there be men aspiring to freedom." Gilder and *Arbeiterbund* president August Vecchioni read aloud the resolutions ratified by his organization. Attorney and Turner leader Sigismund Kaufmann dwelt on the Clayton amendment and predicted a massive German reaction against the Nebraska bill's politician supporters.

But the clear popular favorite that evening was unquestionably J. A. Försch, who was called to the podium by hundreds of voices and greeted by a prolonged ovation. When finally able to make himself heard, he declared the thousands gathered at Washington Hall that evening representative of the views of German immigrants throughout the United States, "wherever their sturdy arms were laboring for its wealth and prosperity in the work-shop and the fields." They were responding to the needs of "Freedom—the impulse of a bold and hardy race against all slavery, whether white or black." Loud applause interrupted him, after which Försch challenged Douglas's claim that his "popular sovereignty" formula would give the people of the Nebraska Territory the right democratically to determine their own social order. Just who, he asked, would be allowed to exercise that right? "Do you think the black men will be asked if they consent to such an arrangement? Not at all." The slaveowners would make the decision for blacks just as nativist politicians sought to restrict the rights of immigrants. "They say the Dutchman is stupid," Försch said, and "so is the negro; but *we* are smart. A hundred stupid men [equal] just one smart slaveholder. That is their calculation." Once Douglas had sought the votes of supporters of land reform by offering a watered-down version in a homestead bill. Since then, however, "Mr. Douglas has been at St. Petersburg, he has been at Rome to kiss the slippers of the Pope, and the Empress of Russia has stroked his cheeks. Then he forgot all about land reform, but he produced another Christmas gift, and that was the Nebraska bill."

Like Douglas himself, Försch continued, those German-Americans who endorsed the Nebraska bill had betrayed their people and principles for base and avaricious reasons. Prior to the meeting called a week earlier to endorse Douglas and his bill, Försch recalled

> there came to me a certain Nesseler, who was once a *gendarme* in Germany. He requested me to appear at the meeting and speak in favor of the Nebraska bill. Of course, I was obliged to refuse. Thereupon he imagined that it was with me as it was with him, and that the clink of dollars would, perhaps, soften my heart, so he laid 25 dollars on the table. I said, very quietly, "Now I am still less inclined to do it." [Renewed applause interrupted his story.] When he perceived that he could do nothing with me, he said, "Försch! have you not yet become knowing? The Nebraska bill is a humbug, and everything in the United States is a humbug. Come, then, make money!" I looked at my wife and said, quietly: "Charlotte, turn the humbug out of doors."

The time had passed, Försch asserted, for further legislative compromise with slavery. A week earlier, the Turners had given the pro-Douglas Germans the "sore heads" they deserved. Resolute measures of that kind were now the only ones worth taking. "In this country as well as in the Old World," he exclaimed, "we have to start the cry, 'Revolution!'" The word evoked the same enthusiasm that it had during the tailors' strike four years earlier: the crowd cheered lustily. Försch concluded, "We know that nothing can be effected now by forebearance, therefore let us send men to Congress who will revolutionize—who will dare to tell the slave breeders to their faces who they are. Let us stand together firmly and faithfully, and the loafers at Washington will get their 'sore heads.'"

The crowd voted unanimously to adopt the proposed resolution, after which it flowed out the doors and formed up as a mass demonstration. With banners flying, three bands playing, and torches illuminating the transparencies that had been displayed at the meeting, marchers proceeded down the Bowery to Chatham Square and then into the park near Tammany and City Hall to show the Democratic leadership the strength of German anti-Nebraska feeling. By the time they reached City Hall, their numbers exceeded five thousand.

As was its general practice, the *Staats-Zeitung* dismissed the actions of the anti-Nebraska Germans as the work of freshly landed and therefore politically unseasoned "greenhorns." The greenhorns responded on Monday, March 6, with a charivari, that old ritual traditionally used to focus popular ridicule upon violators of community standards. The marchers' updated version included invocations of 1848 and expressed pride in having but recently arrived in the United States and loyalty to a rather modern set of values. Four to five thousand anti-Nebraska Germans stepped off from the beer hall owned by Gustav Lindenmüller (a well-known forty-eighter refugee who had helped eject pro-Douglas Germans from Washington Hall on February 23) and headed for the *Staats-Zeitung*'s offices on Frankfort Street. Many of the greenhorn demonstrators defiantly sported sprigs of evergreen on their hats, and their banners, demanding "No Slavery" and "No Nebraska," waved from evergreen boughs. Reaching the *Staats-Zeitung* headquarters, the paraders serenaded the editors with "cat music" and cast down their "greenness" at the front door. Then passing the offices of the anti-Nebraska press (the *Tribune,* the *Abendzeitung,* and the *Demokrat*), they raised a friendly cheer.[11]

Newark: "We Are Generally Enemies of Slavery"

Physical proximity and economic links to New York City—coupled with comparatively low rent and cost of living—helped make Newark, New Jersey, one of the country's principal manufacturing cities in the 1850s and an attractive beacon for growing numbers of immigrants. While in 1835 Germans were still numerically negligible in Newark, by 1850 nearly 4,000 German-born residents constituted about 10 percent of the city's total population. By 1860 the Germans numbered

10,600—some 15 percent of the city's quickly growing population. The German community developed its own churches, periodicals, voluntary associations, and political leaders. As elsewhere, Germans made up a disproportionate part of Newark's craftworker population—about a fourth—and in certain crafts, such as shoemaking, blacksmithing, saddle making, and trunk making, the Germans accounted for between 30 and 40 percent of the work force.[12]

Newark's local histories boast of the contribution the Germans made to the city and wax equally proud that the city offered a haven to those fleeing the oppression and privation of Germany. The city's identification with the European revolution was highlighted in 1852 when the Hungarian nationalist leader Lajos Kossuth visited Newark during his tour of the United States. The city's recent German immigrants gave him a particularly fervent salute. On Kossuth's first day in the city, April 21, he was officially welcomed and feted by the city fathers. Attorney Emil Schöffner brought special greetings in the name of the German community. Schöffner had been a jurist and republican journalist in Saxony. Chosen in 1848 as alternate district delegate to the *Reichversammlung* at Frankfurt, Schöffner subsequently joined the Dresden insurrection and was forced to flee Germany in the summer of 1850. The next night saw Newark's Library Hall tightly packed with an audience of Germans expectantly awaiting an address from Kossuth in their native tongue. Though Kossuth arrived late, the excited crowd—which had formed early—showed no signs of diminished enthusiasm. Rev. Frederick August Lehlbach, another veteran of 1848 and now pastor of the First German Reformed Church on Mulberry Street, introduced Kossuth and expressed hopes that "the tyranny of Europe might be broken."[13]

When Rev. Lehlbach concluded his introduction, Kossuth thanked the crowd for its warm welcome and invoked the bond between revolutions in Germany and Hungary, to which his listeners responded with "nine tremendous cheers." Later the same night, a torchlight parade of Germans once again marched through Newark's streets down to City Hall, where they begged Kossuth for another speech. At length, the mayor came out to address the throng. Kossuth, he reported, was deeply gratified by this additional show of support, but he was also quite exhausted and begged his German friends to excuse him for not coming out to greet them personally. But exclamations of disappointment finally induced Kossuth to deliver a few remarks in the German language. "The immense masses gathered in the streets and the glow of a thousand torches, the cheers which continually rent the air" clearly impressed the *Newark Daily Mercury* that night. Later that year forty-eighter merchant Leonhard Roos represented the Germans of Newark at the Wheeling, Virginia, conference of the *Volksbund für die Alte und Neue Welt.* Five years later Newark still boasted a "Robert Blum Society," which took its name from the famous left-wing deputy of the Frankfurt Assembly killed resisting the counterrevolution in Vienna.[14]

Among the many forty-eighter leaders who settled in Newark, the most active, influential, and radical in their views were Friedrich (Fritz) and Mathilde Giesler Anneke, both of whom had impressive revolutionary credentials. Fritz Anneke had sacrificed a promising career as a Prussian officer by organizing revolutionary societies of soldiers and workers. As a member of the Communist League, he helped found the Cologne Workers Association in 1848, served as a member of the Rhenish district of the plebeian Democratic party, and coedited the *Neue Kölnische Zeitung.*[15] His activities as an organizer and journalist eventually led to his paper's suppression and his own imprisonment (on charges of inciting insurrection). Finally acquitted, Anneke served as a lieutenant-colonel in one of the revolution's final military campaigns (in the Baden-Palatinate), commanding twelve hundred troops at the battle of Ubstadt.[16]

Mathilde Giesler married Anneke in 1847 and tried to keep the *Neue Kölnische Zeitung* appearing during her husband's imprisonment. When the censor finally made this impossible, Mathilde published a new paper, the *Frauenzeitung.* With the final defeat of the revolutionary forces in 1849, the Annekes fled through Switzerland to the United States, settling first in Milwaukee, and then, in 1852, in Newark, where they remained for the next six years. With the proceeds from Mathilde's extensive speaking tour that summer, the couple purchased a press. Before long the monthly *Frauenzeitung* and the daily *Newarker Zeitung* began to appear.[17]

Unlike most of the country's German-language newspapers, and despite the ardent courtship of both Democrats and Whigs, the *Newarker Zeitung* declared its hostility to both major parties. The overwhelming German-American support for the Democratic party it attributed largely to a "want of fundamental knowledge of the existing party relations." Contrary to immigrant suppposition, Fritz Anneke wrote, there was no kinship between the Democratic party of the 1848 Revolution and the organization sporting the same name in the United States. "From our own observation," Anneke declared in mid-1853, "we have long since arrived at the conclusion that no difference, or at most a trifling difference of principle exists between the whig party and the democratic party; that the one is as much or as little democratic as the other." Real social progress demanded a new political party in which "German Americans will probably be very strongly represented . . . for the simple reason that they are not so closely united with the old parties as the native born."[18]

But the issue that did, in fact, trigger such a partisan reorganization—the conflict over chattel slavery—confronted the city of Newark and its working people with a problem. Some of the city's largest and most prosperous industries were heavily dependent on the southern trade, including the manufacture of clothing, harnesses and saddles, and jewelry—all centers of German employment. For many, this dependence militated against antagonizing the slaveowners in any way. "While many portions of the Union are heaving with convulsions which threaten the dismemberment of the States," a self-described "mechanic" observed complacently in a February letter to the Democratic *Daily Eagle*, "the people of Newark gaze on the 'so called manifestations' of popular feelings without alarm, perfectly convinced that government will persue [*sic*] the 'even tenor of its ways,' the anti-Nebraska denunciations to the contrary notwithstanding." The writer was candid about his considerations: "Standing as we do at the head of the manufacturing interests of the State, it behooves her Mechanics and Workingmen to pause and reflect ere they embark in [*sic*] any movement that effects [*sic*] their own interests. The question arises, What would this place be if not for the South? What would become of the millions of manufactured goods annually exported [southward] from this city?"[19]

The editor of the anti-Nebraska *Newark Daily Mercury* had to acknowledge that "the city of Newark possesses but little anti-slavery sentiment, and is firmly bound by its business relations to the southern states." But he could not believe that "our people" were "disposed to look on calmly while so large a portion of the Union now consecrated to freedom is given over to the evils which slavery ever brings in its train." "Cannot some effort be made to get a clear and emphatic expression of the view of our citizens in reference to this monstrous scheme for the expansion of slavery?" Surely, at least, "a small Committee might prepare a remonstrance, which would be printed and circulated everywhere in our City."[20]

The first and most resolute response in Newark arose from the German population. The *Newarker Zeitung* considered the bill to be the central issue of American politics, next to which "all other questions dwindle into comparative insignificance." This was no isolated incident, Anneke argued, but part of a larger and longer-range offensive by the slaveholders and their northern friends, "the beginning of a series of victories which aims to lay the confederacy of the United States in chains at their feet."[21]

The March 9 All-German Anti-Nebraska Meeting

A call to a German anti-Nebraska meeting came from a committee including Fritz Anneke, Leonhard Roos, Frederick A. Lehlbach, Emil Schöffner, Ludwig Greiner, and Fridolin Ill. As a young professor of jurisprudence at the University of Munich, Greiner became a central leader of the republican movement in Rhenish Bavaria in 1848; it was he who signed Fritz Anneke's commission in the *rheinpfälzischen Volkswehr*. Greiner's prominence ultimately earned him a death sentence. Escaping from jail with the help of friends, he reached the United States in 1851. Fridolin Ill, a politically active liberal physician, found himself sentenced to six years in prison by the victorious counterrevolution; he, too, fled abroad. Also affixed to the call was the name of Rochus Heinisch, an Austrian-born cutlery producer, an immigrant of the 1820s, possibly the first substantial German manufacturer in the city, and a former Whig. While Heinisch played no further discernible role in the meeting, his endorsement symbolized an attempt to expand the social and political base of the city's German anti-Nebraska protest.[22]

On Thursday evening, March 9, 1854, Independence Hall hosted the meeting initiated by this call. As usual, the number actually attending was disputed. The Democratic *Eagle*, which viewed all such demonstrations with a jaundiced eye, reported "about 150" there. The approving New York *Tribune* counted twice as many.[23] A variety of data attest to the predominance of forty-eighters and plebeians among the meeting's organizers, officers, and speakers (see tables 18 and 19). Among these, craftsmen composed the largest single occupational group (35.7 percent), closely followed by owners of small commercial establishments, including restaurants and saloons (35.7 percent). Six leaders had professional or white-collar occupations (21.4 percent), including the five prominent forty-eighters in the group—Greiner, Ill, Schöffner, Lehlbach, and Anneke. Only one leader came from the economic elite, and only one was an unskilled laborer (each accounting for a 3.6 percent share of the total leadership).

Wealth data presented in table 19 confirm the profile. In the 1850 census returns (which recorded information about real property alone), more than half the anti-Nebraska Germans listed claimed less than $1,000 worth of real property. None reported property in excess of $4,000. The scope of the 1860 data is wider, including figures for

Table 18
Occupations of Leaders of Newark's All-German Anti-Nebraska Meeting,
March 9, 1854

Occupational Group	(N)	(%)
Economic elite	1	3.6
Professional and white-collar	6	21.4
Small commercial proprietors	10	35.7
Craftsmen	10	35.7
Unskilled	1	3.6
Total accounted for	28	
Not accounted for	4	

Sources: U.S. Census, population schedules for Essex County, N.J., seventh (1850) and eighth (1860) censuses; F. J. Urquhart, *A History of the City of Newark, New Jersey* (New York: Lewis Historical Publishing Co., 1913), esp. William von Katzler, "The Germans in Newark," pp. 1057–87; Joseph Atkinson, *The History of Newark, New Jersey, Being a Narrative of Its Rise and Progress* (Newark: William B. Guild, 1878); David Lawrence Pierson, *Narratives of Newark* (Newark: Pierson Publishing Co., 1917); and Newark city directories.

Table 19
Property Ownership among Leaders of Newark's All-German Anti-Nebraska Meeting, March 9, 1854

	Census Returns	
Value of Property	1850	1860
None	4	0
$1–$499	0	4
$500–$999	1	1
$1,000–$4,999	3	7
$5,000–$9,999	0	1
$10,000–$19,999	0	2
$20,000–$49,999	0	0
$50,000 and above	0	0
Total accounted for	8	15

Note: The 1850 data represent real property alone while the 1860 data include both real and personal property. Twenty-two of the 32 German leaders were found in either the 1850 or 1860 returns; only one was found in both returns.
Sources: U.S. Census, population schedules for Essex County, N.J., seventh (1850) and eighth (1860) censuses.

personal as well as real property, and absolute figures for total property owned are correspondingly higher overall. Even so, roughly 80 percent of the March 9 leaders listed reported total property worth less than $5,000, and one-third reported less than $1,000. (As noted below, this property-holding pattern contrasted sharply with that of the leaders of the citywide anti-Nebraska meeting held a few weeks later, who, as we will see, were generally much wealthier.)

Census data also clarify the status of those ten leaders of the March 9 meeting identified with the crafts and so listed in table 18. Five of these men were traced to the manuscript returns of 1850, the other five to the returns of 1860. Of the ten craftsmen, six claimed property worth $200 or less. Of the remaining four, three reported property worth $2,000, and one claimed property worth $7,000. Thus, four of the ten evidently possesed appreciably greater wealth than did the other six. The wide chasm separating those claiming property valued at $200 or less from those claiming property worth $2,000 or more strongly suggests a distinction here between journeymen and masters.[24] It thus appears that perhaps 60 percent of the March 9 immigrant artisans were employed journeymen and 40 percent were masters—another indication of the socially heterogeneous composition of the anti-Nebraska movement.

Emil Schöffner called the March 9 meeting to order at 8:00 P.M., with Leonhart Roos serving as president and Ludwig Greiner as vice president.[25] Following Roos's brief introductory remarks, Lehlbach, Greiner, and Schöffner each addressed the assembly and denounced the Nebraska bill, its authors, and its supporters. Lehlbach's remarks reflected the forty-eighters' deepening disillusionment with their land of exile. The man who had welcomed Kossuth to freedom's sanctuary in North America now noted (as related in a newspaper account) that when he "came to this country, five years ago, after the defeat of the unfortunate [i.e., ill-fated] revolutionary struggle in Germany, he never expected to be compelled one day to raise his voice, in this country of freedom, against tyranny."

Following Lehlbach's remarks, Ludwig Greiner presented a resolution drafted by the meeting's initiators. The resolution's forty-eighter inspiration was apparent in its strong language, its condemnation on principle of chattel slavery, its concern with the bill's meaning for immigrant and other working people, its democratic internationalism, and its open threat to carry the fight against the Nebraska bill into the electoral arena. "We are generally enemies of Slavery," it declared, "and therefore so much more against the formation of new Slave states." The Douglas bill was "a daring enterprise of the slave breeders" and "their friends" that would "withdraw arable lands of the territory from immigration" by turning them into slave plantations. The bill thus "endangers the freedom of the whole people." The free worker was particularly menaced, since "in a Slave State labor is regarded as unworthy of a freeman, and the free laborer is deprecated."

The resolution also voiced concern about the bill's impact on the democratic cause in Europe. Leonhart Roos had attended the 1852 Wheeling Convention that had urged the United States to champion the cause of liberty internationally. Two years later, however, the course being steered by the U.S. government seemed to point in precisely the opposite direction. By strengthening the hand of aristocracy in America, the resolution asserted, "the European reaction [is also] supported." It closed with this warning: "We, at any election hereafter, to none of our Representatives who declares himself for the Nebraska bill, will give our voice or support."

During the discussion following the reading of the draft, attempts were made to modify it, particularly to remove its blunt threat to oppose all pro-Nebraska politicians. The first such proposal was easily defeated. Emil Schöffner then rose to offer another resolution. "Notwithstanding all circulating rumors," it read, "we confidently expect that President Pierce will hereafter bear himself as a man and a good republican, and veto the Nebraska bill, if it should pass."

All in attendance that night would have liked to see the bill killed, whether by Congress or the White House. But not all were ready to second Schöffner's confidence in Franklin Pierce. (And in fact, as noted above, Pierce had privately promised to support the bill even before Douglas brought it to the Senate floor.) Ludwig Greiner introduced an "amendment" to Schöffner's resolution that replaced praise with a slap at the Democracy's top officeholder, declaring concisely: "We deem the mistrust everywhere expressed of President Pierce wholly justified." Fridolin Ill and Fritz Anneke both urged caution. Each expressed sympathy with Greiner's sentiments but opposed the latter's amendment as inappropriate and irrelevent to the specific purposes of the meeting. The Germans assembled at Independence Hall, however, were in no mood for moderation of any sort and promptly endorsed Greiner's angry, defiant language.

The April 3 "General" Anti-Nebraska Meeting

In its animating political outlook, as well as in the social profile of its leadership, the German meeting of March 9 contrasted vividly with the only other anti-Nebraska meeting to occur in Newark that year.

Table 20
Occupations of German Leaders of Newark's "General" Anti-Nebraska
Meeting, April 3, 1854

Occupational Group	(N)	(%)
Economic elite	20	40.8
Professional and white-collar	16	32.6
Small commercial enterprise	6	12.2
Craftsmen	6	12.2
Farmers	1	2.0
Total accounted for	49	
Not accounted for	2	

Sources: U.S. Census, population schedules for Essex County, N.J., seventh (1850) and eighth (1860) censuses; Katzler, "Germans in Newark"; Urquhart, *History of Newark;* Atkinson, *History of Newark;* and Pierson, *Narratives of Newark.*

Held a month later, on April 3, it was initiated, guided, and shaped by a sector of the city's elite. Among the signatures affixed to the public call, the names of prominent and well-to-do Newark figures strike the eye, as they do in the roster of officers and speakers at the meeting itself. The anti-Nebraska press gloried in the involvement of some of "the worthiest" and "most substantial citizens" of Newark. Mayor Horace J. Poinier presided, and the meeting was called to order by Marcus L. Ward, a well-known Whig financier who would later become, successively, governor of the state, chairman of the Republican National Committee, and a member of the U.S. House of Representatives. Also among the speakers was former New Jersey governor William Pennington, who had distinguished himself in the North by endorsing strict enforcement of the Fugitive Slave Law of 1850. In 1859 the Republican minority in the House would succeed in electing Pennington as speaker largely because of the congressman's impeccably conservative reputation.[26]

A variety of supporting data confirm journalistic reports that the leadership of the April 3 meeting was primarily drawn from Newark's economic elite (see tables 20 and 21). Out of 49 leaders accounted for, 20 men belonged to this category, accounting for 40.8 percent of the total leadership. They included financiers, large-scale merchants, building contractors, and manufacturers (such as coach manufacturer James H. Quimby, who claimed real estate valued at $80,000 in 1850 and nearly $200,000 worth of real and personal property in 1860). Thirteen of these twenty men were either officers or directors of banking and insurance companies. Table 20, in fact, actually un-

Table 21
Property Ownership among Leaders of Newark's "General" Anti-Nebraska
Meeting, April 3, 1854

	Census Returns	
Value of Property	1850	1860
None	5	3
$1–$499	0	0
$500–$999	1	1
$1,000–$4,999	1	2
$5,000–$9,999	3	6
$10,000–$19,999	10	3
$20,000–$49,999	8	5
$50,000 and above	2	7
Total accounted for	30	27

Note: The 1850 data represent real property alone, while 1860 data include both real and personal property. Forty-one of the 51 leaders of the general (April 3) anti-Nebraska meeting were found, 16 of whom showed up on both sets of returns.
Sources: U.S. Census, population schedules for Essex County, N.J., seventh (1850) and eighth (1860) censuses.

derstates this elite presence. Four individuals listed in occupational categories other than those of the elite (two attorneys, one physician, and one grocer) were also affiliated with the city's financial institutions, and another attorney was counsel for the New Jersey Railroad Company. Only about one in eight of the April 3 leaders were involved with the crafts, and only another eighth owned small commercial enterprises. (These last two categories, it will be recalled, accounted for almost three-fourths of the all-German leadership of the March 9 meeting.)

In terms of sheer wealth (as depicted in table 21), three-quarters of the April 3 leaders traced to the 1850 census returns claimed real property worth $5,000 or more, and fully two-thirds appraised their holdings at $10,000 or greater. In the more comprehensive 1860 data, more than half of those listed reported total property worth at least $10,000, while more than 40 percent claimed property equal to or greater than $20,000. The top fourth acknowledged holdings of at least $50,000. Indeed, the collective prosperity thus revealed might have been more imposing still, except that some of the wealthiest individuals involved (judging from 1850 data) could not be found in the 1860 returns.

As its advance publicity had promised, the April 3 meeting was a decidedly mild-mannered affair. Its organizers hoped to persuade southern leaders to withdraw the Kansas-Nebraska bill and thereby stem the growth of militant antislavery sentiment in the North and head off a full-scale sectional confrontation. Attorney Joseph P. Bradley set the meeting's tone. Unlike those at the all-German meeting the previous month, who had reviled the "slavebreeders," Bradley was at pains to assure all that he and his associates felt "no disposition to call hard names." On the contrary, he explained: "We look upon our Southern brethren as brethren—we would not injure their feelings or their institutions." Governor Pennington similarly "regretted very much [that] this question had arisen" at all. "Slavery was always a difficult and delicate subject, and calculated to excite angry and intemperate discussion." Personally, he "had hoped after the Compromise of 1850, [that] this whole project would have been suffered to sleep, at all events, for many years to come." Attorney J. P. Jackson also feared "the agitation on the subject of slavery, which it [the bill] had so unfortunately renewed, and which was now rapidly increasing. This was greatly to be deplored, as the most fraternal feelings have been forming and strengthening throughout the whole country since the Compromise of 1850." Alone among the evening's speakers, attorney Cortland Parker forthrightly opposed slavery as "an evil" (although, he was ready to concede, it might not technically be a sin).

The meeting's prevailing atmosphere of caution was reflected in the resolution it approved. The Douglas bill was regrettable because it would "open anew the whole controversy and conflict between the free and slaveholding states; thus dividing, unhappily, the American people into two great parties, the *'pro slavery'* and *'anti slavery'*," a polarization "destructive of peace and harmony of the States, dangerous to the interests of the Republic, and causing serious apprehensions for the perpetuity of the Union." Naturally, since the worst thing about the bill was its tendency to force a showdown over slavery, the architects of the April meeting advocated nothing likely to accelerate partisan realignment over that issue. Neither the resolution nor any of the speeches seconded or even took note of the Germans' earlier call for an electoral boycott of pro-Nebraska politicians.

In all these respects, comparison of the two meetings bears out the recollection of a Newark German newspaper editor—that the free-soil protests of German immigrants "were abolitionistic, but more popular and clear, more genuine[,] without demagogical under-current than the declamations of the English-speaking opponents of slavery."[27] Still, underlying political differences survived among Douglas's German-American critics, too. The presence of *Dreissiger* entrepreneur Rochus Heinisch at Newark's more conciliatory "general" anti-Nebraska meeting quietly symbolized that divergence. Characteristically, reaction was more dramatically diverse in New York's big, heterogeneous, and volatile *Kleindeutschland*. What would now occur, observers wondered, in the Midwest, the home of Stephen A. Douglas?

7

The Response in the West

"There is a power in this nation greater than either the North or the South," Stephen Douglas had proclaimed in 1850, "a growing, increasing, swelling power." That power was "the country known as the great West—the Valley of the Mississippi, one and indivisible from the Gulf to the Great Lakes, and stretching, on the one side and the other, to the extreme sources of the Ohio and the Missouri—from the Alleghenies to the Rocky Mountains."[1]

As one of the West's leading political representatives—and one, moreover, who harbored strong national ambitions—Douglas might be expected to exaggerate the import of his electoral base. But a firm reality underlay this grandiloquent rhetoric. Though fewer than one in seven Americans lived in the West at the turn of the nineteenth century, that proportion exceeded one in three in 1860, by which time the West boasted more residents than the Northeast. As Douglas declared, "To those vast multitudes, who wish to change their condition, and select new homes, the promised land is westward." Germans were moving into the region at an even swifter rate than native-born migrants and were soon referring to themselves as "the pioneers of the West." By 1860, 40 percent of the United States' total German-born population could be found in Ohio, Illinois, Wisconsin, Indiana, and Michigan.[2] This chapter examines reactions provoked by the Kansas-Nebraska bill among German residents of two of the West's most important urban centers, Cincinnati and Chicago.

Dubbed "the Queen City of the West," Cincinnati did indeed reign over the region's explosive development. Its strategic position on the Ohio River connected it to the entire Mississippi River system, and by the late 1830s the city was linked to New York City as well, through the Ohio and Miami canals, then Lake Erie, and finally the Erie Canal. The 1840s saw extensive railroad construction, and the commercial and population growth that ensued stimulated industrial development. Workshops multiplied and grew in size, flanked by factories employing steam-driven machinery. An English visitor observed around mid-century that the "character of these manufacturing districts" was making the Queen City "one of the wonders of the New World." By 1860 its 160,000 residents made it one of the nation's ten most populous cities, and—more impressively—the third-ranked industrial city in the country. The palpable promise of economic opportunity attracted immigrants in great numbers. Already in 1840, perhaps 15 to 20 percent of the city's population was German-born. By 1850, more than 40 percent of all Cincinnatians were evidently of either German birth or German parentage.[3]

Chicago's development began later. In 1830 it was still only a village, home to fewer than 100 people. Only in the next decade did its population reach 4,500, as Chicago became a secondary commercial center for the upper Midwest. Its first industries—such as cattle slaughtering and meat-packing, tanning, and soap and candle manufacture—served agriculture and processed its products. Then, during the late 1840s and early 1850s, the ongoing settlement of the northern Illinois countryside stimulated the articulation of canal and railroad networks that turned Chicago into a boomtown. The Illinois River and the Illinois and Michigan Canal together gave the city direct access to the Mississippi and thus to the agricultural countryside and to St. Louis. The Rock Island and Illinois Central railroads provided still cheaper and more dependable routes to the interior.[4]

Once again, commercial boom encouraged the growth of population and manufactures. By 1850 the city had grown to 30,000 people, and within four years it reached 66,000. By then local newspapers were bragging of a manufacturing work force of 5,000 annually producing goods worth $8 to $10 million. Both figures reportedly doubled between 1854 and 1856.[5]

As already established industries flourished, new ones sprouted luxuriantly. Enterprises of growing scale turned out raw iron and steel, locomotive engines, rails and cars, stoves, carriages, wagons, and agricultural implements, prefabricated doors and windows, furniture and cabinetry, shoes, assorted brass and copper products, and saddles, harnesses, and other finished leather goods. Modest breweries and distilleries grew into major enterprises.[6]

As in Cincinnati, immigrants supplied much of the labor needed. And while in 1850 the weight of the Irish-born in the population (20 percent) exceeded that of the Germans (17 percent), a single decade reversed the relative importance of these two groups. By 1860, the Irish-born proportion of Chicago's population had declined to 18 percent while that of the Germans had risen to 20 percent. Half of all German-born adult males in that year held skilled or semiskilled jobs; these immigrant craftworkers, in turn, accounted for upwards of one-half of the work force in many craft occupations. Two thousand Germans accounted for 30 percent of the city's unskilled labor pool.[7]

By thus contributing to the settlement and economic development of the West, these German immigrants reinforced Stephen Douglas's confidence in this region's future preeminence. He was equally certain that—as "the heart and soul of the nation and continent"—the West would play a pivotal role in the nation's political life. With important connections to both the Northeast and the South, and as a prime beneficiary of national unity, the West seemed ideally suited to act as sectional peacemaker, as an arbiter that could "speak the law to this nation." "To save the Union," Douglas declared, was thus "the mission of the great Mississippi Valley." And his constituents were all the better qualified for that role for being free of any strong feelings about slavery. "We indulge no ultraisms—no sectional strifes—no crusades against the North or the South."[8]

Cincinnati: Against "Popery" and Slavery

A major test of Douglas's political assessment of the West was to occur in Cincinnati. German immigrants had played important and visible roles in the city's development almost from its founding in 1788. Its first mayor, revolutionary war officer David Ziegler, for example, was a native of Heidelberg. Between his arrival in Cincinnati in 1795 and his death in 1831, Martin Baum became one of the city's wealthiest citizens, for a time presiding over the town council, serving as board member for the local branch of the Second Bank of the United States, and launching the Miami Exporting Company, an enterprise heavily involved in both commerce and transportation. Sebastien Myer, Jacob Kornblüth, and others prospered in Cincinnati's important ready-made clothing industry. The "granddaddy" of Cincinnati coppersmiths, Jeremiah Kiersted, was plying his trade in the city by the century's second decade. During the 1830s his business passed into the hands of his son Hezekiah. Business throve, bringing the younger Kiersted community respect and a seat on the city council. In 1860 he presided over the Democratic party's local convention, which nominated him for the post of city commissioner. Hanoverian Frederick Rammelsberg, in the meantime, was pioneering the mechanization of furniture production. Early in the 1850s businessman and booster Charles Cist rhapsodized about the new six-floor factory built by Rammelsberg and Robert Mitchell, which annually turned out nearly $250,000 worth of furniture.[9]

The big *Dreissiger* immigration also left a deep impression on the politics of German Cincinnati, providing the city with an able, sophisticated, and energetic group of liberal intelligentsia, many of whom were scions of prosperous German families. In their front ranks stood Karl Reemelin, Heinrich Rödter, Stephan Molitor, and Johann Stallo.

Born in Heilbronn, Württemberg, in 1814, Karl Gustav Reemelin would eventually become the most prominent immigrant politician in the antebellum Queen City. Reemelin's father was a well-to-do businessman who "read with me, or rather, made me read to him, history and geography, and conversed with me on political economy." For his part, young Karl "was but too happy to be the recipient of . . . the ripe politico-economic counsels he gave me." In economics, "it was [then] that I imbibed what some would call . . . free-trade ideas." On the political plane, he learned "how much mischief is caused by false government, and incompetent administration." But Karl Reemelin yearned for a more stimulating life. That quest soon led the young man abroad, and in 1833 he settled in Cincinnati, where he managed to combine prosperity with stimulation as a merchant, real estate investor, railroad promoter, journalist, and political leader. Attracted to the free-trade, hard-money doctrines of the Jacksonian Democratic party and repelled by the nativist and sabbatarian bent of the Whigs, Reemelin helped establish the Democratic *Volksblatt* in 1836 and won election first to the state house of representatives and then to the state senate. Admitted to the bar in the late 1840s, Reemelin served in 1850 as a delegate to Ohio's constitutional convention.[10]

Born in 1805 in Neustadt-on-the-Hardt in the Rhenish Palatinate, Heinrich Rödter entered his father's paper mill business at an early age. Like Reemelin, however, Rödter found his family's business dreary and stifling; after experimenting with a military career, he undertook the study of law. Subsequently involved in the liberal-democratic agitation in Germany inspired by France's July 1830 revolution, Rödter had to flee the fatherland in 1832. In the United States he, too, came strongly to identify with the Jacksonian Democracy, and between 1836 and 1840 he managed and edited the Democratic *Volksblatt*. Thereafter he divided his time between commerce (including an interest in a Columbus paper mill), law, politics, and journalism (returning briefly to the *Volksblatt* in 1842, and between 1850 and 1854 publishing the small *Demokratisches Tageblatt*). Rödter served on the board of education, the city council, and in both houses of the state legislature. He died a Democrat in 1857, having recently been elected justice of the peace.[11]

Stephan Molitor was born in 1806 in Chestlitz, Oberfranken, and studied law and philosophy in Germany before migrating to the United States in 1830. Here he found employment first on the staff of the *New Yorker Staats-Zeitung* and then with Buffalo's *Weltbürger*. In 1837 Molitor moved to Cincinnati. Within a decade, he, too, had been elected to the state legislature. Like Heinrich Rödter, however, Molitor's real métier was journalism. Indeed, Molitor went into partnership with Rödter on the *Volksblatt* shortly after settling in Cincinnati and became sole proprietor in 1840. He retained that position for more than twenty years, earning a reputation as a skillful polemicist and an aggressive businessman.[12]

Johann Bernhard Stallo was the youngest of this group of civic leaders. Born in the Duchy of Oldenburg in 1823 to a family of Frisian schoolmasters, he acquired a secondary education at a Catholic normal school and would for some time pursue a career in Catholic academia. But he also began to develop strong liberal democratic views early in life and left the fatherland at the age of sixteen. In Cincinnati he taught German and mathematics for a while at St. Xavier's College before accepting accepting a professorship at St. John's College in New York during the late 1840s. Thereafter he returned to Cincinnati, took up jurisprudence, and was for four years (1849–53) Heinrich Rödter's junior law partner. In 1853 Ohio's governor appointed Stallo to an uncompleted term on the Hamilton County court of common pleas. The voters gave him a full term in that office at the next election. It was apparently in this period that Stallo finally broke with any residual Catholicism. The most reflective and scholarly of the Cincinnati *Dreissigers*, he refined and propagated his own brand of Hegelian-derived philosophical idealism in a series of published works.[13]

As their biographies indicate, these men plunged quickly, successfully, and decisively into the bustling community life of German Cincinnati. In 1834, shortly after their arrival in the city, Karl Reemelin and Heinrich Rödter helped found one of the West's early institutional expressions of German-American liberalism, the German Society. Patterned after successful eastern models, the new association aimed to assure "that as citizens of the United States we can take part

in the people's government which our duty and right commands."
Economic difficulties would be ameliorated through the volunteer efforts of community members.[14] In 1843 Rödter and Molitor helped
found Cincinnati's *Deutsche demokratische Verein* (the German Democratic Association), which dedicated itself both to uniting the city's
German population behind the Democratic party and to holding the
latter to liberal democratic principles—"Equal rights and complete
justice for all men, irrespective of religious or political beliefs." With
the aid of institutions like the German Society, the German Democratic Association, and the *Volksblatt,* Cincinnati's prominent *Dreissiger* sought to rally the rest of their countryfolk behind their social-
political philosophy.[15]

Although these civic leaders have attracted much attention from
historians, it was the German immigrants who worked with their hands,
and who came in far larger numbers, who made Cincinnati's economic growth and development possible. As the case of the Mitchell
and Rammelsberg furniture firm suggests, many of these immigrant
working people labored in the employ of fellow *Landsleute*. By 1840
about one in five members of the Cincinnati work force was German-
born, and as the wave of immigration grew during the 1840s, Germans more than doubled their share of the city's total labor force,
raising it above 43 percent by 1850. Although many Germans worked
as unskilled laborers, it was the imposing German presence in the
skilled trades that struck observers most forcefully. "The Germans almost monopolise the handicraft trades," reported the Englishwoman
Isabella Lucy Bird during her 1854 visit to the city.[16]

The immigrants of the late 1840s and early 1850s brought more
than strong backs and skilled hands to Cincinnati. As one Cincinnati
chronicler later recalled, the new arrivals included "many heroic spirits
that had been embittered by those injustices which had provoked the
rebellion of 1848." By the mid-1850s immigrant radical democrats
were reshaping the features of German Cincinnati. "Skilled, educated,
and intellectual," Bird reported, they "constitute an influence of which
the Americans themselves are afraid."[17]

That much became clear in March 1854, when representatives from
Turner-, Freimänner-, and *Arbeitervereine* and kindred organizations
from throughout Ohio gathered in Cincinnati to formulate a common
declaration of principles. The state convention met in Freemen's Hall,
located on the corner of Vine and Mercer streets in the heart of the
"Over the Rhine" district. Delegates attended from Toledo, Cincinnati, Dayton, Columbus, Akron, Cleveland, Norwalk, Hamilton,
Rossville, Sandusky, Chillicothe, Massillon, Portsmouth, Concordia,

Black River, and Wapakoneta. They bore credentials from working-men's associations, Freemen chapters, discussion clubs, singing societies, reading circles, *Turnvereine* (although evidently not Cincinnati's), farmers' societies, ad hoc mass meetings, and ethnically defined affiliates of broader fraternal organizations (such as Chillicothe's Lodge No. 6 of the Order of the Sons of Liberty). Among Cincinnati's representatives were the tailor Kaspar Gams and the sometime cabinet-maker Gottlieb Wiest for the *Arbeiterverein,* a Freemen contingent led by Hassaurek that included two trunkmakers and a cigarmaker, and (representing the German Discussion Society) William Renau, a teacher in the city's Jewish school.[18]

In two days of deliberation, the delegates hammered out a platform similar in most respects to the Louisville platform. Thousands of copies of the "Cincinnati platform" were distributed in both English and German versions.[19] A number of its planks emphasized the rights and interests of the foreign-born, seeking to speed their enfranchisement and protect them while they traveled abroad. The United States' long-standing refusal to intervene in European affairs—a source of special frustration to political refugees—drew correspondingly withering fire. To make the American political system more representative and responsive, the convention demanded direct election and recall of all public officials and the sharp reduction of their salaries, and declared universal, free, compulsory schooling through the age of fourteen essential.

The convention at Freemen's Hall placed church-state relations in this republican context.[20] "The constitution guarantees freedom of thought," the delegates declared, and this included religious—or irreligious—belief. Moreover, religion ought to be a private matter, and there should be no religious test for those wishing to hold office or give testimony in court; the Bible should no longer be used as a text in the public schools; and "Sunday laws" should be abolished. While the delegates thus strove to curb the temporal power of Puritan and evangelical Protestantism, they identified the Roman Catholic hierarchy as an even greater threat. "In the interest of the Republic," they demanded "that the Pope's exercise of power in the United States through the medium of bishops and other agents be ended, that his interference in the affairs of the nation's citizens be energetically resisted and that the Jesuit order be treated as an open enemy of the Republic."

Other proposals aimed to limit the concentration of wealth and improve the condition of the working population. These included calls to reduce the working day to ten hours, pass a mechanics' lien law,

and initiate a "thorough reform" of poor houses and public infir-
maries. Delegates also asserted that the then-projected Pacific Railroad—the capstone of the era's transportation revolution—should be
publicly rather than privately owned. As for the vast public lands of
the West, the convention urged that these be neither given nor sold
to states or private corporations but instead "granted outright to actual settlers." On the issue of slavery, the Cincinnati convention took
up a radical free-soil position.

This "German reform convention" provoked cries of indignation
from conservative-minded opponents. The Democratic *Cincinnati Daily
Enquirer* found the very "idea of men banding themselves politically
together, according [to] the place of their nativity or the language
which they speak" anathema, because it "exhibits a clannishness of
spirit." "It should be the object of all foreigners who arrive in this
country," the editor instructed, "to become American citizens as soon
as possible, and not to perpetuate their nationalities by acting together
as Germans, or Irish, in political matters." The Cincinnati platform
seemed to the editor a natural product of so essentially un-American
a meeting. The Sunday law he defended as a proper "feature of a
Christian government." The right of recall was a "perfectly wild and
visionary idea" that "would introduce anarchy into the Government
at once." The convention's fundamental error, summarized the *Enquirer,* was to remain fixated upon "an European rather than an
American model" of democracy. "The European idea of Democracy,"
the editor explained, "has always been essentially different from the
American, and has never succeeded so well in actual trial. The former
carries it to a point where it borders on anarchy and unbridled license."

The Bedini "Riot"

In the waning weeks of 1853, German radicals in Cincinnati demonstrated something of their strength and combativeness as well as
their continued devotion to the cause of 1848. In late December the
Queen City became the scene of the largest of the many protests across
the country against the visit of Gaetano Bedini and his cordial reception at the White House. A papal nuncio, Bedini was accused of complicity in the bloody suppression of the Italian revolution of 1848
and, more specifically, in the torture and execution of Garibaldi's associate and chaplain, Ugo Bassi. As already noted, this was by no
means the first conflict to pit the city's Catholic church (or, for that
matter, evangelical Protestants) against German critics. But the sheer
size—and dénouement—of this protest set it apart and catapulted

Cincinnati's immigrant radicals into local and national headlines. The late Carl Wittke, dean of historians of German America, labeled the protest "a disgraceful demonstration by German Turners," and similar attitudes have characterized other accounts.[21]

Bedini's tour brought him in December 1853 to Cincinnati, where he took up temporary residence with Archbishop John Baptist Purcell on Eighth Street in a rectory adjoining the St. Peter-in-Chains Cathedral. To radical democratic partisans of the 1848 Revolution, Bedini's presence was an unbearable provocation. A meeting convened hastily at Freemen's Hall on Christmas morning, Sunday, December 25. In the mistaken belief that Bedini planned to depart the following day, the Freemen decided to take action that same Christmas night. They would march in procession to the archbishop's residence, then continue down to Fifth Street, and there burn Bedini in effigy. Hurried preparations for the impending demonstration, including the manufacture of effigy, gallows, and banners, consumed Sunday afternoon and evening. Messengers circulating through the German community visited the *Arbeiterverein* and the *Turngemeinde*. The workers' association quickly met and dispatched a contingent of about twenty people to join the demonstration. The Turners held no meeting but informed their members of the planned protest, some of whom joined the march as well.[22]

As it turned out, the protesters were not the only ones active that Christmas Sunday. Word of the intended march reached the ears of Cincinnati's police chief and police judge. On the grounds that the marchers intended to harm Bedini personally, these officials detailed a large body of watchmen (police) to intercept and break up the demonstration. Unaware of these developments, the protesters gathered, organized their ranks, and stepped off from Freemen's Hall at approximately 10:00 P.M. Bilingual banners borne aloft reflected the Jacobin-like cast of their republicanism. "Liberty, Equality, Love and Fraternity," read one. "No Priests, No Kings, no Popery," demanded another. Others simply read "Down with Bedini" and "The Gallows-Bird Bedini." A stocky German carried the gallows frame on which Bedini's effigy was to be hanged. Estimates of the number of participants varied from 600 to 1,200, including women and children. The *Cincinnati Daily Gazette* could only presume that so many "ladies of intelligence" had participated in a boisterous evening street demonstration because they had been "carried away with the intense excitement of disgust and indignation of their husbands and brothers."[23]

As planned, the marchers headed down to Ninth Street. There, however, they ran afoul of some one hundred members of the Cincinnati police force, who suddenly charged the demonstrators, beat them with clubs, tore down their banners, fired into their ranks at point-blank range, arrested those they could hold, and pursued those who fled through the streets. "The stampede was complete," by one account, "—husbands were separated from their wives, and screams and shouts added to the confusion of the noise of firearms." Police claimed that a marcher had fired the first shot. *Freimänner* representatives rejected that claim, adding that no one in authority had even bothered to call upon the demonstrators to disperse before ordering the police charge.[24]

All told, the police crowded more than sixty Germans into the police station, *Freimännerverein* leader Friedrich Hassaurek among them. Fourteen of those arrested had sustained bullet wounds, and twenty-six-year-old Palatine native Karl Eggerlin subsequently died of his injuries. At least five marchers who escaped arrest were also wounded. On the other side, one policeman was shot in the leg. Police claimed to have confiscated a total of three pistols, one dagger, three canes, one sword cane, a sheathed butcher knife, and a few other weapons.[25]

This bloody confrontation triggered a tremendous public uproar. Prominent citizens and most English-language newspapers at first blamed the demonstrators for the violence. So did some respected German-Americans. Prosperous coppersmith and alderman Hezekiah Kiersted initially believed "that the procession should have been intercepted before reaching the bishop's house" and offered personally to arrest the "ringleader" (evidently meaning Hassaurek). But as the Freemen energetically presented their version of the night's events, public reaction shifted. On Monday, Freemen and others were on the streets throughout the city handing out circulars and posting placards explaining and defending their motives and conduct the previous night. When Eggerlin died, sympathizers organized a huge funeral procession in his honor, in effect a demonstration in support of the remaining sixty-three defendants. At length, in a move furiously denounced by the mayor, the prosecuting attorney himself asked the court to dismiss the case for lack of evidence of criminal misconduct; the court agreed.[26]

The whole affair had redounded against both the Catholic hierarchy and city officials. When the Freemen established a fund to aid those wounded during the so-called "Weihnachts riot," Archbishop Purcell donated ten dollars, explaining that "when there is a question of relieving those who suffer and are poor, all differences of faith or opinion should be forgotten." But the Freemen would not be mollified. *Verein* president Edward Steffens replied that "the blood of a brother, barbarously murdered, stands between you and us." Nor could the Freemen accept the archbishop's donation, "persuaded as we are, by a long train of historical facts, and by the late occurrences, that a Jesuit under the guidelines of the despotic King of Rome can never mean good, nor deal with sincerity toward men known to cherish republican opinions and sentiments of justice, and brotherly affection for mankind, as we do. We beg to return the ten dollar bill to you, which you will find herein enclosed."[27]

The momentum of the anti-Bedini protest increased during subsequent days. Following the dismissal of charges against him and his fellows, Friedrich Hassaurek turned the tables on his accusers and pressed charges of his own against 109 policemen, the police chief, and the police judge. In the meantime, the German singing societies of Cincinnati gave a concert at Freemen's Hall to raise money to defray the legal costs arising from all this litigation.[28]

The German Fight against the Nebraska Bill

In the anti-Bedini campaign, Cincinnati's radical German democrats reaffirmed their dedication to the cause of 1848 and their tenacious hostility to perceived enemies of liberty and republicanism as they understood those principles. Within weeks, however, the Bedini uproar would be eclipsed by the controversy over the future of chattel slavery. For on January 4, as Cincinnati debated the *Weihnachts* imbroglio, Democrat Stephen A. Douglas of Illinois presented his Kansas-Nebraska bill to the U.S. Senate.

The response in German Cincinnati was remarkable on a number of counts. First, despite their previous support for the national Democratic party and for Douglas as a prominent party spokesman, far more Germans mobilized against the bill than in favor of it, and Germans made up a significantly larger proportion of the city's anti-Nebraska movement than its pro-Nebraska movement. Second, the social composition of the German pro- and anti-Nebraska forces diverged in significant ways. German craftsmen figured far more centrally in the movement to oppose the bill and resist slavery's expansion. Germans with political and white-collar positions, in contrast, figured more centrally in the attempts to uphold Douglas, his bill, and the national Democratic administration. Finally, some of the state's principal forty-eighter organizations took stands on slavery and the rights of black Americans that were far more abolition-minded than those typical of the North's anti-Nebraska mainstream.

For some time, supporters of Douglas and Pierce in the Queen City denied that any anti-Nebraska movement even existed. The Democratic *Enquirer* assured readers in late February that no significant protest against the Douglas bill had arisen or would arise, even though certain people "seem to imagine that there is a terrible popular excitement upon the subject of Nebraska." Such a presumption, it added, "is a great delusion having its origin in the heated brain and distempered fancy of our contemporaries. Never was an opposition more signally unsuccessful in rallying popular sentiments to its aid."[29]

If pronouncements like these comforted their authors and some readers, they had little to do with reality. Four days before the *Enquirer* pronounced the anti-Nebraska movement stillborn, Cincinnati's first anti-Nebraska meeting occurred. It was organized and attended almost exclusively by Germans, and it convened the evening of Friday, February 24, at the *Turnhalle*. The anti-Nebraska *Gazette* found the crowd assembled there "large and enthusiastic." A committee including tailor and *Arbeiterverein* leader Kaspar Gams, the German Discussion Society's William Renau, and Adolf Gerwig, a rationalist minister, forty-eighter veteran, and democratic activist, proposed a series of resolutions that the assembly adopted unanimously. These resolutions shunned conciliatory language and denounced the Douglas bill as a violation of the Constitution and the Missouri Compromise of 1820, a "disgrace to America and this age," and "solemnly protest[ed] against it in the name of humanity, liberty, and justice." Stephen Douglas himself had "forfeited the esteem of every citizen who has the interests of liberty in his heart."[30]

About ten days later, on a rainy Tuesday evening, March 7, a large nonpartisan anti-Nebraska crowd assembled at Cincinnati's Mechanics' Hall. In composition and tone, it strongly resembled the "general" anti-Nebraska meeting that would be held in Newark on April 3 (recall the discussion in chapter 6). This March 7 meeting was apparently called, officered, and attended primarily by "the first men of the County of Hamilton," most of whom were non-Germans. It was meant to demonstrate (as the *Gazette* put it) that "public opinion of Cincinnati is not tinctured with fanaticism or polluted with sentiments disloyal to the Union."[31] The first speaker, an attorney named Walker, appropriately began his remarks by assuring all assembled that "I am not now and never have been an Abolitionist in the common acceptation [*sic*] of that word. That is, I have always felt that we of the North were bound to keep our faith in the South, so far as it was pledged by the Federal Constitution, either expressly or by clear implication, and ought not, therefore, to interfere by any other than moral means, with Slavery in the States where it was already established." Because the institution of slavery now threatened to extend itself, however, Walker considered it "a sacred duty to exert all the powers I possess" to avoid that prospect. He devoted the balance of his remarks to demonstrating the legal inadmissibility of the Nebraska bill.

Charles Reemelin was the meeting's principal German speaker. Cincinnati's leading *Dreissiger* politician, Reemelin was no more an abolitionist than Walker.[32] But the Kansas-Nebraska Act had evidently roused his ire. Though Reemelin had supported the Compromise of 1850, the speech he delivered at Mechanics' Hall sounded a far more militant antislavery note. He was no longer for "any compact made with slavery; none could be made that ought to be kept." We of the North, he said, "had been deluded with the idea that slavery was temporary" and would remain geographically confined. The Douglas measure, however, showed that the South considered slavery "permanent and national" in character. "The South thinks they are secure," he concluded, "but let them pass this bill, and the whole slavery question will again be open."

The meeting closed by endorsing unanimously an anti-Nebraska resolution, parts of which echoed those ratified by the earlier *Turnhalle* meeting. The territories were free, "intended by the God of Nature for free men," they said, "and we will never consent that they shall be wrested from their hands to be exhausted by slave labor, and to become the stronghold of oppression." In at least two respects, however, the Mechanics' Hall resolutions differed from those passed earlier at the *Turnhalle*. First, in condemning the Douglas bill for allowing the South "to introduce their negroes within the Territories," those gathered at Mechanic's Hall implied a hostility not simply to slavery but to black people themselves, an attitude common among midwestern anti-Nebraska forces. Second, despite Reemelin's individual remarks, the meeting's threats to fight the bill's passage and implementation were liberally intermixed with conciliatory overtures to the slaveholders. "It is both for the honor and interest of the South," the resolution urged, "to maintain her plighted faith with reference to the Missouri Compromise." No such formulas had been considered necessary by the earlier German anti-Nebraska meeting.[33]

The contemptuous attitude that Democratic regulars continued to display toward the anti-Nebraska movement received an even sharper jolt in late March, when the *Enquirer* itself felt obliged to print a call to a public meeting at Greenwood Hall the evening of Friday, March 24. Entitled "Nebraska: For Freedom and Free Labor," that call bore the names of nearly one thousand individuals who identified themselves as "members of the Democratic party . . . who desire that Ne-

Table 22
Occupations of Cincinnati's Democratic Anti-Nebraska Leaders

Occupational Category	Total Identified (N)	(%)	German (N)	(%)	Non-German (N)	(%)
Economic elite	35	10.1	15	6.8	20	15.5
Professional and white-collar	45	12.9	24	10.0	21	16.3
Officeholders	11	3.2	5	2.3	6	4.7
Small proprietors	48	13.8	30	13.7	18	14.0
Craftsmen	179	51.4	125	57.1	54	41.9
Unskilled	30	8.6	20	9.1	10	7.8
Total accounted for	348		219		129	
Not accounted for	603		472		131	

Sources: Cincinnati city directories. The call appeared in the *Cincinnati Daily Enquirer* of March 23, 1854.

braska should be reserved for free labor, and who oppose its colonization by negro slaves, and who are prepared to resist the repeal of the Missouri Compromise." Judging by the names alone, at least 70 percent of the signatories were of German ancestry, once again suggesting the strength of opposition to slavery's expansion among this part of the city's population. Unable now to deny the magnitude and breadth of anti-Nebraska sentiment, the *Enquirer* acknowledged that the call had been signed "by a considerable number of our political friends, who have always been attached to the principles and organization of the party" and that "there are many others on the list whose Democracy is of an equally unquestionable and adamantine character."[34]

City directories and other sources identify the occupations of 348 (about 37 percent) of the 951 people who signed the Democratic anti-Nebraska call. Of these, 219 had German names, while the remaining 129 did not (see table 22). Most of these 348 people were plebeians, and this was most dramatically true of its German component. More than 60 percent were either craftsmen (57.1 percent) or unskilled laborers (9.1 percent); fewer than 7 percent belonged to the city's economic elite (bankers, major merchants, and industrialists). If we add the category of government officeholders to the economic elite, the proportion still remains below 10 percent.

The prominent physician and Democratic congressman George Fries presided over the meeting at Greenwood Hall.[35] His introductory remarks aimed narrowly at the issue of slavery's geographical expansion. "We have met, Gentlemen," Fries emphasized, "*not* for the purpose of re-opening the dangerous and exciting subject of slavery agitation, with which to disturb the peace and quiet of the community. That work has been more unfortunately done by other parties, and in other quarters, where such treason to all the Compromises for the pacification of this vexed question was least of all to be expected." The Kansas-Nebraska Act was held to be a violation of "Democratic" principles and "democratic" doctrine, especially the doctrine of free soil. "It withholds from the pioneer settlers of this vast country all those rights held sacred by freemen throughout the world, and especially sacred to the true Democracy of the United States," Fries declared.

Charles Reemelin, who again delivered the evening's main address, had evidently cooled down considerably since his earlier, nearly abolitionist speech. He now strove primarily to prove that the Douglas bill was "not in accordance" with the 1820 and 1850 compromises. According to newspaper accounts, Reemelin now acknowledged that "he had acquiesced reluctantly in the compromise of 1850, and if Pierce and Douglas had stuck to it, he would have kept still. He would not have lifted his voice against an administration for which he had voted." At length, however, he turned to some more general considerations. "This country has been called the asylum of the oppressed," Reemelin noted. "If this bill should pass, it might be called the home of the oppressed, for certainly, if the oppressed were at home anywhere, it would be here."

The resolution subsequently adopted by the meeting was drafted by a committee of six individuals, including at least one German, Stephan Molitor. Like the one passed at the predominantly non-German meeting of March 7 at Mechanics' Hall, this resolution struck a balance between more militant and more cautious tendencies. Declaring its hatred for slavery as such, the resolution nevertheless pinpointed the question of slavery's extension as the central issue of the moment. Compromise with the South was earnestly desired, but if "the Slave states are not satisfied with the Missouri Act, and the large additional concessions we have since made, in which we have done violence to our feelings and our principles, but are determined again to become aggressors upon our well established rights and liberties," if "they are determined to draw the sword upon us," that is, then "we shall not hesitate to throw the scabbard away" either. Finally, the assembly took a bold step and resolved that "at the ensuing October election we will vote against any candidate for a seat in the House of Representatives of Congress, who shall not in a public and explicit manner declare his unqualified hostility to the Nebraska bill." The meeting endorsed the resolution and adjourned.

One important component of the German anti-Nebraska constituency was conspicuously absent from the dissident Democratic meeting and from the list of names affixed to its call. Prominent German-American residents such as well-to-do coppersmith Hezekiah Kiersted had helped intitiate and organize the meeting at Greenwood Hall, as had such liberal *Dreissiger* professionals as Stephan Molitor, Charles Reemelin, and J. B. Stallo.[36] But Friedrich Hassaurek, Gottlieb F. Wiest, Kaspar Gams, and other well-known immigrant radicals took no discernible part in the meeting's organization or conduct. They were attending the statewide March convention of German radicals discussed earlier, which was still in session in Cincinnati when the Greenwood Hall gathering occurred. The radicals nonetheless made their sentiments plain on the Nebraska issue. In a resolution sent to and read at Greenwood Hall, the immigrant radicals declared themselves "fully in favor of the object of your meeting . . . as an expression of indignation against the monstrous Nebraska fraud, and promise our hearty cooperation against every extension of slavery."[37]

At their own convention, however, Ohio's German radicals took a considerably more militant, uncompromising stand against slavery and in favor of black rights. "Whigs and Democrats," they declared, "have united around slaveholding, manhunting, and the Nebraska betrayal and have consolidated this firm alliance under the aegis of the southern slaveholders themselves." It was time to turn away from such politicians, they added, declaring that "we are sick of and have forever broken with the old parties." The radical German democrats not only opposed the extension of slavery but went on to demand repeal of the 1850 Fugitive Slave Law, branding it a violation of the letter and spirit of the Declaration of Independence. Even more boldly, they called for the end of slavery itself throughout the United States.[38]

Still the convention had not finished with the general issue. It explicitly separated itself from all attempts to turn free-soil doctrine into an instrument for the exclusion of blacks per se from the states and territories. The convention's general demand that public lands be set aside for settlement by smallholders also stipulated that these lands be distributed to all qualified applicants, "irrespective of color." In antebellum America this was a revolutionary demand, particularly when raised on the Kentucky border; it was championed only by abolitionists and radical free-soilers such as Chase and Giddings. It contrasted vividly with the much narrower concept of free soil expounded by others and with the apparent silence on the subject in the decade-old platform of the *Deutsche demokratische Verein.*

If this radical convention in general angered the pro-Douglas and pro-administration Democrats, its antislavery resolutions left them frankly dumbfounded. The call for outlawing slavery throughout the United States, protested the editor of the *Enquirer,* was "an abolition one, of the most ultra character," and its implementation would violate the federal constitution. The same was true of demands to repeal the Fugitive Slave Law, a measure "guaranteed to the slave holder in that instrument by an express provision." The editor continued: "Another abolition peculiarity is a declaration in favor of giving negroes a free homestead upon the public domain as well as whites. The true policy of this country is to discourage free negroes from remaining in the Union, and to offer every inducement for them to emigrate to other climes, where they can enjoy greater social advantages."[39]

Supporters of the Kansas-Nebraska bill in Cincinnati rallied their forces the following month. The April 5 edition of the *Enquirer* featured a call for a public meeting to endorse Douglas's bill. The wording of the call, however, revealed the defensive stance into which the Pierce administration's supporters had been forced. "We, the undersigned, Democratic citizens of Hamilton County," it announced, "considering as we do the existence of Negro Slavery to be an evil, entailed upon this country by British avarice, and deeming it our duty to resist the extension of that evil by all CONSTITUTIONAL means— do, at the same time hold the usurpation by Congress, of UNCONSTITUTIONAL power, for that or any other purpose, to be a greater EVIL than Negro Slavery itself, pernicious alike to the freedom of the people and to the preservation of this glorious Union." It was thus federal antislavery legislation that constituted the main threat to American liberty. "Therefore," the call concluded, "all those of our fellow-citizens, who value the freedom of the people higher than the treacherous doctrines of abolitionism" should attend a "Mass Meeting of the Democracy" on the evening of Thursday, April 6, at the marketplace on Court Street, at half past seven o'clock."[40]

The list of the call's sponsors is interesting in a number of ways. First, only about 300 people signed the call, fewer than one-third the number who had initiated the anti-Nebraska meeting two weeks earlier. Second, only about one-third of the names on the list were German, compared with more than two-thirds of those listed on the anti-Nebraska call analyzed earlier (see table 22). True, the fact that 101 Germans, including well-to-do and prestigious community members,

Table 23
Occupations of Cincinnati's Democratic Pro-Nebraska Leaders

Occupational Category	Total Identified		German		Non-German	
	(N)	(%)	(N)	(%)	(N)	(%)
Economic elite	14	10.9	3	9.4	11	11.5
Professional and white-collar	42	32.8	9	28.1	33	34.4
Officeholders	13	10.2	5	15.6	8	8.3
Government employees	2	1.6	1	3.1	1	1.0
Small commercial proprietors	13	10.2	6	18.8	7	7.3
Craftsmen	37	28.9	6	18.8	31	32.3
Unskilled	7	5.5	2	6.3	5	5.2
Total accounted for	128		32		96	
Not accounted for	164		69		95	

Sources: Cincinnati city directories; *Cincinnati Daily Enquirer,* April 5, 1854.

had endorsed a pro-Nebraska meeting discounted the *Gazette*'s glib assertion in late February that the Germans opposed the bill "almost to a man."[41] The fact that no more than this number had signed, on the other hand, reinforces the impression that anti-Nebraska views were much more prevalent among the city's Germans than pro-Nebraska sentiment. Finally, occupational analysis indicates important social differences between the pro- and anti-Nebraska German coalitions (see table 23).

Occupations were determined for 128 of the pro-Nebraska signatories, 96 of whom were apparently non-German, 32 apparently German. Compared with the anti-Nebraska list analyzed earlier, this one had a considerably weaker base among skilled producers. Fewer than one in five of the identified German signatories worked in the crafts. Adding unskilled laborers only raises the proportion to one in four. The same occupational groups, in contrast, had accounted for more than half of the identified anti-Nebraska German Democrats. Corresponding to the relatively weak representation of the crafts among the German pro-Nebraska signatories was the relative strength of those with professional and white-collar occupations, primarily clerks and bookkeepers (28.1 percent), and Democratic party leaders and officeholders (15.6 percent).

Once again, the contrast with the anti-Nebraska Germans is marked. Among the latter, very few had been Democratic officials (2.3 percent), and only 10 percent had held professional or white-collar occupations. In a letter to the *Gazette,* an opponent of the bill claimed to find in the pro-Nebraska list few "of the popular element" but many "intimately connected with the wire-pulling of the party," including those employed by the federal government. The occupational analysis presented here lends credence to that writer's accusation. So did the *Enquirer*'s own account, which boasted of the prominence at the meeting of representatives of the Democratic "Old Guard," men whose "names are associated with the history of the party in this city back to its earliest days."[42]

Those gathered at the meeting itself heard and voted for a series of resolutions defending the Douglas bill in the name of popular sovereignty, states' rights, anti-abolitionism, party loyalty, and confidence in the Pierce administration. George Pugh, the new senator from Ohio, explained that the meeting itself "never would have been called had only the Whigs and Abolitionists [opposed] the Nebraska bill. But a meeting of the professed Democracy of Hamilton County had been held to oppose the measure of the Administration and to condemn the President of our choice." This made it necessary for the "true Democracy to assemble and express its sentiments." The *Columbian* pegged attendance at only 500, while the *Gazette* acknowledged the presence of 700. An enthusiastic *Enquirer* found the gathering "immense," attracting upwards of 3,000 people.[43]

Interestingly, however, the *Enquirer* ventured no similarly upbeat assertions concerning the number of Germans present. That subject was broached only in an oblique, but perhaps no less telling, manner—in the paper's coverage of a German anti-Nebraska meeting held simultaneously at the *Turnhalle* (i.e., on April 5). Friendly observers reported a sizable crowd in attendance there, filling the main hall, the galleries, and the antechamber of the saloon. Instead of denying the substantial turnout, the *Enquirer* tacitly acknowledged it, denouncing the meeting as a deliberate ploy to reduce German attendance at the pro-Douglas meeting. Anti-Nebraska German leaders, charged the editor, "well knew that many of their falsehoods and misrepresentations about the character of the Nebraska Bill would be exposed [there], and as they did not want to have the eyes of their deluded votaries opened to the impositions practiced upon them, resorted to the expedient of keeping them away."[44] This was the sound of frustration. It would be heard again.

Chicago: "Beggarly Sans Culottes!"

In early February 1854, a still-confident Stephen Douglas foretold that when the "provisions and principles" of the Kansas-Nebraska Act "have been fully developed and become well understood," his initiative would prove "as popular at the North as at the South." Within a month that prophecy seemed in process of fulfillment as the legislature of Douglas's home state of Illinois formally endorsed his bill.[45]

The senator hoped for similar success in Chicago, where his personal following had always been large and devoted. Although some of its citizens held strong antislavery feelings, Douglas had already proven more than a match for that element. Almost four years earlier antipathy toward the terms of the 1850 Compromise had led the Chicago common council to declare the new Fugitive Slave Law null and void within the bounds of the city. Douglas, as a principal framer of the compromise, had responded personally to this challenge, presenting himself two days later before a large and hostile Chicago crowd. When Douglas concluded his speech that day, that audience voted to repudiate the common council's stand.[46]

Douglas's self-confidence was hardly shaken by the rapid subsequent growth of the city's immigrant population. Here as elsewhere, Irish voters adhered firmly to the welcoming Democratic party. And as recently as 1852, German community leaders—including Körner, Schneider, and land-reform champion Dr. Karl Hellmuth (who had supported the Free Soil party in 1848)—vigorously and successfully stumped for Democratic candidates, including Stephen Douglas. During that campaign, Schneider, the forty-eighter editor of the city's principal German-language newspaper, stressed that triumph for the Democrats would translate into "aid to German patriots."[47]

When in 1854 Douglas once more found himself under attack for his stand on the issue of slavery, he again turned for assistance to native- and foreign-born Democratic stalwarts. In Illinois these included Isaac Cook, a Chicago postmaster and saloon owner, and Alois Zotz, who edited the German-language *Illinois Banner* in Peoria. In Chicago Douglas's strongest ally among the Germans proved to be alderman Michael Diversey, a Catholic immigrant who had arrived during the 1830s. As co-owner (with William Lill) of the Chicago Brewery—the largest such enterprise in the West, capitalized at $300,000—Diversey was now reputed to be the city's wealthiest German resident. He was also a staunch opponent of social and political "ultraism," including antislavery. When Stephen Douglas later sought funds to launch a new German-language newspaper in Chicago, he naturally turned to Diversey. Just as naturally, Diversey obliged. The result was the *National Demokrat,* which the *New Yorker Staats-Zeitung* greeted as a welcome ally.[48]

Michael Diversey's unwavering support for the Democrats grew in value as the Nebraska bill alienated previously dependable German

Table 24
Occupations of Chicago's Anti-Nebraska Petitioners

Occupational Category	All Petitioners		German Names		Non-German Names	
	(N)	(%)	(N)	(%)	(N)	(%)
Economic elite	4	2.8	4	3.4	0	0.0
Professional and white-collar	23	16.0	15	12.7	8	21.1
Small commercial proprietors	13	9.0	13	11.0	0	0.0
Craftsmen	87	60.4	72	61.0	15	57.7
Unskilled	15	10.4	13	11.0	2	7.7
Government employees	1	0.7	0	0.0	1	3.8
Officeholders	1	0.7	0	0.0	0	0.0
Total accounted for	144		118		26	
Not accounted for	621		583		38	

Sources: Chicago city directories.

Chicagoans. One artifact of this defection was a petition against the Nebraska bill submitted to the state legislature in 1854 that bore the signatures of more than 750 names, most of them German (see table 24).[49] Of those Germans whose occupations could be determined, more than 60 percent were craftsmen, notably shoemakers, tailors, carpenters, cabinetmakers, harness makers, and stoneworkers of various kinds—all leading trades of the immigrant craftworkers. If we add those identified as unskilled laborers and small commercial proprietors (principally owners of groceries, taverns, restaurants, and boardinghouses), the percentage climbs above 80. Major merchants, manufacturers, and financiers (the economic elite) accounted for just under 4 percent.[50]

This occupational breakdown highlights two important social-economic characteristics of German anti-Nebraska opinion in Chicago. First, it crossed class lines, as it did generally in the North. Second, its core strength lay in the skilled crafts.

The German anti-Nebraska movement was also diverse in political terms. It involved a coalition between two principal ideological currents, one professing liberal ideals while struggling to restrain the forces of political polarization and social upheaval, and the other, the left wing, which took a more radical and militant stance. The liberal current calls to mind Rosenstein and Dietz in New York City, Heinisch in Newark, and Reemelin, Molitor, and their colleagues in Cincinnati. In Illinois this current's most consistent, articulate, and influential representative was Gustav Körner, one of the country's outstanding liberal emigrés of the 1830s. Körner made his home in the old German community of Belleville, Illinois, situated in downstate St. Clair County, some fifteen miles southeast of St. Louis, just across the Mississippi River. There Körner studied law, and his practice flourished as the leading *Dreissiger* families of southern Illinois found in him an effective advisor and spokesman. Eventually extending his ambitions and constituency statewide, Körner deftly scaled the Democratic ladder, reaching the state supreme court in 1845 and the lieutenant governorship seven years later.[51]

The archetype *Dreissiger* liberal, Körner helped organize his sympathizers' ideological resistance to the forty-eighter radicals. His own stance on chattel slavery grew organically out of his moderately progressive *Weltanschauung*. "I always hated slavery," he could honestly record, but then added with equal accuracy that "constitutionally I saw no way of abolishing it." Like Cincinnati's Charles Reemelin, Körner greeted the Compromise of 1850 with relief, despite its inclusion of a new Fugitive Slave Law, as a way of peacefully resolving this perennial conflict. The *Belleviller Zeitung*, which served as Körner's sounding board in those days, defended the compromise against "the fanaticism of North and South" and in particular excoriated its German-American critics. Among the recent immigrants, asserted the *Zeitung*, antislavery zeal reflected the same extremism that had ultimately doomed the German Revolution—the same "excessiveness, speculation and phrasemongering have ruined everything in the old country."[52]

Four years later, the *Belleviller Zeitung* temporized on the Nebraska bill, taking a clear stand in opposition only after the bill had become law. Körner opposed the Kansas-Nebraska Act on the grounds that— by nullifying previous compromises—it would bring "agitation, strife, and bloodshed, if not . . . civil war." But Körner had canvassed the state in tandem with Stephen Douglas during the 1852 campaign and had become lieutenant governor that year on a Democratic state ticket expressly designed to soothe downstate pro-South sensitivities. These considerations led Körner to keep his own counsel on the Nebraska controversy during much of the year and thus to decline to play a leading role in the developing anti-Nebraska movement.[53] That role he left to his colleague, Francis A. Hoffmann.

Born in Westphalia in 1822, Francis Hoffmann settled in northern Illinois and became a practicing Lutheran minister by 1840. By 1847 he was postmaster of rural Schaumburg Township in Cook County, and in 1851—having left the pulpit, citing ill health—he became county clerk. In that same year Hoffmann moved to Chicago, where he took up the law, then plunged into real estate and soon founded a successful banking house. In 1853 voters in the Eighth Ward elected him to the common council.[54]

In 1854 Alderman Hoffmann shared Körner's displeasure with Douglas's bill but evidently felt freer to act on that sentiment. Hoffmann's prominence and respectability in the German-American population made him a prized speaker at anti-Nebraska meetings, upon which he sought to exert a restraining influence. His speeches commonly combined a moral denunciation of slavery with a defense of the South's constitutional right to maintain it, strong criticism of Stephen Douglas with cautions against precipitously breaking with Douglas's party.

The left wing of the German anti-Nebraska coalition was personified by Eduard Schläger, a forty-eighter veteran and one of the country's most iconoclastic emigré activists. Schläger spent his first years in the United States in Boston, where he edited the *Neu England Zeitung* with Bernhard Domschke (a refugee, freethinker, and cosignatory of the Louisville platform who eventually became president of the national *Turnverein*) and Philip Wagner (a refugee and leader of Boston's *Deutsche Revolutionsverein*).The *Zeitung* quickly became renowned for its generalized democratic radicalism and antislavery fervor; it was one of the very few German-language papers in the country to withhold support from Democratic presidential candidate Franklin Pierce in 1852, campaigning instead for the free soil (Free Democratic) candidate, John P. Hale. That same year, Eduard Schläger served as secretary and Boston delegate to the German Wheeling Conference. Moving on to Chicago soon afterward, he again became well known as an advocate of extreme democratic views. (Gustav Körner singled him out in his memoirs as "a half crazy reformer who made a great noise.") After trying to launch a journal of his own (the *Deutsch-Amerikaner*), Schläger joined the editorial staff of the *Illinois Staats-Zeitung* in 1854, where he remained through the outbreak of the Civil War. Under the direction of emigré Palatine republicans George Schneider and George Hillgärtner, the *Staats-Zeitung* opened its pages (and editorial board) to a spectrum of progressive German figures, from liberal through radical democratic and beyond.[55] Joining Schläger later on was Theodor Hielscher, the schoolteacher noted for his prominence in the Berlin uprising of 1848. Hielscher had first settled in Baltimore, where he helped lead the *Freimännerverein*. He then moved to Indianapolis, where he edited the *Freie Presse* and played an active part in the Turner chapter. At the end of the decade, he moved on to Chicago, where he quickly rose into the leadership of the *Arbeiterverein*.[56]

Chicago's first mass German protest against the Nebraska bill occurred on March 16, 1854, at North Market Hall in the heart of the immigrant Eighth Ward. Its resolutions, roster of officers, and speaker list reflected the political diversity of the coalition that the gathering represented. The meeting's prime mover was Eduard Schläger, who also co-drafted its resolutions and presented a speech of his own. The evening's principal orator, however, was Francis Hoffmann.[57]

Tension between the meeting's liberal and radical democratic participants was apparent all evening. Resolutions cast in a decidedly free-soil rather than abolitionist mold announced an intention to reduce "the slaveholding interest from its present position of a leading power to what it really is, a local institution existing by sufferance."[58] No attempt was made, on the other hand, to minimize the gravity or broader significance of the Nebraska dispute. Resolutions pointedly characterized Douglas's bill as "not a solitary measure, but a logical consequence of similar previous acts, and an ominous prophecy of further attacks upon Northern liberty." So was the Clayton amendment, which—by "reducing the free foreigner to the position now occupied by the slave, who is politically without any rights, and depriving him of all influence against the phalanx of slaveholders" in the territories—betrayed "a spirit, particularly inimical to us Germans, pioneers of the West, as we are." It was thus "high time to make war, not only against the Nebraska Bill, but in general to stand on the offensive" against all such attempts "to increase the preponderance of the slaveholding interest in the union."

The resolutions also blistered those held responsible for this attempt "to introduce Slavery into the Nebraska Territory." Singling out Douglas "as an ambitious and dangerous demagogue" and a "blemish upon the honor of the State of Illinois," the meeting added its "deepest condemnation at the servile manner" in which the Illinois legislature had endorsed Douglas's bill. Still more wide-ranging was the assertion that "the Democratic party and its leaders have, by their sycophancy to the South, called forth this outrage," with the result that "we have lost our confidence, and must look with distrust upon the leaders of the Democratic party, to whom, hitherto, we had confidence enough to think, that they paid some regard to our interests." Angry as this wording was, however, it stopped short of calling explicitly for the Democratic party's destruction. No such call could have received the unanimous endorsement of the body that night.

Francis Hoffmann's speech demonstrated that fact. "We have no inclination whatever to interfere in the rights of the South," Hoffmann stressed, and "though it may be beyond our comprehension how a freeman can enslave his fellow man, yet we will submit. We peaceably submit to what the politicians call the rights of the South." It was only the Nebraska bill's threat to bring slavery "to the free ground of the North," he continued, that compelled men like him to draw the line and warn, "So far, but no further." Stephen Douglas the individual, heretofore "always held in the utmost respect, I might say adoration," had proven himself an apostate, Hoffmann observed, and now "we weep for the fall of a great man of Israel. Henceforth we cannot acknowledge his claims to our esteem."

But Hoffmann was not yet prepared to leave the ranks of the Democratic party itself. It was one thing, after all, to excommunicate a lone heretic. It was something else again to declare a schism in the church. As with Körner, Hoffmann's ties to the Democratic party were strong. "I have been a faithful adherent of the democratic party for the last fourteen years," he recalled. "I honestly and firmly believe that the principal doctrines of that party are truly republican." If in the future, Hoffmann granted, the party were to demand that its office-holders and local organizations endorse "measures at which humanity shudders and against which justice cries out," then it would be necessary to "break the chains that fetter us to that party." But, he insisted, that point had not yet been reached: "This is not a party test, nor a party measure."[59]

Eduard Schläger's speech provided counterpoint. He ventured beyond the wording of the common resolutions to urge an outright break with the Democratic party, just as he and his colleagues on the *Neu England Zeitung* had in 1852. "The time has gone by," he declared that evening, "when it was only necessary to play the fiddle to make the Germans dance to any given tune." The smooth phrases and glib promises of politicians had deluded the immigrants too long. It was "high time the German population ceased being led by the nose by the demagogues of the Democratic Party."[60]

The meeting's aftermath revealed even more starkly the fragility of the sponsoring coalition and especially the volatility of its plebeian base. Following the formal adjournment, a large group of the participants organized themselves into a column and marched from North Market Hall through the German neighborhoods and into the center of the city, stopping at Court House Square. On the way their ranks were swollen by what the *Chicago Daily Tribune* called "swarms" of

Landsleute recruited from the streets. At the square, marchers took
hold of a banner bearing a caricature of Stephen Douglas, tied it to
a rope, hoisted it overhead, and set it ablaze "amidst the hisses, groans,
and hurrahs of the largest number of people ever before assembled in
the city on any public occasion."[61] While "others might talk and write
about these [pro-slavery legislative] acts as if they were merely ordi-
nary acts," one sympathetic observer noted, these German demonstrators, "as consistent republicans," sought to demonstrate "the
intensity of their scorn" with "the very strongest expression of condemnation" that remained "within the limits of the law."[62]

Within months, this scene would be repeated accross the nation.
By summer Douglas himself would ruefully observe, "I could travel
from Boston to Chicago by the light of my own effigy. All along the
Western Reserve of Ohio I could find my effigy on every tree we
passed." But in the middle of March, this early outburst of popular
immigrant fury still appeared to many a startling and disquieting development. Among the native-born, the most negative reactions naturally came from the Democratic press, which had previously courted
the Germans so ardently. The pro-Douglas *Cleveland Plain Dealer* cursed
these immigrant "beggarly sans culottes" as "enemies of peace and
order—of government human or divine." "Such acts," warned another like-minded writer, "are but the first phase of violence and mob
law" and displayed a spirit portending "the direst . . . consequences
that can well be conceived."[63]

Southern senators pointed to the effigy burning to justify restricting the immigrant franchise and excluding prenaturalized aliens from
the benefits of pending homestead legislation. "I ask the senators to
cast their eyes over this country," urged Mississippi's Stephen Adams,
to observe "the number of foreigners . . . see the riots in our cities—
look at their protest," now "see them hang in effigy an American
Senator for having the honesty and independence to mete out equal
justice to all sections of the confederacy." Look at all of this, Adams
challenged, "and then tell me if you do not see a danger." Germans
newspapers duly reported such reactions to their readers.[64]

The spectacle at Court House Square called forth a mixed response
even within the anti-Nebraska camp. The *Chicago Daily Journal* found
it "strange" to see "our German fellow-citizens" burn the effigy of
"their idol, whom they had so long worshipped." "We have yet to
hear the first word in approval of that act," declared the *Daily Democratic Press* more pointedly. "Every citizen from whom we have heard
an expression of opinion at all in relation to the matter condemns it

in unmeasured terms," it noted, adding: "Excesses of this character are sure to injure the cause they are intended to advance."[65]

The debate raged within German Chicago as well. George Schneider of the *Illinois Staats-Zeitung* reportedly "deprecated" the effigy burning; another German opposed to the Nebraska bill also denounced and disowned the action in a public letter, insisting that "the whole thing was managed by a few abolitionist Germans." That letter was answered by another German, however, who ridiculed the "inconsistency" of the first, "who pretends to hate the Nebraska *treason* while he does not dare crush the *traitor*." Fortunately, the reply contended, "the Germans [are] in general . . . not cold-blooded enough to make such nice distinctions."[66]

In the following months, differences within Chicago's German anti-Nebraska movement continued to manifest themselves. One such occasion was a conference called in Peoria that May to unite German democrats across the state. From Chicago came unions of journeymen carpenters and tailors founded during the strike wave of the previous year, as well as organizations of Freemen and Turners. The failure to attract delegates from downstate made the conference a more dependable gauge of the Chicago contingent's views. The platform adopted contained more than a dozen familiar planks—ranging from immigrant rights through religious freedom and including specific demands for expanded public education and a shorter working day. None of these individual subjects, however, was deemed more pressing than that of chattel slavery. On the contrary, the delegates asserted, "We consider the agitation against slavery the most important issue of all." No one was surprised that the convention called for the exclusion of slavery from both Kansas and Nebraska. More remarkable, however, was the conference's forthright denunciation of the state's exclusionary antiblack laws, a position that sharply distinguished the delegates' brand of anti-Nebraska-ism from the more racist variety so prevalent among native-born midwesterners.[67]

Postscript: "Bleeding Kansas"

The ratification of Douglas's bill in the spring of 1854 for a while shifted the locus of struggle over slavery's future into the Kansas Territory itself. There, even settlers initially more concerned with the practical tasks of homesteading than with politics soon became embroiled in the escalating conflict. The thousands of Germans who entered the territory during the 1850s proved no exception. Among those avowed "free-staters" who set out for Kansas from Chicago under the leadership of Vermont-born free-soiler D. J. Gibbs, many were Germans. Turners organized a Kansas settlement society (*Ansiedlungsverein*) of their own. A *Kansas-Zeitung* that styled itself "an organ for free speech, free land, and free men" began publication in the summer of 1857 and apparently continued to appear at least through late 1860.[68]

Although free-soil residents of Kansas enjoyed numerical superiority as early as the fall of 1855, Democratic President Franklin Pierce granted recognition to a territorial government dominated by pro-slavery forces. On May 21, 1856, elements of the latter, bolstered by Missouri reinforcements, invaded the free-state settlement of Lawrence, destroyed its two newspapers, and demolished or looted nearby homes and businesses. Republican journalists apprised German readers elsewhere in the country of the involvement and fate of their *Landsleute* there. During the raid on Lawrence, the *Weekly Chicago Democrat* reported, one German free-stater was taken prisoner by pro-slavery forces while another was "dragged through the streets . . . and most shamefully abused." Both English- and German-language readers learned from one member of the Turners' *Ansiedlungsverein* that "all the Germans in the territory go with the Free State party to a man."[69]

Like most such generalizations, however, this one was an oversimplification that concealed divisions within the local German-born population. To be sure, zealous free-state supporters did include numbers of German immigrants. Among them were Jacob Benjamin, Theodore Wiener, and Charles (Karl) Kaiser, the latter a German-born veteran of the Hungarian Revolution. Another was August (Anshl) Bondi, the youngest member of Vienna's Academic Legion in 1848, whose father and mother now worked, respectively, in a furniture factory and clothing shop in Louisville, Kentucky. All four men joined the partisan band led by John Brown. But the fiercest slave-state partisans in Kansas also included German immigrants like the Sherman brothers, "Dutch Bill" and "Dutch Henry."

Born in Oldenburg, these two men had grown wealthy in Kansas during the previous decade as proprietors of a trading post and tavern catering to westward-bound migrants. Though not slaveowners themselves, the Shermans hated blacks, looked forward to Kansas becoming a "southern" state, and assisted the Missouri-based "border ruffians" who enforced the writ of the pro-slavery territorial government at Lecompton. August Bondi later recalled of these fellow countrymen that they "never shrank from perpetrating crime if it were done in the interests of the pro-slavery cause." They "had been going from house to house of the free-state men, and had threatened that shortly the Missourians would be there and make a clean sweep of them." The Shermans specifically advised Bondi that remaining in Kansas would endanger his health. In the event, it was William Sherman who succumbed: he was among those whom John Brown's party executed in May 1856 at Pottawatomie Creek in retaliation for attacks upon free-staters.[70] In this case, at least, an intraethnic political divide had become a line of blood.

PART IV

"The Second Fight for Freedom"

8

"The Content of Freedom": Germans, Republicans, and Democrats

The Kansas-Nebraska Act and its aftershocks shattered the consensual and organizational foundations of the compromise era. Throughout the country the conviction grew that the future prospects of both labor systems—and of the whole constellation of social relations and values that characterized each of them—would be decided in the new territories. Northern Whigs begged their southern colleagues to oppose the Nebraska bill in the interests of party cohesion; but a secret conference of southern Whig congressmen resolved instead to support the measure. Divisions within the Democratic party deepened, too. Longtime loyalists (such as immigrant banker Francis Hoffmann) watched helplessly as their earnest pleas for tolerance of intraparty differences were impatiently brushed aside. By May, Democratic leaders were declaring Douglas's bill both a party measure and a party test; dissent became heresy. When anti-Nebraska German Democrats tried to raise the issue again a few months later at a downstate Illinois party convention, Douglas stalwarts howled them down.[1]

These developments—and they were the norm rather than the exception—forced a reevaluation of old assumptions, including those concerning partisan alliances and loyalties. In the fall of 1854 makeshift anti-Nebraska electoral tickets representing various coalitions of free-soil Democrats, Whigs, and Americans ("Know-Nothings") appeared on the ballot in a number of of free states. The crystallization of a full-fledged antislavery party climaxed in the Republican presidential campaign of John C. Frémont in 1856. The first national Republican platform denounced the repeal of the Missouri Compromise, called for the admission of Kansas as a free state, and branded slavery "a relic of barbarism" that Congress was duty-bound to exclude from all territories. Despite the victory of Democrat James Buchanan, the presidential campaign mounted by the fledgling Republican party proved a stunning success: Frémont carried eleven out of the sixteen free states with 45 percent of that section's popular vote. Four years later, Lincoln garnered 54 percent of the popular presidential vote outside the slave South, winning every free state but New Jersey.[2]

German-American radicals became intimately involved in this process of party realignment. As we have seen, many had grown dissillusioned with the so-called second party system at an early date—including Karl Heinzen, J. A. Försch, Friedrich Hassaurek, Eduard Schläger, Gustav Struve, August Willich, Joseph Weydemeyer, and Fritz Anneke. If even prior to 1854 Anneke's *Newarker Zeitung* had judged that "the old parties are on the verge of dissolution," the Kansas-Nebraska confrontation only stiffened its stance as "a decided opponent of all the existing political parties" along with his conviction that "the formation of a new genuine party of progress" was "indispensably necessary." Congress's subsequent ratification of Douglas's bill, Anneke believed, rendered that necessity self-evident. "If any proof were still wanting that this [D]emocracy and the slave power is one and the same thing," he wrote, "this proof has now been given." The news coming out of Kansas during the next few years only seemed to add to that proof.[3]

Now, however, new and more specific issues had to be addressed. Exactly what would the "new party of progress" look like? What would it stand for? Who would lead it, and who would support it? Questions like these took center stage in U.S. politics during the 1850s. German-Americans of various social classes and political outlooks brought their own concerns into the resulting debates.

Leaders of the the *Amerikanische Arbeiterbund* had hoped in 1853 to unite American wage earners politically and organize them independently of the nation's dominant propertied classes—whether southern slaveholders or northern capitalists. This was to be accomplished by founding a party based on the working class and its institutions. The *Arbeiterbund's* 1854 call for an independent "organization of working men" to fight the Nebraska bill was evidently conceived as a step in that direction.

Even this interim goal, however, proved unattainable. It was difficult enough to unite the working class in the antebellum era even on the comparatively modest basis of common economic problems and aspirations, as both Weitling and Weydemeyer learned in practice. Differences among native- and British-born, Irish-born, and German-born workers continued to run deep, as did those between skilled workers as yet little affected by economic change and those affected more profoundly. In general, craftworkers cast their lot with unskilled laborers only episodically and briefly.

Durable agreement on fundamental political issues—above all on the issue of slavery—proved even more elusive, and the working-class national anti-Nebraska organization projected by the *Amerikanische Arbeiterbund* never came into being. The stance taken by the most numerous single group of immigrant workers in the nation—the Irish Catholics—captures part of the reason. Few Irish-American workers seem to have participated in the anti-Nebraska protests at all.

Complementing the political disunity of the working class were powerful ideological affinities, already described, between most radical-minded German craftworkers and the more consistently liberal democratic members of the propertied German-American middle class of well-to-do professionals and middling proprietors. Although certain trade-union struggles had already shaken this democratic coalition, few had yet drawn profound political conclusions from that fact. In light of the deep divisions within the working class, indeed, most considered this cross-class alliance of "progressives" too precious to risk in pursuit of the chimera of an independent party of labor.

Joseph Weydemeyer and his associates reluctantly acknowledged these realities and reoriented their policies accordingly. August Willich reached similar conclusions and dismissed talk in the late 1850s of building a specifically working-class party on a national basis. Such a project was precluded, he explained, partly because of the deep-going political disagreements among different ethnic components of the working class. Even the German craftworkers—whom Willich regarded as the most ideologically advanced group in the nation—seemed to him a shaky prop for proletarian political independence.[4]

To these general, long-term factors was added another, conjunctural one. The anti-Nebraska movement and the party it spawned arose at a moment of working-class demobilization. The labor organizations initiated or expanded during the 1853 upsurge were already declining again when Stephen Douglas brought his bill into the Senate. By the time mass protests got underway, unions and other labor organizations had become even weaker. The economic crisis of 1854–55 then delivered a coup de grace, and an even more severe downturn followed in 1857. Only in 1858 did the trade unions, the German organizations included, begin to revive. The Republican party thus took shape and made its first presidential bid when when the labor movement was in disarray, even less capable than previously of formulating (much less imposing) its own political program.

These facts defined the political options of antislavery craftworkers and their associates during the rest of the 1850s. Those who considered the slavery question primary tended to act as members of the broader German plebeian democratic movement, which had its own place within the still more diverse political coalition that supported and strove to influence the young Republican party.

Among the immigrant democratic organizations, the colorful *Turnvereine* were most conspicuous in their support for Republicanism. Members marched and rallied for party candidates in Detroit, Chicago, Cincinnati, Pittsburgh, Philadelphia, Newark, and elsewhere, sometimes dressed in their own distinctive garb, sometimes in the uniform of Republican "Wide-Awakes." Five hundred Turners attended one Frémont rally in New York City. Throughout the free states, crowds of immigrants gathered in open-air meetings and torchlit nighttime rallies to hear men identified with the 1848 Left exhort them to support the Republican party.[5]

These early Republican partisans in New York City included Herman Raster's *Abend-Zeitung,* Rudolph and Felix Lexow's *New Yorker Criminal Zeitung und Belletristisches Journal,* and the *New Yorker Demokrat,* which had played a central role in the anti-Nebraska mobilizations. The last named—edited at various times by Wilhelm Schlüter, Joseph Hartmann, Adolph Douai, Wilhelm Kopp (formerly of the Boston *Arbeiterverein,* later editor of the *Sociale Republik*), and Philip Wagner (lithographer, bookkeeper, and another Struve associate)—became, in Wagner's words, "the house organ of German Republicans." Germans attending Republican rallies in New York listened to speeches from journalists like these as well as from J. A. Försch, Friedrich Kapp, Julius Fröbel, Karl Heinzen, and Fritz Jacobi.[6] The Cincinnati *Hochwächter* rallied early to the new party as well. In Chicago George Schneider, Eduard Schläger, and Caspar Butz (recently transferred from Detroit, where he had helped lead the *Arbeiterverein* and bring out Esselen's *Atlantis*) spoke for the Republicans.[7]

In Philadelphia leading German Republicans included such veteran labor leaders as mechanic Franz Arnold and shoemakers C. Ludwig (Louis) Mahlke and T. Conrad Liebrich as well as Friedrich Schünnemann-Pott (a one-time baker's apprentice who had become speaker, or lay leader, of the Philadelphia *freie Gemeinde*), and freethinking businessman Nikolaus Schmitt. The city's first meeting of German Republicans took place in the *Arbeiterhalle* at the corner of Third and Green streets.[8] Newark labor activists and sometime *Arbeiterverein* leaders who campaigned for the Republicans included Fritz Anneke, G. Schäfer, and Hermann Kreitler. These men, in turn, collab-

orated with other forty-eighters who had played a prominent role in
the city's anti-Nebraska protests—most notably Ludwig Greiner,
Friedrich Lehlbach, and Fridolin Ill.[9] Theodor Hielscher—renowned
for his outspoken role in Berlin in 1848 and later a founder of Baltimore's *Verein freier Menschen*—now edited the *Indiana Volksblatt* in
Indianapolis. Hielscher was one of the most outspoken and consistent
Republicans in the city.[10] Maryland's only Republican newspaper was
printed in German. The Baltimore *Wecker* (Alarm) enjoyed the further distinction of being the only German Republican newspaper in
the entire South in 1856. The *Wecker* appeared under the editorial
direction of Carl Heinrich Schnauffer (veteran of the armed struggle
in Baden), Wilhelm Rapp (Schnauffer's old comrade-in-arms), and
August Becker (Cologne Communist Trial defendant and later an editor of the Cincinnati *Hochwächter*). It enjoyed close ties with the city's
Sozialistischer Turnverein. In 1860 the Republican party's first mass
meeting in the city took place at the *Turnhalle*.[11]

Campaign Themes

In 1856 and afterward, German radicals campaigning for Republicanism among their *Landsleute* stressed two interrelated themes. At
the most general level, they emphasized political and philosophical
consistency and continuity with the ideals of 1848. The national *Turn-
Zeitung* explained its support for Lincoln in such ideological terms:
"We Turners fight against slavery, Nativism, or any other kind of restriction based on color, religion, or place of birth, since all this is
incompatible with a cosmopolitan viewpoint."[12]

Forty-eighter radicals had long argued (against nativist and even
immigrant critics) that their own outlook and goals were basically the
same as those historically associated with the American Revolution
and American democracy. During the second half of the 1850s this
argument was turned around; radical German Republicans depicted
resistance to slavery as the duty of all honest partisans of European
democracy and foes of aristocratic reaction. Gustav Struve called upon
his "comrades of 1848 and 1849" to fight for freedom in the New
World "in the spirit of the martyrs of the German Revolution." Adolph
Douai trusted that his fellow Germans had not "lost the hatred of
every kind of slavery" that impelled them to travel abroad and would
therefore still "acknowledge freedom for everyone." The editor of the
Syracuse, New York, *Demokrat* affirmed at a Republican mass meeting that "the men who fought in Germany for freedom will in this

country also fight for freedom." Have "we become so degraded," Friedrich Kapp demanded on one occasion of between three and four thousand listeners, "as to conclude a peace here with the same party against whom we fought in Europe?" "No! No!" his audience reassured him. In New York, Pittsburgh, Chicago, Buffalo, and elsewhere, Friedrich Hecker warned massive crowds that failure to vote for the Republicans would be "a betrayal of their flag and their past." On these occasions, the singing of the *Marseillaise*—a common part of mass meetings of German Republicans—served to underline the kinship between European and American democracy.[13]

Rich in drama, symbolism, and logical rigor, this line of argument nonetheless remained rather abstract. German Republican speakers and writers strove to concretize it by emphasizing the practical implications for immigrant plebeians of the decade's electoral struggle. No less than despots and aristocrats in the Old World, they argued, the so-called Democrats and their slaveholding masters endangered the rights and living standards of German working people in the United States in a more immediate, palpable way. In the face of that threat, the Republicans, for all their failings, offered free laborers the only protection available. Radical German Republicans began stressing the practical appeal of Republicanism for plebeians at an early date. "Kansas Belongs to Labor, not to Slavery," proclaimed Brooklyn's German Republicans in 1856. The national *Turn-Zeitung* couched its endorsement of Frémont in the same language: the Pathfinder was the "candidate of labor and the settler."[14]

The most effective Republican appeals to German voters combined the abstract theme with the more practical one. Frémont supporters meeting at Philadelphia's *Arbeiterhalle* in June 1856 raised their voices in a new "*Republikanische Marseillaise.*" Written by the head of the *freie Gemeinde,* the anthem exhorted,

> Raise this battle cry
> In the holy freedom war:
> Free speech! Free press!
> And land and men both free!
> Frémont! With him to victory!

The song quickly caught on and was heard in other cities as well.[15]

A huge rally in New York City that fall once more exemplified this juxtaposition of abstract and concrete.[16] Seven to ten thousand German natives thronged the Academy of Music on Tuesday, October 7, at the call of the German Central Republican Committee. "Most of the Germans here," declared the committee's president, Friedrich Kapp, had "taken part in the late struggle for independence" from autocracy in their homeland, so the huge turnout that day was only "to be expected from the men who followed the republican banner in the old country and [who] will be its true followers in their adopted home." Gustav Struve declared it "a day of rejoicing for thousands who, driven from their native soil and suffering here in exile, assemble in this free soil to greet the rising of a new day of freedom." The fruits of victory would nourish the hopes of those left behind as well, Struve asserted, since "if Freedom shall be restored" in America, "the oppressed of Europe will look confidently to this hemisphere as a new area of liberty."

Friedrich Hecker also expressed satisfaction at the opportunity "to again address" so many "old friends, who in former years had battled for freedom" in their fatherland. Hecker ridiculed the slaveowners who called themselves and their party Democratic; they "made the name of Democracy nothing but a byword." The so-called Democrats were not friends but deadly enemies of free laborers. How could "a man who would be free" help them "to steal territories for the Southern barons from free labor"? The victory of the proslavery party, indeed, would make European oppression seem benign by comparison. "The tyranny of the slaveholders is worse than the despotism of the czar of Russia," Hecker warned his audience. So "if the Slave Democracy should win the victory, then go, go my [listeners], to Russia! There, in that country of despotism, you will be freer than here!"

"The Content of Freedom"

Some major differences set German democrats apart from the Republican party mainstream. Most radical German Republicans, for example, looked upon the so-called social question in a manner that distinguished them from the great majority of native-born party leaders. As Eric Foner notes, Republican leaders, including those affiliated with its most abolition-minded wing, were generally "satisfied with the economic and social order they perceived in the North." They "saw the people's needs and desires through the eyes of the vigorous new elite of manufacturers and promoters," David Montgomery adds.[17]

The response of the German-American Left, however, to the economic shocks of 1854–55 and 1857 bespoke distinct assumptions and priorities that set it apart from the Republican party. Some of Frémont's most ardent immigrant partisans—including Peter Rödel and J. A. Försch in New York and Fritz Anneke in Newark—in these years supported demands by unemployed workers for municipal employment and sustenance. In the first issue of the *Sociale Republik* (New York), the editors defined their relationship to Republican party leaders as follows: "Along with them, we want a free Kansas, but not only that. We want a free Union! Freedom of the soil, freedom for labor, freedom for immigration." Their specific demands included the prohibition of exorbitant interest rates on loans, a struggle against government corruption, and both education and health care for the poor. In short, "We want not only the form but also the content of freedom as expressed in the words 'Welfare and Education for All!'" August Willich's *Cincinnati Republikaner* waged war upon "Whig principles in the Republican party." German trade unionists and other democrats in Cincinnati wanted government measures to discourage land speculation and sought an end to the chartering of banks of issue. The Chicago *Arbeiterverein*, which assumed leadership of the national German-American labor movement in early 1860, called for a new mechanics' lien law. Sharply divergent views were expressed on the subject of protective tariffs. But the concrete demand that attracted the most fervent and universal support among plebeian German Republicans was the call for land reform, a plank still absent from the party's national platform in 1856.[18]

As for slavery and its future—the Republican party's founding and defining issue—German radicals often found themselves in agreement with the party's "Radical" wing. Following the election of 1856, some Republican leaders attributed Frémont's defeat to his failure to win the confidence of more conservative-minded (especially Whig) voters in such free states as Illinois, Indiana, and Pennsylvania. Republican victory, these men argued, required (among other things) softening and downplaying the Republican stance on slavery. The falling-out between Stephen Douglas and James Buchanan over Kansas in 1857–58 seemed to point the way. A number of prominent eastern Republicans endorsed Douglas's bid for reelection to the Senate in 1858, and the *New York Daily Times* even counseled Republicans to abandon categorical opposition to the admission of any new slave states in favor of the popular sovereignty formula.[19]

More resolute antislavery elements throughout the party dug in their heels. For their part, German democrats in the party cited their European experiences to urge rejection of temporizing counsel. If southern planters and their political allies evoked the European counter-revolution, indeed, then Republican compromisers called to mind Frankfurt's ineffectual liberal majority. August Bondi dismissed vacillators among the free-state forces in Kansas as "cowards" who "belonged to that class with whom interest always counts for more than principle, as was the case in 1848 in Germany." The very first issue of the *Sociale Republik* complained that "the American Republicans strongly resemble the European liberals of the pre-1848 years." Theodor Hielscher drew the same parallels in early 1860. Conservative Republicans, he charged, "would nominate a ticket and make a platform for which even the slaveholders of Georgia could vote and on which even they could stand." Men like these always lacked the foresight and firmness required for victory in sharp conflicts. "In 1848," he recalled acidly, "during the revolution in Germany, there was [*sic*] also such men." "Though others could see that the kings, dukes and princes had formed a secret league in order to overthrow the popular will, these gentlemen boldly asserted that they were 'unable' to see the signs of the gathering storm. . . . And yet I remember having met one of these men who could not see a 'reaction,' as it was called in 1848, fleeing before the bayonets of the soldiers in 1849, and all he had to say, when I asked him whether he was now able to see the 'reaction,' was 'Who would have throught it possible!' " Hielscher and those who shared his sentiments determined not to repeat that experience, not to permit trimmers to mislead and disarm the progressive movement in the new world.[20]

Far from supporting a retreat from the 1856 Republican program, indeed, German democrats fought to defend and deepen the party's antislavery policy. The central committee of the *Allgemeine Arbeiterbund von Nord-Amerika*—which included such longtime craftworker activists as the tailor leader Victor Pelz and shoemaker leaders Philip Stoppelbein and Peter Rödel—called in the fall of 1858 for completing the work begun in 1776 and 1848 in America, thereby turning this "glorious country of freedom, with all its abundant land, into a free state for all free men." In such "a free democratic republic . . . slaveholders will brandish no whips" nor break up any more families on the auction block. Repeal of the Fugitive Slave Law was a necessary first step in that direction. German Republicans in Newark agreed and insisted on no further expansion of slavery. In association with the *Turnverein* and other democratic societies, Cincinnati's *Socialer Arbeiterverein* called a series of meetings repeatedly pressing these same demands and criticizing the Republican party for soft-pedling the slavery issue. The Supreme Court's proslavery decision in the Dred Scott case (1857) provoked the demand for "a reorganization of the federal judiciary, which must be elected by the people."[21]

The stress placed on the Fugitive Slave Law was neither arbitrary nor fortuitous. It involved these German democrats in what was, as

Eric Foner has noted, one of "the most strident controversies" to occur within antebellum Republicanism, a controversy that pitted the party's more ardently antislavery elements against its conservatives and moderates. A commitment to preserve and honor the Fugitive Slave Law would signify a continued belief in the viability of compromise over slavery and, more than that, it would mean acknowledging property rights in human beings and the obligation of state and federal governments to enforce those rights.[22]

John Brown's Raid

The same antislavery ardor that scorned Republican conciliators and repudiated the Fugitive Slave Law also expressed itself in response to John Brown's raid on Harpers Ferry in 1859. August Bondi's scorn for Frankfurt-type vacillators in Kansas had led him to join John Brown's partisans in that territory. A few years later, the *Turn-Zeitung,* now edited and published by members of a Baltimore chapter under considerable pressure to moderate their antislavery principles, hastened to distance itself from the Harpers Ferry raid. That decision, however, called forth angry denunciations from Turner chapters in the free states. The German Republican newspaper of Davenport, Iowa, believed Brown would find "an outstanding place in the history of this Republic." Karl Heinzen praised Brown as the "pride and disgrace of this Republic, its most courageous martyr and hero in the cause of liberty." The organ of the national *Allgemeine Arbeiterbund von Nord-Amerika* declared Brown and his comrades to be "martyrs for freedom."[23]

Nor were such inflammatory sentiments confined to the printed page. Chicago's German Jefferson Club convened a public gathering where Caspar Butz praised Brown for being ready to fight for his principles not only with words but also with deeds. Brown, moreover, "had shown Virginia that the handwriting is on the wall—a writing not to be obliterated till the giant wrong of slavery was obliterated." In so doing, Eduard Schläger added, "John Brown had turned his own defeat into a great victory." A meeting of German Republicans in Milwaukee warned more bluntly that "if the last means to solve that slavery question in a peaceful manner fails, it would . . . be perfectly justifiable to gain that end in revolutionary ways," in which case "all responsibility for such a necessary step will rest on the heads of those who persistently refuse to abolish, by means of reform, an institution that disgraces our century and this republic."[24]

One of the most dramatic meetings took place in Cincinnati's German "Over the Rhine" district. On Sunday afternoon, December 4, 1859, a gentleman strolling through that neighborhood came upon an unusually large crowd filing into the building long shared by the *Freimänner-* and *Arbeitervereine*. Curious, he entered, too, later describing what he found in a published account signed only, "Spectator."[25]

The main floor and galleries of the hall were packed, Spectator reported. Some two-thirds of those present were Germans; most of the rest were black—"lineal descendants of Ham." Black-red-gold banners hung from the gallery, and on the main stage were the Stars and Stripes, "with a stalwart nigger as standard bearer." The purpose of this singular gathering became clear when Spectator turned toward the speaker's platform. It was draped in the black crepe of mourning and bore the words, "In Memory of John Brown." Among those who spoke was the Unitarian minister Moncure Daniel Conway, destined to become the outstanding advocate of Thomas Paine's ideas and the editor of his works. John Brown, Conway asserted on this occasion, was "the last apostle and martyr" of "Paine's creed." After Conway came Peter A. Clark, the black abolitionist principal of the Western District Colored School. Clark was gratified to "address a meeting of the only freedom-loving people of this city," the only ones who were prepared "to do justice to his race" and to "to vindicate the principles of freedom."

But Spectator seemed most shaken by the words of a third speaker—August Willich, leader of the city's *Arbeiterverein* and editor of its newspaper. Spectator listened in stunned disbelief as Willich not only mourned Brown and denounced slavery, the Democratic party, and its supporters but also "exhorted his hearers to whet their sabers and nerve their arms for the day of retribution, when Slavery and Democracy would be crushed in a common grave." No less alarming than these speeches was the reaction of the interracial crowd. The fiery words delivered from the podium, Spectator reported indignantly, "received the rapturous applause of the motley gathering." Indeed, he continued, "the fiercer the denunciations of slavery and Democracy, the more uproarious were the woolly-heads and their allies."

In its quest for German standard-bearers, the Republican party found recruits outside the circle of radical democrats. The crisis of the second party system split the ranks of German moderates during the later 1850s. Some—and particularly those whose ties to the Democratic leadership were fraying even before 1854—joined the Republican party in its first period of existence. Prominent among them was the founder and patriarch of Missouri's Germania, Friedrich Münch of St. Louis. Johann Stallo, Stephan Molitor, and the Cincinnati *Volksblatt* also shifted their allegiance at an early stage in the Republican party's development. So did Philadelphia counterparts Theodore Pösche (coauthor of *The New Rome*) and George Seidensticker.[26]

For others, however, political principles combined with more pragmatic considerations—especially a mutually satisfactory partnership with native-born Democratic leaders—to make conversion to Republicanism slower and more difficult. Gustav Körner's example illustrates this general pattern. As late as February 1856, Körner was still spurning nomination to the Illinois Republican central committee, although by then even so cautious a group of men as ex-Democrats Francis Hoffmann and Lyman Trumbull and former Whigs Orville H. Browning and Abraham Lincoln had joined the new party. While "a mere opposition party may please those who have their eyes upon political preferment," Körner explained in self-justification, it "does not satisfy me." The words were a bit disinguous. When he uttered them, Körner was Illinois's lieutenant governor, having attained that enviable post of "political preferment" through loyal service to the Democratic party. He was loath to abandon that partisan relationship. More instructive were Körner's caveats of principle; he could not "cooperate with any party" that was unwilling to "affirmatively maintain that the Constitutional rights of the Southern states should never be interfered with."[27]

Eventually swept into Republican ranks by the accelerating political polarization that he had earnestly resisted, Körner was gratified to find the new party firmly in the hands of men with whom he saw eye to eye on many issues. Former Whigs and former Democrats, these men agreed on the need (as Browning phrased it in a letter to Lyman Trumbull in 1856) "to keep the [Republican] party in this state under the control of moderate men—and conservative influences—[for] if we do, the future destiny of the state is in our hands and victory will inevitably crown our exertions; on the other hand, if rash and ultra counsels prevail, all is lost." At the state and national levels, native-born Republican moderates retained control of the party from 1856 through 1860. That fact facilitated the recruitment of additional German moderates as well.[28]

For native-born moderate Republican leaders, the recruitment of immigrant liberals such as Körner, Hoffmann, and Molitor offered a dual advantage. They allowed the party to turn a friendly face toward German voters, including those hostile to the more radical-minded among their own countryfolk. It was Körner, thus, who cautioned Lincoln about Friedrich Hecker's liability as a campaign speaker;

"amongst the Catholicks [*sic*] and even orthodox protestants," Körner advised, Hecker "is considered the very Anti-Christ." At least equally important was the assistance that immigrant moderates offered in diluting the intraparty influence of more "rash and ultra" German Republicans.[29]

Such considerations helped clear a path for German moderates to positions of considerable "political preferment" within the new party. The Illinois organization offered Francis Hoffmann its nomination for lieutenant governor in 1856. By the fall, Gustav Körner—having more tardily rallied to the cause—was a highly touted speaker at party rallies and demonstrations who worked diligently both to muster German voters and to keep them in line. His speech in Chicago the night of June 4, 1856, faithfully reflected this dual goal. The *Turnverein* had just led thousands of German residents on an enthusiastic campaign demonstration through the city's streets. That march fed into a crowd waiting to hear speakers promote the cause of free soil, free labor, and Frémont. Körner declared that while "the Germans . . . were for free territory," they "were not given to fanaticism of any kind. They would oppose the fanaticism of the North just as they were now opposing the fanaticism of the South." John Brown's October 1859 raid on the federal arsenal at Harpers Ferry, Virginia, brought such differencess into sharp relief. Körner considered the raid "a totally insane attempt" carried out by a "monomaniac, insane on this one point." More shocking to Körner were those who praised Brown and his motives even while rejecting the raid itself as illegal and unwise. Worst of all, however, were "some of the German radical press [who] went so far as to exalt, not only the man, but the act itself."[30]

Divergences over policy between radical and moderate German Republicans transcended the issues of sectional conflict. We have already surveyed some of the more deep-seated social-political divisions in German America. Affiliation of both radical and moderate Germans to Republicanism carried these differences into the new party. The economic crisis of 1857 cast a bright spotlight upon them. Hermann Kreismann, a liberal attorney appointed Chicago city clerk by the new Republican mayor, John Wentworth, helped to dissuade German workers from seeking "work or bread" from the city government. Demands such as these, Kreismann argued, were both un-American and antirepublican and were put forward "to prejudice the German citizens against the city government and, if possible, the cause of law and order." That road led only to ruin. The immigrant jobless, he emphasized, must avoid all "extreme action." Republican leaders clearly appreciated Kreismann's efforts. Those who had raised the divisive class demands in the first place, asserted the Republican editor of the *Chicago Daily Tribune,* had tried to foment "revolutionary proceedings in our midst." The retreat from these demands, on the other hand, reflected the presence of "staid, quiet, and order-loving citizens" among the foreign-born who were able to give the meetings of the unemployed the "the proper direction" and thereby "save the German name from the discredit that might otherwise have been brought upon it." The editor added the hope—cherished alike by "all the American friends of the Germans"—that "the proposition laid down in Kreismann's practical speech may be adhered to at all hazards." In short: "Let us have no European socialism here." (Ideological affinities such as these, moreover, had a way of becoming firm political and personal alliances. State Republican chairman Norman Judd soon took young Kreismann under his wing, and when Judd later received the coveted post of ambassador to Berlin, Kreismann became his embassy secretary.)[31]

The German Democrats

Whatever differences divided them, German Republicans united against those strongly rooted and influential elements in the immigrant population who fought to keep the German vote Democratic. The core of the German-American Democratic leadership included large numbers of earlier immigrants—notably substantial mercantile and manufacturing elements, newspaper publishers, and the more conservative clergy—who were more firmly tied to the economic, political, and ideological status quo than most newcomers. Such people confronted Carl Schurz during his campaign tours, those "ingrained partisans of the opposite creed . . . who, in some instances, had established a partisan leadership." When "impudent young intruders" tried to present the Republican case in those communities, Schurz recalled, entrenched immigrant Democratic leaders resisted "not seldom with a sort of fanatical ferocity." They feared and resented "everything that seemed to threaten the power and prestige of their party" and so "dared to invade the circle of their influence." Irish Democrats, Frederick Douglass believed, should "be pitied as well as blamed," since "some excuse perhaps may be found" for their actions in poverty, ignorance, and degradation. "Far otherwise is it with the Germans," however. Among German Democratic leaders, Douglass noticed, there were men "entirely independent as to means" whose political ties could be explained only by reference to "base and sordid" motives.[32]

As it happens, the most influential German-born Democrat in this period was indeed one of the wealthiest of his countrymen—the financier August Belmont. Legend has it that in 1856 Belmont presented $50,000 of his own funds to aid the Democratic campaign in Pennsylvania, more than twice the sum that New York's entire Republican organization managed to raise to assist Frémont's efforts there. Whatever the actual size of his donation, Belmont's sympathies were clear. Merciless in his denunciation of the "abolitionist" Republicans, Belmont congratulated the victorious Buchanan lavishly. Belmont remained loyal to the White House when even Stephen Douglas balked at Buchanan's openly proslavery policy in the Kansas territory. He finally switched from Buchanan to Douglas only in 1859, and then, it seems, principally because Buchanan had disappointed Belmont's ardent hopes for a diplomatic appointment. In the aftermath of Harpers Ferry, Belmont cosponsored a mass meeting at the New York Academy of Music called to repudiate abolitionism, Republicanism, "John Brownism," and all other (antislavery) threats to national unity. In 1860 Belmont energetically pushed Stephen Douglas's bid for the presidency and was himself elected chairman of the Northern Democratic party's Central Committee. In New York he convinced scions of the Astor dynasty and other Douglas Democrats of the merits of "fusion"—that is, of confronting Republicans with a single slate representing Douglas, Breckinridge, and Bell—and then presided over the great citywide fusion rally of November 2, 1860.[33]

Gustav A. Neumann of the *New Yorker Staats-Zeitung* and the Customs House worked closely with Belmont as leader of the Democratic party's German Central Committee in the city. As the de facto organ of New York's prosperous German-American businessmen, the *Staats-Zeitung* fought against Republicanism with all the influence and invective at its command. Its editors spoke in New York and elsewhere in support of the Democratic administration in both 1856 and 1860 while they railed in editorial columns against the "black Republican Nigger love" of *Achtundvierziger* newspapers, which they dismissed as "*Niggerblätter.*" German Democrats meeting at New York's Cooper Institute in October 1860 boasted a roster of officers and speakers that included the *Staats-Zeitung*'s Oswald Ottendorfer, various local Democratic officeholders, plus (in the envious words of the Republican *Times*) "many of the most prominent German merchants and business men of the City," among them Leopold Bamberger and auctioneer William A. Kobbe.[34]

Other German papers that remained Democratic included Cincinnati's *Wahrheits-Freund* and *Volksfreund,* the Cleveland *Germania,*
Milwaukee's *Banner und Volksfreund* and its Catholic newspaper, the
Seebote, Detroit's *Michigan Demokrat,* the Louisville *Anzeiger,* Indianapolis's *Indiana Volksblatt,* and the Buffalo *Demokrat.* In Chicago
the liberal forty-eighter and banker Heinrich Greenbaum stood by
Stephen Douglas throughout the decade. In 1855 Douglas secured
the financial sponsorship of a group including wealthy German brew-
master and alderman Michael Diversey for a new Democratic German-language organ, as mentioned earlier. When President Buchanan's extreme pro-slavery policy in Kansas finally forced Douglas to
part ways with the White House, Diversey and the *National Demokrat*
broke with Douglas (and most Chicago Democrats) rather than abandon Buchanan. By 1860 the advancing isolation of German Democrats in Illinois (as in Missouri, western Pennsylvania, and elsewhere)
left them heavily dependent upon out-of-state speakers for their campaign rallies. The forty-eighter and antislavery *Wecker* did not speak
for all Germans in Baltimore. The principal organ of the city's German-American elite, the *Correspondent,* remained staunchly Democratic. So did immigrant tobacco merchants who formed the core of
Baltimore's exclusive Germania Club and who prized their good relations with planters.[35]

Reflecting the high stakes and strong feelings involved in the decade's partisan contests, confrontations often escalated beyond rhetoric. As Carl Schurz toured the country, he later recalled, German
Democrats "tried all sorts of means, even by threats, to keep people
away from my meetings. They interrupted my speeches by catcalls and
other disturbing noises. Occasionally they went so far as to break the
windows of the halls in which I spoke by throwing stones or even
more disagreeable missiles." Radical German Republicans could respond in kind. In Newark, Fritz Anneke greeted Democrats who were
assaulting a Frémont rally with a hail of paving stones. In Chicago,
die-hard German Democrats fought bitterly and desperately against a
German Republican groundswell. In 1856 they tried disrupting German Republican mass meetings, burned an effigy of the editor of the
Illinois Staats-Zeitung, marched on that paper's editorial offices, and
finally threatened to seize the premises and put all to the torch. Only
the timely arrival of armed Chicago Turners induced the would-be
arsonists to reconsider. "One of the Turners went to the door with
a revolver in his hand and invited the gay Nebraskals to 'mob,'" the
Staats-Zeitung gleefully recounted, "provided they should intend to
digest the lead contents of his six-shooter."[36]

Although many German-American liberals went over to the Republican party and quickly rose in its ranks, others—especially those of *Dreissiger* vintage—held back. Among them were individuals who had opposed the Kansas-Nebraska Act in 1854 but balked at joining a new party defined on that basis. In the face of the overwhelming support for Republicanism expressed by forty-eighter publications, indeed, the *New Yorker Staats-Zeitung* took pride in the number of *Dreissiger* newspapers and politicians who remained within the German Democratic fold. The Columbus *Westbote,* having voiced its criticisms of the Nebraska bill in 1854, thus returned to the Democratic ranks in 1856 and denounced "German confusionists" who did otherwise. George Dietz, a prodigal editor of the *New Yorker Staats-Zeitung* who had addressed an anti-Nebraska meeting in 1854, not only rallied to Buchanan in 1856 but spoke for the Democratic party in cities where German Democrats were scarce. Joseph Fickler, a liberal Catholic freethinker and forty-eighter emigré from Constanz who became a New York hotel owner, stood by the Democrats in 1856 and backed John Bell in 1860. Dr. Edward Morwitz, a liberal physician who had fled Danzig and had published the *Demokrat* in Philadelphia, kept that paper in the Democratic column, too. *Dreissiger* John Laible, a sponsor of Newark's anti-Nebraska protests, remained loyal to the Douglas Democrats through 1860, when he joined prominent fellow brewers Adolph and Herman Shalk in publicly endorsing the Democratic ticket. Milwaukee's Francis Hübschmann, a leading liberal freethinker and a founder of the city's German Democratic Association, stayed with the Democratic party, as did others of his circle.[37]

In Cincinnati the prominent *Dreissiger* liberal Heinrich Rödter remained an active Democrat till the day of his death in 1857. The well-to-do coppersmith Hezekiah Kiersted, who had joined the anti-Nebraska movement in 1854, nonetheless strove energetically throughout the decade to keep the city's Germans in the Democratic camp. Other prominent Democratic stalwarts in Cincinnati included Frank Höffer (a *Dreissiger* realtor and agent who had served as the first vice president of the German Democratic Association in 1846) and General August Moor (a liberal *Dreissiger* military officer who achieved distinction and local hero status during the Mexican War).[38]

Their fellow Cincinnatian Karl Reemelin had been quite outspoken and active in the 1854 protests, but his antislavery ardor perceptibly cooled over the course of that year. In 1856 Friedrich Hassaurek engineered Reemelin's selection as delegate to the preliminary Republican convention in Pittsburgh, attempting thereby to broaden the party's German base of support. Reemelin reluctantly accepted but then removed himself from the campaign proper by taking a European tour. By 1860 his political about-face was unmistakable. Surveying the four presidential candidates in the field that year, Reemelin dismissed Stephen Douglas out of hand. John Bell, although the candidate of the Constitutional Unionist party formed by pro-Compromise Whigs and Know-Nothings, seemed better. At least, Reemelin judged, Bell's election would not bring "any serious trouble upon the country." Ultimately, however, Bell's nativism disqualified him in Reemelin's eyes. Briefly impressed with Lincoln, Reemelin at last rejected the Republican as too ready to employ federal power in the service of antislavery. This process of elimination left only Vice President John C. Breckinridge, candidate of the Southern Democrats, whose platform promised federal guarantees for the sanctity of slave property in all territories, "faithful execution of the Fugitive Slave Law," and "acquisition of the Island of Cuba" (a longtime goal of southern fire-eaters). Reemelin nevertheless endorsed him in the conviction that Breckinridge "was no pro-slavery man, that he desired a settlement, which would have left us the integrity of our constitution and saved personal liberty; all without war and its bloody and other false solutions." Nor did Reemelin keep this decision quiet; he stood as a Breckinridge elector in Cincinnati.[39]

Democrats managed to hold the allegiance even of some individuals identified with the German-American Left. One of these was Karl Hellmuth, the Chicago physician, land reformer, early editor of the *Illinois Staats-Zeitung,* and supporter of the Free Soil party in 1848. Hellmuth had opposed the Nebraska Act in 1854 but was once again lending his name to the Democratic cause in 1856. Wilhelm Wagner of the Freeport, Illinois, *Deutscher Anzeiger,* also remained a Democratic loyalist. So did Conrad Hollinger, the forty-eighter editor of Newark's *Volksmann,* who had ties to the city's *Arbeiterverein.* Gottlieb Kellner, formerly involved in the *Amerikanische Arbeiterbund* and coeditor of the New York *Die Reform,* subsequently moved to Philadelphia, became editor-in-chief of the anti-Republican *Demokrat,* and spoke for the Democratic ticket elsewhere in the state as well. Wilhelm Rosenthal, Philadelphia freethinker, former president of the *Arbeiterverein,* and former editor of the *Freie Presse,* also spoke for the party in 1856.[40]

In the spring of 1858 a group led by one William Benque briefly vied for the leadership of the German-American labor movement and published a newspaper entitled *Der Arbeiter* in New York's *Kleindeutschland.* Pro-Republican leaders of the Newark *Arbeiterbund* refused to collaborate with this group, citing the latter's initial attempt to evade the issues of political action and slavery. Thereafter *Der Arbeiter* began devoting considerable column space to a multipart series entitled "Sklaverei" that elaborated views similar to those propounded by the *New Yorker Staats-Zeitung*. *Der Arbeiter* denounced the agitation of abolitionists and repeated the assertions of southern congressmen that slaves were treated better than northern wage earners. Refusing to condemn slavery on principle or even its westward expansion, the paper called only for a crackdown on the already illegal Atlantic slave trade. It also insisted that all slaves manumitted in the United States be promptly colonized abroad. Critics in the labor movement now branded *Der Arbeiter* as an agent of Tammany Hall (and possibly of the Prussian government as well), and Benque and his associates soon found themselves expelled from the *Allgemeine Arbeiterbund*.[41]

The fight with Benque was no marginal incident. As sectional and partisan conflict mounted, the issue of slavery and its future pushed steadily toward the center of German-American political life.

9

"The Spirit of 1848": Nationality, Class, and the Fight for Votes

Northern Democrats did not, to be sure, depict themselves as enthusiastic champions of slavery's expansion. They took their stand, rather, as dauntless guardians of national unity, popular rights, and regional and cultural diversity. Buchanan and Douglas were thus the legitimate heirs of Thomas Jefferson and Andrew Jackson; Democrats alone would defend the rights of the multitude against the designs of any would-be privileged elite. Cast in this light, popular sovereignty was no mere legislative device but the embodiment of a basic principle—that of democratic self-government. As such, it once again demonstrated the Democratic party's basic "trust in the intelligence, the patriotism, and the discriminating justice of the American people." Promising to "abide by and adhere to a faithful execution" of both the 1850 compromise measures and the Kansas-Nebraska Act, moreover, only the Democratic party would defend the nation against threats of "civil war and disunion."[1]

This line of argument proved persuasive not only among the native-born voters but among German immigrants as well. As in the past, the Democratic party depicted itself as the natural home of the foreign-born and the national guarantor of their aspirations for liberty, democracy, and opportunity. Only the Democrats, thus, were ready to protect the rights of all white residents, native and immigrant alike, regardless of religious faith. The platform proudly asserted its support for the rights of the foreign-born, declaring that "the liberal principles embodied by Jefferson and the Declaration of Independence, and sanctioned by the Constitution, which makes ours the land of liberty and the asylum of the oppressed of every nation, have ever been cardinal principles in the Democratic faith, and every attempt to abridge the privilege of becoming citizens and the owners of soil among us, ought to be resisted with the same spirit which swept the alien and sedition laws from our statute-books." Newspapers, speeches, and campaign banners translated these platform planks into German. A typical meeting of German Democrats held in New York City in 1860 thus promised "No decrease in naturalization rights" and "Support of the Union as the bulwark of Freedom on Earth." These principles were then linked to the party's stand on slavery and the Kansas-Nebraska Act: "Opposition to Sectionalism, which stirs up fanaticism and disturbs public peace and prosperity" so essential to "the general good." The *Wahrheits-Freund* proclaimed that " 'The Union: No South, No North, No East, No West,' is the motto of this great party," which attracts "all friends of the constitution, all true patriots."[2]

Nor did the Democratic appeal end here. The party also reminded immigrant plebeians that it was the only dependable friend of the producing classes of all nationalities. As in the age of Jackson, its platform of 1856 declared, the Democratic party was "continuing to resist all monopolies and exclusive legislation for the benefit of the few at the expense of the many." German Democrats expounded on the theme, "Buchanan: Friend of the Worker." The panic of 1857 offered an opportunity to concretize that claim. In November the German editor of Chicago's *National Demokrat* attended meetings of the city's German jobless, where he advocated sending a workers' delegation to City Hall, there to demand "work or bread" for the unemployed. In New York Democratic mayor Fernando Wood demonstratively affirmed the legitimacy of the same type of demands and promised to expand the city's public works program to accommodate them. The Republican English-language press predictably howled with rage, denouncing Mayor Wood's promises as dangerous anti-Republican demagoguery calculated to foment among "the laboring population a spirit of envy, hatred and defiance toward all who are not in the same condition as themselves." An ally of Wood's hastened to draw out the lessons before an audience of unemployed workers. The "black republicans," he noted, "whilst they still professed to be great friends of the workingman," in truth "were his greatest enemies."[3]

Democratic spokesmen stressed economic issues in another way, too. They tirelessly pointed out that key sectors of the North's manufacturing population depended heavily upon southern markets—among them thousands of German craftworkers (notably, but not only, tailors). A Republican victory at the polls, they warned, would certainly destroy this essential North-South commerce by triggering southern boycotts of northern firms—or even the South's outright withdrawal from the Union. This appeal to the most immediate concerns of hard-pressed craftworkers was a powerful one. Victor Pelz, a central leader of New York City's German tailors' union and labor movement, later acknowledged that he had voted Democratic in 1856 partly to protect his livelihood.[4]

In this respect, too, the panic of 1857 seemed to corroborate Democratic arguments by underlining the German *Handwerker*'s stake in good intersectional relations. The cotton kingdom fared better during the crisis and rebounded more quickly from it than the national economy did. Indeed, the South's comparatively sustained effective demand for northern goods during this difficult period had helped pace the national recovery. What would the removal of the southern market mean in the next crisis? In the immediate aftermath of the panic, William Benque's *Der Arbeiter* again reminded German craftworkers of their stake in retaining friendly relations with the South: "The so-called slavery question is for us German Americans an extremely dangerous one." Some anti-Republican employers brought home the same point at election time. New York City clothing houses reportedly distributed the following notice in 1860 to German tailors in their employ: "The here enclosed Union [i.e., Douglas-Breckinridge-Bell fusion] Ticket is the one that you, on the 6th day of November, *must put in the ballot box*. By doing this you will take care of yourself and family, you will get plenty of work and good prices. But if the Republican candidate for President is elected the South with withdraw its custom from us, and you will be able to get little work, and at bad prices."[5]

Citing the imminent prospect of severed North-South commerce in the fall of 1860, employers such as these began reducing production levels and discharging employees. In Newark the clothing firm of Lewis, Garthwaite and Co. placed notices in the cloth distributed to their outworking German employees warning simply, "The man who fails to vote for the Union ticket will get no more work." At the end of October the *New Yorker Staats-Zeitung* and a widely distributed handbill calling upon German tailors of Williamsburg, Brooklyn, who were concerned about their jobs to a meeting at Henry Berger's beerhall. Those who attended were greeted by German-speaking advocates of the Democratic and anti-Republican Fusion tickets, who urged support for their candidates as the surest form of job security.[6]

Republicans denounced such counsel as contemptible, empty, and hypocritical: contemptible, because it tried to gain votes through fear and intimidation; empty, because the slaveowners' threats of retribution would prove hollow were the North to find the courage to stand up; and hypocritical, because those in the North posing as the friends of labor were actually supporting and abetting the expansion of a system that degraded all working people. "Look at the advertisements in Southern papers [offering] 'A carpenter for sale,'" Friedrich Hecker urged a German crowd. This enslavement of one group of workers undermined the position of all others. That is why, he added, "wages are much lower in the South than in the North." The refusal to "work for ten cents a day" crystallized this line of argument. Only if the North's free laborers sent Republicans to Washington, moreover, would they create a government capable of protecting their interests.[7]

In New York City, where fears of southern economic warfare ran high, pro-Republican leaders of the German tailors' union mobilized members and friends to attend the October 1860 meeting in Williamsburg convened by German Democrats.[8] The result recalled the scene six years earlier when the *Staats-Zeitung* had attempted to hold a pro-Nebraska meeting in *Kleindeutschland*. German Democrats who tried to convene the meeting at Berger's hall found themselves faced (in the words of one opponent) with "many revolutionary tailors" who expressed "their intention to adorn the lamp posts with the [Democratic] conspirators." Just as in 1854, an antislavery majority replaced the Democratic chairman with one of its own choosing and jeered pro-Democratic speakers. Tailor and *Arbeiterbund* leader Victor Pelz took the floor to castigate German Democrats for their dire warnings about the consequences of a Republican victory. Pelz had himself heeded such warnings in 1856 and voted for Buchanan. That ballot, he recalled now, had won nothing for tailors. This year, therefore, "he would vote for Lincoln, so help him God, and take the consequences."

A second tailor (referred to in the press as "Bornhard") then spoke. This was apparently the same man whose deep distrust of the clothing manufacturers and hostility toward them led him to urge a revolutionary general strike during the 1850 tailors' struggle. An intervening decade of conflict over the slavery issue led him now to invoke the same sentiments in support of another course of action. The present meeting, Bornhard asserted, had been engineered by elite cutters and foremen employed by New York garment houses. Was it not suspicious, he asked, that such people, "who had always abused and tyrannized over the tailors," were suddenly showing such concern for the tailors' welfare "just before election?" Let the tailors look not to such traditional enemies but to the Republican party, he went on, for a genuine solution to labor's economic problems—in the form of homestead laws and tariff protection for industry.

Bornhard's speech, we are told, elicited stormy applause. The insurgent chairman declared the meeting adjourned, and most of the tailors then departed, cheering Lincoln as they left. Days later, a Republican labor activist expressed the tongue-in-cheek hope that the Democrats would "not be discouraged" by the evening's events. "We will assist them if they want to gain any more such victories over the tailors and mechanics. I would propose to them to call a meeting of the cabinet makers next."

In fact, however, the evening's outcome proved ambiguous, reminding us once again that New York City's working class (including its German component) remained deeply divided politically. Not all the German tailors present in Berger's hall sided with the Republicans; a group of Democratic tailors remained behind after adjournment was declared. Seeing this, a small body of Republican sympathizers hung back, too, to prevent their opponents from reconvening the meeting. At this point a contingent of Irish Democrats entered the hall and encircled the Republican sympathizers. After a spirited exchange of catcalls and insults, a battle with fists and clubs erupted. This time it was the Republican tailors who found themselves driven out, after which a brief Democratic meeting was in fact held.[9]

Republicanism, Nativism, and Sabbatarianism

The Democratic appeal to the craftworkers' economic self-interest captured a larger theme of that party's campaigns. For decades, and with considerable success, Democrats had counterposed the interests of northern workers to those of southern slaves. Neither solidarity among all laborers nor universal legal equality, Democrats contended, provided the proper formula for social progress. The road forward passed instead through racial solidarity and the restriction of civic equality to whites alone. Campaigning among immigrant voters in the 1850s, they rejected out of hand the assertion by German forty-eighters and others that freedom was indivisible, either theoretically or practically. A Democratic editor in Pittsburgh congratulated the "many Germans" who supported "the great white Race party." A Democratic campaign banner prominently displayed at a huge German-language meeting in New York City typically promised "Justice to White men, native and immigrant."[10]

Democrats depicted the Republicans, in contrast, as exclusionary, predatory, and divisive—run by wealthy and arrogant Yankee puritans, nativists, and temperance and sabbatarian fanatics and their black wards. "In the event of Lincoln's election," speculated a German member of New York's Democratic electoral college delegation in 1860, "the White House would be converted into a sort of negro asylum for the dissemination of Republican philanthropy" at the expense of all other Americans. Indeed, it was added, the same Republicans who championed black freedom expressed only contempt for the great mass of white immigrant wage earners and small proprietors. German Democrats variously charged German Republicans with being nativists—a "Know-Nothing German 'Republican' clique" (*Nichtswisserlich* "*republikanische*" *Deutscherklique*)—or of selling themselves to nativism for personal gain. Keep up the pressure on this theme, Stephen Douglas instructed his supporters: "That will bring the Germans and all other foreigners and Catholics to our side." "Frémont's Platform," proclaimed one typical pro-Buchanan banner, was "Down with the Foreigner, And Up With the Nigger." A sympathetic newspaper described the banner's accompanying illustration: "Frémont was represented . . . with his foot upon a prostrate foreigner, while a negro stood proudly alongside the candidate, laughing impudently in his face." "You know yourselves of what elements the so-called Republican party is composed," Milwaukee's Catholic *Seebote* warned its readers. "Temperance men, abolitionists, haters of foreigners, sacrilegious despoilers of churches, Catholic-killers, these are the infernal ingredients of which this loathesome Republican monstrosity is composed."[11]

Democrats did find allies among the Catholic and more conservative Protestant clergy. C. F. W. Walther's large and influential Missouri Synod of the Lutheran church, which traced its lineage back to the Saxon "Old Lutherans," became a pole of attraction for religiously and socially conservative German Protestant clergy and laity. Unlike some other branches of the Lutheran church in the United States, the Missouri Synod steadfastly refused to take a stand against slavery throughout the antebellum era and continued to find justification for modern bondage in the Bible.[12]

Catholic theologians had for centuries regarded servile status as but one of many unfortunate but natural products of humankind's fall from grace. Like German Democratic papers generally, Cincinnati's Catholic *Wahrheits-Freund* looked forward to the eventual end of slavery but cautioned readers that in the meantime "it is the citizen's duty to accept things as they are and conduct themselves accordingly. Slavery exists among us and is accepted and recognized by the Constitution, and is in some areas tightly interwoven with the whole social order." The utmost care, calm, and patience was therefore necessary when dealing with this volatile issue. By rejecting such counsel, the *Wahr-heits-Freund* added, the Republican party revealed itself to be but a new incarnation of radical abolitionism and European-style red republicanism. The party's alleged program of "quick and immediate emancipation of the Negro slaves" threatened a reenactment on North American soil of the horrors of the Haitian Revolution. Words like these gratified Alexander Stephens, Georgia Whig and future Confederate vice president, who noted of the Catholic clergy that "they have never warred against us or our peculiar institutions. No one can say as much of New England Baptists, Presbyterians, or Methodists; the long roll of abolitionist petitions, with which Congress has been so agitated for the past years, come not from the Catholics; their pulpits at the North are not desecrated every Sabbath with anathemas against slavery."[13]

Most Republican leaders heartily reciprocated the enmity of the Catholic church. Some were repelled solely or principally by the Catholic hierarchy's political conduct and program.[14] The anti-Catholicism of many others, however, was less narrowly and sharply focused. Their hostility was fed by an assortment of political, economic, and cultural grievances, including the widespread belief that the heavy immigration of the 1850s was responsible for many problems besetting the nation. Such sentiments had sparked the phenomenal upsurge in 1853–54 of the American party, whose more strongly antislavery wing subsequently gravitated toward Republicanism. In 1856 a convention of these so-called "North Americans" placed John C. Frémont's name atop its own electoral ticket, and the Republican candidate accepted the nomination.

At the state level, relations between Republicans and antislavery Know-Nothings during the following years took various forms. In some cases the parties remained independent while backing some of the same candidates (as they did in 1856). In other cases the two parties' local organizations fused outright. Whether merging, allying, or competing for votes with the Republicans, however, free-soil nativists encouraged the already strong anti-Catholic and anti-immigrant inclinations of numerous Republican party leaders and supporters.[15]

This trend became most pronounced in certain states, where Republicanism became identified with initiatives aimed at limiting the political power of the foreign-born, weakening Catholic church institutions, or prohibiting the manufacture and consumption of alcohol. Wisconsin's Republican leadership was largely Whig in origin, and in 1855 the Republican-dominated state legislature passed temperance legislation. In 1860 the Republican state ticket received and welcomed Know-Nothing endorsement. Iowa's Republican party had strong nativist and prohibitionist roots and inclinations. Among leaders of Indiana Republicanism, as George Julian later recalled, "Know-Nothings and Silver-Grey Whigs of the state were recognized as brethren" in 1856, and the party's "political managers even went so far as to suppress their own electoral ticket during the canvass, as a peace-offering to old Whiggery and Know-Nothingism." Indiana Republicans demanded revocation in 1856 of policies that had permitted resident aliens to vote before the end of their five-year federal naturalization period.[16]

Nativism played a conspicuous role in the early history of Ohio Republicanism, too. Salmon P. Chase became governor in 1855 at the head of a ticket containing the names of eight open Know-Nothings. Thereafter Republican leaders in the state strove to mute nativist forces in their midst and to concentrate the party's fire upon the Catholic church rather than upon immigrants generally. Measures designed to curb the political power of Catholicism, however, injured (and antagonized) others as well, such as an 1857 law aimed at the Irish that tightened voter registration requirements. Michigan Republicans pushed through a similar law in 1859.[17]

In New York the efforts of Horace Greeley, Thurlow Weed, and William Seward at first kept Republicanism comparatively free of nativist associations. But when an independent Know-Nothing ticket helped defeat the Republican slate in 1855, the state party reconsidered its policy. Indeed, the New York Republican organization soon became one of the most nativist in the country. In 1858 the state party's platform endorsed both a voter registration law and extension of the period between naturalization and enfranchisement. In 1860 a prominent former Know-Nothing headed the Republican list of presidential electors. "Sometimes I despair," Seward confessed. "The natural course for the Germans is to sustain free labor. But except for myself all our free labor public men either directly or indirectly join the Know Nothings in persecuting Germans."[18]

The New Jersey organization was strongly nativist in inclination as well. Its earnest attempts in 1856 to fuse with the state's Know-Nothing party were frustrated only because of the latter's rebuff. In Newark even that English-language Republican newspaper overtly friendliest to antislavery Germans nonetheless campaigned zealously against German drinking and sabbath behavior. "Against this species of foreign influence" the editors of the *Daily Mercury* and their allies were proudly "ranged as one man." And nowhere did nativists exercise more power within Republican ranks than in Pennsylvania. There the Republican boss Simon Cameron (an ex-Democrat, ex-Know-Nothing financier) brazenly dismissed or squelched all intraparty opposition to his aggressively anti-immigrant policy. In 1856 the state party's platform denounced "foreign influence of every kind" in national politics. In 1860 Pennsylvania's Republican gubernatorial candidate sported Know-Nothing credentials.[19]

But most damaging of all to Republican prospects among foreign-born voters was Massachusetts's so-called Two-Year Amendment. In 1855 the state legislature approved an amendment to the state constitution that would bar immigrants from voting during a full twenty-one years following naturalization. In 1857 and again in 1858 Republicans (by then in control of the legislature) passed a diluted version of that measure, which provided for a waiting period of two years. The change appeased few if any immigrant voters. Acutely sensitive to the danger, some Republican leaders from midwestern states urged their Massachusetts brethren to reconsider and rescind. In the spring of 1859, however, Massachusetts voters formally approved the amendment.[20]

German Democratic leaders naturally made the most of this Republican-nativist connection. German Republicans countered that anti-German sentiments were at least as strong in the Democratic party as in the Republican. In fact, evidence of anti-immigrant animus in the Democratic party was becoming increasingly plentiful. Southern Democrats in the Senate had championed the nativist Clayton amendment to the Kansas-Nebraska bill in 1854. Southern Democrats in the same body then supported another Clayton initiative, an amendment to the pending homestead bill that would deny its benefits to any foreign-born person who had not yet been naturalized. Immigrant homesteaders, the southerners feared, would range themselves against slavery in the territories. Senator Andrew P. Butler of South Carolina preferred to see the West's institutions "moulded by the American mind, accustomed to and disciplined under, the dominion of English law" and not by "the mass of the German, Irish, and other foreign population coming here and going upon your Territories, [who] do not understand your institutions." Mississippi's Stephen Adams complained that "the whole education of the foreigners and their prejudices when they come to this country are against the institution of slavery." Militant anti-Nebraska demonstrations mounted by German-born residents helped convince Adams that the United States ought to "cease to hold out any further inducements" to "further immigration from other countries." By December 1854, indeed, Adams and others were pressing a bill of their own that would extend the federal naturalization period from five to twenty-one years.[21]

Developments like these—widely and repeatedly cited in the Republican press—did little to advance the Democratic party's interests among German-born voters. Continued Democratic hegemony, Friedrich Kapp warned, would mean that "the future of this country shall be shaped by the will of the slaveholders; free immigration shall be stopped [and] this Union shall be compelled to trample into dust the principles which constitute the elements of its political greatness." "The pro-slavery party called itself Democratic," said Gustav Struve. "But it had no title to that noble name. It was the veriest aristocratic party, a party of slaveholders, [in relation] to whom the poor members were themselves slaves." That party's slaveholding leaders valued the foreign-born only as workhorses or voting cattle. "A Southerner is like a baron," Hecker insisted, searching for compelling parallels. "He looks upon an emigrant as he would look upon a nigger." Immigrants who wished instead to assert their humanity and defend their interests had no future in a party led by such men.[22]

With such appeals German Republicans sought to turn the attention of other German voters away from issues such as nativism, temperance, and sabbatarianism and back toward those of slavery and the West. Here was the major difference between the parties and the real hub around which American politics had come to revolve, they argued—and here the interests of Republicans and immigrant plebeians coincided. The Republican party was committed to keeping the West free. "Frémont is a democrat through and through, a democrat in the best sense of the word," asserted Theodor Hielscher's *Freie Presse von Indiana* in 1856. As president, Frémont "will exclude only slavery from the free territories" and "protect . . . the rights of free workers" and the "liberties of the immigrants." "The issue that the people are about to decide," the paper reiterated four years later, "is not between free trade and tariffs, between paper money and coin, but rather this: in the politics of this land, shall supremacy go to slavery or the interests of human rights and freedom?"[23]

Since slavery had become the central and most important issue on the political agenda, moreover, some German Republicans asserted that it was not only permissible but necessary for those in agreement here to join forces regardless of differences on other matters. Free-soil Germans thus properly belonged in the same party with free-soil nativists. In fact, argued the *Illinois Staats-Zeitung,* "such union of different elements for the attainment of one common and good end" was an elementary principle of all effective political action, as partisans of European freedom should know. Only readiness to cooperate despite disagreements, after all, made it possible for "emigrants from the different States of Europe" to cooperate in exile—as "when they strive to unite the [purely] politico-revolutionary" with "the socialistic and communistic parties, into *one great republican party*." (Under George Schneider's editorship, the *Illinois Staats-Zeitung*'s editorial staff and group of contributors embodied just such a coalition.) "And this *very same* 'fusion' we want to achieve by establishing a great American 'liberty party.' "[24]

Friedrich Hecker made the same point. "Wrong and misled" as they were, Hecker "would yet prefer Temperance men and Know-Nothings to the hordes of Ruffians which attack the liberties of our people alike on the borders of our Territories and at the nation's Capital—and which made the name of Democracy nothing but a by word." "Even supposing that the party of freedom in this country does not in every single question come up to what we may consider the fullest extent of liberty and right," agreed Friedrich Kapp at a mass German rally a few months later, "we are still bound to make common cause with this party against a common enemy." This was the more logical because a Republican triumph would hasten an end to the conditions that bred nativism in the first place. Here German Republicans put to their own use of a line of argument earlier popularized by Hermann Kriege and the *Association der Social-Reformer*. In eastern cities, Kapp asserted, "the native laborers" blamed their economic hardships on "the great emigration, which, as they believe, takes the work from them." A Republican victory, however, by barring the further spread of slavery, thereby "opens the lands of the West to emigration" and "in this manner saves for us and our children free land and [free] labor sufficient to prevent our being placed in want by each crisis." The inclusion of an explicit homestead plank in the Republicans' national platform in 1860 made such arguments still more persuasive, and Republicans that year circulated a German translation of their proposed land law widely.[25]

But no matter how doggedly and eloquently presented, arguments such as these could not silence qualms about deeply rooted Republican sabbatarian, temperance, and nativist propensities. Pointing out the mote in the southern Democrat's eye could not conceal the beam in the northern Republican's. German-American champions of the Republican party felt concern at two levels. First, the Republican-sponsored proscriptive measures constituted attacks on rights about

which German immigrants generally—and German democrats and laboring people specifically—felt strongly. Second, the identification of
these attacks with Republicanism threatened to trap many antislavery
German immigrants within the pro-slavery Democratic ranks.[26] The
New York German Republican Central Committee heatedly denounced Massachusetts's "Two-Year Amendment." That legislation,
protested a meeting of German-born Republicans in Toledo, Ohio,
"strikes at the very root" of the "fundamental principle of the Republican party that all citizens had equal rights before the law without
any distinction of color or birth." The assemblage vowed "never more
[to] lend our help to elevate a party to power which tramples us under
foot." Democratic newspapers, English- and German-speaking alike,
delighted in reprinting protests like these.[27]

Arbeitervereine, Turnvereine, and *Freimännervereine* denounced proscriptive Republican rhetoric and legislation with the same vehemence
and, often enough, in the same terms that they directed against human bondage. The 1855 Buffalo convention that formally declared
the *Sozialistischer Turnerbund*'s revulsion toward chattel slavery also
emphasized that "the Turners are against all temperance laws as undemocratic in principle and unjust and impractical in practice." In 1856
the *New York Criminal Zeitung und Belletristisches Journal* vehemently
protested Frémont's acceptance of the American party's presidential
nomination and agonized over "the many complications involved in
the approaching election." The *Sociale Republik* could see little difference between the philosophies of nativism and slavery. In 1854 New
York's German anti-Nebraska protesters linked antislavery and anti-
temperance themes, then carried this combination of concerns into
the process of party realignment. In 1856 a pro-Frémont meeting of
between four and five thousand New York Germans thus demanded
not only "No expansion of slavery," but also "No temperance," and
"No extension of the naturalization period."[28]

Even the firmest opponents of slavery among German radicals repeatedly warned native-born anti-Nebraska, and then Republican,
leaders that nativism and sabbatarianism would alienate otherwise
sympathetic immigrant workingmen. Like Kapp, Hecker, and Hielscher,
Christian Esselen was prepared "to submit to annnoying measures"
rather than "than betray the grand principles of liberty." But Esselen
himself quickly discovered that few of his Wisconsin *Landsleute* agreed
with those priorities: "If the curse of slavery is mentioned [to them],
for which that [Democratic] party conducts its propaganda, if one
points to Kansas and Missouri, it is replied that all that has nothing
to do with the Democratic party of Wisconsin; that Wisconsin has

no slavery." In any case, such people would add, it was better to be governed by Wisconsin Democrats "than virtuous Puritans that will load us down with temperance legislation." "The general horror of Know-Nothings," Esselen found, "seems to be the principal occupation of Germans in Wisconsin."

Fritz Anneke encountered similar problems in the East as he campaigned for the Republican party among those immigrant working people "whose mental horizon is limited, who have no profound spiritual cultivation." "It is an easy thing," he reported, "to explain to the moderately intelligent laborer the Nebraska disgrace of the cut-purse Douglas, and to awaken his feeling against it." But for those "who combat year after year for the necessities of life," the "prohibition of a beverage, the political intervention in the natural functions of daily life is felt [more] immediately" than a still "theoretical" hostility to the comparatively "remote" issue of slavery in the western territories. The danger was serious, therefore, that in a conflict between supporting antislavery and antiprohibition, many who belonged with the former would cast their lot with the latter. Anneke challenged the Republican leadership: "Would you remove such a danger, you who have a deep, earnest, moral interest in the support of the cause of freedom, give up all prohibitory laws against beverages and not cripple your efforts with a fanatical Temperance cause; you will then have all the German votes on your side. Oppose the evil of intemperance in every mode except the senseless, tyrannical prohibitory laws, and every intelligent German will cooperate with you."[29]

Frustration with Republican attitudes toward slavery, immigrant rights, and social-economic issues in the North encouraged talk of abandoning the Republicans altogether and launching "a new party of freedom." In 1858, thus, the central committee of the recently formed *Allgemeine Arbeiterbund von Nord-Amerika* called for the organization of a new "social-republican party." But while a number of forty-eighter newspapers endorsed the proposal, it failed to attract enough support to become viable. Talk of abandoning Republicanism was loudest in those locales (especially in the East) where nativists and social conservatives exercised greatest control over the Republican organizations. But most immigrant Republicans—radicals as well as moderates—regarded plans for a third, primarily German party as hopeless, foolhardy, and dangerously divisive of the "progressive" electorate.[30]

The fight for a stronger stand against nativism and slavery and in favor of land reform, however, continued, and these demands evolved into a tacit "minimum program" for German radicals, who used it as a litmus test with which to judge aspirants for public office. The New

York *Arbeiterverein* and *Turnverein* cosponsored mass meetings to oppose the anti-immigrant actions of the Republican party. German labor activists and Turners helped organize meetings in Newark that
resolved to support only those candidates for office sworn to support
a homestead law, oppose the extension of slavery, and resist encroachments on naturalization rights and public conduct on the sabbath.
Similar meetings also took place in Cincinnati in the late 1850s, where
similar resolutions were passed.[31]

The struggle over the soul of the Republican party—and over its
platform and presidential nomination—came to a head in 1860. Some
in the party's most conservative wing (and some opportunists like
Horace Greeley) championed the nomination of Edward Bates of
Missouri, who had supported the Know-Nothing campaign for Fillmore in 1856. Another name floated was that of Massachusetts governor Nathaniel Banks, who was identified with his state's nativist
"two-year amendment."[32]

Opposition to candidates such as these united most Republican
radicals and moderates. At the Indiana Republican State Convention
in February 1860, Theodor Hielscher introduced a resolution in-
structing delegates to the forthcoming Republican National Convention to refuse support to any candidate who had failed to back the
Republicans in 1856. The party needed "no conservative men,"
Hielscher argued, "but we need one, like old Jackson, that would not
be afraid of saying, 'By the Eternal I will put down treason wherever
it shows its head!'" On March 7, Turners and other German Republicans in Davenport, Iowa, formally rejected Bates's candidacy because
of his previous Know-Nothing connections and his stated support for
the Fugitive Slave Law. A meeting of Cincinnati Republicans in Turner
Hall endorsed the Davenport resolutions on March 21.[33]

A week earlier, on March 13, the German Republican Club of New
York City "invite[d] all similar organizations to unite upon the following or similar resolutions," specifying general adherence to the party's
1856 platform, "determined opposition to all efforts for the extension
and perpetuation of slavery," defense of naturalization and other rights
of the foreign-born, an end to "the pernicious, usurious land policy
and the squandering of the federal domain by speculators," and a "reasonable" protective tariff. These criteria were couched in the form of
an ultimatum: "We can go hand in hand with the Republican party
only when it nominates decided and reliable representatives of the
above principles for the offices of president and vice president."

Soon afterward the newspaper of Cincinnati's *Socialer Arbeiterverein*
outlined its own approach to the coming elections. The *Republikaner*'s

editor, August Willich, listed "the qualifications of the man whom we can support for President," the man with "the proper material to make a President of the People—*a Working Men's President.*" Such an individual, the paper declared, must recognize that "the great struggle now going on in every civilized nation of the earth [was] *the conflict of labor against monopoly.*" (Like Hielscher, Willich held up Andrew Jackson as a model.) Such a man must "place himself on the side of the laborer, of the producing classes, as against the monopolists." To be free to do so, the candidate must be beholden to no "political clique organizations." By the same token, he must himself be a man of the people; whatever wealth he possessed must be the fruit of his own efforts: "He must have laid the foundation of his own fortunes upon *his own labor,* and must never have stained his escutcheon through connivance with monopoly." Two days later, on the evening of March 19, three thousand members and allies of the *Arbeiterverein* marched from its hall down to the Findlay Marketspace. There Friedrich Oberkline, a leader of the *Verein* and corresponding secretary of the iron molders' union, read approvingly from the *Republikaner* editorial, concluding in his own words that those must be placed in office "who represent the masses—men from the loom and the workshop."[34]

The next day the German Republican Central Committee of New York moved to mobilize and organize sentiments such as these to counter the pressure of both nativist and conciliationist forces within the party. The New Yorkers called upon German Republicans from around the country to send delegates to a meeting of their own in Chicago in mid-May, to coincide with the Republican National Convention already slated for that city. Prime movers behind this initiative included Wilhelm Kopp of the *New Yorker Demokrat* and Karl Heinzen and Adolf Douai of Boston. The German gathering, according to this call, would seek to influence the party's national convention, oversee the work of German delegates thereto, and secure the nomination of an acceptable presidential candidate.[35]

As James M. Bergquist notes, "geography, more than degree of radical ideology," influenced the response to this initiative. Once again, those most frustrated by their local Republican organizations tended to greet the call enthusiastically. Thus, on April 10 Newark's German Republicans responded positively, stressing the need to press the Republicans for a homestead bill, protective tariff, abolition of the Fugitive Slave Law, a policy of firm exclusion of slavery from all territories, and "vigorous protection of all citizens [while] abroad." Those German-Americans, on the other hand, whose relations with local Republican parties were warmer tended to view the call with skepticism, suspecting the framers of seeking a full-scale split from the Republican party. Those voicing such views, therefore, included not only such Illinois liberals as Körner and Kreismann but also the more radical Caspar Butz and Joseph Weydemeyer, the latter by now editing a newspaper (*Stimme des Volkes*) for the Chicago *Arbeiterverein*.[36]

This division of opinion nearly wrecked the German meeting (which convened at Chicago's Deutsches Haus on May 14) and did prevent it from playing the decisive role in the national party's deliberations that its initiators had intended. Still, the conference participants did finally agree on a set of resolutions "requesting" that German delegates to the Republican convention press there for the following policies: a formal endorsement of the party's principled opposition to the spread of slavery and the application of those principles "in a sense most hostile to slavery," for the admission of Kansas as a free state, for defense of the civil rights of immigrants, and for a homestead bill that would use western lands to satisy the needs of "the people" rather than "the greed of the speculators." This platform represented a multilateral compromise among most German Republican leaders, East and West, radical and liberal, which may help explain its silence concerning the Fugitive Slave Law and a protective tariff.[37]

In the end, the Republican National Convention did satisfy many of the Deutsches Haus concerns. It is true that some of the more fiery denunciations of slavery contained in the 1856 platform were deleted at the convention, and the raid on Harpers Ferry was branded a "lawless invasion." But the delegates denounced the Dred Scott decision, labeled threats of secession "contemplated treason," condemned the existence of slavery in any territory as unconstitutional, and championed Kansas's admission as a free state. In addition, the platform demanded that the "satisfactory homestead legislation which has already passed the House" be enacted by the Senate, and it opposed "any change in our naturalization laws" (along with "any state legislation by which the rights of citizens hitherto accorded to immigrants from foreign lands shall be abridged or impaired").[38] If the party's more radical potential candidates were passed over, so were Bates and Banks. The nomination went to Abraham Lincoln, a moderate Republican with limited national standing but a record of opposing nativism, despising slavery, and speaking for the "common man." The St. Louis *Anzeiger des Westens* waxed particularly enthusiastic on this last point. The *New Yorker Demokrat* expressed its general satisfaction as well: "Next to the adoption of the well approved platform of the Republican Convention, . . . no nomination for the Presidential office could be more welcome than that of Abraham Lincoln, the spirited and successful opponent of Douglas. The struggle [against] a corrupt clique . . . which had smuggled a narrow-minded Know-Nothingism into the very bosom of free and honest Republican principles . . . has been already fought out upon the field of the Republican nomination."[39]

Much of the German labor press responded with caution. If the convention's outcome left something to be desired, they generally concluded, that fact by no means precluded support. The *Stimme des Volkes* of the *Chicagoer Arbeiterverein* thus judged the the national party platform "certainly something short of a radical one, and a little lukewarm," but one nevertheless "that in general satisfies the demands we make upon it." It believed Lincoln was "the choice of the conservative wing of the Republican Convention" but vowed to support him as the "lesser of two evils." Willich's *Republikaner* took the party's preference for Lincoln over an outright radical as "a stunning blow." But at least, it noted, Lincoln was free of Know-Nothing taint, and if not as forthright a defender of the foreign-born as Chase and Seward, still opposed to changes in naturalization laws. "If Lincoln is not enshrined in the hearts of the people, like Frémont, he has nonetheless labored among the people all his life—he is truly a self-made man!"[40]

At the Ballot Box

How did the mass of German-Americans respond to the conflicting appeals of Democrats and Republicans in 1856 and 1860? An investigation of their voting behavior provides some indication, but it must be approached with care, with due sensitivity to both analytical and contextual complications. Specific political influences active at the state and local levels complicate attempts to describe national patterns. So does the mosaic of suffrage laws and practice. Many recent immigrants were barred from voting during the five-year federal naturalization period. But the requirement that voters be federal citizens was waved or ignored in certain states, cities, election wards, and even precincts. The analytical problem thus posed is further aggravated by the fact that ethnically or occupationally homogeneous voting districts were virtually unknown in the cities of the 1850s, and attempts to identify voters' religious affiliations is even more fraught with perils. Finally, historians can only speculate about the actual number of eligible voters in any given ethnic, religious, or occupational category that actually cast a ballot at election time.[41] None of these methodological pitfalls makes election analysis impossible; taken together, however, they should remind us of the uncertainties involved and the tentative character of the conclusions reached.

The data available indicate that, overall, support for the Republican party grew significantly among German working people between 1856 and 1860. During these years both party leaders and voters tested one another's responses to a succession of dramatic events and struggled to evaluate political issues and prioritize them according to their importance. Particular factors in specific locales influenced the local results—and especially the pacing—of this sorting-out process.

Though some individuals and newspapers associated with the forty-eighter Left remained with the Democratic party, they constituted the exception rather than the rule. Despite both ethnic and class qualms, most organized German craftworkers and other radical democratic organizations evidently supported Lincoln in 1860. The Democratic party, on the other hand, found strong German support among rural voters generally and those urban dwellers (such as unskilled laborers) less identified with social and political radicalism and more closely tied to the Catholic and conservative Protestant clergy. Unskilled immigrants were probably also more susceptible to Democratic warnings about job competition from former slave fieldhands than were their more highly skilled *Landsleute*—and more dependent upon the services of Democratic party machines.[42]

But (as Fritz Anneke and others had warned) the willingness of German workers to abandon the Democratic party also varied according to the degree that they felt menaced locally by Republican proscriptive and repressive tendencies. Antislavery sentiments among Germans translated into Republican votes most readily where Republicans resolutely and effectively cleansed themselves of antiforeign and sabbatarian taint. A similar, though not identical, point can be made concerning Republican anti-Catholicism: where it seemed a constituent element of narrow, xenophobic, and conservative hostility to the foreign-born in general, antislavery German voters responded with the most widespread hostility. Where, on the other hand, progressive-minded German voters could view Republican anti-Catholicism as something focused upon the papacy and the church hierarchy and springing from a democratic, republican outlook—in such cases Republican candidates fared better among them.[43]

New Jersey, the only free state to withhold some of its electoral votes from Lincoln in 1860, contained a Republican organization heavily weighted with nativists and sabbatarians. But while an anti-Republican fusion ticket defeated Lincoln in Newark, the new party's share of the vote grew substantially between 1856 and 1860 from 29 percent to 45 percent of the totals. Republican gains among the Germans seem to have been commensurate. Newark's Sixth Ward, which by 1860 contained about one-third of the city's adult German male population, gave 29 percent of its ballots to Frémont in 1856 and 48 percent to Lincoln in 1860. The Republican *Daily Mercury,* once strongly linked to the nativist party, praised the "activity and vigilance" of the German Republican organizers.[44]

The picture was similar across the Hudson. The notoriously nativist Republican organization of New York City garnered only 23 percent of the citywide presidential vote in 1856, though the *New York Daily Times* was surprised to find that "in several of the strong German wards of this city probably *full one-third* of all Germans voted with the Republicans."[45] In 1860, when the citywide vote for Republicanism reached 35 percent, the four wards of *Kleindeutschland* (the Tenth, Eleventh, Thirteenth, and Seventeenth) gave Lincoln between 32 and 42 percent of their ballots. Specific precincts registered still stronger Republican support. Some additional perspective is provided here, as elsewhere, by the behavior of Irish voters, whose loyalty to the Democratic party was stronger and who evidently cared less about free soil and more about Republican nativism than the Germans. The heavily Irish "Bloody Ould Sixth" Ward in Manhattan gave Lincoln only 12 percent of its votes in 1860. In the strongly German wards in Williamsburg (the Sixteenth and Eighteenth), Lincoln received 49 to 55 percent of the vote.[46]

In Wisconsin, where Republican nativism was strong, Lincoln apparently attracted only about one-sixth of the total German vote. In Milwaukee, the three most heavily German wards supported Douglas in 1860. Here too, however, Republicans achieved significant inroads: the heavily German Eighth Ward went Republican in 1860, while the Democratic vote in the heavily German Second Ward dropped from about 85 percent of the total in 1856 to about 60 percent four years later. (The Irish Third Ward, in contrast, gave Democrats their largest margin of victory in 1860.)[47]

Pennsylvania Republicanism was even more strongly nativist. "The Republican Party, therefore," *Pittsburgh Gazette* editor D. N. White had warned, "can only represent a portion of the anti-Nebraska sentiment" in the city. It is interesting to note, however, that even in this setting, German support for the Democratic party declined markedly in 1856 and 1860 compared with 1852. "In no county of the State," the Democratic *Pittsburgh Post* observed, "is there so large a proportion of German voters." Though Democrats had striven hard to enlighten these voters, explained the editor, too large a share of the immigrants had stubbornly "refused to know the truth." The Republicans had successfully "deceived" many in the city's German electorate by campaigning on "the Kansas humbug," and it was "perfectly clear that we lost a large proportion of it in a body."[48]

The Indiana and Iowa Republicans—also heirs to their states' nativist currents—failed to win over many German voters. Michigan Democrats retained their greatest German strength among rural Catholics and Lutherans. In Detroit, however, the Democrats lost their previous majorities in 1860 in three of four heavily German wards; in a fourth, the Democratic vote declined from a former high of 64 percent in 1856 to 53 percent in 1860. Fearing such an outcome, the Democratic *Detroit Free Press* had recalled that "it was in the German wards of Detroit last fall that the black republicans made all the gains by which their Mayor was elected."[49]

In Ohio, when Salmon P. Chase won the governorship in 1855 on a ticket loaded with Know-Nothings, German Cincinnatians gave him only about one in ten of their ballots. The state's rural German vote apparently remained Democratic throughout the 1850s. But energetic attempts to mute specifically sabbatarian, protemperance, and antiforeign forces in the Republican organization evidently had an impact in the larger cities. Democratic observers grudgingly conceded that radical forty-eighters had campaigned with considerable success for Republican candidates in both Cleveland and Cincinnati. Nearly half of Cleveland's German voters apparently cast their ballots for the Republicans in both 1856 and 1860.[50] In Cincinnati, Frémont won about half the German votes cast and big majorities in two of its German wards (the Tenth and Eleventh). Democrats felt betrayed. "It must be very encouraging and consoling to those [native-born] American Democrats who risked their lives and property, and involved themselves in lifetime disputes with their countrymen, in defense of naturalized citizens," growled the *Daily Enquirer*, "to find so large a number of that very class against them." Nor did Democratic fortunes revive "Over the Rhine." In 1860, when Lincoln received only 46 percent of all Cincinnati ballots, the combined vote of the heavily German Eleventh and Twelfth wards went 60 percent Republican.[51]

Where nativist influence in the Republican party was weaker, as in Minnesota, Illinois, and Missouri, the party registered stronger and swifter gains among the German rank and file. Minnesota's Republican party, which was relatively free of the nativist stigma and had explicitly gone on record in 1859 against antiforeignism, won a majority of the state's German voters in 1860. In the 1856 Chicago mayoral race, fusion between Republicans and Know-Nothings played an important role, and the Democratic candidate carried the heavily German Seventh Ward by more than 80 percent. But by summer the state Republican organization was explicitly repudiating the politics of nativism, now brandishing banners promising "No prescription on Account of Birthplace." In a study of statewide voting patterns, Stephen Hansen found Illinois's Germans giving about 70 percent of their votes to both Frémont and Lincoln. And James Bergquist estimated that while Chicago as a whole gave Lincoln a 55 percent majority, Germans of the North Side's Seventh Ward voted 75 percent Republican in 1860.[52] In Missouri, Frémont was not on the ballot in 1856, so St. Louis voters were faced with a choice between Buchanan and the independent nativist candidate. Some 60 percent of German voters in the city apparently abstained. In 1860, however, the Germans gave Lincoln more than 80 percent of their votes.[53]

The observations of Christian Esselen and Fritz Anneke thus proved valid. Republican organizations fared best among urban Germans when they could demonstrate convincing democratic credentials by rejecting, or at least subordinating, the politics of conservative nativism and sabbatarianism. In such cases, German plebeians opposed to slavery's expansion felt freest to translate that impulse into electoral support for Republican candidates. As the Republican party nationally moved in this direction—and as events from "Bleeding Kansas" and the Dred Scott decision to Harpers Ferry dramatized the stakes in the sectional conflict—the affinity of German-born workers grew firmer still.

Secession and Revolution

In the four months between Lincoln's election and inauguration, the secession movement in the South reactivated northern conciliationists—Democratic and Republican alike—who agitated vigorously in behalf of compromise measures such as those proposed in Congress by Republican representative William Kellogg of Illinois and old-line Whig senator John J. Crittenden of Kentucky. To forestall disunion, Crittenden offered a series of resolutions and constitutional amendments that would have strengthened the Fugitive Slave Law, protected the interstate slave trade, and permanently guaranteed the sanctity of slavery in all existing or "hereafter acquired" territories south of the old Missouri Compromise line. As Kenneth Stampp noted, "the compromise drive was always spearheaded by eastern merchants and manufacturers." A contemporary observer commented drily that Crittenden's champions were "men who are well to do worldly speaking,

. . . usually found in warm parlors, . . . remarkable for good feeding, . . . sleek and comfortable. I notice that they pay great attention to the price of stock." A sharp commercial downturn during the winter of 1860–61 registered mercantile apprehensions about the effects of secession and further increased support for compromise.[54]

These last-ditch attempts at sectional compromise also found supporters outside the North's economic elite, including among important segments of the northern working class. Among them were such pioneer leaders of organized labor as Robert Gilchrist, Uriah Stephens, and William Sylvis. Sylvis, a founder and first treasurer of the National Iron Molders Union, voiced the sentiments of many others. A staunch Douglas Democrat, he disliked slavery but blamed abolitionists and Republicans for preciptating a crisis that threatened the beloved federal Union. Some of Sylvis's friends and fellow molders helped organize a large procompromise meeting in Louisville, one of many held throughout the country. Those meetings culminated in a national labor convention held in Philadelphia on Washington's birthday, February 22, 1861, that endorsed the Crittenden proposals.[55]

Compromise also found German-American advocates, such as New York's August Belmont and the editors of Chicago's *National Demokrat*. Cincinnati's Karl Reemelin viewed the secession of southern states tolerantly; to him it appeared merely "an act of desperation, to protect themselves, against being victimized."[56] It seems probable that some German craftworkers also favored conciliating the South. Any such voices, however, were drowned out by the chorus of German Republicans vehemently opposed to conceding anything in their party's 1860 platform. Immigrant liberals led by Carl Schurz and Gustav Körner branded secession as treason and compromise as futile or worse. More radical-minded immigrant forces, having already organized and mobilized in behalf of a militant party platform, were well prepared to carry on that struggle in the election's aftermath. A large crowd thus gathered in the Philadelphia *Arbeiterhalle* in response to a call from the city's German Republican Club in late November and there resolved "against any dilution of the Chicago platform, to surrender not even an iota of principle for the sake of compromise but rather to fight harder than ever for freedom, progress, and improving the condition of the working classes." In Chicago, German Republican organizations led by a carpenter, a shoemaker, a window maker, and a laborer voiced their contempt for the "several Chicago meat packers and grain merchants" who, because "they probably are not able to buy as much pork and flour as they were wont," were "doing everything they possibly can during the current week to support the compromisers in the Senate and House of Representatives." Fears of a secessionist assault on the nation's capital led Turners in both Chicago and Washington, D.C., to form rifle companies in January, and Turners joined Lincoln's personal bodyguard on Inauguration Day.[57]

In early February, en route to that inauguration, Lincoln passed through Cincinnati. Approximately two thousand German workingmen came to greet him at his hotel one evening during his stay. Their spokesman was the iron molder Friedrich Oberkline, who voiced sentiments considerably at variance with those of William Sylvis. Oberkline bluntly reminded the president-elect that he had won the votes of "the German free workingmen of Cincinnati . . . as the champion of Free Labor and Free Homesteads." And unlike those who wished "to create an impression that the mass of workingmen were in favor of compromise between the interests of free labor and slave labor, by which the victory just won would be turned into a defeat," the Germans present "spurn[ed] such compromises" and "firmly adhere[d] to the principles which directed our votes in your favor." They therefore trusted "that you . . . will uphold the Constitution and the laws against secret treachery and avowed treason." Furthermore, Oberkline pointedly offered, "if to this end you should be in need of men, the German free workingmen, with others, will rise as one man at your call, ready to risk their lives in the effort to maintain the victory already won by freedom over slavery."[58]

Lincoln declined to respond as directly to these remarks, cautiously preferring "to wait and see the last development of public opinion before I give my views or express myself at the time of the inauguration." The Democratic *Daily Enquirer* was less reticent, ridiculing the *Arbeiterverein*'s offer of military service. "We imagine we see them crossing the Ohio into Kentucky," led there by men "who got up a revolution in their own country . . . leaving it in a worse condition than it was before." Once in Kentucky, the editors continued, "we imagine we see them most soundly thrashed, as they would undoubtedly be, by the Kentuckians."[59]

Events would shortly compel a change in Lincoln's tactics and submit the newspaper's wry musings to practical tests. South Carolina artillery forced the surrender of Fort Sumter on April 14, and the next day Lincoln called for 75,000 volunteers to quash the rebellion. The protracted era of compromise over chattel slavery was coming to an explosive end in a second American Revolution—the conflict that Fritz Anneke called "America's second fight for freedom."[60]

For many German-Americans, this latest conflict recalled other antecedents, too. Once Karl Reemelin saw war on the horizon, he promptly "took steps . . . to keep easily out of the toils of war both myself and my family." He was, as his memoirs ruefully recall, "too well versed in the history of my native land to ever become personally involved in a civil war by my own free will." Other of his countryfolk invoked similar historical parallels in order to draw very different practical conclusions. "The American people," declared Friedrich Kapp, were now "fighting the same battle in which the European nations are engaged. . . . Yes! The conflict on the eve of decision in the United States is neither more nor less than one of the manifold phases of the struggle between aristocracy and democracy."[61]

All told, some 200,000 (or roughly one-tenth) of those who served in the Union army during the war were German-born, and 36,000 of these soldiers served in all-German units under German commanders. The *Turnvereine* were particularly active in recruiting and organizing these forces. The Turners' training, youth, social composition, and political complexion made them particularly suited to the tasks at hand. In fact, Turners and former Turners alone supplied seven to eight thousand troops and whole army units in Ohio, New York, Illinois, and Pennsylvania. Among the first to act were the Turners of Baltimore, who sped to Washington to guard it against attack pending further reinforcements. When news of this fact filtered back to Baltimore, a pro-Confederate crowd attacked the *Turnhalle*, overwhelmed its defenders, and sacked the building. The neighboring premises of the Republican *Wecker* suffered the same fate.[62]

Two days after Lincoln's call for volunteers, meanwhile, German-Americans met in Cincinnati's Turner Hall to form Ohio's all-German Ninth Infantry Regiment. In another twenty-four hours the muster rolls were overflowing. Nearly 70 percent of the volunteers were craftworkers, and four of the ten companies raised had been signed up at the *Arbeiterhalle* itself. August Willich was elected adjutant, later major; Friedrich Oberkline enlisted as a sergeant and subsequently rose to second lieutenant. In Newark, too, the *Turnverein* organized volunteers, its efforts supplemented by a separate meeting of "German workingmen" from the Sixth and Thirteenth wards. Similar scenes occurred in Chicago, Milwaukee, Indianapolis, Philadelphia, and New York (where the *Sozialistischer Turnverein* formed the Twentieth [United Turner Rifles] Regiment).[63] "The spirit of 1848," exulted a veteran of the German Revolution, "has once more awakened."[64]

10

"When Poor Men's Sons Must Sacrifice": The War and Beyond

Evaluations of the German-American military performance varied widely. Hostile northerners blamed German-born troops for the Union defeat at Chancellorsville. On the other hand, contrary to the predictions of the Democratic *Cincinnati Daily Enquirer,* Germans of that city's Ninth Ohio Regiment helped secure Union victories in Kentucky at Rowletts Station, Mill Springs, and Perryville. The *New York Daily Times* credited German soldiers with preventing a complete rout at the second Battle of Bull Run by standing and fighting while native-born Union troops fled. Critics dismissed German troops as mechanical, plodding, and slow to take the initiative. But some Confederate prisoners of war reportedly "say the damned Dutch stand like rocks," that "there is no giving ground in them." Other southerners accused the "bloody Dutch," those "Dutch Devils," of savage brutality. One southern newspaper editor longed to "hang every Dutchman captured" and then use the corpses "to manure the sandy plains and barren hillsides of Alabama, Tennessee, and Georgia."[1]

The North's German communities followed the progress of their countrymen in uniform closely, with great and touchy pride. Newspaper dispatches, soldiers' letters to relatives, friends, and newspapers, and word-of-mouth reports kept the home front informed about life in the Union army. These accounts detailed victories, heroism, fear, and tragedy, but more as well: nativism seemed to follow immigrants into military life. German soldiers sometimes accused native-born superiors of keeping them out of action, treating them as mere cannon fodder, passing them over for promotion, blaming them for problems common to the army as a whole, and denying them equal access to food and supplies.[2] At home, relatives, friends, neighbors, and *Lands-*

leute generally responded by reinforcing their support for the German troops. Local committees formed to press the claims of individual German officers or to raise money to purchase clothing, medical supplies, and food for immigrant units "shamefully neglected" by others. Efforts such as these won support from a broad social and political spectrum of German-Americans. Particularly prominent, however, were male leaders of the *Turngemeinde* and *Arbeitervereine* and their wives.[3]

The war's first year was bitter for the Union as a whole. By the summer of 1862, a string of battlefield defeats and costly victories had driven the morale of both the army and the civilian population sharply downward. The spirits of the German-born sank even further—under the weight of perceived neglect, indignity, and misuse. Enlistment rates fell steadily as demands grew louder for a more equitable distribution of the war's military costs. The German-born father of one Union soldier gave eloquent voice to a widespread sentiment when he objected that "we plebeians have done our share. The patricians . . . need not think that only the sons of plebeians are fit and worthy to be slaughtered and that the wealthy can sidestep their obligations as citizens of the United States and evade the rigors and hardships of military life." Nor did paying bounties to induce the laboring population to enlist in even greater numbers mollify class resentments like these. "What good is a hundred or even a thousand dollars," the man demanded, "when poor men's sons must sacrifice life and limb under the leadership of these ignorant patrician generals?" To achieve a more equitable distribution of the war's military burdens among all social classes, the Chicago *Arbeiterverein* called for universal military conscription. The federal law of March 1863, which allowed individuals to avoid the draft for a $300 commutation fee, was unsatisfactory; the *Arbeiterverein* repeated its demand for a draft formula "placing rich and poor on the same level."[4]

The inequitable draft system aggravated other wartime grievances. During the first years of the fighting, inflation ate away at the living standards of wage-dependent families in the North. The development of a labor shortage subsequently permitted the labor movement—including its German-speaking component—to rebuild and help restore some of the lost purchasing power. The resulting pressure on profits and managerial prerogatives, however, provoked an employers' counteroffensive against the reconstituted unions. Citing the demands of the war effort, local, state, and federal officials as well as Union commanders threw their weight behind the employers. State legislatures in New York, Ohio, Illinois, and Massachusetts passed laws circumscribing the freedoms of trade unions. In April 1864, the military

commander of St. Louis, General William S. Rosecrans, ordered an
end to all strikes and labor organizations generally in war-related industries, threatening to try offenders in military courts. Rosecrans's
decree called forth expressions of outrage, but a month later General
Stephen Burbridge issued a second such edict in Louisville. A leader
of the *Chicagoer Arbeiterverein* regarded such abuse of martial law as
a menace to northern democracy. Security on the home front, he held,
would more safely be policed by a network of citizen defense organizations.[5]

Northern Democrats and their German-born advocates (including
the editors of the *New Yorker Staats-Zeitung* and Cincinnati's *Volksfreund*) sought to capitalize on German discontent on the home front.
With the fall of Fort Sumter, men like August Belmont and Oswald
Ottendorfer had taken a stand for defense of the Union. Before very
long, however, they were attacking Lincoln for waging "a war of extermination" against the South, and in 1864 the two men supervised
the campaign of Democratic presidential candidate George McClellan
among German voters. Belmont opened his party's convention that
year with the proclamation that "four years of misrule by a sectional,
fanatical and corrupt party have brought our country to the very verge
of ruin."[6]

The New York City riots of mid-July 1863 seemed to reveal a
growing receptivity to such Democratic rhetoric. Iver Bernstein notes
that some Germans joined in the more orderly and circumscribed protests against the draft that occurred on Monday, July 13. But the Germans largely withdrew from the streets as the draft protests degen-
erated into looting sprees and murderous attacks on black citizens. In
both New York and Newark, meanwhile, rioters targeted individuals
as well as buildings identified with German Republicanism, and members of New York's *Turnvereine* and *Schutzenvereine* joined others in
patrolling *Kleindeutschland* "to protect lives and property." On Manhattan's Seventh Avenue, a crowd that lynched a black man reportedly
hung a sign around the victim's neck branding him a "Black Dutchman."[7]

As these examples suggest, fundamental differences in purpose distinguished the stance of German democrats from that of leading German Democrats. In and out of uniform, the former maintained a steady
drumfire during the war in favor of a more aggressive, egalitarian,
and straightforwardly antislavery program than the one enunciated by
Lincoln, and they raised demands that often brought them into close
collaboration with congressional Radical Republicans. "We criticize
the Administration because it offers too little resistance against the

Rebels," emphasized one committee of German Republicans early in the war, "not because it opposes them too forcefully." As for German-born Copperheads, the Cincinnati *Arbeiterverein* considered them "deserving [of] the contempt of every loyal citizen."[8]

The Chicago *Arbeiterverein* had agreed to provide national leadership to German-American labor at the end of the 1850s, and kept its promise during the war and postwar years. The summer of 1861 found its members debating not about the merits of last-ditch compromise with the South, but whether "the current war against the slaveholders [is] worthy of support so long as it does not openly aim at slavery's abolition or have that as its certain consequence." General John C. Frémont's August order emancipating all Rebel-owned slaves in Missouri drew enthusiastic applause in this quarter. Frémont's initiative had inspired Germans "to report for military duties in large numbers," reported the *Socialer Arbeiterverein* of Chicago's Tenth Ward. By promptly rescinding Frémont's order, Abraham Lincoln made a great many enemies. The *Chicagoer Arbeiterverein*'s Joachim Kersten, a tailor, chaired a protest meeting at the *Arbeiterhalle* in September 1861. A full year before Lincoln's preliminary Emancipation Proclamation, the German-Americans at this gathering declared that "slavery existing in the southern states of the Union is the cause of the present war" and that "the peace of the Union cannot be restored unless this infamous institution is completely abolished." Only in that way could the South be defeated quickly; the administration's lack of firm antislavery principles lay behind indecisive, temporizing military tactics that prolonged the war and its attendant suffering. The Tenth Ward *Socialer Arbeiterverein* went further, asserting that "Lincoln's mutilation of General Frémont's proclamation" was nothing less than "treason against our country."[9]

A few months later, Lincoln defied these sentiments and removed Frémont from command altogether. Some German troops in Missouri threatened mutiny. Frémont's replacement, General Henry Halleck, though himself of German ancestry, was appalled by the political complexion of these immigrant enlisted men. "Officered in many cases by foreign adventurers or perhaps refugees from justice and having been tampered with by political partisans for political purposes," he wrote McClellan in January of 1862, they "constitute a very dangerous element in society as well as in the army."[10]

The *Chicagoer Arbeiterverein* embraced Lincoln's Emancipation Proclamation and celebrated it in public meetings. Those meetings demonstrated, as one speaker put it, that "this society recognizes that this battle is a battle of workers." Northern Democrats again warned that emancipation would flood the North with low-wage black laborers whose competition for work would drive down the living standards of poor (and especially immigrant) whites. German Republicans replied that, on the contrary, the former slave would remain in the South "if his human rights are respected" there. But the *Arbeiterverein* repudiated Illinois's attempts to exclude blacks by law as "a disgrace to a free state." In July 1863 the *Arbeiterverein*'s leaders denounced "the atrocities committed against defenseless people, the murders, robbberies, looting, and arson" in New York City, adding that those "who incited men to riot must also be classed as friends of the Rebels." A committee elected by the society's membership (which by now exceeded one thousand) firmly endorsed the suppression of the draft riot "with several bullets."[11]

Lincoln's decision to free the slaves in states still in rebellion pleased but did not satisfy Radical Republican critics. Eventually the desire for a still more aggressive and consistently abolitionist policy led some to seek an alternative presidential candidate for the 1864 elections. Members of the *Chicagoer Arbeiterverein*, meeting in March 1864, were "perfectly willing to acknowledge the good personal qualities of our present [Chief] Executive" but nonetheless complained that "his administration has been a vacillating one, without any system." As a result of Lincoln's dilatory and passive policies, the nation "more than once has been carried to the abyss, the war prolonged, the sacrifices multiplied." Reviewing possible replacements for Lincoln, it added, "no one has such a deep hold upon the sympathies of the majority of the German citizens as John C. Frémont."[12]

Frémont's German supporters drafted a comprehensive political platform. They demanded protection of popular liberties in the North, specifying that "the rights of free speech, press, and the habeus corpus, be held inviolable save in districts where martial law has been proclaimed." They also demanded a Radical Republican war policy premised on the Confederacy's unconditional surrender, the nationwide abolition of slavery, congressional supervision of Reconstruction, and legislation ensuring "all men absolute equality before the law" and "confiscation of the lands of the rebels and their distribution among the soldiers and actual settlers."[13]

German partisans of Frémont's candidacy rallied in a number of states. Fritz Anneke, a harsh critic of Lincoln, reported that "a large number of Germans who are true to their principles oppose the reelection of the weak-headed, unprincipled log-splitter." Other German Republicans encountered the same phenomenon, though often greeting it with less enthusiasm. In Pittsburgh, a German editor critical of Frémont was "astonished to see how unanimous classes of people are in their resolve to support" the Pathfinder's challenge. Gustav Körner, who had become a Lincoln confidant, also "regretted . . . that so many Germans were found in opposition to Lincoln." (Such people, Körner explained in his memoirs, were simply "highly impractical idealists." They were "most radical on the slavery question, and Lincoln was too slow for them.") Lincoln himself, already sensitized to political currents among German voters, feared their support for Frémont would split the Union (Republican) vote deeply enough to throw Illinois, Wisconsin, and New York to McClellan, and with them the presidency.[14]

Ultimately the Frémont movement collapsed. General William T. Sherman's crucial capture of Atlanta on September 2, 1864, represented a major improvement in the Union's military fortunes and initiated a correspondingly sharp revival in the Lincoln administration's popularity. All at once the president seemed both willing and able actually to crush the foe. In the meantime, Frémont had proved himself less radical than his platform and his would-be constituents, specifically rejecting reform proposals that entailed large-scale confiscation of landed property.[15]

Frémont announced the end of his campaign on September 22, 1864, and German democrats generally returned to the Republican fold, where they once more bolstered its Radical wing. Their vocal support for emancipationist policies brought them repeatedly into collision with conservative forces. Lincoln's 1864 reelection induced a recalcitrant House of Representatives to approve a constitutional amendment (the Thirteenth) that outlawed slavery nationwide. One of the few northern states to refuse its endorsement was New Jersey. Four weeks before Appomatox—on Sunday evening, March 19, 1865—antislavery Germans in Newark's Sixth Ward assembled to insist upon ratification. Unsympathetic city fathers dispatched police to break up the meeting, claiming that it violated Newark's sabbatarian laws. The flow of events, however, could not be deflected. The German meeting simply reconvened at Turner Hall a few days later, and Republicans eventually captured the New Jersey state legislature, which then ratified the Thirteenth Amendment. In 1866 the national convention of the Turner movement passed a resolution in favor of strong federal civil rights legislation and supported Congress's struggle against Andrew Johnson over the nature and future of Reconstruction.[16]

At last the road seemed open toward the future envisioned by Fritz Anneke early in 1864. "When the rebellion is crushed," he wrote, "the United States will take a quite unprecedented upturn. In a few years the South will be thickly populated, especially by soldiers and industrialists of the north, and be settled by this immigration and the free negroes; and agriculture, trade, industry will flourish as never before. But that is not all. We shall decisively influence the politics of Europe and the globe. We shall appear with propaganda and support the Revolution wherever it may appear, and . . . by '67 it [Europe] may be republican."[17]

The Contradictions of Victory

The triumph of the Union did initiate an "unprecedented upturn" in the development of industrial capitalism in the United States. Victory over the planter class removed a major barrier to the free extension and development of the free labor economy. Industrialization, urbanization, and immigration made rapid strides in the next decades. In just twenty years (1870–90), the nation's manufacturing work force more than doubled in size while manufacturing investment tripled. The average number of workers employed per firm grew by about 50 percent, an aggregate figure that conceals much sharper rates of concentration in particular firms and industries. The United States replaced Great Britain as the world's premier industrial nation.[18]

These changes had major political consequences. Contradictions within the republican (and Republican) ideologies of free labor that had begun to emerge in the antebellum era now asserted themselves with greater force. As the social chasm widened between those who freely hired labor and those free to labor for them, observers with diverse political views grew alarmed. "Our late war resulted in the building up of the most infamous monied aristocracy on the face of the earth," warned William Sylvis (president of the new National Labor Union) in 1869, and "this monied power is fast eating up the substance of the people." The conservative Republican *New York Daily Times* noted that same year that little workshops were "far less common than they were before the war" and that "the small manufacturers thus swallowed up have become workmen [for] wages in the greater establishments." Industrial America thus stared into the face of "a system of slavery as absolute if not as degrading as that which lately prevailed [in] the South," one in which "manufacturing capitalists threaten to become the masters, and it is the white laborers who are to be slaves." "He is blind to facts and figures," the *Times* declared, "who does not see this antagonism between the employing capitalists and the workingmen of this country increasing daily in bitterness." The Republican *Illinois Staats-Zeitung* joined the chorus soon afterward, worrying that "as factory industry develops and population becomes more dense, the misproportion between fixed wages and increasing capital will increase," one result of which would be the rise of "an obtuse, savage, ignorant and violent mass of proletarians." Meanwhile, in the states of the former Confederacy, dreams of replacing the slave labor system with a society based on either independent small-peasant cultivation or an idealized version of free wage labor foundered.[19]

In this corrosive atmosphere, the social and intellectual foundations of the old German-American radical democracy began to disintegrate. Some, unprepared for these consequences of the Union victory, became embittered and discouraged, withdrawing to the political sidelines. Many others—guided by personal prosperity, evolving philosophies, or both—became increasingly convinced that the defense of civil liberty required the most zealous enforcement of property rights and social order.

For enterprising individuals, the postwar era abounded in personal opportunities. Compendia of notable German-Americans and many state and city histories written in the late nineteenth and early twentieth centuries brim over with the names of "successful" immigrant artisans, small shopkeepers, and professionals whose children and grandchildren steadily ascended the ladders of economic, social, and political prominence. The Republican party in particular offered unprecedented career opportunities to talented and energetic individuals. Friedrich Engels had warned Joseph Weydemeyer years earlier that the "greatest obstacle" to Weydemeyer's political progress in the United States would be "the fact that reliable Germans, those who are worth anything, readily become Americanised." Influenced by "special American circumstances," including "the necessarily rapid, indeed ever more rapid, increase in the country's prosperity," they soon come "to regard bourgeois conditions as the *beau idéal*." In 1871 Eduard Schläger depicted the later evolution of many forty-eighters in similar terms. Once proud of their own traditions, he noted, such people now evinced growing "indifference to specific German endeavors" and greater respect for "American methods"—particularly "the disagreeable ones, the greed for gold and the business shrewdness." These "Greens" had in this respect followed in the footsteps of the once-despised "Grays."[20]

This conservative drift was strengthened by unforeseen developments in the old country, too. Expectations that German unity would occur on a republican basis were confounded. Unification imposed from above by King (and then Emperor) Wilhelm I and Bismarck for the first time made it possible during the 1860s and 1870s to link the chariot of all-German patriotism to the horses of political and social conservatism. Even Fritz Anneke, once a staunch and optimistic republican, had by the summer of 1870 drawn drastic conclusions. "The Republic is not to be thought of for the time being," he wrote Mathilde. But "old William takes a very noble and fine position, and I can forgive him everything. He is now the representative of the only Germany, and as prince a worthy representative."[21]

The impact of these unexpected transformations on German America manifested themselves in the postwar history of the Turners. Renamed the *Amerikanischer Turnerbund,* the national federation turned further and further away from its radical roots. The movement's social composition began to change, too; small businessmen, officeholders, and professionals made up a rising proportion of the membership. While an activist stratum and individual Turner chapters continued to champion reform, the organizational life of the Turners, on the whole, revealed a declining interest in social or political change. "The later history of the *Turnerbund,*" observes an official account, "consists chiefly . . . of the various gymnastic festivals and conventions which, though eminently successful, are of particular interest only to those who are intimately identified with the organization." The passage of time left its mark on the forty-eighter press as well. The *Illinois Staats-Zeitung*—purchased by Anton C. Hesing, who became a political boss in Chicago—grew increasingly hostile to social radicalism. "America," it insisted, "with its vigorous realism, is just the place for separating the legitimate components of the labor movement from the anti-rational and confused fantasies with which it surrounds itself in Europe."[22]

No one, however, personified this rightward political shift better than Carl Schurz, who may fairly be called its pioneer. In 1848 Schurz was the proud protégé of the radical democrat Gottfried Kinkel, and he became a Radical Republican during the Civil War. Over the following decade, however, Schurz evolved into a spokesman for a "Liberal Republican" movement that demanded an end to Reconstruction, an embrace of laissez-faire economic policy, and a government apparatus guided (like the economy) by society's "best men" of culture, breeding, and wealth.

By 1872 Schurz was complaining that in the Reconstruction South "the rule of unprincipled and rapacious leaders at the head of the colored population has resulted in a government of corruption and plunder and gives no promise of improvement." It was the freedmen's support for the era's Republican state governments in the South, he now asserted, that left them unable to reach "a good understanding with their white neighbors." Schurz subsequently opposed federal support for civil rights and federal resistance to Ku Klux Klan terror "as transgressing the limits with which the Constitution hedges in the competency of the National Government, and as encroaching upon the sphere of State authority." As Rutherford B. Hayes's Secretary of the Interior, Schurz fought the attempt by federal employees to secure an eight-hour working day. He concluded from the great strikes of 1877 that since local militias were too weak and undependable to deal with civil disturbances, the nation needed to maintain a larger standing army. Schurz's later years also brought him delight in "the friendly contact I have had with Prince Bismarck and other German statesmen" who "have spoken to me with such frankness and confidence."[23]

Nationality, Class, and the Politics of Tradition

In 1898 Schurz memorialized his generation of immigrant reformers in a speech celebrating a half-century since the abortive German Revolution. "Surely no one will deny," Schurz presumed, "that these German representatives of the movement of '48 who have sought a new home in America have always been good and conscientious citizens of their new fatherland." Indeed, he added, "most of them have proved that the revolutionary agitators of 1848 could become reliable and conservative citizens under a free government."[24]

Many subsequent chroniclers of German-American history followed Schurz's lead, portraying the German immigrants' experience in antebellum America as a mere prelude to the illustrious careers of Schurz and others like him. In such hands, German-American history became a sort of ethnic Horatio Alger tale. Its heroes were hard-working immigrants whose efforts stimulated the growth of industry, commerce, and mainstream cultural and political institutions in their adoptive land. In return for their notable contributions, these foreign-born individuals achieved varying degrees of personal prosperity and social prominence, both of which could be bequeathed to proud descendants.

This sanitized view of the past appealed strongly to those descendants, as it did more broadly to members of a German-American middle class anxious to achieve and maintain respectability and acceptance among their Anglo-American neighbors. This historical perspective was also useful to a certain stratum of German-American politicians, businessmen, editors, and others who functioned as ethnic intermediaries, or brokers, between immigrant countryfolk and the nation's English-speaking elite. The uncontroversial contributions of earlier German-Americans proved the intrinsic worthiness (and Americanism) of the broker's current constituents; they also justified political and economic demands made on their behalf (or, at least, in their name). And by touting success stories of "good and conscientious" German-American forebears, ethnic brokers encouraged hopeful newcomers to accept their own "reliable and conservative" counsel and leadership.[25]

In these circles, radical democratic and socialistic traditions had little or no value or utility. They did not add up to a "usable past," for either ethnic brokers or upwardly mobile German-Americans more generally. Those antecedents, on the contrary, became a source of embarrassment, matters best minimized, dismissed (as products of youthful utopianism or anachronistic European habits of mind), and then forgotten as soon as possible. The anti-German hysteria of World War I, which (as John Higham noted) was "thoroughly interwoven" with antiradicalism, only reinforced this attitude among German-Americans. The *Turnerbund* of the 1920s was content to record that "the impetuosity of the early days has given way to the thoughtful deliberation of later years." More and more German-American historians now stared perplexedly at the "queer resolutions" of the 1840s and 1850s, as though fingering the mysterious artifacts of some ancient and lost civilization. Albert B. Faust's landmark two-volume study *The German Element in the United States,* concluded that the "queer resolutions" endorsed by "socialistic, anarchistic, and humanitarian" groups of early immigrants were, in fact, insignificant, and urged readers "not [to] take them too seriously."[26]

In their repudiation of and selective amnesia concerning German-American radicalism, these writers of German immigrant stock were only repeating the behavior of mid-nineteenth-century Anglo-Americans, who had successfully forgotten the strength of Paine-ite, Jacobin currents in earlier decades—the more confidently to denounce immigrant radical democrats as altogether alien to American life and traditions.

That this view of German-American history won wide acceptance is attested to, ironically, by that iconoclast and champion of German values, H. L. Mencken. He caustically asserted in 1928 that "the influence of the Germans upon American life is very slight . . . and they have left no impression upon American ideas." Their principal claim to fame, Mencken added, was the introduction into the English language of a handful of words, most of them related to food and drink. "I can see no reason," he concluded, "why Germans should waste their time bemoaning the loss of the German-Americans." This scrubbed, manicured, and perfumed version of "the contributions and influence of German Americans" has also attracted champions of the "consensus" interpretation of the national experience—as the neoconservative scholar Thomas B. Sowell recently demonstrated in his survey *Ethnic America: A History*. "Germans did little political organizing," Sowell affirmed, and "politics never became a consuming interest of German Americans." But "nineteenth-century German immigrants and their offspring were responsible for establishing leading businesses in many American industries." They also made a notable impact on American culture, and "along with the Christmas tree, the frankfurter, the hamburger, and beer became fixtures of the American way of life," as had "Philadelphia scrapple, German chocolate cake, cole slaw, and sauerkraut." In fact, "one of the most important social changes wrought by the German immigrants was their promotion of numerous forms of innocent public family entertainment. Music, picnics, dancing, card playing, swimming, bowling, and other physical activities were among the American pastimes, now taken for granted, but introduced or promoted by Germans in the nineteenth century." In this connection, Sowell did note, "they organized gymnastic clubs called *Turnvereine*—or Turner societies—throughout the United States, stressing athletic activity, patriotism, and mental development."[27]

In 1982, a year after Professor Sowell's book appeared, Congress created a German-American Tricentennial Commission to celebrate three centuries of German settlement in North America. The commission's charge and composition reflected the influence of the homogenized, conservative version of the immigrant experience in America. Among the commission's tasks was to honor, as a congressional resolution put it, "the immeasurable human, economic, political, social, and cultural contributions to this country by millions of German immigrants over the past three centuries" and, in so doing, "to focus on the democratic values that bind us together." The commission itself was top-heavy with corporate officers; President Ronald Reagan selected Richard V. Allen as chair, his own former assistant for national security affairs, who subsequently had become a fellow of the Heritage Foundation and senior foreign policy advisor to the Republican National Committee.[28]

Neither Carl Schurz, Thomas Sowell, nor Ronald Reagan could find much room in the ethnohistorical pantheon for those nineteenth-century German-Americans who strove hard and long to transform their adopted homeland.[29] Led in some cases by veterans of the 1840s and 1850s and reinforced by huge postwar infusions of immigrant industrial workers and farm laborers, such people constituted a bridge between the socially heterogeneous radical democratic movements of the antebellum era and the more specifically working-class movements of later years (trade unionism, socialism, anarchism, and anarcho-syndicalism), with which many German-Americans became identified.

German-American workers played prominent roles in the historic nationwide upsurge of organized labor that occurred in the late 1860s and early 1870s and produced the National Labor Union (NLU). The NLU made Eduard Schläger (delegate of the *Chicagoer Arbeiterverein*) a vice president. In New York City, too—as a young Dutch-English immigrant named Samuel Gompers discovered—"forty-eight-ers" remained prominent in the postwar labor movement. Indeed, of the seven New York trade unions represented at the the NLU's second national convention, four were headed by Germans. New York's Labor Union No. 5 included Friedrich Sorge as well as leaders of the German tailors', cabinetmakers', and cigarmakers' unions. German-American craftworkers provided strong bases of support for sections of the International Workingmen's Association in St. Louis, Cincinnati, Baltimore, Philadelphia, Pittsburgh, Newark, Buffalo, and Detroit; New York City's Labor Union No. 5 doubled as Section 1 of the First International.[30]

The depression of 1873 put an end to the first postwar mobilization of American labor, but it did not sever all lines of continuity. German workers were ubiquitous in the mass strikes that shook the country in 1877. Afterward, Carl Schurz's frequent collaborator, E. L. Godkin of the *Nation,* urged "the well-to-do and intelligent classes of the population" to take note of "the profound changes which have during the last thirty years been wrought in the composition and character of the population, especially in the big cities. Vast additions have been made to it within that period, to whom American political and social ideals appeal but faintly, if at all, and who carry in their very blood traditions which give universal suffrage an air of menace to many of the things civilized men hold dear."[31]

German labor organizations also played key roles in the full-scale labor revival of the 1880s and the agitation for an eight-hour workday that provided the backdrop for the Haymarket affair in Chicago. Six of the eight Haymarket defendants were German-Americans, and the *Chicago Times*—once the proudly antinativist organ of Stephen Douglas—insisted that in general "the enemy forces are not American at all" but rather "rag-tag and bob-tail cutthroats of Beelzebub from the Rhine, the Danube, the Vistula, and the Elbe." On this point, at least, the Republican *Chicago Daily Tribune* heartily concurred. Chicago's problems, the *Tribune* held, was that it "has become the rendezvous of the worst elements of the socialistic, atheistic, alcoholic European classes."[32]

Radicalized German-American workers resisted attempts to write them—or their concerns and values—out of the American experience and out of U.S. history. They invoked an alternative set of outlooks, symbols, and memories that commonly combined themes carried forward from the old plebeian democracy with the sharper consciousness of class differences inspired by the hard conditions of life on both sides of the Atlantic in the later nineteenth century. They aimed to root the doctrine of class struggle in North American conditions and thereby to emphasize the fundamental identity of immigrant and native-born political traditions.

This stubborn alternative approach was apparent in the earliest postbellum era, as when Eduard Schläger urged the National Labor Union to separate from both the Democratic and Republican parties and form an independent labor party. Schläger appealed to the antebellum free-soil experience, citing it as an object lesson for the labor movement. "We are shy of fighting the old political parties but should not be," he argued. "The Free Soil Party originated with a few thousand voters; but if it had not been formed, Lincoln would never have been elected President of the United States."[33]

A few years later, in 1872, the platform adopted by the International's U.S. affiliates retained both goals and phraseology familiar since the 1840s and 1850s: "equal rights and duties," "complete political and social equality for all, without distinction of sex, creed, color, or condition," and "the principles of associative production, with a view to the complete supercession of the present system of capitalist production." Social changes in the interim had simply necessitated modifications in strategy and doctrine. A successful fight for these democratic, egalitarian goals (so the American Internationalists now held) required a type of movement and political orientation distinct from the old, socially diverse plebeian democracy. The platform asserted that "the emancipation of the working classes must be accomplished by the working classes themselves," who would in the process effect the "total abolition of all class rule and all class privileges."[34]

Four years later—in the midst of the nation's centennial celebration and on the eve of the 1877 strike wave—a July Fourth meeting attended in Chicago by left-wing Turners, a German labor militia (the *Lehr und Wehr Verein*), and members of the cabinetmakers' and other trade unions cheered the bilingual reading of a socialist "Declaration of Independence." The declaration denounced the abuse of such "self-evident" and "inalienable Rights" of workers as "Life, Liberty, and the full proceeds of their Labor." The authors looked forward to the day when "mass misery" and "social and political servitude . . . will be eliminated for all time . . . in a 'social republic.' " For that change to occur, however, it was necessary "for the members of one class of people to dissolve the political and social bands which have connected them with the others." A decade later in Chicago, the prison auto-biographies of the German Haymarket defendants rang with similar ethnopolitical themes. August Spies expressed pride in his long membership in Chicago's working-class "Aurora" chapter of the Turner movement. Spies's comrade Oscar Neebe traced his own hostility to organized religion back to a youthful study of Thomas Paine. Adolph Fischer invoked the antislavery struggle to belittle the hope "that the modern slave-holders—the capitalists—would voluntarily, without being forced to do so, give up their privileges and set free their wage slaves."[35]

The line of ethnic, cultural, and political continuity captured in these episodes did not lend itself readily to more familiar celebrations of successful adjustment, individual opportunity, and upward mobility. Much less did it prove the universal appeal over time of any national political consensus. It was, instead, part of an alternative tradition, one that valued not Carl Schurz but his less illustrious compatriots and contemporaries, a tradition whose latter-day adherents—such as Socialist Party historian Hermann Schlüter—would look upon the antebellum generation of immigrant activists as "pioneers of the modern radical wing."[36]

Appendix

Table A
Employment in Leading U.S. Industries, Both Sexes, 1850

	All Hands	Male	Female
Boots and shoes	105,254	73,305	32,949
Cottons and weavers	98,888	36,072	62,816
Clothiers and tailors	96,551	35,051	61,500
Lumber, sawing and planing	52,218	51,766	452
Woolens, carding, fulling	45,895	—	—
Machinists and millwrights	27,892	27,834	58
Blacksmiths	25,002	24,983	19
Tanners, curriers, morocco dr's	24,542	24,247	295
Flour and grist mills	23,310	23,260	50
Cabinetware	22,010	20,997	1,013
Iron furnaces	21,054	20,847	207
Iron foundries	18,969	18,938	31
Carpenters and builders	15,282	15,276	6
Hats and caps	15,200	6,974	8,226
Coal mining	15,118	15,112	6
Agricultural implements	7,220	7,211	9
Tobacconists	14,236	12,261	1,975
Coaches and carriages	14,040	13,982	58
Saddles and harnesses	12,958	12,598	360
Ship and boat building	12,629	—	—
Coopers	11,916	11,900	16
Wheelwrights	11,549	11,542	7
Stone and marble quarries	10,001	9,996	5
Iron forges	7,775	7,698	77
Tin and sheet iron	7,393	7,365	28

Source: C. G. Kennedy, *Abstract of the Statistics of Manufactures of the Seventh Census* (Washington, D.C.: Government Printing Office, 1858).

Table B
Selected U.S. Manual Occupations, White and Free Black Males, 1850

	Number of Individuals
Carpenters and builders	185,898
Cordwainers	130,473
Black- and whitesmiths	99,703
Miners	77,410
Masons and plasterers	63,392
Tailors and clothiers	55,849
Joiners, cabinet- and chairmakers	50,031
Coopers	43,694
Weavers and spinners	37,564
Machinists, millwrights	33,708
Wheelwrights	30,693
Painters and glaziers	28,166
Millers	27,795
Lumbermen, sawyers, woodcutters	23,366
Saddle- and harnessmakers	22,779
Butchers	17,733
Tanners, curriers, morocco dressers	16,911
Coach- and wagonmakers	15,599
Printers	14,740
Bakers	14,256
Stone and marble cutters, quarry	15,978
Tinsmiths	11,747
Brickmakers	11,514
Hat and cap manufacturers	11,024
Tobacconists and cigarmakers	10,823

Note: The data are for legally free males fifteen years of age or older.
Source: DeBow, *Statistical View of the United States, Compendium of the Seventh Census.*

Table C
Average Annual Wages in Selected Trades, 1850 and 1860

	1850	1860
Carpenters	$366	$430
Tailors	$156	$173
Shoemakers	$205	$251
Upholsterers	$242	$298
Tanners, curriers, leathermakers	$248	$313
Bakers	$291	$320
Cabinetmakers	$302	$329

Note: Rounded off to the nearest whole dollar, these average wages represent crude calculations. They have been obtained simply by dividing the total work force into the total annual wage bill in each industry. No attempt is made to distinguish between male and female workers or between full- and part-time workers.
Sources: Kennedy, *Abstract of the Statistics of Manufactures of the Seventh Census;* Secretary of the Interior, *Manufactures of the United States in 1860* (Washington, D.C.: Government Printing Office, 1865).

Table D
Property Ownership among Leading Anti-Nebraska Germans in Newark

Craftsman	1850 Data	1860 Data
Tailor I	No property	—
Harnessmaker	No property	—
Cabinetmaker	No property	—
Stonecutter	—	$100
Tailor II	—	$200
Blacksmith	—	$200
Cutler	—	$2,000
Jeweler	$2,000	—
Ropemaker	$2,000	—
Chairmaker	—	$7,000

Sources: U.S. Census, population schedules for Essex County, N.J., seventh (1850) and eighth (1860) censuses.

Notes

Introduction: "Either Social or Political Refugees"

1. Oscar Handlin, *The Uprooted: The Epic Story of the Great Migrations that Made the American People* (New York: Grosset and Dunlap, 1951), p. 3; Maldwyn Allen Jones, *American Immigration* (Chicago: University of Chicago Press, 1960), p. 1.

2. Jones, *American Immigration,* p. 1; John Higham, "Another Look at Nativism," *Catholic Historical Review* 44 (July 1958), reprinted in *Pivotal Interpretations of American History,* ed. Carl N. Degler (New York: Harper and Row, 1966), vol. 2, pp. 142–53.

3. These figures are derived from the table data in Stanley Lebergott, "The Pattern of Employment since 1800," in *American Economic History,* ed. Seymour Harris (New York: McGraw-Hill, 1961), p. 292. Michael Reich calculates that of (legally free) "income recipients who participated directly in economic activity," 80 percent were self-employed and 20 percent subsisted on wages or salaries in 1780, while a century later the respective percentages were 37 and 62 ("The Evolution of the United States Labor Force," in *The Capitalist System: A Radical Analysis of American Society,* ed. Richard C. Edwards et al. [Englewood Cliffs, N.J.: Prentice-Hall, 1972], p. 175). David Montgomery estimates that in 1870, 33 percent of the work force were self-employed and 67 percent worked for wages. The three calculations thus vary in detail, but all three conform to the same general historical trends (*Beyond Equality: Labor and the Radical Republicans, 1862–1872* [New York: Alfred A. Knopf, 1967], pp. 448–56).

4. Joseph C. G. Kennedy, *Population of the United States in 1860; Compiled from the Original Returns of the Eighth Census* (Washington, D.C.: Government Printing Office, 1864), pp. xxxi–xxxii; Niles Carpenter, *Immigrants and Their Children, 1920* (Washington, D.C.: Government Printing Office, 1927), pp. 62, 77, 324; E. P. Hutchinson, *Immigrants and Their Children* (New York: John Wiley, 1956), p. 2; Jones, *American Immigration,* p. 117; and

Marcus Lee Hansen, *The Atlantic Migration, 1607–1860: A History of the Continuing Settlement of the United States* (New York: Harper and Row, 1961), p. 180.

5. Rowland Berthoff, *An Unsettled People: Social Order and Disorder in American History* (New York: Harper and Row, 1971), pp. 182–83, 477–78. On the international significance of the migrations, see Klaus J. Bade, ed., *Auswanderer, Wanderarbeiter, Gastarbeiter: Bevölkerung, Arbeitsmarkt und Wanderung in Deutschland seit der Mitte des 19. Jahrhunderts* (Ostfildern: Scripta Mercaturae, 1984) and the publications of the Labor Migration Project based at the University of Bremen, headed by Professor Dirk Hoerder.

6. "New York Industrial Exhibition. Special Report of Mr. George Wallis. Presented to the House of Commons . . . February 6, 1854," in *The American System of Manufactures,* ed. Nathan Rosenberg (Edinburgh: Edinburgh University Press, 1969), p. 208; Ford is reprinted in *Historical Aspects of the Immigration Problem,* ed. Edith Abbott (Chicago: University of Chicago Press, 1926), pp. 382–83; letter of August 20, 1871, from the North American Central Committee of the International Workingmen's Association (IWA) to the London Conference, in the Letterbooks of the General Council, IWA Papers, State Historical Society of Wisconsin, Madison; H. Gerth, ed., *The First International: Minutes of the Hague Congress of 1872 with Related Documents* (Madison: University of Wisconsin Press, 1958), pp. 197–99; Rev. Samuel Lane Loomis, *Modern Cities and their Religious Problems* (New York: Baker and Taylor, 1887), pp. 65–66, 73.

7. Herbert G. Gutman and Ira Berlin, "Class Composition and the Development of the American Working Class, 1840–1890," in Gutman, *Power and Culture: Essays on the American Working Class,* ed. Ira Berlin (New York: Pantheon Books, 1987), pp. 382–91. See also David Montgomery, "To Study the People: The American Working Class," *Labor History* 21 (1980): 502–3.

8. Gutman and Berlin, "Class Composition," p. 394.

9. By 1890, the United States' 2.8 million German-born residents constituted about 30 percent of the nation's total recorded foreign-born population. The Irish-born numbered 1.9 million and represented about 20 percent of the foreign-born total. The massive "new immigration" that made itself felt during the 1890s reduced but did not eliminate the German plurality by 1900. See U.S. Bureau of the Census, *Historical Statistics of the United States, Colonial Times to 1970* (Washington, D.C.: Government Printing Office, 1975), vol. 1, pp. 8–9, 117–18.

10. *New York Daily Tribune,* April 23, 1850; Friedrich Sorge, *The Labor Movement in the United States,* ed. B. Chamberlin and P. Foner (Westport, Conn.: Greenwood Press, 1977), p. 199. This work was originally published in Berlin in 1891–95.

11. Isabella Lucy Bird, *The Englishwoman in America* (1856; repr., Madison: University of Wisconsin Press, 1966), pp. 119–20; Thomas R. Whitney, *A Defence of the American Policy, as Opposed to the Encroachments of Foreign*

Influence, and Especially to the Interference of the Papacy in the Political Interests and Affairs of the United States (New York: Dewitt and Davenport, [1856]), pp. 167–69.

12. R. R. Palmer, *The Age of the Democratic Revolution* (Princeton, N.J.: Princeton University Press, 1969), vol. 1, pp. 4–5.

13. Carl Schurz, *The Reminiscences of Carl Schurz*, 2 vols. (New York: Doubleday, Page and Co., 1909), vol. 1, p. 137.

14. See, for example, George Rudé, *Debate on Europe, 1815–1850* (New York: Harper and Row, 1972) and *Ideology and Popular Protest* (New York: Harper and Row, 1980); Charles Breunig, *The Age of Revolution and Reaction, 1789–1850* (New York: W. W. Norton and Co., 1970); Eric J. Hobsbawm, *The Age of Revolution, 1789–1848* (New York: New American Library, 1962); Staughton Lynd, *Intellectual Origins of American Radicalism* (New York: Vintage Books, 1969); Barrington Moore, Jr., *Social Origins of Dictatorship and Democracy: Lord and Peasant in the Making of the Modern World* (Boston: Beacon Press, 1967); Richard D. Brown, *Modernization: The Transformation of American Life, 1600–1865* (New York: Hill and Wang, 1976); Alfred F. Young, ed., *The American Revolution: Explorations in the History of American Radicalism* (DeKalb: Northern Illinois University Press, 1976); Lewis B. Namier, *1848: The Revolution of the Intellectuals* (Oxford: Oxford University Press, 1946); Charles Morazé, *The Triumph of the Middle Classes: A Political and Social History of Europe in the Nineteenth Century* (Garden City, N.Y.: Anchor Books, 1968); Margaret Jacob and James Jacob, eds., *The Origins of Anglo-American Radicalism* (London: Allen and Unwin, 1984); Theodore S. Hamerow, "History and the German Revolution of 1848," *American Historical Review* 55 (1954–55): 27–44; Andreas Dorpalen, "Revolutions of 1848," in *Marxism, Communism, and Western Society*, ed. C. C. Kerring (New York: Herder and Herder, 1973), vol. 7, pp. 244–53; Donald J. Mattheisen, "History as Current Events: Recent Works on the German Revolution of 1848," *American Historical Review* 88 (1983): 1219–37; Dieter Langewiesche, "Einleitung," in *Die deutsche Revolution von 1848/49*, ed. Langewiesche (Darmstadt: Wissenschaftliche Buchgesellschaft, 1983).

15. Hobsbawm, *Age of Revolution*, p. 86; see also Hobsbawm's *The Age of Capital, 1848–1875* (New York: New American Library, 1975), pp. 16–18; E. P. Thompson, *The Making of the English Working Class* (New York: Pantheon Books, 1963), p. 262.

16. See Marcus Lee Hansen, "The Revolution of 1848 and the German Emigration," *Journal of Economic and Business History* 2 (August 1930): 630–31. Hansen's thesis reappeared almost verbatim in his influential posthumous summation, *The Atlantic Migration*, p. 274. See also Hildegard Binder Johnson, "Adjustment to the United States," in *The Forty-Eighters: Political Refugees of the German Revolution of 1848*, ed. A. E. Zucker (1950; repr. New York: Russell and Russell, 1967), p. 43. Cf. Günter Moltmann, "German Emigration during the First Half of the Nineteenth Century as a Social Protest Movement," in *Germany and America*, ed. Hans Trefousse (New York:

Brooklyn College Press, 1980), and see also P. H. Noyes's observations in *Organization and Revolution: Working-Class Associations in the German Revolution of 1848–49* (Princeton, N.J.: Princeton University Press, 1966), p. 2.

17. Friedrich Kapp, quoted in the *New York Daily Times,* August 22, 1856.

18. Eugen Seeger, *Chicago: The Wonder City* (Chicago: Gregory, 1893), pp. 105–7; George von Skal, *The History of the German Immigration to the United States and Successful German-Americans and their Descendants* (New York: F. T. and J. C. Smiley, 1908), p. 28; Carl Wittke, *Refugees of Revolution: The German Forty-Eighters in America* (1952; repr., Westport, Conn.: Greenwood Press, 1970), p. 341.

19. Charles A. Beard and Mary R. Beard, *The Rise of American Civilization* (New York: Macmillan, 1930); James M. McPherson, *Battle Cry of Freedom: The Civil War Era* (New York: Oxford University Press, 1988); Eric Foner, *Politics and Ideology in the Age of the Civil War* (New York: Oxford University Press, 1980) and *Reconstruction: America's Unfinished Revolution, 1863–1877* (New York: Harper and Row, 1988).

20. F. B. Sanborn, ed., *The Life and Letters of John Brown, Liberator of Kansas, and Martyr of Virginia* (1885; repr., New American Library, 1969), p. 146; Philip S. Foner, ed., *The Life and Writings of Frederick Douglass,* 5 vols. (New York: International Publishers, 1975), vol. 2, p. 50; Wendell Phillips, *Speeches, Lectures, and Letters,* ed. Theodore C. Pease, 2d ed. (Boston: Lee and Shepard, 1891), p. 29; Roy P. Basler, ed., *The Collected Works of Abraham Lincoln,* 8 vols. (New Brunswick, N.J.: Rutgers University Press, 1953), vol. 4, p. 438, and vol. 7, p. 14.

21. Montgomery, *Beyond Equality,* p. 91.

22. Some notable exceptions are John Jentz, "Artisans, Evangelicals, and the City: A Social History of Abolition and Labor Reform in Jacksonian New York" (Ph.D. diss., City University of New York, 1977); Jonathan A. Glickstein, " 'Poverty Is Not Slavery': American Abolitionists and the Competitive Labor Market," in *Antislavery Reconsidered: New Perspectives on the Abolitionists,* ed. Lewis Perry and Michael Fellman (Baton Rouge: Louisiana State University Press, 1979); and Eric Foner, "Abolitionism and the Labor Movement in Ante-bellum America," in his *Politics and Ideology;* and Edward Magdol, *The Antislavery Rank and File: A Social Profile of the Abolitionists' Constituency* (Westport, Conn.: Greenwood Press, 1986), which focuses on the 1830s.

23. Frederick Douglass, "Adopted Citizens and Slavery," *Douglass's Monthly* (August 1859); William E. Dodd, "The Fight for the Northwest, 1860," *American Historical Review* 16 (1910): 786–88; Donnal V. Smith, "The Influence of the Foreign-born of the North West in the Election of 1860," *Mississippi Valley Historical Review* 19 (September 1932): 200.

24. Joseph Schafer, "Who Elected Lincoln?" *American Historical Review* 47 (September 1941): 58; John A. Hawgood, *The Tragedy of German-America: The Germans in the United States of America during the Nineteenth Century—and After* (New York: G. P. Putnam's Sons, 1940), p. 52; Frank L.

Klement, *The Copperheads in the Middle West* (Chicago: University of Chicago Press, 1960), p. 13; Robert Kelley, *The Cultural Pattern in American Politics* (New York: Alfred A. Knopf, 1979), pp. 16, 27.

25. The quoted phrase comes from Carl Degler's summary of the "ethnocultural" argument in his essay, "Remaking American History," *Journal of American History* 67 (June 1980): 17–18.

Chapter 1: "So Deeply Interwoven": General Crisis and Emigration

1. *Historical Statistics of the United States: Colonial Times to 1970,* vol. 1, pp. 8–9; Mack Walker, *Germany and the Emigration, 1816–1885* (Cambridge, Mass.: Harvard University Press, 1964), p. 157.

2. Wilhelm Mönckmeier, *Die deutsche überseeische Auswanderung: Ein Beitrag zur deutschen Wanderungsgeschichte* (Jena: Verlag von Gustav Fischer, 1912). p. 7; Wolfgang Köllmann and Peter Marschalck, "German Emigration to the United States," *Perspectives in American History* 7 (1973): 517, 522, 531–32; Walker, *Germany and the Emigration,* pp. 70–74; F. Burgdörfer, "Migration across the Frontiers of Germany," in *International Migrations,* ed. Walter F. Wilcox (New York: National Bureau of Economic Research, 1931), pp. 317–18, 346–48.

3. Köllmann and Marschalck, "German Emigration," pp. 523–24, 530, 532; Walker, *Germany and the Emigration,* pp. 47, 51, 64, 74–78, 160; Hildegard Rosenthal, *Die Auswanderung aus Sachsen im 19. Jahrhundert (1815–1871),* p. 88; Clifford Neal Smith, *Emigrants from Saxony (Grandduchy of Sachsen-Weimar-Eisenach) to America, 1854, 1859* (pamphlet) (DeKalb, Ill.: Westland Publications, 1974); Helmut Sedatis, *Liberalismus und Handwerk in Südwestdeutschland* (Stuttgart: Klett-Cotta, 1979), pp. 122, 124; J. D. B. DeBow, `Statistical View of the United States, Compendium of the Seventh Census* (Washington, D.C.: Beverley Tucker, 1854), p. 123. Among Mecklenburgers departing in 1854, 45 percent were laborers, 12 percent were farmers, and 31 percent were craftworkers. For 1855–57, 67 percent were laborers, and 23.5 percent were craftworkers (Mönckmeier, *Deutsche überseeische Auswanderung,* pp. 154–60). A classic, and still invaluable, example of immigration studies that focus on professionals and the well-to-do is Gustav Körner's *Das deutsche Element in den Vereinigten Staaten von Nordamerika, 1818–1848* (Cincinnati: Verlag von A. E. Wilde and Co., 1880).

4. William Howitt, *The Rural and Domestic Life of Germany: with Characteristic Sketches of its Cities and Scenery, Collected in a General Tour, and during a Residence in the Country in the Years 1840, 41 and 42* (Philadelphia: Carey and Hart, 1843), pp. 55–56, 81.

5. Adna Ferrin Weber, *The Growth of Cities in the Nineteenth Century: A Study in Statistics* (Ithaca, N.Y.: Cornell University Press, 1963), pp. 15, 82, 84–86, 144; Phyllis Deane and W. A. Cole, *British Economic Growth, 1688–1959* (Cambridge: Cambridge University Press, 1967), p. 142; Friedrich-Wilhelm Henning, *Die Industrialisierung in Deutschland, 1800 bis 1914* (Paderborn: Ferdinand Schöningh, 1973), pp. 20, 130; Diedrich Saalfeld, "Le-

bensverhältnisse der Unterschichten Deutschlands im Neunzehnten Jahrhundert," *International Review of Social History* 29 (1984): 218; Helmut Böhme, *An Introduction to the Social and Economic History of Germany: Politics and Economic Change in the Nineteenth and Twentieth Centuries* (New York: St. Martin's Press, 1978), pp. 1–8.

6. Reinhart Koselleck, *Preussen zwischen Reform und Revolution: Allgemeines Landrecht, Verwaltung und soziale Bewegung von 1791 bis 1848*, 2d ed. (Stuttgart: Klett-Cotta, 1981), pp. 23–51, 78–115; Friedrich Lütge, *Deutsche Sozial- und Wirtschaftsgeschichte: Ein Überblick*, 3d ed. (Berlin: Springer-Verlag, 1966), pp. 344–86, 445–53; Jürgen Kocka, "Entrepreneurs and Managers in German Industrialization," in *Cambridge Economic History of Europe*, 7 vols. (Cambridge: Cambridge University Press, 1978), vol. 7, part 1, p. 512; Knut Borchardt, "Germany, 1700–1914," in *The Fontana Economic History of Europe*, 5 vols. (London: Collins/Fontana Books, 1972), vol. 4, part 1, pp. 85–88, 101–2; Theodore S. Hamerow, *Restoration, Revolution, Reaction: Economics and Politics in Germany, 1815–1871* (Princeton, N.J.: Princeton University Press, 1966), pp. 21–55; Hugo C. Wendel, *The Evolution of Industrial Freedom in Prussia, 1845–1849* (Allentown, Pa.: H. Ray Haas and Co., 1918); Martin Kitchen, *The Political Economy of Germany, 1815–1914* (London: Croom Helm, 1978), pp. 18–20, 63.

7. Eda Sagarra, *A Social History of Germany, 1648–1914* (London: Methuen and Co., 1977), p. 175; T. Hodgskin, *Travels in the North of Germany: Describing the Present State of the Social and Political Institutions, the Agriculture, Manufactures, Commerce, Education, Arts and Manners in that Country, Particularly in the Kingdom of Hanover*, 2 vols. (Edinburgh: Archibald Constable and Co., 1820), vol. 2, pp. 193, 198–99; R. H. Tilly, "Capital Formation in Germany in the Nineteenth Century," in *Cambridge Economic History of Europe*, vol. 7, part 1, p. 411; B. R. Mitchell, *European Historical Statistics, 1750–1975*, 2d ed. (New York: Facts on File, 1980), pp. 606–7; Borchardt, "Germany, 1700–1914," pp. 84–85.

8. W. G. Hoffmann, "The Take-off in Germany," in *The Economics of Take-off into Sustained Growth*, ed. W. W. Rostow (London: Macmillan and Co., 1964), p. 118; Mitchell, *European Historical Statistics*, pp. 455–56. See also Jacques Droz, *Les Revolutions Allemandes de 1848* (Paris: Presses Universitaires de France, 1957), pp. 72–73.

9. J. J. Lee, "Labour in German Industrialization," in *Cambridge Economic History of Europe*, vol. 7, part 1, p. 442; Lütge, *Deutsche Sozial- und Wirtschaftsgeschichte*, pp. 419–21; Walther G. Hoffmann, Franz Grumbach, and Helmut Hesse, *Das Wachstum der deutschen Wirtschaft seit der Mitte des 19. Jahrhunderts* (Berlin: Springer-Verlag, 1965), p. 172; Jonathan Sperber, "State and Civil Society in Prussia: Thoughts on a New Edition of Reinhart Koselleck's *Preussen zwischen Reform und Revolution*," *Journal of Modern History* 57 (1985): 293–94. My understanding of the nature and evolution of work and labor in early nineteenth-century Germany has been heavily influenced by the works of Frederick D. Marquardt and by Jürgen Kocka's masterful

synthesis, *Lohnarbeit und Klassenbildung: Arbeiter und Arbeiterbewegung in Deutschland, 1800–1875* (Berlin: Verlag J. H. W. Dietz, 1983).

10. Kocka, *Lohnarbeit und Klassenbildung,* pp. 33–34; Thomas C. Banfield, *Industry of the Rhine,* 2 vols. (London: Charles Knight and Co., 1846), vol. 1, pp. 46, 231; Wolfram Fischer, *Der Staat und die Anfänge der Industrialisierung in Baden, 1800–1850* (Berlin: Duncker and Humblot, 1962), p. 299; Carl Jantke, "Zur Deutung des Pauperismus," in *Die Eigentumslosen: Der deutsche Pauperismus und die Emancipationskrise in Darstellungen und Deutungen der zeitgenössischen Literatur,* ed. C. Jantke and D. Hilger (München: Verlag Karl Alber Freiburg, 1965), pp. 7–47.

11. Werner Conze, "Die Wirkungen der liberalen Agrarreform auf die Volksordnung in Mitteleuropa im 19. Jahrhundert," *Vierteljahrschrift für Sozial- und Wirtschaftsgeschichte* 38 (1949): 6–17; Wilhelm von Laer, "Bericht über die Lage der arbeitenden Klassen des Kreises Herford an das Kgl. Preuss. Landes-Ökonomie-Kollegium 1851," and Georg Ludwig Wilhelm Funke, "Zur Lage der Heuerleute," both in *Die Eigentumslosen,* pp. 93–111.

12. Helga Schultz, "Landhandwerk und ländliche Sozialstruktur um 1800," *Jahrbuch für Wirtschaftsgeschichte* 2 (1981): 11–49; Jean H. Quataert, "The Shaping of Women's Work in Manufacturing: Guilds, Households, and the State in Central Europe, 1648–1870," *American Historical Review* 90 (December 1985): 1122–48; Howitt, *The Rural and Domestic Life of Germany,* pp. 90–91; Conze, "Wirkungen der liberalen Agrarreform," pp. 6–7; Kocka, *Lohnarbeit und Klassenbildung,* pp. 85–89. Some writers have given different names to different stages in the process by which these producers were subordinated, referring to the logically prior phase as the *Kaufsystem* and the later as the *Verlagsystem.* That distinction is analytically useful. Because the first "system" tended to evolve into the second unevenly, in different ways and at different rates, however, this study employs the term *Verlagsystem* (or outwork, or cottage industry) to refer more broadly to all small-scale handicraft production linked to mass markets through the medium of third parties (merchants or other producers). Cf. Jürgen Schlumbohm, "Relations of Production—Productive Forces—Crises in Proto-Industrialization," in *Industrialization before Industrialization: Rural Industry in the Genesis of Capitalism,* ed. Peter Kriedtke et al. (Cambridge: Cambridge University Press, 1981), esp. pp. 98–107; and W. O. Henderson, *The Rise of German Industrial Power, 1834–1914* (Berkeley, Calif.: University of California Press, 1975), p. 63.

13. Howitt, *The Rural and Domestic Life of Germany,* pp. 56–60; Kocka, *Lohnarbeit und Klassenbildung,* pp. 37–39, 89–90, 96–101.

14. Fischer, *Der Staat,* p. 275; Schlumbohm, "Relations of Production," pp. 98–101; Karl Heinrich Kaufhold, "Handwerk und Industrie 1800–1850," in *Handbuch der deutschen Wirtschafts- und Sozialgeschichte,* ed. Hermann Aubin and Wolgang Zorn (Stuttgart: Ernst Klett Verlag, 1976), vol. 2, pp. 322–28, 353–58; Wolfgang Köllmann, *Bevölkerung in der industriellen Revolution: Studien zur Bevölkerungsgeschichte Deutschlands* (Göttingen: Vanden-

hoeck and Ruprecht, 1974), p. 226; Wolfram Fischer, Jochen Krengel, and Jutta Wietog, *Sozialgeschichtliches Arbeitsbuch* (München: Verlag C. H. Beck, 1982), vol. 1, pp. 54–55.

15. Hans Rosenberg, *Bureaucracy, Aristocracy, amd Autocracy: The Prussian Experience, 1660–1815* (Boston: Beacon Press, 1958), pp. 202–28; Frederick D. Marquardt, "The Manual Workers in the Social Order in Berlin under the Old Regime" (Ph.D. diss., University of California, 1973), pp. 456–57.

16. Henning, *Industrialisierung in Deutschland,* pp. 37–50; Conze, "Wirkungen der liberalen Agrarreform," pp. 17–26; Lütge, *Deutsche Sozial- und Wirtschaftsgeschichte,* pp. 433–45; Sperber, "State and Civil Society," pp. 284–87.

17. Conze, "Wirkungen der liberalen Agrarreform," pp. 9–14; Elisabeth Fehrenbach, "Verfassungs- und Sozialpolitische Reformen und Reformprojekte in Deutschland unter dem Einfluss des Napoleonischen Frankreich," *Historische Zeitschrift* 228 (April 1979): 289–316; Rainer Koch, "Die Agrarrevolution in Deutschland 1848. Ursachen—Verlauf—Ergebnisse," in *Die deutsche Revolution von 1848/49,* ed. Dieter Langewiesche (Darmstadt: Wissenschaftliche Buchgesellschaft, 1983), pp. 362–94; Sperber, "State and Civil Society," pp. 287–89, 292–94. The quotation is from William Jacob, "A History of Agriculture, Manufactures, Statistics and State of Society of Germany and Parts of Holland and France," in *Documents of European Economic History,* ed. S. Pollard and C. Holmes, 3 vols. (London: Edward Arnold, 1968), vol. 1, pp. 35–36.

18. Borchardt, "Germany, 1700–1914," pp. 98–99; Saalfeld, "Lebensverhältnisse," pp. 218, 220; Weber, *Growth of Cities,* p. 144; Hoffmann, "Takeoff in Germany," p. 101; Jacob, "A History of Agriculture," p. 36. In Badenese agriculture between 1829 and 1844, the number of those in the lowest tax group increased four times faster than the agrarian population as a whole (Fischer, *Der Staat,* p. 299).

19. These statistics are based on data in Saalfeld, "Lebensverhältnisse," p. 218, and Henning, *Industrialisierung in Deutschland,* p. 130.

20. Tilly, "Capital Formation in Germany," p. 411; Borchardt, "Germany, 1700–1914," pp. 104–9; Kitchen, *Political Economy of Germany,* pp. 34–44.

21. Tilly, "Capital Formation in Germany," pp. 419, 427; Henderson, *Rise of German Industrial Power,* pp. 53–61; Henning, *Industrialisierung in Deutschland,* pp. 111–26.

22. Kitchen, *Political Economy of Germany,* pp. 53, 55, 57–8; Fischer, Krengel, and Wietog, *Sozialgeschichtliches Arbeitsbuch,* vol. 1, p. 79; Henderson, *Rise of German Industrial Power,* pp. 66–69; Sidney Pollard, *Peaceful Conquest: The Industrialization of Europe, 1760–1970* (Oxford: Oxford University Press, 1981), pp. 78–83.

23. Henderson, *Rise of German Industrial Power,* pp. 28–29, 53; Frank B. Tipton, *Regional Variations in the Economic Development of Germany during the Nineteenth Century* (Middletown, Conn.: Wesleyan University Press, 1976).

24. Fischer, Krengel, and Wietog, *Sozialgeschichtliches Arbeitsbuch*, vol. 1, p. 41; Pollard, *Peaceful Conquest*, pp. 70, 103; Tipton, *Regional Variations*, pp. 37, 185; Hartmut Zwahr, *Zur Konstituierung des Proletariats als Klasse: Strukturuntersuchung über das Leipziger Proletariat während der industriellen Revolution* (Berlin: Akademie-Verlag, 1978), ch. 1, esp. pp. 30–31, 36, 84–86; Hubert Kieswetter, "Bevölkerung, Erwerbstätige und Landwirtschaft im Königreich Sachsen 1815–1871," in *Region und Industrialisierung: Studien zur Rolle der Region in der Wirtschaftsgeschichte der letzten zwei Jahrhunderte*, ed. Sidney Pollard (Göttingen: Vandenhoek and Ruprecht, 1980), pp. 89–106; Köllmann, *Bevölkerung in der industriellen Revolution*, pp. 73, 88.

25. Klara Van Eyll, "Wirtschaftsgeschichte Kölns von Beginn der Preussischen Zeit bis zur Reichsgründung," in *Zwei Jahrtausende Kölner Wirtschaft*, ed. Hermann Kellenbenz (Köln: Greven Verlag, 1975), vol. 2, pp. 183–86, 190–91, 198.

26. Berlin locksmiths and machine fitters (the latter trade having developed out of the former) generally worked in large machine tool and locomotive factories, some of which employed more than one thousand workers apiece by 1850. A few textile establishments employed between two and three thousand employees each, and cloth printers (like nail makers) found the nature and pace of their work heavily affected by the use of machines. See Lothar Baar, "Probleme der industriellen Revolution in grosstädtischen Industriezentren: Das Berliner Beispiel," in *Wirtschafts- und Sozialgeschichliche Probleme der frühen Industrialisierung*, ed. Wolfram Fischer (Berlin: Colloquium Verlag, 1968), pp. 529–42; Otto Büsch, "Das Gewerbe in der Wirtschaft des Raumes Berlin/Brandenburg 1800–1850," *Untersuchungen zur Geschichte der frühen Industrialisierung vornehmlich im Wirtschaftsraum Berlin/Brandenburg* (Berlin: Colloquium Verlag, 1971), pp. 52, 56–57; Frederick D. Marquardt, "Sozialer Aufstieg, sozialer Abstieg und die Entstehung der Berliner Arbeiterklasse, 1806–1848," *Geschichte der sozialen Mobilität seit der industriellen Revolution*, ed. Hartmut Kaelble (Königstein: Athenäum, Hain, Scriptor, Hanstein, 1978), p. 146; Marquardt, "Labor Relations and the Formation of the Working Class: Masters and Journeymen in Berlin, 1760–1848" (unpublished paper, 1983), pp. 17–18; Marquardt, "A Working Class in Berlin in the 1840's?" in *Sozialgeschichte Heute*, ed. Hans-Ulrich Wehler (Göttingen: Vandenhoek and Ruprecht, 1974), p. 194.

27. Banfield, *Industry of the Rhine*, vol. 2, pp. 140, 152–53, 232, 234, 245; Köllmann, *Bevölkerung in der industriellen Revolution*, p. 43; Pierre Aycoberry, "Probleme der Sozialschichtung in Köln im Zeitalter der Frühindustrialisierung," in *Wirtschafts- und Sozialgeschichtliche Probleme*, p. 513; David S. Landes, *The Unbound Prometheus: Technological Change and Industrial Development in Western Europe from 1750 to the Present* (Cambridge: Cambridge University Press, 1969), p. 167; Lee, "Labour in German Industrialization," p. 473; Borchardt, "Germany, 1700–1914," pp. 104–6; Eyll, "Wirtschaftsgeschichte Kölns," pp. 183, 244–45; Kaufhold, "Handwerk und Industrie," pp. 340–41.

28. Fischer, Krengel, and Wietog, *Sozialgeschichtliches Arbeitsbuch,* vol. 1, pp. 56–57; Fischer, *Der Staat,* pp. 297, 321; Borchardt, "Germany, 1700–1914," p. 111.

29. Tipton, *Regional Variations,* pp. 15; Pollard, *Peaceful Conquest,* pp. 98–99; Banfield, *Industry of the Rhine,* vol. 2, pp. 75, 152–53; J. H. Clapham, *The Economic Development of France and Germany, 1815–1914* (Cambridge: Cambridge University Press, 1921), p. 85; Droz, *Les Revolutions Allemandes de 1848,* pp. 84–87. The historian of Bochum found that this "industrial metropolis" of the late nineteenth-century Ruhr district was still a "backwater country town" in the 1840s. See David F. Crew, *Town in the Ruhr: A Social History of Bochum, 1860–1914* (New York: Columbia University Press, 1979), pp. 11–12, 17, 59.

30. Zwahr, *Zur Konstituierung des Proletariats als Klasse,* pp. 36, 45, 69, 94–95; Eyll, "Wirtschaftsgeschichte Kölns," pp. 183, 244–45; Marquardt, "Sozialer Aufstieg," p. 146; Marquardt, "Labor Relations," pp. 4–5; Baar, "Probleme der industriellen Revolution in grosstädtischen Industriezentren," p. 535.

31. Aycoberry, "Probleme der Sozialschichtung in Köln," pp. 521–22; Wolfgang Köllmann, *Sozialgeschichte der Stadt Barmen im 19. Jahrhundert* (Tübingen: Mohr, 1960), pp. 103–5; Friedrich Lenger, *Zwischen Kleinbürgertum und Proletariat: Studien zur Sozialgeschichte der Düsseldorfer Handwerker 1816–1878* (Göttingen: Vandenhoek and Ruprecht, 1986); Henning, *Industrialisierung in Deutschland,* pp. 130; Fischer, *Der Staat,* pp. 290, 303.

32. Noyes, *Organization and Revolution,* pp. 25–26, 70–72; Marquardt, "Labor Relations," p. 6; Gustav Schmoller, *Zur Geschichte der deutschen Kleingewerbe im 19. Jahrhundert. Statistische und nationalökonomische Untersuchungen* (Halle: Verlag der Buchhandlung des Waisenhauses, 1870), pp. 358, 369–70; Fischer, Krengel, and Wietog, *Sozialgeschichtliches Arbeitsbuch,* vol. 1, p. 140.

33. Aycoberry, "Probleme der Sozialschichtung in Köln," p. 523; Zwahr, *Zur Konstituierung des Proletariats als Klasse,* pp. 25–114; Kaufhold, "Handwerk und Industrie," pp. 339–41; Marquardt, "Sozialer Aufstieg," p. 151; Lee, "Labour in German Industrialization," p. 483.

34. Stephan Born, "Programmatische Einleitung zu den Statuten des Berliner Zentralkomitees für Arbeiter," in *Arbeiterbewegung: Sozialer Protest und Kollektive Interessenvertretung bis 1914,* ed. Helga Grebing (München: Deutscher Taschenbuch Verlag, 1985), p. 136; Noyes, *Organization and Revolution,* p. 147.

35. Aycoberry, "Probleme der Sozialschichtung in Köln," p. 521; Eyll, "Wirtschaftsgeschichte Kölns," p. 183; Hans Stein, *Der Kölner Arbeiterverein (1848–1849): Ein Beitrag zur Frühgeschichte des rheinischen Sozialismus* (Cologne: Gilsbach and Co., 1921), pp. 10–13; Marquardt, "Sozialer Aufstieg," pp. 146–49; Marquardt, "Manual Workers," pp. 467–69; Friedrich Lenger, "Polarisierung und Verlag: Schumacher, Schneider und Schreiner in Düsseldorf

1816–1861," in *Handwerker in der Industralisierung: Lage, Kultur und Politik vom späten 18. bis ins frühe 20. Jahrhundert,* ed. Ulrich Engelhardt (Stuttgart: Klett-Cotta, 1984), pp. 127–45; Dieter Bergmann, "Die Berliner Arbeiterschaft in Vormärz und Revolution 1830–1850: Eine Trägerschicht der beginnenden Industrialisierung als neue Kraft in der Politik," in *Untersuchungen zur Geschichte der frühen Industrialisierung,* p. 460.

36. Across Prussia as a whole, in contrast, there was approximately one master for every forty residents. Schmoller, *Zur Geschichte der deutschen Kleingewerbe,* pp. 71, 274, 358–59, 367, 370–71; Fischer, *Der Staat,* p. 301; David Blackbourn, "Between Resignation and Volatility: The German Petite Bourgeoisie in the Nineteenth Century," in *Shopkeepers and Master Artisans in Nineteenth-Century Europe,* ed. Geoffrey Crossick and Heinz-Gerhard Haupt (London: Methuen, 1984), p. 39.

37. Schmoller, *Zur Geschichte der deutschen Kleingewerbe,* p. 166; Sedatis, *Liberalismus und Handwerk,* p. 129; Marquardt, "Manual Workers," pp. 466–67; Carola Lipp, "Württembergische Handwerker und Handwerkervereine im Vormärz und in der Revolution 1848/49," in *Handwerker in der Industralisierung,* pp. 353–59; Edward Shorter, "Middle-Class Anxiety in the German Revolution of 1848," *Journal of Social History* 2 (1969): 206–9.

38. Kocka, *Lohnarbeit und Klassenbildung,* pp. 101–6; Sedatis, *Liberalismus und Handwerk,* p. 123.

39. Kitchen, *Political Economy of Germany,* pp. 23, 84–85; Werner K. Blessing, "'Theuerungsexcesse' im vorrevolutionären Kontext—Getreidetumult und Bierkrawall im späten Vormärz," in *Arbeiterexistenz im 19. Jahrhundert: Lebensstandard und Lebensgestaltung deutscher Arbeiter und Handwerker,* ed. Werner Conze and Ulrich Engelhardt (Stuttgart: Klett-Cotta, 1981), pp. 356–84; Karl Heinrich Kaufhold, "Grundzüge des handwerklichen Lebensstandards in Deutschland im 19. Jahrundert," in *Arbeiter im Industrialisierungsprozess: Herkunft, Lage und Verhalten,* ed. Conze and Engelhardt (Stuttgart: Klett-Cotta, 1979), pp. 146–48; Jürgen Bergmann, "Das Handwerk in der Revolution von 1848: Zum Zusammenhang von materieller Lage und Revolutionsverhalten der Handwerker 1848/49," in *Untersuchungen zur Geschichte der frühen Industrialisierung,* pp. 325–29.

40. Hamerow, *Restoration, Revolution, Reaction,* p. 87; Walker, *Germany and the Emigration,* pp. 80, 131; Hansen, *Atlantic Migration,* p. 252.

Chapter 2: "Social Freedom and Independent Existence": Labor and Revolution

1. Rudolph Stadelmann, *Social and Political History of the German 1848 Revolution,* trans. James G. Chastain (Athens: Ohio University Press, 1948), pp. 81–84; Veit Valentin, *Geschichte der deutschen Revolution von 1848–49,* 2 vols. (Berlin: Verlag Ullstein, 1931), vol. 2, pp. 356–57; Noyes, *Organization and Revolution,* p. 57; Droz, *Les Revolutions Allemandes de 1848,* pp. 151–56; Hamerow, *Restoration, Revolution, Reaction,* pp. 102–9.

2. Adolf Wolff, *Berliner Revolutionschronik: Darstellung der Berliner Bewegung im Jahre 1848 in politischer, sozialer und literarischer Beziehung,* ed. C. Gompertz (1848; repr., one-volume ed., Berlin: Ferd. Dummlers Verlagsbuchhandlung, 1898), pp. 83–109; J. Bergmann, "Das Handwerk in der Revolution von 1848," pp. 334–36; Ruth Hoppe and Jürgen Kuczynski, "Ein Berufs- bzw. auch Klassen- und Schichtenanalyse der Märzgefallenen 1848 in Berlin," in *Die Konstituierung der deutschen Arbeiterklasse von den dreissiger bis den siebziger Jahren des 19. Jahrhunderts,* ed. Hartmut Zwahr (Berlin: Akademie-Verlag, 1981), pp. 343–61.

3. Valentin, *Geschichte der deutschen Revolution,* vol. 2, p. 578; Hamerow, *Restoration, Revolution, Reaction,* pp. 99–102; Stadelmann, *Social and Political History,* pp. 55–62; Wolff, *Berliner Revolutionschronik,* pp. 110–39.

4. Dieter Langewiesche, *Liberalismus und Demokratie in Württemberg zwischen Revolution und Reichsgründung* (Düsseldorf: Droste Verlag, 1974), pp. 345–47; Rainer Koch, "Die Agrarrevolution in Deutschland," pp. 362–94 passim; Droz, *Les Revolutions Allemandes de 1848,* pp. 151–56.

5. Manfred Botzenhart, "Die Parlamentarismusmodelle der deutschen Parteien 1848/49," in *Die deutsche Revolution von 1848/49,* pp. 291–321; Hamerow, *Restoration, Revolution, Reaction,* pp. 61, 127–28, 215; Noyes, *Organization and Revolution,* pp. 92–93, 96, 334; Walker, *German Home Towns* (Ithaca, N.Y.: Cornell University Press, 1971), pp. 366–67; Schurz, *Reminiscences,* vol. 1, pp. 142–43.

Even the "broad democratic basis" that Schurz referred to, however, was granted only under pressure. Gagern and his colleagues strove persistently to restrict the suffrage to men of property. Since at least 1830, the liberal Rhenish industrialist David Hansemann—now Prussia's Minister of Finance—had distinguished sharply between government by the majority and government for the majority, between laws "determined by counting heads" and rule by "the true strength of the nation, which, while it is also to have no interest other than that of the numerical majority, yet differs essentially from it, since by its better education, greater insight, and its property it has a larger stake in the maintenance of a stable, vigorous, and good government." In late 1848 Hansemann was still branding universal manhood suffrage "the most dangerous experiment in the world." It was an experiment upon which he and those who shared his thinking were compelled to embark against their better judgment. Donald G. Rohr, *The Origins of Social Liberalism in Germany* (Chicago: University of Chicago Press, 1963), p. 96; James J. Sheehan, *German Liberalism in the Nineteenth Century* (Chicago: University of Chicago Press, 1978), p. 74.

6. Hamerow, *Restoration, Revolution, Reaction,* pp. 127–28; Rohr, *Origins of Social Liberalism,* pp. 95–96.

7. Dr. Rudolph Virchow is quoted in Hamerow, *Restoration, Revolution, Reaction,* p. 102. See Noyes, *Organization and Revolution,* pp. 59, 118, 124–25, 152, 154–55, 300, 307n; Stephan Born, *Erinnerungen eines Achtundvierzigers mit dem Bildnis dem Verfassers,* 3d ed. (Leipzig: Verlag von Georg

Heinrich Meyer, 1898), pp. 191–93; W. Ed. Biermann, *Karl Georg Win-kelblech (Karl Marlo). Sein Leben und sein Werk,* 2 vols. (Leipzig: A. Deichert'sche Verlagsbuchhandlung, 1909), vol. 2, pp. 284–86; Stein, *Kölner Arbeiterverein,* pp. 33–50; Lipp, "Württembergische Handwerker," pp. 348–50, 372–77; Frolinde Balser, *Sozial-Demokratie 1848/49–1863: Die erste deutsche Arbeiterorganisation: "Allgemeine deutsche Arbeiterverbrüderung" nach der Revolution,* 2 vols. (Stuttgart: Ernst Klett Verlag, 1965), vol. 1, pp. 339–51; Uhlrich Engelhardt, "Gewerkschaftliches Organisationsverhalten in der ersten Industrialisierungsphase" in *Arbeiter im Industrialisierungsprozess: Herkunft, Lage und Verhalten,* ed. Conze and Engelhardt (Stuttgart: Klett-Cotta, 1979), p. 387.

8. Kocka, *Lohnarbeit und Klassenbildung,* pp. 167–73; Werner Conze and Dieter Groh, *Die Arbeiterbewegung in der nationalen Bewegung* (Stuttgart: Ernst Klett Verlag, 1966), pp. 25–31; Engelhardt, "Gewerkschaftliches Organisationsverhalten," pp. 372–86; D. Bergmann, "Die Berliner Arbeiterschaft," pp. 30–50, 475–79; Lipp, "Württembergische Handwerker," pp. 348–52, 367–72; Michael J. Neufeld, "German Artisans and Political Repression: The Fall of the Journeymen's Associations in Nuremberg, 1806–1868," *Journal of Social History* 19 (1986): 492–93.

9. Born, *Erinnerungen,* pp. 136–37; Balser, *Sozial-Demokratie 1848/49–1863,* vol. 1, pp. 66–72; Noyes, *Organization and Revolution,* pp. 127, 131, 135, 139, 150, 158, 193, 200–203, 256, 271; Marquardt, "Manual Workers," pp. 471–73.

10. Noting the high number of tailors in the league, Engels recalled that "even in the big metropolises, the man who exploited them was usually only a small master. The exploitation of tailoring on a large scale, what is now called the manufacture of ready-made clothes, by the conversion of handicraft tailoring into a domestic industry working for a big capitalist, was at that time even in London only just making its appearance. On the one hand, [then,] the exploiter of these artisans was a small master; on the other hand, they all hoped ultimately to become small masters themselves." That this was not simply a post facto assessment is clear from Engels's prerevolutionary correspondence with Marx. Friedrich Engels, "On the History of the Communist League," in K. Marx and F. Engels, *Selected Works,* 2 vols. (Moscow: Progress Publishers, 1962), vol. 2, pp. 343–44, 356. The quotation in the text is from Marx and Engels, *Collected Works,* vol. 38 (New York: International Publishers, 1982), p. 154. See also James A. Schmiechen, *Sweated Industries and Sweated Labor: The London Clothing Trades, 1860–1914* (Urbana: University of Illinois Press, 1984), pp. 7–23.

11. Biermann, *Karl Georg Winkelblech,* vol. 2, pp. 444–45; Hans Meusch, ed., *Die Handwerkerbewegung von 1848/49: Vorgeschichte, Verlauf, Inhalt, Ergebnisse* (Eschwege: Gildverlag Hans-Gerhard Dobler, 1949), pp. 54–55; Noyes, *Organization and Revolution,* pp. 127, 203, 245.

The claims of organized journeymen in 1848 included demands to limit the number of apprentices per master, to ban outright the employment of nonresidents of the city, and to fire unskilled workers from jobs considered appropriate only for recognized journeymen (Marquardt, "Labor Relations," p. 25; Marquardt, "A Working Class in Berlin," p. 199; "Forderungen des Zentralkomitees für Arbeiter in Berlin an die Nationalversammlungen in Frankfurt und Berlin," in Grebing, *Arbeiterbewegung*, p. 137).

12. Karl Obermann, *Die deutschen Arbeiter in der Revolution von 1848*, 2d ed. (Berlin: Dietz Verlag, 1953), p. 106; Noyes, *Organization and Revolution*, p. 248.

13. Noyes, *Organization and Revolution*, pp. 218, 308–10; Engels to Marx, January 14, 1848, *Collected Works*, vol. 38, pp. 152–55; Kocka, *Lohnarbeit und Klassenbildung*, pp. 94–96.

14. Franz Mehring, *Geschichte der deutschen Sozialdemokratie* (1897; repr. Berlin: Dietz Verlag, 1960), p. 433.

15. Lenger, *Zwischen Kleinbürgertum und Proletariat*, pp. 150–69; Noyes, *Organization and Revolution*, pp. 153.

16. Stein, *Kölner Arbeiterverein*, pp. 26–28; Marquardt, "A Working Class in Berlin," p. 202.

17. Meusch, ed., *Die Handwerkerbewegung*, pp. 69–76; Hamerow, *Restoration, Revolution, Reaction*, pp. 145–46.

18. Noyes, *Organization and Revolution*, pp. 177–90; Walker, *German Home Towns*, p. 365.

19. Jürgen Kocka, "Problems of Working-Class Formation in Germany: The Early Years, 1800–1875," in *Working-Class Formation: Nineteenth-Century Patterns in Western Europe and the United States*, ed. I. Katznelson and A. Zolberg (Princeton, N.J.: Princeton University Press, 1986), p. 312.

20. Balser, *Sozial-Demokratie 1848/49–1863*, vol. 1, pp. 47–152; Grebing, *Arbeiterbewegung*, pp. 45–46; Biermann, *Karl Georg Winkelblech*, vol. 2, pp. 270–71; Noyes, *Organization and Revolution*, pp. 205–6.

21. J. Bergmann, "Das Handwerk in der Revolution von 1848," pp. 340–46; Noyes, *Organization and Revolution*, p. 209.

22. Biermann, *Karl Georg Winkelblech*, vol. 2, p. 455.

23. Rohr, *Origins of Social Liberalism*, pp. 78–96, 132–35.

24. Sedatis, *Liberalismus und Handwerk*, esp. pp. 49–50; Valentin, *Geschichte der deutschen Revolution*, vol. 1, pp. 472–81, vol. 2, pp. 313–18; Carl Wittke, *Against the Current: The Life of Karl Heinzen (1809–1880)* (Chicago: University of Chicago Press, 1945), p. 65; Noyes, *Organization and Revolution*, pp. 221–32, 250–53, 260–77, 342–45; Gustav Lüders, *Die demokratische Bewegung in Berlin im Oktober 1848* (Berlin: Walther Rothschild, 1909), pp. 70–110, 141–56, 160–63; Droz, *Les Revolutions Allemandes de 1848*, pp. 445–51, 457–58; Leonore O'Boyle, "The Democratic Left in Germany, 1848," *Journal of Modern History* 33 (1961): 374–83.

25. Wolfgang Schieder, "Die Rolle der deutschen Arbeiter in der Revolution von 1848/49," in *Die deutsche Revolution von 1848/49*, pp. 322–40; Lüders, *Demokratische Bewegung in Berlin*, pp. 164–67; Sheehan,

German Liberalism, p. 62; Hermann Josef Rupieper, "Die Sozialstruktur demokratischer Vereine im Königreich Sachsen 1848–55," *Jahrbuch des Instituts für deutsche Geschichte* 7 (1978): 457–68; Lipp, "Württembergische Handwerker," pp. 364, 372–77; John L. Snell, *The Democratic Movement in Germany, 1789–1914* (Chapel Hill: University of North Carolina Press, 1976), pp. 90–91; J. Bergmann, "Handwerk in der Revolution von 1848," pp. 338–40. Radicals also registered major successes in Westphalia and the Rhineland in 1849. Cf. Jonathan Sperber, *Popular Catholicism in Nineteenth-Century Germany* (Princeton, N.J.: Princeton University Press, 1984), p. 50.

26. Hans Rosenberg, "Theologischer Rationalismus und vormärzlicher Vulgärliberalismus," *Historische Zeitschrift* 141 (1930): 531–32. On the general point, see Wolfgang Schieder, "Religion in the Social History of the Modern World: A German Perspective," *European Studies Review* 12 (July 1982): 289–99; and Sagarra, *Social History of Germany,* pp. 203–4.

27. H. Daniel-Rops, *The Church in an Age of Revolution, 1789–1870* (New York: E. P. Dutton and Co., 1965), pp. 214–15, 244–45, 250, 281–85; Joseph N. Moody, ed., *Church and Society: Catholic Social and Political Thought and Movements, 1789–1950* (New York: Arts, Inc., 1953), p. 230; Kenneth Scott Latourette, *The Nineteenth Century in Europe: Background and the Roman Catholic Phase* (New York: Harper and Row, 1958), pp. 256–60, 270–78; William L. Langer, *Political and Social Upheaval: 1832–1852* (New York: Harper and Row, 1969), pp. 519, 526, 533.

28. Jonathan Sperber, "Competing Counterrevolutions: Prussian State and Catholic Church in Westphalia during the 1850s," and Vernon Lidtke, "Catholics and Politics in Nineteenth-Century Germany: A Comment," *Central European History* 9 (March 1986): 45–52, 117–18; Moody, ed., *Church and Society,* pp. 232–34.

29. Opposed to the fusion, the sect of "Old Lutherans" thus became advocates of greater church-state separation. In other respects, however, the Old Lutherans clung firmly to the most socially, politically, and theologically conservative doctrines. Allowed to emigrate, they became influential in American Lutheranism, notably in the Missouri Synod (Walker, *Germany and the Emigration,* p. 78; Sagarra, *Social History of Germany,* pp. 204–11; Frederick C. Luebke, "The Immigrant Condition as a Factor Contributing to the Conservatism of the Lutheran Church—Missouri Synod," in his *Germans in the New World: Essays in the History of Immigration* [Urbana: University of Illinois Press, 1990]).

30. Robert M. Bigler, *The Politics of German Protestantism: The Rise of the Protestant Church Elite in Prussia, 1815–1848* (Berkeley: University of California Press, 1972), pp. 3–52, 109; William O. Shanahan, *German Protestants Face the Social Question* (Notre Dame, Ind.: University of Notre Dame Press, 1954), vol. 1, pp. 193, 195; Hartmut Lehman, "Pietism and Nationalism: The Relationship between Protestant Revivalism and National Renewal in Nineteenth-Century Germany," *Church History* 51 (March 1982): 39–53.

31. Sperber, *Popular Catholicism,* pp. 15–47; Howitt, *The Rural and Domestic Life of Germany,* p. 191. On economic, legal, and religio-intellectual changes among German Jews, see David Sorkin, *The Transformation of German Jewry, 1780–1840* (New York: Oxford University Press, 1987); Jehuda Reinharz and Walter Schatzberg, eds., *The Jewish Response to German Culture* (Hanover, N.H.: University Press of New England, 1985); and Eric E. Hirschler, *Jews from Germany in the United States* (New York: Farrar, Strauss and Cudahy, 1955).

32. Catherine Magill Holden [Prelinger], "A Decade of Dissent in Germany: An Historical Study of the Society of Protestant Friends and the German-Catholic Church, 1840–48" (Ph.D. diss., Yale University, 1954), pp. 151, 209, 339; Valentin, *Geschichte der deutschen Revolution,* vol. 1, pp. 45–47, 107–8, 149–51, 191, 221–23; Droz, *Les Revolutions Allemandes de 1848,* pp. 61, 108–12, 481–512.

33. Holden Prelinger, "Decade of Dissent," pp. 94, 217–18, 259, 332, 334, 338, 362–63, 381; Bigler, *Politics of German Protestantism,* pp. 217–18; Rosenberg, "Theologischer Rationalismus," p. 534; Lenger, *Zwischen Kleinbürgertum und Proletariat,* pp. 153–62, 217–27.

34. Holden Prelinger, "Decade of Dissent," pp. 206, 210, 216–17, 341–42, 347, 360, 377; Bigler, *Politics of German Protestantism,* p. 55; Jacques Droz, "Religious Aspects of the Revolutions of 1848 in Europe," in *French Society and Culture Since the Old Regime,* eds. Evelyn M. Acomb and Marvin L. Brown, Jr. (New York: Holt, Rinehart and Winston, 1966), pp. 134–48; Lehman, "Pietism and Nationalism," pp. 47–50; Hans-Arthur Marsiske, *"Wider die Umsonstfresser": Der Handwerkerkommunist Wilhelm Weitling* (Hamburg: Ergebnisseverlag, 1986), pp. 81–86; Carl Wittke, *The Utopian Communist: A Biography of Wilhelm Weitling, Nineteenth-Century Reformer* (Baton Rouge: Louisiana State University, 1950), esp. chaps. 1 and 4; Rolf Engelsing, "Zur Politischen Bildung der deutschen Unterschichten, 1789–1863," *Historische Zeitschrift* 206 (1968): 349–53. Decades later, Social Democratic workers would still think of Jesus as the revolutionary offspring and advocate of the laboring classes (Vernon Lidtke, "Social Class and Secularisation in Imperial Germany: The Working Classes," *Leo Baeck Institute Year Book* 25 [1980]: 26–31).

35. Bigler, *Politics of German Protestantism,* p. 107.

36. Snell, *The Democratic Movement in Germany,* pp. 66–71; Noyes, *Organization and Revolution,* p. 48; Holden Prelinger, "Decade of Dissent," pp. 424–26; Lüders, *Demokratische Bewegung,* pp. 135–40, 152–56, 164–67; Balser, *Sozial-Demokratie 1848/49–1863,* vol. 1, pp. 347–48. This combination of religious, social, and political loyalties had a tradition of its own. The works of rationalist democrat Thomas Paine, in German translation since the turn of the century, thus found an appreciative audience in these circles. In 1847 Hermann Kriege brought out a new German-language selection of Paine's writings; Hecker lavished praise on the deist *Age of Reason* in his foreword to an 1852 German edition of *The Rights of Man* (Mark O. Kistler,

"German-American Liberalism and Thomas Paine," *American Quarterly* 14 [Spring 1962]: 82–84).

37. Walker, *Germany and the Emigration,* pp. 160–61.

Chapter 3: "Where Nobody Need Be Poor": Immigrants and Industry in America

1. Carl Schurz, *Speeches, Correspondence, and Political Papers,* ed. Frederic Bancroft, 6 vols. (1913; repr., New York: Greenwood Publishing Co., 1969), vol. 1, pp. 49–50.

2. Gottfried Duden, *Report on a Journey to the Western States of North America and a Stay of Several Years along the Missouri (during the Years 1824, '25, '26, 1827)* (1834; repr., Columbia: University of Missouri Press, 1980); Banfield, *Industry of the Rhine,* vol. 1, p. 86; Walker, *Germany and the Emigration,* pp. 62–63; Philip Schaff, *America: A Sketch of Its Political, Social, and Religious Character,* ed. Perry Miller (1855; repr., Cambridge, Mass.: Harvard University Press, 1961), pp. 219–20. See also Victor R. Greene, *American Immigrant Leaders, 1800–1910: Marginality and Identity* (Baltimore: Johns Hopkins University Press, 1987), pp. 42–45.

3. Walker, *Germany and the Emigration,* p. 155; Gottfried Menzel, *Die Vereinigten Staaten von Nordamerika mit besonderer Rücksicht auf deutsche Auswanderung dahin* [Berlin, 1853], reprinted in *Historical Aspects of the Immigration Problem,* p. 137; Leo Schelbert, "On Interpreting Immigrant Letters: The Case of Johann Caspar and Wilhelmina Honneger-Hanhart," *Yearbook of German-American Studies* 16 (1981): 144.

4. Karl Büchele, *Land und Volk der Vereinigten Staaten von Nord-Amerika* (Stuttgart: Hallberger'sche Verlagshandlung, 1855), p. 403.

5. Menzel, *Deutsche Auswanderung,* in *Historical Aspects of the Immigration Problem,* pp. 139–40 and passim.

6. Douglass C. North, *The Economic Growth of the United States, 1790–1860* (New York: Norton, 1966), p. 99; Secretary of the Interior, *Statistics of the United States, (Including Mortality, Property, &c.), in 1860; Compiled from the Original Returns and Being the Final Exhibit of the Eighth Census* (Washington, D.C.: Government Printing Office, 1866), p. xx; Paul David, "The Growth of Real Product in the United States before 1840: New Evidence, Controlled Conjectures," *Journal of Economic History* 27 (June 1967): 164–66, 169–70, 196–97; David, "New Light on a Statistical Dark Age: U.S. Real Product Growth before 1840," *American Economic Review* 57 (May 1967): 295–99, 302–86; Frederick von Raumer, *America and the American People,* trans. William W. Turner (New York: J. and H. G. Langley, 1846), p. 170.

7. Secretary of the Interior, *Statistics of the United States in 1860,* p. xx. On population density, see Kennedy, *Population of the United States in 1860;* p. xlix; and Stuart Bruchey, *The Roots of American Economic Growth, 1607–1861: An Essay in Social Causation* (New York: Harper and Row, 1968), p. 75.

8. See Stanley Lebergott, "Labor Force and Employment, 1800–1960," in *Output, Employment, and Productivity in the United States after 1800,* vol. 30 in Studies in Income and Wealth (New York: National Bureau of Economic Research, 1966), pp. 118–19. Some of the figures in table 11 may have to be adjusted in light of findings reported in Thomas Weiss, "Revised Estimates of the United States Workforce, 1800–1860," in *Long-Term Factors in American Economic Growth,* ed. Stanley L. Engerman and Robert E. Gallman (Chicago: University of Chicago Press, 1986). The overall trends portrayed in this table, however, seem unaffected.

9. Francis Grund, *The Americans in their Moral, Social, and Political Relations* (1837; repr., New York: Johnson Reprint Corp., 1968), pp. 204, 311–12; North, *Economic Growth of the United States,* p. v; Marvin Fisher, *Workshops: The European Response to American Industrialization, 1830–1860* (New York: Oxford University Press, 1967), p. 45; Alexis de Tocqueville, *Democracy in America,* ed. Phillips Bradley (1835; repr., New York: Alfred A. Knopf, 1945), vol. 2, p. 165.

10. Fisher, *Workshops,* p. 69.

11. Jones, *American Immigration,* pp. 92–94.

12. In contrast, few Germans resided in New England, and most of the small minority who ventured into the slave states settled in the urban South and upper South, making a living in the mixed economies there (Kennedy, *Population of the United States in 1860,* pp. xxix–xxxii; Secretary of the Interior, *Statistics of the United States in 1860,* p. lvii). The comparatively small size of the South's towns and cities—and the native-born southern white population's preference for rural life—transformed even this small number of immigrants into a major proportion of the region's urban population. On this point, see Ira Berlin and Herbert G. Gutman, "Natives and Immigrants, Free Men and Slaves: Urban Workingmen in the Antebellum American South," *American Historical Review* 88 (December 1983): 1175–1200.

13. The Menzel quotation is from *Historical Aspects of the Immigration Problem,* p. 141. In 1860, 38 percent of all German-Americans lived in one of the nation's 44 largest cities; only 11 percent of the native-born did (Kennedy, *Population of the United States in 1860,* pp. xxviii–xxix, xxxi–xxxii). As for the West, about 17,000 German-Americans labored in agriculture in 1870 in New York, New Jersey, and Pennsylvania combined. Roughly the same number worked the land in just Iowa alone, more than twice as many did so in Illinois, more than four times as many in Wisconsin (Francis A. Walker, *Statistics of the Population of the United States in 1870,* pp. 698–99, 704–5). See Paul W. Gates, *The Farmer's Age: Agriculture, 1815–1860* (New York: Harper and Row, 1968), p. 96; Gates, *Agriculture and the Civil War* (New York: Alfred A. Knopf, 1965), pp. 277–80. See also Clarence H. Danhof, "Farm-Making Costs and the 'Safety Valve': 1850–1860," *Journal of Political Economy* 49 (June 1941): 317–59; and Danhof, *Change in Agriculture: The Northern United States, 1820–1870* (Cambridge, Mass.: Harvard University Press, 1969), pp. 110–29. The U.S. Census did not begin to gather and

report data on farm tenancy until 1880. On immigrants who did become farmers in the United States after a period in urban centers, see Walter D. Kamphoefner, *The Westfalians: From Germany to Missouri* (Princeton, N.J.: Princeton University Press, 1987), esp. chap. 5.

14. Stanley Nadel, "Kleindeutschland: New York City's Germans, 1845–1880" (Ph.D. diss., Columbia University, 1981), pp. 214–50; Theodor Griesinger, *Lebende Bilder aus Amerika in humoristischen Schilderungen* (Cincinnati: Max Weil and Co., 1861), pp. 56–64, 73–80, 190–98, 237–44; Griesinger, *Freiheit und Sclaverei unter dem Sternenbanner, oder Land und Leute in Amerika* (Stuttgart: A. Kroner, 1862), pp. 685–707; Max Burgheim, *Cincinnati in Wort und Bild: Nach authentischen bearbeitet und zusammengestellt* (Cincinnati: Burgheim Publishing Co., 1891); Rudolf A. Hofmeister, *The Germans of Chicago* (Champaign, Ill.: Stipes Publishing Co., 1976), pp. 114–28; Hartmut Keil, "Immigrant Neighborhoods and American Society: German Immigrants on Chicago's Northwest Side in the Late Nineteenth Century," in *German Workers' Culture in the United States, 1850 to 1920*, ed. H. Keil (Washington, D.C.: Smithsonian Institution Press, 1988), pp. 25–58; Hartmut Keil and John B. Jentz, eds., *German Workers in Chicago: A Documentary History of Working-Class Culture from 1850 to World War I* (Urbana: University of Illinois Press, 1988), pp. 5–6, 176–79, 236–37; William von Katzler, "The Germans in Newark," in *A History of the City of Newark, New Jersey*, ed. F. J. Urquhart (New York: Lewis Historical Publishing Co., 1913), pp. 1057–87; Kathleen Neils Conzen, *Immigrant Milwaukee, 1836–1860: Accommodation and Community in a Frontier City* (Cambridge, Mass.: Harvard University Press, 1976), pp. 126–48, 154–91; Conzen, "The Paradox of German-American Assimilation," *Yearbook of German-American Studies* 16 (1981): 153–60.

15. Lee H. Soltow, *Men and Wealth in the United States, 1850–1870* (New Haven, Conn.: Yale University Press, 1975), p. 149; Nora Faires, "Occupational Patterns of German-Americans in Nineteenth-Century Cities," in *German Workers in Industrial Chicago, 1850–1910: A Comparative Perspective*, ed. Keil and Jentz (DeKalb: Northern Illinois University, 1983), pp. 37–51; Conzen, *Immigrant Milwaukee*, pp. 70–74.

16. *Hunt's Merchant's Magazine* 19 (1848): 43; *North American Review* 82 (1856): 265; Büchele, *Land und Volk der Vereinigten Staaten*, p. 284; Nadel, "Kleindeutschland," pp. 135, 163–74; Robert Ernst, *Immigrant Life in New York City, 1825–1863* (New York: Kings Crown Press, 1949), pp. 33, 91, 94–95, 165, 256n; Conzen, *Immigrant Milwaukee*, pp. 38–39, 65–68, 83, 102–5, 113–23, 204–6; Dieter Cunz, "The Baltimore Germans and the Year 1848," *American-German Review* 10 (October, 1943): 30; Audrey Louise Olson, "St. Louis Germans, 1850–1920: The Nature of an Immigrant Community and Its Relation to the Assimilation Process" (Ph.D. diss., University of Kansas, 1970), pp. 32–36; George Helmuth Kellner, "The German Element on the Urban Frontier: St. Louis, 1830–1860" (Ph.D. diss., University of Missouri–Columbia, 1973), pp. 300–301; Clyde Griffen and

Sally Griffen, *Natives and Newcomers: The Ordering of Opportunity in Mid-Nineteenth-Century Poughkeepsie* (Cambridge, Mass.: Harvard University Press, 1978), pp. 90–91, 121, 147.

17. George Rogers Taylor, *The Transportation Revolution, 1815–1860* (1951; repr., New York: Harper and Row, 1968), p. 250.

18. *New York Daily Tribune,* November 6, 1845; "Annual Report of the NYAICP" for 1852 in *Historical Aspects of the Immigration Problem,* pp. 325–26; Victor S. Clark, *History of Manufactures in the United States* (1929; repr., New York: Peter Smith, 1949), vol. 1, pp. 391–92; Norman Ware, *The Industrial Worker, 1840–1860: The Reaction of American Industrial Society to the Advance of the Industrial Revolution* (1924; repr., Chicago: Quadrangle Books, 1964), pp. 67–70; Ernst, *Immigrant Life in New York City,* pp. 65–66; Christine Stansell, *City of Women: Sex and Class in New York, 1789–1860* (New York: Alfred A. Knopf, 1986), pp. 44, 150, 157; *Statistics of the United States in 1860,* p. 312; Bessie Louise Pierce, *A History of Chicago* (New York: Alfred A. Knopf, 1940), vol. 2, p. 500; Conzen, *Immigrant Milwaukee,* pp. 87–90; James Matthew Morris, "The Road to Trade Unionism: Organized Labor in Cincinnati to 1893" (Ph.D. diss., University of Cincinnati, 1969), p. 12; Thomas W. Gavett, *The Development of the Labor Movement in Milwaukee* (Madison: University of Wisconsin Press, 1965), p. 8; *Hunt's Merchant's Magazine* 32 (1855): 693; *New York Daily Times,* March 4, 1853.

19. Walker, *Statistics of the Population in 1870,* pp. 710–15.

20. Wallis is reprinted in Rosenberg, ed., *American System of Manufactures,* p. 208; "Seventeenth Annual Report of the NYAICP" for 1860, in *Historical Aspects of the Immigration Problem,* p. 833.

21. Walker, *Statistics of the Population in 1870,* pp. xxxi–xxxii; Ernst, *Immigrant Life in New York City,* pp. 214–17; Sean Wilentz, *Chants Democratic: New York City and the Rise of the American Working Class, 1788–1850* (New York: Oxford University Press, 1984), p. 112. New York City as then constituted (i.e., the island of Manhattan) plus Brooklyn contained as many German immigrants as the next three largest settlement centers combined—St. Louis, Cincinnati, and Philadelphia: 138,217 versus 138,084.

22. In Philadelphia, the nation's second manufacturing city, Germans comprised only some 6 percent of all residents at mid-century, and 8 percent in 1860. But because about one-third of all German-born males in the labor force concentrated in four industries, they composed one-fifth of the city's boot and shoemakers, almost one-third of its clothing and furniture workers, and more than two-fifths of its food preparation and handling workers. In Newark, the nation's sixth-ranked manufacturing city, Germans supplied 15 percent of the population by 1860, but 20 percent of its tanners and curriers, 25 percent of its jewelers, 30 percent of its blacksmiths, one-third of its shoemakers and saddlers, and 40 percent of its numerous trunkmakers.

Nor did this general pattern differ farther west. Even before the influx of the 1840s and 1850s, German-born residents of Cincinnati (the country's third-ranking manufacturing center) constituted about one-fourth of the total population, 30 percent of its tanners and curriers, and nearly two-fifths of its tailors, shoemakers, and hatters combined. In 1870 the German-born still composed about one-fourth of the population, but now accounted for 35 percent of the city's work force and 40 percent of all those engaged in "mining, manufacturing, [or] mechanical" occupations. By that date, one in three Cincinnatians employed in the garment industry was German-born, while among cigarmakers, furniture makers, blacksmiths, bakers, and boot and shoemakers, the proportion rose to about one in two. Among tanners, curriers, leather finishers, and coopers, it ran between six and seven in ten. In St. Louis, where Germans composed some 30 percent of the total population in 1850, they made up almost half of all those engaged in the skilled crafts; a decade later, their slightly lower share of the urban population (26.5 percent) now included about seven out of every ten tradespeople employed in the city. In Pittsburgh, Germans made up about 20 percent of all family heads in 1850 and comparable proportions of those working in the crafts, and represented roughly 40 percent of all shoemakers, tailors, and bakers. In neighboring Allegheny City, Pennsylvania, in the same year, Germans composed 13 percent of the population, 43 percent of the shoemakers, and 56.5 percent of the tailors. In 1860 in Chicago, Germans made up one-fifth of the total population but between one-half and three-quarters of all tailors, shoemakers, cabinetmakers, bakers, and butchers. Even in places like Buffalo and Milwaukee, where Germans constituted an even higher proportion of the urban population—between 35 and 40 percent by the late 1850s—their representation in key trades rose higher still. In both cities they accounted for between 60 and 80 percent of all cabinetmakers, tailors, butchers, ironworkers, masons, coopers, and shoemakers.

On the general pattern, see E. P. Hutchinson, *Immigrants and Their Children, 1850–1920* (New York: John Wiley, 1956), pp. 79, 81; Theodore Hershberg et al., "Occupation and Ethnicity in Five Nineteenth-Century American Cities: A Collaborative Inquiry," *Historical Methods Newsletter* 7 (1974): 174–216; and Faires, "Occupational Patterns," passim. For the specific data cited in this note, see Walker, *Statistics of the Population in 1870,* pp. 704–801; Kennedy, *Population of the United States in 1860,* p. 610; Bruce Laurie and Mark Schmitz, "Manufacture and Productivity: The Making of an Industrial Base, Philadelphia, 1850–1880," in *Philadelphia: Work, Space, Family, and Group Experience in the 19th Century,* ed. Theodore Hershberg (New York: Oxford University Press, 1981), pp. 54–55; Susan E. Hirsch, *Roots of the American Working Class: The Industrialization of Crafts in Newark, 1800–1860* (Philadelphia: University of Pennsylvania Press, 1978), pp. 47, 49; Steven J. Ross, *Workers on the Edge: Work, Leisure, and Politics in Industrializing Cincinnati, 1788–1890* (New York: Columbia University Press, 1985), pp. 74, 136; J. D. B. DeBow, *Statistical View of the United States* (1854), p. 399; *The Seventh Census,* (1853), p. lii; Frederick Anthony Hodes, "The Urbanization of St. Louis: A Study in Urban Residential Patterns in the Nineteenth Century" (Ph.D. diss., St. Louis University, 1973), pp. 72–

73. See also Kellner, "The German Element on the Urban Frontier," pp. 272–75; Laurence Glasco, "Ethnicity and Occupation in the Mid-Nineteenth Century: Irish, Germans, and Native-born Whites in Buffalo, New York," in *Immigrants in Industrial America, 1850–1920,* ed. Richard L. Ehrlich (Charlottesville: University Press of Virginia, 1977), pp. 152–56; Conzen, *Immigrant Milwaukee,* pp. 99–101, 106–8. For data on Pittsburgh and Chicago, I am indebted to Nora Faires and the late Herbert Gutman respectively.

Close intercity comparisons are difficult, because different studies use different statistical bases (state vs. federal censuses, manufacturing vs. population censuses, 1850 vs. 1855 vs. 1860 vs. 1870, total work force vs. male work force vs. adult work force vs. household heads). But the overall tendency of German immigrants to cluster and thereby achieve disproportionate weight in particular skilled crafts is clear. Moreover, nearly all these figures understate the German-American presence in the trades because they miss those children of the immigrants who were reaching adulthood by the time of the Civil War.

23. Thomas P. Kettell (formerly editor of *Hunt's Merchant's Magazine*), "Manufacturing," in *Eighty Years' Progress of the United States, from the Revolutionary War to the Great Rebellion: Showing the Various Channels of Industry through which the People of the United States Have Arisen from a British Colony to their Present National Importance* (New York: New National Publishing House, 1864), pp. 360–68; Ross, *Workers on the Edge,* pp. 69–71, 78–81; Roger W. Clark, "Cincinnati Coppersmiths," *Cincinnati Historical Society Bulletin* 23 (October 1965): 257–72; Ernst, *Immigrant Life in New York City,* pp. 80–81, 83; *New York Daily Tribune,* April 23, 1850, April 12, 1853; Wilentz, *Chants Democratic,* pp. 112–13, 115–16; A. T. Andreas, *History of Chicago from the Earliest Period to the Present Time* (Chicago: A. T. Andreas Co., 1886), vol. 3, pp. 756–61; Hofmeister, *Germans of Chicago,* pp. 129–33; Edwin T. Freedley, *Philadelphia and Its Manufactures: A Hand-Book Exhibiting the Development, Variety, and Statistics of the Manufacturing Industry of Philadelphia in 1857* (Philadelphia: Edward Young, 1858), esp. pp. 185–86, 272–73; Hirsch, *Roots of the American Working Class,* pp. 24–25, 31–32; Katzler, "The Germans in Newark," pp. 1049, 1059–60.

24. Secretary of the Interior, *Statistics of the United States in 1860,* p. 312; Faires, "Occupational Patterns," passim; Nadel, "Kleindeutschland," pp. 145–47, 168; Wilentz, *Chants Democratic,* pp. 115, 405; Robert A. Christie, *Empire in Wood: A History of the Carpenter's Union* (Ithaca, N.Y.: Cornell University Press, 1956), p. 23; William Haber, *Industrial Relations in the Building Industry* (Cambridge, Mass.: Harvard University Press, 1930), pp. 274–75; Hermann Schlüter, *The Brewing Industry and the Brewery Workers' Movement in America* (1910; repr., New York: Burt Franklin, 1970), pp. 42–59; W. L. Downard, *The Cincinnati Brewing Industry: A Social and Economic History* (Athens: University of Ohio Press, [1973]), pp. 5–25; Griffen and Griffen, *Natives and Newcomers,* pp. 184–85; Conzen, *Immigrant Milwaukee,* pp. 99–100, 104–5; *New York Daily Tribune,* November 8, 1845; Ross, *Workers on*

the Edge, pp. 120- 24; Eugen Seeger, *Chicago, the Wonder City* (Chicago: George Gregory, 1893), p. 115; *Chicago und sein Deutschthum* (Cleveland: German-American Biographical Publishing Co., 1901–1902), p. 94; Hoffmeister, *Germans of Chicago,* pp. 133–35; Freedley, *Philadelphia and Its Manufactures,* pp. 195–98.

An analysis of the 1850 and 1860 manufacturing censuses gives a rough but suggestive picture of the economic ranking of some of these crafts (see appendix table C). The consistency of the gap in wages over the decade— and the supporting testimony of literary evidence—strengthens confidence in the pattern that emerges. In both 1850 and 1860 the average carpenter's wage was about 20 to 30 percent higher than the average cabinetmaker's, 25 to 35 percent higher than the average baker's, 35 to 50 percent higher than the average leather worker's, 45 to 50 percent higher than the average upholsterer's, 70 to 80 percent higher than the average shoemaker's, and 135 to 150 percent higher than the average tailor's. Differences in cost of living (it was evidently lower in the Midwest than in the Northeast) did not affect the ranking. On cost of living, see Philip R. P. Coelho and James F. Shepherd, "Differences in Regional Prices: The United States, 1851–1880," *Journal of Economic History* 34 (September 1974): 551–91; Coelho and Shepherd, "Regional Differences in Real Wages: The United States, 1851–1880," *Explorations in Economic History* 13 (1976): 203–30.

25. Wilentz, *Chants Democratic,* pp. 115, 137–39; Ernst, *Immigrant Life in New York City,* p. 87; Conzen, *Immigrant Milwaukee,* pp. 101, 107–8.

26. "Autobiography of George Puchta," 1933, George Puchta Collection, Hamilton County Public Library, Cincinnati; Rev. Charles Frederic Goss, *Cincinnati: The Queen City, 1788–1912* (Chicago: S. J. Clark Publishing Co., 1912), vol. 4, pp. 918–19; Melvin G. Holli and Peter d'A. Jones, *Biographical Dictionary of American Mayors, 1820–1980* (Westport, Conn.: Greenwood Press, 1981), pp. 297–98.

27. *New York Daily Tribune,* September 5, November 11, 1845; "Seventeenth Annual Report of the NYAICP," in *Historical Aspects of the Immigration Problem,* p. 833; *New York Daily Times,* March 3, 1854; *Chicago Daily Tribune,* March 7, 1854.

28. Fisher, *Workshops,* pp. 66–69; Moritz Busch, *Travels between the Hudson and the Mississippi, 1851–1852,* trans. and ed. Norman H. Binger (Lexington: University Press of Kentucky, 1971), p. 141.

29. *New York Daily Tribune,* September 5, 1845; *Republik der Arbeiter* (New York), May 7, 1853; Busch, *Travels,* p. 141

30. Schwenck letter of November 7, 1857, in Keil and Jentz, eds., *German Workers in Chicago: A Documentary History,* p. 29; Menzel in *Historical Aspects of the Immigration Problem,* pp. 141–42.

31. *Illinois Staats-Zeitung* (Chicago), July 26, 1861; *Volks-Tribun* (New York), October 31, 1846; Conzen, *Immigrant Milwaukee,* p. 113; *Die Reform* (New York), May 4, 1853.

32. Alan Dawley, *Class and Community: The Industrial Revolution in Lynn* (Cambridge, Mass.: Harvard University Press, 1976), pp. 29–30, 76–78;

and Paul G. Faler, *Mechanics and Manufacturers in the Early Industrial Revolution: Lynn, Massachusetts, 1780–1860* (Albany: State University of New York Press, 1981), pp. 78–80; *New York Daily Tribune,* September 9, 1845. Much additional data cited in descriptions of this and the following industries are taken from the manufacturing censuses of 1850 and 1860.

33. Wilentz, *Chants Democratic,* pp. 115, 125–26, 405; Ernst, *Immigrant Life in New York City,* p. 78; Kettell, "Manufacturing," p. 317; *Republik der Arbeiter* (New York), May 7, 1853; *New York Daily Tribune,* April 9, 1850, April 12, 1853.

34. Dawley, *Class and Community,* p. 30; *New York Daily Tribune,* September 3, 5, 9, 1845; *Eighty Years' Progress,* p. 325; Wilentz, *Chants Democratic,* p. 404.

35. Ernst, *Immigrant Life in New York City,* p. 214; *Report of the Committee of the Senate upon the Relations between Labor and Capital, and Testimony Taken by the Committee* (Washington, D.C.: Government Printing Office, 1885), vol. 1, pp. 413–17 (henceforth cited as *Report on Labor and Capital*); *New York Daily Tribune,* September 9, 1845, April 9, 1850.

36. Freedley, *Philadelphia and Its Manufactures,* pp. 185, 187; *Eighty Years' Progress,* p. 324; J. Leander Bishop, *A History of American Manufactures from 1608 to 1860,* 3 vols., 3d ed. (1868; repr., New York: Johnson Reprint Corporation, 1967), vol. 3, p. iii; Hirsch, *Roots of the American Working Class,* pp. 25–28, 59–62; *Newark Daily Advertiser,* June 22, 1854.

37. Margaret Walsh, *The Manufacturing Frontier: Pioneer Industry in Antebellum Wisconsin, 1830–1860* (Madison: State Historical Society of Wisconsin, 1972), pp. 198–99; Andreas, *History of Chicago,* vol. 1, p. 571; Conzen, *Immigrant Milwaukee,* p. 102; *Hunt's Merchant's Magazine* 25 (1851): 510 and 32 (1855): 693; *Annual Review of the Commerce, Manufactures, Public and Private Improvements of Chicago for the Year 1854* (Chicago: Daily Democratic Press, 1854), p. 46; *Eighth Annual Review of the Trade and Commerce of the City of Chicago, for the Year 1859* (Chicago: Chicago Daily Press and Tribune, 1860), p. 32; *Twelfth Annual Review of Chicago, 1860* (Chicago: Chicago Daily Tribune, 1861), p. 36; Ross, *Workers on the Edge,* pp. 27, 37–38, 113, 136; Charles Cist, *Sketches and Statistics of Cincinnati in 1851* (Cincinnati: Wm. H. Moore and Co., 1851), pp. 176–77; "Autobiography of George Puchta"; Cist, *Cincinnati in 1841: Early Annals and Future Prospects* (Cincinnati: author, 1841), p. 54; Cist, *Sketches and Statistics of Cincinnati in 1859* (Cincinnati: author, 1859), p. 259; Walker, *Statistics of the Population in 1870,* p. 783; Morris, "The Road to Trade Unionism," pp. 45–47.

38. Cist, *Cincinnati in 1851,* p. 177.

39. Ware, *The Industrial Worker,* p. 48. Only about one-third of all tailors listed in the population census failed to show up in the manufacturing census (compared with 40 to 45 percent of all shoemakers) in both 1850 and 1860.

40. Egal Feldman, *Fit for Men: A Study of New York's Clothing Trade* (Washington, D.C.: Public Affairs Press, 1960), pp. 4, 6–7, 11–16, 35, 96,

104. According to Feldman, at least half of all garments manufactured in New York City were destined for southern consumers. See also Wilentz, *Chants Democratic*, pp. 120–21, 124, 404–5; Jesse Eliphalet Pope, *The Clothing Industry in New York* (New York: Columbia University Press, 1905), p. 12; Nadel, "Kleindeutschland," p. 141.

41. *Hunt's Merchant's Magazine* 20 (1849): 347–48.

42. Feldman, *Fit for Men*, pp. 99, 102, 109; Pope, *The Clothing Industry in New York*, pp. 12–15.

43. In an ethnic breakdown closely paralleling that of the boot and shoe industries, Germans made up more than half of New York's tailors in 1855, and the Irish accounted for another third. See Ernst, *Immigrant Life in New York City*, pp. 71–78, 214; Nadel, "Kleindeutschland," pp. 141–43; *New York Daily Tribune*, August 14, 1845, July 29, 1850, June 8, 1853; *Republik der Arbeiter* (New York), March 12, 1853; Pope, *The Clothing Industry in New York*, 31–35; Feldman, *Fit for Men*, pp. 113–16; Wilentz, *Chants Democratic*, pp. 404–5; Virginia Penny, *How Women Can Make Money, Married or Single* (Philadelphia: McKinney and Martin, 1870), pp. 111–14. (This work was first published in 1863 under the title, *Employment of Women: A Cyclopedia of Women's Work*.) The family system of labor encouraged a drastic undercount of the number of wives and children employed by the clothing industry, which may help explain why Irish women (most of whom were probably unmarried) so radically outnumber German women in census tabulations.

44. Isaac Lippincott, *A History of Manufactures in the Ohio Valley to the Year 1860* (1914; repr., New York: Arno Press, 1973), p. 168; *New Yorker Staats-Zeitung*, September 4, 1846; *Fifth Annual Review of the Commerce, Manufactures, and the Public and Private Improvements of Chicago, for the Year 1856* (Chicago: Daily Democratic Press, 1857), p. 40; *Hunt's Merchant's Magazine* 32 (June 1855): 693; Gavett, *Labor Movement in Milwaukee*, pp. 8–9; Walsh, *The Manufacturing Frontier*, pp. 195–98; Conzen, *Immigrant Milwaukee*, pp. 99, 101–3, 112; *Newark Daily Mercury*, November 1, 1860; Hirsch, *Roots of the American Working Class*, pp. 59–60; Andreas, *History of Chicago*, vol. 3, pp. 720–24; Freedley, *Philadelphia and Its Manufactures*, pp. 220–25; Ross, *Workers on the Edge*, pp. 38, 131–33; Cist, *Cincinnati in 1851*, pp. 184–85; Cist, *Cincinnati in 1859*, p. 271.

45. Bishop, *History of American Manufactures*, vol. 2, p. 425; *New York Daily Tribune*, March 7, August 14, November 7, 1845, April 27, May 6, 1850; Stansell, *City of Women*, pp. 122, 145; Hirsch, *Roots of the American Working Class*, pp. 26, 29, 31, 34–36, 47; Cist, *Cincinnati in 1851*, p. 212; Morris, "The Road to Trade Unionism," pp. 72–74; Ross, *Workers on the Edge*, p. 148; Hermann Schlüter, *Die Anfänge der deutschen Arbeiterbewegung in Amerika* (Stuttgart: J. H. W. Dietz, 1907), p. 133.

46. In addition to the population and manufacturing censuses of 1850 and 1860, see Ware, *Industrial Worker*, pp. 66–67.

47. Ernst, *Immigrant Life in New York City*, p. 215; Elizabeth Ingerman, "Personal Experiences of an Old New York Cabinetmaker," *Antiques* 84 (No-

vember 1963): 576–80; *New York Daily Tribune,* November 11, 1845; Wilentz, *Chants Democratic,* pp. 127–28, 404–5.

48. Wilentz estimates that less than 2 percent of the industry's work force was employed in factories making use of power-driven machinery (Wilentz, *Chants Democratic,* pp. 404–5). See also Clark, *History of Manufactures in the United States,* vol. 1, p. 421; Ingerman, "Personal Experiences," p. 580; Schlüter, *Die Anfänge,* p. 134; Ernst, *Immigrant Life in New York City,* p. 80. Data on Philadelphia furniture manufacture can be found in Laurie and Schmitz, "Manufacture and Productivity," and Laurie, Hershberg, and Alter, "Immigrants and Industry," as well as in Freedley, *Philadelphia and Its Manufactures,* pp. 272–75; Elizabeth Page Talbott, "The Philadelphia Furniture Industry: 1850 to 1880" (Ph.D. diss., University of Pennsylvania, 1980), pp. 27, 57–66, 83; and the *New York Daily Tribune,* April 22, 1850.

49. Clark, *History of Manufactures,* vol. 1, pp. 421–22; Cist, *Cincinnati in 1851,* p. 201; Donald C. Peirce, "Mitchell and Rammelsberg: Cincinnati Furniture Makers, 1847–1881" (Ph.D. diss., University of Delaware, 1980), pp. 47–49; Talbott, "Philadelphia Furniture Industry," pp. 152–54, 233, and passim; *Republik der Arbeiter* (New York), March 12, 1853. In 1850 only 42 percent of the number of "joiners, cabinet-, and chairmakers" noted in the population census showed up in the manufacturing census. A decade later, the proportion had risen to 54 percent.

50. Cist, *Cincinnati in 1851,* pp. 201–2; Ross, *Workers on the Edge,* pp. 37, 100–101.

51. Cist, *Cincinnati in 1851,* pp. 201–3, 208; "Report of Mr. George Wallis" in *American System of Manufactures,* p. 294; Busch, *Travels,* p. 140; Peirce, "Mitchell and Rammelsberg," pp. 44–52; Jane E. Sikes, *The Furniture Makers of Cincinnati, 1790 to 1849* (Cincinnati: author, 1976), pp. 196–99. By the end of the 1850s, the Cincinnati firm of Clawson and Mudge was occupying two eight-story factory buildings (connected by walking bridges) that boasted both a considerable increase in power machinery as well as steam elevators to ease the flow of work (Cist, *Cincinnati in 1859,* pp. 292–95).

52. Walsh, *Manufacturing Frontier,* pp. 201–3; Conzen, *Immigrant Milwaukee,* pp. 108, 111; Andreas, *History of Chicago,* vol. 1, p. 570, vol. 3, pp. 733–42; William J. Cronon, "To Be the Central City: Chicago, 1848–1857," *Chicago History* 10 (Fall 1981): 130–40; *Annual Review of Chicago, 1854* (Chicago: Daily Democratic Press, 1854), pp. 41, 43; Sharon Darling, *Chicago Furniture: Art, Craft, and Industry: 1833–1983* (New York: Norton, 1984), pp. 14–20; *Hunt's Merchant's Magazine* 32 (June 1855): 693. The flood of low-priced, high-quality cabinetware made in the West was squeezing many New York cabinetmakers out of business by the 1860s. The New York firm of Meier and Hagen did eventually prosper, but only because (as Ernest Hagen recalled) "by mere accident we got a private trade among some of the old New York familys [*sic*]" and could therefore quit ready-made production altogether (Ingerman, "Personal Experiences," p. 580). For the impact on Philadelphia, see Talbott, "Philadelphia Furniture Industry," pp. 8–9.

53. Lippincott, *History of Manufactures in the Ohio Valley,* pp. 170–72; Hirsch, *Roots of the American Working Class,* pp. 25–26; Louis C. Hunter, "The Heavy Industries before 1860," in *The Growth of the American Economy,* ed. Harold F. Williamson, 2d ed. (New York: Prentice-Hall, 1951), p. 179; Constance McLaughlin Greene, "Light Manufactures and the Beginnings of Precision Manufacture," in *Growth of the American Economy,* p. 200; Peter Schmitt, Sr., "Family Record" (1888), Peter Schmitt Papers, Cincinnati Historical Society; David A. Hounshell, *From the American System to Mass Production, 1800–1932: The Development of Manufacturing Technology in the United States* (Baltimore: Johns Hopkins University Press, 1984), pp. 154–59; Laurie and Schmitz, "Manufacture and Productivity," and Laurie, Hershberg, and Alter, "Immigrants and Industry," passim; William H. Shaw, *History of Essex and Hudson Counties, New Jersey* (Philadelphia: Everts and Peck, 1884), vol. 1, p. 563; Conzen *Immigrant Milwaukee,* p. 100; Cist, *Cincinnati in 1851,* p. 49; Cist, *Cincinnati in 1859,* p. 256; Pierce, *History of Chicago,* vol. 2, p. 500.

54. Kettell, "Manufacturing," pp. 360–61, 368; Andreas, *History of Chicago,* vol. 1, p. 569, vol. 3, p. 743; *Annual Review of Chicago, 1854,* pp. 38–39; Freedley, *Philadelphia and Its Manufactures,* pp. 444–45, 447–49, 451; *Hunt's Merchant's Magazine* 26 (1852): 509, and 32 (1855): 693; Cist, *Cincinnati in 1851,* pp. 183, 252; Cist, *Cincinnati in 1859,* pp. 268, 335; Schmitt, "Family Record."

55. Bishop, *History of American Manufactures,* vol. 2, p. 176; Clark, *History of Manufactures,* vol. 1, p. 472; *Hunt's Merchant's Magazine* 17 (1847): 321–22, and 36 (1857): 765–66; Cist, *Cincinnati in 1851,* p. 49; Cist, *Cincinnati in 1859,* p. 271; Franklin E. Coyne, *The Development of the Cooperage Industry in the United States, 1620–1940* (Chicago: Lumber Buyers Publishing Co., 1940), pp. 15–16; Hounshell, *From the American System to Mass Production,* p. 51; Conzen, *Immigrant Milwaukee,* pp. 97, 106–7; *Cincinnati Daily Enquirer,* March 22, 1847; *New York Daily Times,* March 25, April 2, 1853.

56. The Morocco leather-making industry processed goat and lambskins and employed even more workers per firm (*Chicago Daily Tribune,* December 17, 1852); *Hunt's Merchant's Magazine* 26 (1852): 509, and 32 (1855): 693; Clark, *History of Manufactures,* vol. 1, p. 495; Hirsch, *Roots of the American Working Class,* pp. 25, 29–31; Bishop, *History of American Manufactures,* vol. 2, pp. 425, 446; Kettell, "Manufacturing," pp. 317–24.

57. Freedley, *Philadelphia and Its Manufactures,* pp. 357–60; Charles B. Kuhlmann, "Processing Agricultural Products in the Pre-Railway Age," in *Growth of the American Economy,* pp. 160–61; Kettell, "Manufacturing," pp. 317–19; Cist, *Cincinnati in 1851,* pp. 49, 261; Cist, *Cincinnati in 1859,* pp. 332, 344; *Chicago Daily Tribune,* December 17, 1852; *Annual Review . . . of Chicago for the Year 1854,* pp. 44–46; *Hunt's Merchant's Magazine* 26 (1852): 509, and 32 (1855): 693; Conzen, *Immigrant Milwaukee,* pp. 97, 106. As usual, the average capitalization and labor force size was considerably greater

in the major industrial cities. By 1860, for example, almost two-thirds of Newark's leather makers worked in firms with upwards of one hundred hands, and nearly 80 percent worked for firms with steam-powered equipment (Hirsch, *Roots of the American Working Class,* p. 31).

58. Hirsch, *Roots of the American Working Class,* p. 31; *Eighty Years' Progress,* pp. 316–24; Kuhlmann, "Processing Agricultural Products," pp. 159–61.

59. Freedley, *Philadelphia and Its Manufactures,* pp. 375–76; Hirsch, *Roots of the American Working Class,* pp. 25–26, 29, 47; *Newark Daily Advertiser,* March 16, 1850; Cist, *Cincinnati in 1851,* p. 235; Cist, *Cincinnati in 1859,* p. 328; *Hunt's Merchant's Magazine* 32 (June 1855): 693.

60. Willis N. Baer, *The Economic Development of the Cigar Industry in the United States* (Lancaster, Penn.: [Art Printing Co.], 1933), pp. 38–43; Edith Abbott, *Women in Industry* (New York: D. Appleton and Co., 1910), pp. 186–96; Ernst, *Immigrant Life in New York City,* p. 91; Samuel Gompers, *Seventy Years of Life and Labour: An Autobiography* (1925; repr., New York: Augustus M. Kelley, 1967), vol. 1, pp. 33–34; Kuhlmann, "Processing Agricultural Products," in *Growth of the American Economy,* p. 168; Freedley, *Philadelphia and Its Manufactures,* pp. 388–89; Cist, *Cincinnati in 1851,* pp. 244–45; Cist, *Cincinnati in 1859,* p. 333; Burgheim, *Cincinnati in Wort und Bild,* pp. 146–47.

61. *New York Daily Tribune,* April 9, 23, 25, May 13, 1850; *Republik der Arbeiter* (New York), May 7, 1853; Nadel, "Kleindeutschland," p. 143; Wilentz, *Chants Democratic,* p. 140; Ernst, *Immigrant Life in New York City,* p. 88; Laurie and Schmitz, "Manufacture and Productivity," and Laurie, Hershberg, and Alter, "Immigrants and Industry," passim; Cist, *Cincinnati in 1851,* p. 171; Cist, *Cincinnati in 1859,* pp. 249–50; Andreas, *History of Chicago,* vol. 1, p. 571; *Report on Labor and Capital,* vol. 1, pp. 436–43.

62. Lippincott, *History of Manufactures in the Ohio Valley,* p. 148; Commons, *History of Labor,* vol. 1, pp. 564–65, 600; Ware, *The Industrial Worker,* pp. 31–34, 160, 229, 232; Wilentz, *Chants Democratic,* p. 372; Carl N. Degler, "Labor in the Economy and Politics of New York City, 1850–1860: A Study of the Impact of Early Industrialism" (Ph.D. diss., Columbia University, 1952), p. 11; Ross, *Workers on the Edge,* pp. 142–43, 335n; Thomas Senior Berry, *Western Prices before 1861: A Study of the Cincinnati Market* (Cambridge, Mass.: Harvard University Press, 1943), p. 504; Hirsch, *Roots of the American Working Class,* p. 116; Pierce, *History of Chicago,* vol. 2, p. 155; *New York Daily Times,* March 22, 1853.

63. *New Yorker Criminal-Zeitung und Belletristisches Journal,* January 22, 1855; Leah Hannah Feder, *Unemployment Relief in Periods of Depression: A Study of Measures Adopted in Certain American Cities, 1857 through 1922* (New York: Russell Sage Foundation, 1936), pp. 18–19.

64. Herbert F. Koch, "The Panic of 1857 and Its Effects in Ohio" (M.A. thesis, University of Cincinnati, 1951), pp. 140–45, 150–53, 142, 194; *Sixth Annual Review of Chicago, 1857* (Chicago: Chicago Daily Press, 1858), esp. pp. 31, 47.

65. Keil and Jentz, eds., *German Workers in Chicago: A Documentary History*, pp. 24–27, 31–22, 37; Morris, "The Road to Trade Unionism," p. 105.

66. Büchele, *Land und Volk der Vereinigten Staaten*, p. 403; *New York Herald*, August 5, 1850.

Chapter 4: "The Love of Liberty Is Almost a Religion": Political
Unity and Dissension

1. Nadel, "Kleindeutschland," pp. 228–39; Kathleen Neils Conzen, "Immigrants, Immigrant Neighborhoods, and Ethnic Identity: Historical Issues," *Journal of American History* 66 (December 1979): 608–9, 613–14.

2. *New Yorker Staats-Zeitung*, April 1, 6, 13, 22, May 13, 1848, March 25, 1850; *New York Herald*, February 24, 1854; *New York Daily Tribune*, February 24, 1848; Robert Edwin Herzstein, "New York City Views the German Revolution, 1848: A Study in Ethnicity and Public Opinion," in *The Consortium on Revolutionary Europe: Proceedings, 1976*, ed. Lee Kennett (Athens, Ga.: University of Georgia Press, 1976), pp. 103–4; Carl Wittke, *The German-Language Press in America* (Lexington: University of Kentucky Press, 1957), pp. 62–70; Leonard Koester, ed., "Early Cincinnati and the Turners: From Mrs. Karl Tafel's Autobiography," *Historical and Philosophical Society of Ohio Bulletin* 6 (October 1948): 21–22.

3. *New Yorker Staats-Zeitung*, April 6, March 25, 1848; Wittke, *German-Language Press*, pp. 63–70; Wittke, *Refugees of Revolution*, pp. 199–200; Wittke, *Against the Current*, pp. 43, 57–59; Cunz, *The Maryland Germans: A History* (Princeton: Princeton University Press, 1948), p. 275; Thomas Stockham Baker, *Lenau and Young Germany in America* (Philadelphia: P. C. Stockhausen, 1897), pp. 57–59; James M. Bergquist, "The Political Attitudes of the German Immigrant in Illinois, 1848–1860" (Ph.D. diss., Northwestern University, 1966), p. 97; Audrey Louise Olson, "St. Louis Germans, 1850–1920: The Nature of an Immigrant Community and Its Relation to the Assimilation Process" (Ph.D. diss., University of Kansas, 1970), pp. 155–57; L. A. Wollenweber, "Aus meinem Leben," *Mitteilungen des Deutschen Pionier-Vereins von Philadelphia* (hereafter cited as *Mitteilungen*) 14 (1910): 22; C. F. Huch, "Der patriotische Verein," *Mitteilungen* 17 (1910): 21–25; Huch, "Die Deutschamerikaner und die deutsche Revolution," *Mitteilungen* 17 (1910): 25–33; Huch, "Der Befreiungs-Verein," *Mitteilungen* 17 (1910): 34–37; Huch, "Die Anfänge der Arbeiterbewegung unter den Deutschamerikanern," *Mitteilungen* 17 (1910): 41–42; Pierce, *History of Chicago*, vol. 2, pp. 27–28; *Chicago Daily Journal*, December 5, 6, 8, 1851; John Gerow Gazley, *American Opinion of German Unification, 1848–1871* (New York: Columbia University, 1926), p. 21; Thomas Sergeant Perry, ed., *The Life and Letters of Francis Lieber* (Boston: James R. Osgood and Co., 1882), pp. 213–14; Gustav Körner, *The Memoirs of Gustave Koerner, 1809–1896*, ed. Thomas I. McCormack, 2 vols. (Cedar Rapids: Torch Press, 1909), vol. 1, pp. 516, 533; Busch, *Travels*, p. 239.

4. Phillip Wagner, *Ein Achtundvierziger: Erlebtes und Gedachtes* (Brooklyn, N.Y.: Verlag von Johannes Wagner, 1882), pp. 224–26; *Republik der Arbeiter,* November 29, 1851; Eduard Schläger, "Der Wheelinger Congress im September 1852," *Der Deutsche Pionier* 8 (June 1876): 90–91; Heinrich Rattermann, "Kritik des Wheelinger Congress von 1852," *Der Deutsche Pionier* 8 (July, 1876): 155–59; *Turn-Zeitung,* April 15, 1854; *New Yorker Staats-Zeitung,* May 13, April 13, 15, 22, June 10, 17, 1848; Julius Goebel, "A Political Prophecy of the Forty-Eighters in America," *Deutsch-Amerikanische Geschichtsblätter* 12 (1912): 474–79; Huch, "Deutschamerikaner und die deutsche Revolution," p. 26; C. F. Huch, "Revolutionsvereine und Anleihen," *Mitteilungen* 18 (1910): 1–19; Jakob Müller, *Aus den Erinerungen eines Achtundvierzigers: Skizzen auf der deutsch-amerikanischen Sturm- und Drang-Periode der 50er Jahre* (Cleveland: Rudolph Schmidt Printing Company, 1896), pp. 204–15; *Chicago Daily Journal,* December 5, 6, 8, 1851.

5. *Turn-Zeitung,* January 15, March 1, April 1, 1852; *Republik der Arbeiter,* January 29, 1851; Müller, *Erinerungen eines Achtundvierzigers,* pp. 210–15; *New Yorker Staats-Zeitung,* April 22, 1848; Klaus Wust, *Guardian on the Hudson: The German-American Society of the City of New York, 1784–1984* (New York: German Society of the City of New York, [1984]), p. 30.

6. *Turn-Zeitung,* January 15, March 1, 1852; Samuel S. Busey, *Immigration: Its Evils and Consequences* (New York: De Witt and Davenport, 1856), p. 15; *Republik der Arbeiter,* January 29, 1852; *Hochwächter,* March 10, 1852; Karl Obermann, *Joseph Weydemeyer: Ein Lebensbild, 1818–1866* (Berlin: Dietz Verlag, 1966), pp. 251–54; Baker, *Lenau and Young Germany in America,* pp. 71–72n.

7. Karl J. R. Arndt, "American Incitement to Revolution on the Eve of the Frankfurt Parliament," *American-German Review* 11 (April 1945): 24–25; *New Yorker Staats-Zeitung,* October 22, 1852; Huch, "Revolutionsvereine und Anleihen," pp. 7–8; *New Yorker Staats-Zeitung,* April 22, 29, 1848; Körner, *Memoirs,* vol. 1, p. 535; Schläger, "Wheelinger Congress," pp. 91, 93; Goebel, "Political Prophecy, p. 476.

8. Theodore Pösche and Charles Göpp, *The New Rome; or, The United States of the World* (New York: G. P. Putnam and Co., 1853), pp. 99–100; Baker, *Lenau and Young Germany in America,* p. 71.

9. *New Yorker Staats-Zeitung,* January 19, 1854, October 28, 1856; Wittke, *Refugees of Revolution,* pp. 107, 174, 219–25; *Cincinnati Daily Enquirer,* October 13, 1860.

10. Karl Reemelin, *Life of Charles Reemelin, in German: Carl Gustav Rümelin, From 1814–1892* (Cincinnati: Weier and Daiker, 1892), p. 86; Körner, *Memoirs,* vol. 1, pp. 518, 541, 546–47; Marlin Timothy Tucker, "Political Leadership in the Illinois-Missouri German Community, 1836–1872" (Ph.D. dissertation, University of Illinois, 1968), p. 94; Mary Beth Stein, "American Politics through German Eyes: The Elections of 1856 and 1860 as Reported in the Freie Presse von Indiana," *Studies in Indiana German-Americana* 1 (1988): 60–61 (my translation); Frank Freidel, *Francis Lieber,*

Nineteenth-Century Liberal (1947; repr., Gloucester, Mass.: Peter Smith, 1968), pp. 86, 233; Pösche and Göpp, *The New Rome,* p. 100; *New York Daily Tribune,* April 15, 1850; and Herzstein, "New York City Views the German Revolution," pp. 108–9, 113.

11. Kinkel, Moritz Busch observed, found himself "speaking to a public that is either too 'gray' to be able *still* to offer him enthusiasm or too 'green' for anything *more* than enthusiasm to be expected" (Busch, *Travels,* p. 129). Wittke, *Refugees of Revolution,* pp. 32, 38; Huch, "Die Deutschamerikaner und die deutsche Revolution," pp. 25–33; *New Yorker Staats-Zeitung,* July 7, 1848, April 21, 1849; Wittke, *German-Language Press,* p. 68; Herzstein, "New York City Views the German Revolution," p. 107.

12. *Daily Pittsburgh Gazette,* January 22, 28, 29, 1852; Donald S. Spencer, *Louis Kossuth and Young America: A Study of Sectionalism and Foreign Policy, 1848–1852* (Columbia: University of Missouri Press, 1977), p. 154. The leading Marxist in the United States took a dimmer view of the same phenomenon. Even though "the [German] workers have been taken advantage of in so many different ways" by representatives of the European liberal bourgeoisie, he grumbled in frustration, "most of them" remained readier "to donate a dollar for this hostile [i.e., bourgeois liberal and nationalist] propaganda than to give one cent for the presentation of their own interests." Obermann, *Joseph Weydemeyer: Ein Lebensbild,* p. 248.

13. *Pittsburgh Courier,* translated in the *Pittsburgh Times* and reprinted in John P. Sanderson, *Republican Landmarks: The Views and Opinions of American Statesmen on Foreign Immigration* (Philadelphia: J. B. Lippincott and Co., 1856), pp. 223–25.

14. *New York Herald,* August 5, 1850, January 9, 16, 1855; Keil and Jentz, *German Workers in Chicago,* pp. 29–32.

15. *New Yorker Staats-Zeitung,* May 10, 1854; Sanderson, *Republican Landmarks,* pp. 223–24; *Sociale Republik,* January 29, 1859.

16. Müller, *Erinerungen eines Achtundvierzigers,* pp. 41–42; *New Yorker Demokrat,* July 17, October 29, 1852; *New York Daily Tribune,* July 13, 14, 15, 1855; Carl Wittke, *The Utopian Communist: A Biography of Wilhelm Weitling, Nineteenth-Century Reformer* (Baton Rouge: Louisiana State University Press, 1950), pp. 161; *Newark Daily Mercury,* November 8, 1853, February 9, 1854.

17. *Belleviller Zeitung,* May 1, 1855; Bergquist, "Political Attitudes," p. 173; Seeger, *Chicago: The Wonder City,* pp. 110–12.

18. Carl Schurz, *Reminiscences,* vol. 2, p. 16; Wittke, *Refugees of Revolution,* p. 108.

19. Augustus Prahl, "The Turner," in *The Forty-Eighters,* pp. 79–92; Koester, "Early Cincinnati and the Turners," pp. 21–22.

20. Henry Metzner, *A Brief History of the American Turnerbund,* rev. ed. (Pittsburgh: National Executive Committee of the American Turnerbund, 1924), pp. 7–16; Schlüter, *Die Anfänge,* pp. 199–201; C. F. Huch, "Der Sozialistische Turnerbund," *Mitteilungen* 26 (1912): 4–5; Marion Dexter

Learned, *The German-American Turner Lyric* (Baltimore: C. W. Scheider and Sons, 1897), pp. 21–25; *Turn-Zeitung,* April 1, 1854; William Frederic Kamman, *Socialism in German American Literature* (Philadelphia: Americana Germanica Press, 1917), p. 58; Koester, "Early Cincinnati and the Turners," pp. 18–22; Wilbur D. Jones, "Some Cincinnati Societies A Century Ago," *Bulletin of the Historical and Philosophical Society of Ohio* 20 (January 1962): 40; Alice Reynolds, "Friedrich Hecker," *American-German Review* 12 (April 1946): 4; "Erinnerungen aus der Geschichte des New York Turnverein," Gustav Scholer Papers, New York Public Library; *Chicago und sein Deutschthum,* p. 90; Hildegard Johnson, "German Forty-Eighters in Davenport," *Iowa Journal of History and Politics* 44 (January 1946): 16–18; Huch, "Die ersten Jahre der Philadelphia Turngemeinde," *Miteilungen* 26 (1912): 29–36.

21. *Turn-Zeitung,* November 15, 25, 1851, January 15, 1852, February 1, 1854; Learned, *German-American Turner Lyric,* pp. 21–24; Metzner, *History of the American Turnerbund,* pp. 8–10; Henrietta M. Heinzen, in collaboration with Hertha Anneke Sanne, "Biographical Notes in Commemoration of Fritz Anneke and Mathilda-Franziska Anneke" (typescript, Wisconsin State Historical Society, 1940), p. 28; Huch, "Philadelphia Turngemeinde," pp. 29–36; Huch, "Der Sozialistische Turnerbund," pp. 3–5; Schlüter, *Die Anfänge,* pp. 200–202; Prahl, "The Turner," p. 99. By the end of the decade, Turners of various political stripes probably numbered between nine and ten thousand. *New York Daily Tribune,* October 8, 1856; *Sociale Republik,* October 1, 1859; Katzler, "Germans in Newark," p. 1114; Wittke, *Refugees of Revolution,* p. 225.

22. Kammen, *Socialism in German American Literature,* p. 61. Similar assertions may be found in the *Turn-Zeitung,* April 1, 1853; and the *Sociale Republik,* July 31, 1858.

23. Schlüter, *Die Anfänge,* pp. 201–3; Katzler, "Germans in Newark," p. 1087; Huch, "Der Sozialistische Turnerbund," p. 1; Learned, *German-American Turner Lyric,* pp. 13–14 (original emphasis). The social profiles represented in tables 16 and 17 probably inflate the size of the early Turners' well-to-do sector; at least some of the occupational data reflect the impact of individual upward mobility since the 1840s and 1850s.

24. *Turn-Zeitung,* December 1, 1851, August 1, October 15, 1853; *Republik der Arbeiter,* December 3, 1853; *New Yorker Staats-Zeitung,* January 19, 1854; Eduard Schläger, "Das Freidenkerthum in den Vereinigten Staaten," *Internationale Monatsschrift* 1 (January 1882): 54–58; Huch, "Die freireligiöse Bewegung unter den Deutschamerikanern," *Mitteilungen* 11 (1909): pp. 1–2; Kistler, "German-American Liberalism and Thomas Paine," pp. 81–91; Moncure Daniel Conway, *Autobiography, Memories and Experiences* (New York: Houghton, Mifflin and Co., 1904), vol. 1, pp. 272, 275.

25. Carl Maulshagen, *American Lutheranism Surrenders to the Forces of Conservatism* (Atlanta: University of Georgia, 1936), pp. 99–112; Philip Schaff, *America: A Sketch,* pp. 35–36, 219; Heinrich H. Maurer, "Studies in the Sociology of Religion; Part III: The Problems of a National Church before

1860," *American Journal of Sociology* 30 (March 1925): 546, 549–50, and "Part IV: The Problems of Group-Consensus; Founding the Missouri Synod," *American Journal of Sociology* 30 (May 1925): 665–82; Walter O. Forster, *Zion on the Mississippi: The Settlement of the Saxon Lutherans in Missouri, 1839–1841* (St. Louis: Concordia Publishing House, 1953), pp. 135, 313, 262–67.

26. *Wahrheits-Freund,* March 16, 23, April 13, May 18, 1854, October 18, December 13, 1855, July 17, 1856; "Letters of the Right Reverend John Martin Henni and the Reverend Anthony Urbanek," *Wisconsin Magazine of History* (1926): 91; Jay P. Dolan, *The Immigrant Church: New York's Irish and German Catholics, 1815–1865* (Baltimore: Johns Hopkins University Press, 1975), p. 80.

27. Alfred Steckel, "German Roman Catholic Central Society of the United States of America," *Records of the American Catholic Historical Society of Philadelphia* 6 (1895): 252–65; Emmett H. Rothan, *The German Catholic Immigrant in the United States (1830–1860)* (Washington, D.C.: Catholic University of America, 1946), pp. 108–9. In 1851 a Catholic journal specifically oriented to a craftworker readership (entitled *Handwerker und Arbeiter-Union*) appeared in Cincinnati (*Hochwächter,* October 22, 1851; *Republik der Arbeiter,* October 25, 1851).

28. "Letters of Rev. Henni," pp. 90–91.

29. Busch, *Travels,* p. 31, 48; Schaff, *America: A Sketch,* pp. 35, 224–25; Henry Villard, *Memoirs of Henry Villard, Journalist and Financier, 1835–1900* (Cambridge, Mass.: Houghton, Mifflin and Co., 1904), vol. 1, p. 97; Huch, "Die freireligiöse Bewegung," pp. 1–3; John A. Hawgood, *The Tragedy of German-America: The Germans in the United States of America during the Nineteenth Century—and After* (New York: G. P. Putnam's Sons, 1940), p. 230; Wittke, *We Who Built America: The Saga of the Immigrant* (New York: Prentice-Hall, 1945), pp. 225–27; Nora Faires, "Revolutionaries in a Rationalist Church: Forty-Eighters in the Smithfield Congregation in Pittsburgh," in *German Forty-Eighters in the United States,* pp. 231–41; *Wahrheits-Freund,* April 13, 1854; Goss, *Cincinnati,* vol. 1, pp. 140–41; Körner, *Deutsche Element,* pp. 210–13; Joseph Atkinson, *History of Newark, New Jersey: Being a Narrative of Its Rise and Progress* (Newark: William B. Guild, 1878), p. 203; David Lawrence Pierson, *Narratives of Newark* (Newark: Pierson Publishing Co., 1917), p. 277; Katzler, "Germans in Newark," p. 1051.

30. *Wahrheits-Freund,* April 20, 1854; *Newark Daily Mercury,* August 14, 1857; Wagner, *Ein Achtundvierziger,* pp. 227–29; *Geschichtliche Mittheilungen über der Deutschen Freien Gemeinden von Nord-Amerika* (Philadelphia: Deutschen Freien Gemeinden von Philadelphia, 1877), pp. 1–28; Busch, *Travels,* pp. 46–48; *New Yorker Staats-Zeitung,* March 2, 1850; *Die Reform,* June 23, 31, July 23, October 29, December 1, 1853; J. J. Schlicher, "Bernhard Domschke: I. A Life of Hardship," *Wisconsin Magazine of History* 29 (1945–46): 323–24; Kamman, *Socialism in German American Literature,* p. 54; Wittke, *Refugees of Revolution,* pp. 128–30.

31. Huch, "Die freireligiöse Bewegung," p. 9; Cunz, *The Maryland Germans,* p. 275n; *Belleviller Zeitung,* April 10, 1851; Eduard Schläger, *Die sociale und politische Stellung der Deutschen in den Vereinigten Staaten: Ein Beitrag zu der Geschichte des Deutsch-Amerikanerthums der letzten 25 Jahre* (Berlin: Puttkamer and Mühlbrecht, 1874), p. 14; Müller, *Erinerungen eines Achtundvierzigers,* pp. 41–42.

32. "Association of Freemen of Cincinnati (*Verein freier Männe*)," April 14, 1852, in Hamilton County Incorporation Records, Hamilton County Courthouse, Cincinnati; *Hochwächter,* October 13, 1851, March 10, 1852; *Cincinnati Volksblatt,* December 31, 1853.

33. [Herman Julius Reutnik,] *Berümte deutsche Vorkämpfer für Fortschritt, Freiheit und Friede in Nord-Amerika von 1626 bis 1888* (Cleveland: Forest City Bookbinding Co., 1888), pp. 327–28; *Cincinnati Daily Enquirer,* March 17, 1853, January 11, 1854; *Hochwächter,* November 26, 1851; Carl Wittke, "Friedrich Hassaurek: Cincinnati's Leading Forty-Eighter," *Ohio Historical Quarterly* 68 (January 1959): 4; "Friedrich Hassaurek," *Deutsche Pionier* 17 (1885): 3–20; Körner, *Deutsche Element,* pp. 203–5, 212–14; *Republik der Arbeiter,* January 1, 1853; *Daily Cincinnati Gazette,* December 28, 1853.

34. Tocqueville, *Democracy in America,* vol. 1, p. 316.

35. U.S. House of Representatives, Committee on Foreign Affairs, *Report on Foreign Criminals and Paupers* (Report No. 359), 34th Cong., 1st sess., p. 1; *Newark Daily Mercury,* April 23, June 13, 1853, February 9, 10, 1854.

36. Ray Allen Billington, *The Protestant Crusade, 1800–1860: A Study of the Origins of American Nativism* (1938; repr., Chicago: Quadrangle Books, 1964), pp. 289–303, 331–32; Philip Gleason, *The Conservative Reformers: German-American Catholics and the Social Order* (Notre Dame, Ind.: University of Notre Dame Press, 1968), pp. 15–20; Madeleine Hooke Rice, *American Catholic Opinion in the Slavery Controversy* (1944; repr., Gloucester, Mass.: Peter Smith, 1964), pp. 91; *Daily Pittsburgh Gazette,* February 2, 20, 1854; "Letters of Rev. Henni," p. 89.

37. David Mead, "Brownson and Kossuth at Cincinnati," *Bulletin of the Historical and Philosophical Society of Ohio* 7 (April 1949): 92; Lloyd D. Easton, *Hegel's First American Followers: The Ohio Hegelians: John B. Stallo, Peter Kaufmann, Moncure Daniel Conway, and August Willich* (Athens: Ohio University Press, 1966), p. 61; *Wahrheits-Freund,* December 13, 1855; William A. Baughin, "Nativism in Cincinnati before 1860" (M.A. thesis, University of Akron, 1950), pp. 126n, 154–55; *Cincinnati Daily Enquirer,* January 11, 1854.

38. Billington, *The Protestant Crusade,* pp. 302–4; Rothan, *The German Catholic Immigrant,* p. 117; Sanderson, *Republican Landmarks,* p. 224.

39. *Sociale Republik,* June 26, 1858.

40. Obermann, *Joseph Weydemeyer: Ein Lebensbild,* pp. 269–73, 345–57; David Herreshoff, *The Origins of American Marxism: From the Transcendentalists to De Leon* (1967; repr., New York: Monad Press, 1973), pp. 53–70; Sorge, *Labor Movement,* pp. 3–10; *Der Arbeiter,* April 10, 17, 1858.

41. *Turn-Zeitung,* January 1, September 1, 1852.
42. *Turn-Zeitung,* January 1, 1852; *Sociale Republik,* June 26, July 24, 1858.
43. Metzner, *American Turnerbund,* p. 8; *Turn-Zeitung,* December 1, 1851; Schlüter, *Die Anfänge,* p. 203; *Cincinnati Republikaner,* February 1, 13, March 16, October 3, 1860.
44. Heinrich H. Maurer, "The Earlier German Nationalism in America," *American Journal of Sociology* 22 (January 1917): 530; *Turn-Zeitung,* April 4, 1854; Huch, "Die freireligiöse Bewegung," pp. 9, 15; Wittke, *Refugees of Revolution,* pp. 131–32; *Hochwächter,* October 13, November 26, 1851; Körner, *Memoirs,* vol. 1, p. 567; Schlicher, "Domschke," pp. 319–25.
45. Jutta Schoers Sanford, "The Origins of German Feminism: German Women, 1789–1870" (Ph.D., Ohio State University, 1976), pp. 127, 132–44; Stanley Zucker, "German Women and the Revolution of 1848: Kathinka Zitz-Halein and the Humania Association," *Central European History* 13 (September 1980): 237–54; Catherine M. Prelinger, "Religious Dissent, Women's Rights, and the Hamburger Hochschule für das weibliche Geschlecht in Mid-Nineteenth-Century Germany," *Church History* 45 (March 1976): 42–55. Like the wives of Gustav Struve and Ludwig Blenker, Mathilde Anneke accompanied her husband into battle during the Baden-Palatinate campaign. See Dora Edinger, "A Feminist Forty-Eighter," *American-German Review* 8 (June 1942): 18–19; Maria Wagner, *Mathilde Franziska Anneke in Selbstzeugnissen und Dokumenten* (Frankfurt: Fischer Taschenbuch Verlag, 1980), pp. 35–130; Annette P. Bus, "Mathilde Anneke and the Suffrage Movement," in *German Forty-Eighters in the United States,* pp. 79–84; Heinzen and Sanne, "Biographical Notes," p. 29, 34–35.
46. Wittke, *Against the Current,* pp. 94–95; *Hochwächter,* November 26, 1851, January 28, 1852; Körner, *Memoirs,* vol. 1, p. 567; Sanderson, *Republican Landmarks,* p. 221.
47. Helene Sara Zahler, *Eastern Workingmen and National Land Policy, 1829–1862* (New York: Columbia University Press, 1941); George M. Stephenson, *The Political History of the Public Lands from 1840 to 1862* (Boston: Richard G. Badger, 1917), pp. 103–13; John R. Commons and Associates, *History of Labor in the United States,* vol. 1, pp. 489–535; Roy Marvin Robbins, "Horace Greeley: Land Reform and Unemployment, 1837–1862," *Agricultural History* 7 (1933): 18–41; Roseboom, *Civil War Era,* pp. 32–33, 219.
48. Ware, *Industrial Worker,* pp. 222–26; Wilentz, *Chants Democratic,* pp. 335–43; *New York Daily Tribune,* July 3, 1850; *Newark Daily Advertiser,* October 11, 1850; *Chicago Daily Democrat,* June 7, 8, July 12, 1850; Cincinnati *Nonpareil,* October 19, 22, 24, 26, 29, 1850; *Cincinnati Republikaner,* April 18, 1860; Andreas, *History of Chicago,* vol. 1, p. 389; Joe L. Norris, "The Land Reform Movement," *Papers in Illinois History and Transactions for the Year 1937* (1938): pp. 73–82; Pierce, *History of Chicago,* vol. 2, pp. 183–84; Degler, "Labor," 233–57.

49. *Young America,* October 18, November 8, December 20, 1845; Schlüter, *Die Anfänge,* pp. 20–23, 34, 47–49; Sorge, *Labor Movement,* pp. 76–77; *Volks-Tribun,* January 5, 17, March 7, May 9, 16, 1846; *New Yorker Staats-Zeitung,* September 5, 1846, October 17, 1848, January 3, 1851, March 11, 1854; *New Yorker Demokrat,* October 4, 1850, as reprinted in the *Belleviller Zeitung,* October 24, 1850; *New Yorker Staats-Zeitung,* March 9, June 3, October 7, 1848, January 3, 1851; *New York Daily Tribune,* November 3, 1845; *New Yorker Criminal Zeitung und Belletristisches Journal,* June 4, 1852.

50. *Volks-Tribun,* January 10, 1846; *Republik der Arbeiter,* May 15, July 17, 1852, April 30, 1853; *New Yorker Staats-Zeitung,* September 5, 1846; *Young America,* December 20, 1845; *New York Daily Tribune,* July 3, 6, 29, August 5, 1850; *Chicago Daily Democrat,* June 7, 8, 1850; Cincinnati *Nonpareil,* October 19, 22, 24, 26, 29, 1850; *Turn-Zeitung,* May 1, 1854; Norris, "Land Reform Movement," pp. 78–81; Andreas, *History of Chicago,* vol. 1, p. 389; Bergquist, "Political Attitudes," p. 90; Gazley, *American Opinion,* p. 441; Sanderson, *Republican Landmarks,* p. 221; Arthur C. Cole, *The Irrepressible Conflict: 1850–1865* (1934; repr., Chicago: Quadrangle Books, 1971), p. 137.

51. *Turn-Zeitung,* December 1, 1851; *Young America,* November 8, 1845; *New York Daily Tribune,* November 3, 1845.

52. Hermann Kriege, *Die Väter unserer Republik in ihrem Leben und Wirken* (New York: Verlag von J. Uhl, 1847); *The Free West,* May 18, 1854; *Louisville Daily Democrat,* March 4, 1854.

53. *Sentinel of Freedom* (Newark), April 14, 1854; *Newark Daily Advertiser,* April 14, 1853.

54. Sanderson, *Republican Landmarks,* p. 227.

55. Whitney, *Defence of the American Policy,* pp. 167–71; Busey, *Immigration,* p. 21; Sanderson, *Republican Landmarks,* p. 227; J. Wayne Laurens, *The Crisis: Or, the Enemies of America Unmasked* (Philadelphia: G. D. Miller, 1855), pp. 180–81.

56. *Wahrheits-Freund,* March 16, 1854; *Newark Daily Mercury,* June 8, 1853.

57. Körner, *Memoirs,* vol. 1, p. 567; *New Yorker Staats-Zeitung,* April 6, 1854; *Daily Pittsburgh Gazette,* March 24, 1854; *Newark Daily Advertiser,* June 8, 30, 1853; Maria Wagner, "The Forty-Eighters in Their Struggle against American Puritanism: The Case Study of Newark, New Jersey," in *German Forty-Eighters in the United States,* pp. 219–30.

58. Freidel, *Francis Lieber,* pp. 194–95; Joseph Dorfman, *The Economic Mind in American Civilization, 1606–1865* (1946; repr., New York: Augustus M. Kelley, 1966), vol. 2, pp. 869–72, 874, 877; Robert E. Cazden, *A Social History of the German Book Trade in America to the Civil War* (Columbia, S.C.: Camden House, 1984), p. 195; Theodor Lemke, *Geschichte des Deutschthums von New York von 1848 bis auf die Gegenwart* (New York: Theodor Lemke, 1891), pp. 11–17; Stanley Nadel, "The Forty-Eighters and the

Politics of Class in New York City," in *German Forty-Eighters in the United States,* pp. 51–66.

59. Becker, *Germans of 1849,* p. 43; *New Yorker Staats-Zeitung,* January 19, April 8, May 10, 1854.

60. Schurz, *Speeches,* vol. 1, pp. 5–8; Hans Trefousse, *Carl Schurz: A Biography* (Knoxville: University of Tennessee Press, 1982), pp. 14–19; Pösche and Göpp, *The New Rome,* pp. 162–63.

Chapter 5. "It Is Time to Fight Again": The Organizations of Labor

1. *Cincinnati Volksblatt,* November 15, 1851, quoted in the *Hochwächter,* November 26, 1851; *Chicago Daily Tribune,* November 16, 1857.

2. Reemelin, *Life,* pp. 41–42; *Life and Letters of Francis Lieber,* pp. 171–72; *Cincinnati Daily Commercial,* April 5, 1859; Keil and Jentz, eds., *German Workers in Chicago: A Documentary History,* p. 34; Schaff, *America: A Sketch,* pp. 35–36.

3. J. D. Angell, "German Emigration to America," *North American Review* 82 (1856): 265.

4. Whitney, *Defence of the American Policy,* pp. 167–69; Körner, *Memoirs,* vol. 1, p. 547; Busch, *Travels,* p. 251.

5. During the 1850s, a reorganized German Society modified its views and made room for members and leaders from the recent immigration. Wust, *Guardian on the Hudson,* pp. 14, 26–31; Anton Eickhoff, ed., *In der neuen Heimath: Geschichtliche Mittheilungen über die deutschen Einwanderer in allen Theilen der Union* (New York: E. Steiger and Co., 1884), pp. 89–158; Friedrich Kapp, *Geschichte der Deutschen im Staat New York,* 3d ed. (New York: E. Steiger, 1869), vol. 1, pp. 334–40; Schlüter, *Die Anfänge,* pp. 19–23; Ernst, *Immigrant Life in New York City,* pp. 33, 107, 113; Commons, *History of Labor,* vol. 1, p. 535. Financier and Whig leader Philip Hone, of French-German ancestry, was president of the New York German Society during the late 1820s and 1830s (Allan Nevins, ed., *The Diary of Philip Hone, 1828–1851,* 2 vols. [1927; repr., New York: Kraus Reprint Co., 1969], vol. 1, pp. xiv, 343–44).

6. *Volks-Tribun* (New York), October 10, 31, 1846; *New Yorker Staats-Zeitung,* September 5, 1946, June 17, 1848; *Republik der Arbeiter* (New York), May, 1850, September, 1851; *Turn-Zeitung,* January 15, 1852; *New York Daily Tribune,* July 3, 1850; Schlüter, *Die Anfänge,* pp. 15–19; Huch, "Die Anfänge der Arbeiterbewegung," p. 42.

7. *New Yorker Criminal Zeitung und Belletristisches Journal* (October 5, 1860); *New York Daily Tribune,* July 1, 3, 31, 1850; Burgheim, *Cincinnati in Wort und Bild,* p. 94; Degler, "Labor," pp. 44–45; Wilentz, *Chants Democratic,* pp. 365–66; Wittke, *Utopian Communist,* pp. 173–74, 198, 211; *Republik der Arbeiter,* February, October, November, 1850, June 28, 1851; Incorporation papers, Working Men's Literary and Debating Society, April 17, 1855, Recorder's Office, Hamilton County Courthouse, Cincinnati; Huch, "Die Anfänge der Arbeiterbewegung," pp. 39–42; *Chicago Daily Tribune,*

December 7, 1857; Pierce, *History of Chicago*, vol. 2, p. 167; *Illinois Staats-Zeitung* (Chicago), February 12, 1861.

8. *Chicago Daily Tribune*, December 7, 1857; *Republik der Arbeiter*, March 27, May 1, 15, July 10, 1852; *Illinois Staats-Zeitung*, September 30, 1861, January 6, 1864; *Chicago und sein Deutschthum*, pp. 129–31.

9. *Chicago Daily Tribune*, December 7, 1857.

10. *Republik der Arbeiter*, March, June, 1850, November 29, 1851, March 27, May 1, 15, 1852, November 13, 1852, April 16, December 7, 1853; *New York Daily Tribune*, April 15, 23, 25, June 10, July 3, August 5, 12, 13, 1850, March 2, 1854; *Die Reform* (New York), March 26, May 4, June 1, 11, 25, August 20, September 21, October 27, December 7, 1853; *Sociale Republik* (New York), July 31, 1858; *New Yorker Staats-Zeitung*, March 2, 1850; Katzler, "Germans of Newark," p. 1057; *Daily Democratic Press* (Chicago), April 6, 1853; *Daily Cincinnati Gazette*, March 24, 1854.

11. *Republik der Arbeiter*, February, 1850, April 19, 1851, May 15, August 28, 1852; *Die Reform*, January 24, June 1, July 16, August 20, December 7, 1853; *New York Daily Tribune*, April 26, 27, June 7, 1850; Frederick R. Schmidt, *He Chose: The Other Was a Treadmill Thing* (Santa Fe: Author, 1968); James L. High, "Dr. Ernst Schmidt (1830–1900)," typescript, 1960, Ernst Schmidt Papers, Chicago Historical Society; Katzler, "Germans of Newark," p. 1061; *Illinois Staats-Zeitung*, April 16, 1862. Some declassed intelligentsia were probably among those labor leaders identified as manually unskilled workers.

12. *New Yorker Staats-Zeitung*, May 27, 1848; *Republik der Arbeiter*, May 15, August 22, 28, 1852, April 16, 1853; Katzler, "Germans of Newark," p. 1050; H. B. Johnson, "Caspar Butz of Chicago—Politician and Poet," *American-German Review* 12 (August 1946): 4–7; Ronald P. Formisano, *The Birth of Mass Political Parties: Michigan, 1827–1861* (Princeton, N.J.: Princeton University Press, 1971), p. 184 and n.

13. Sorge, *Labor Movement*, p. 92; Schlüter, *Die Anfänge*, p. 128; Wilentz, *Chants Democratic*, pp. 366–67; Ware, *Industrial Worker*, pp. 185–86; *New York Daily Tribune*, July 29, 1850.

14. *New York Daily Tribune*, April 12, 15, 22, 23, 26, May 6, 14, 1850; *Republik der Arbeiter*, March, 1850, May 10, 31, June 21, 28, November 29, 1851, May 1, August 28, November 3, 1852; *Sociale Republik* (New York), April 24, 1858; Laurie, *Working People of Philadelphia*, pp. 193–94; Schlüter, *Die Anfänge*, p. 85; Wittke, *Utopian Communist*, pp. 31, 172, 179–85, 230–31; Gavett, *Labor Movement in Milwaukee*, pp. 6, 9; Conzen, *Immigrant Milwaukee*, pp. 111–12; Ross, *Workers on the Edge*, p. 159; Commons, *History of Labor*, vol. 1, pp. 566, 569.

15. *Republik der Arbeiter*, February and March, 1850; Sorge, *Labor Movement*, p. 90; Huch, "Die Anfänge der Arbeiterbewegung," pp. 43–45; Ross, *Workers on the Edge*, p. 159; Laurie, *Working People of Philadelphia*, pp. 193–94.

16. *Republik der Arbeiter*, February and March, 1850; Wittke, *Utopian Communist*, pp. 199–201.

17. That such views remained widespread in labor circles generally was made clear in a report submitted the same day by a committee of New York's Industrial Congress. It blamed the sad state of the economy "mainly" on "the intervention of the commission merchant and trader between the producer and the consumer." The middlemen "accumulate fortunes out of their trade" by "contributions laid on commodities *in transit* between the maker and the consumer. . . . Workmen about our cities acquire no practical knowledge of trade, and become dependent on the commission merchant, who undertakes, for the lion's share, to find those in want of the manufactured articles, and to sell on behalf of the original producer." The report therefore sought to "dispense with the intervention of the commission merchant, in transferring wares from the producer to the consumer." *New York Daily Tribune,* August 15, 1850, original emphasis.

18. *New York Daily Tribune,* July 3, 1850; *New Yorker Staats-Zeitung,* September 5, 1846; Schlüter, *Die Anfänge,* pp. 72–75, 88; *Republik der Arbeiter,* May, 1850, 9, 1851; Wittke, *Utopian Communist,* pp. 162, 193; Huch, "Die Anfänge der Arbeiterbewegung," p. 42.

19. Commons, *History of Labor,* vol. 1, pp. 599, 605–6; Morris, "Road to Trade Unionism," pp. 76–77; Ross, *Workers on the Edge,* pp. 148–49.

20. *New York Daily Tribune,* April 15, May 13, 23, 1850; *Republik der Arbeiter,* April 23, 30, 1853; Degler, "Labor," pp. 40–41; Morris, "Road to Trade Unionism," p. 99; *Sociale Republik,* June 19, 1858.

21. *New York Daily Tribune,* May 13, 1850; *New Yorker Staats-Zeitung,* July 27, 1850.

22. Conzen, *Immigrant Milwaukee,* pp. 110–11, 113; *New York Daily Tribune,* April 22, 26, May 14, July 31, 1850, March 22, 1854; *New York Daily Times,* April 13, 1853; *Republik der Arbeiter,* April 16, 1853; *Die Reform,* April 23, 1853. On charivaris and *Katzenmusik,* see Natalie Davis, "The Reasons of Misrule," in *Society and Culture in Early Modern France* (Stanford, Calif.: Stanford University Press, 1975); E. P. Thompson, "Folklore, Anthropology, and Social History," *Indian Historical Review* 3 (January 1978): 247–66; Bryan D. Palmer, "Discordant Music, Charivaris and Whitecapping in Nineteenth-Century North America," *Labour/Le Travailleur* 3 (1978): p. 15 and passim; George Phillips, "Über den Unsprung der Katzenmusiken: Eine canonistisch-mythologisch Abhandlung" [1849], in *Vermischte Schriften* (Wien: Wilhelm Braumüller, 1860), pp. 35–47, 88–92; Eric J. Hobsbawm, "Introduction" to *The Invention of Tradition,* ed. Hobsbawm and Terence Ranger (Cambridge, Mass.: Cambridge University Press, 1983), pp. 1–14.

23. *New York Daily Tribune,* May 17, 1850.

24. *New York Daily Tribune,* September 1, 1853; Degler, "Labor," pp. 28, 32–34; *New York Daily Times,* April 11, 1853. See also Gavett, *Labor Movement in Milwaukee,* pp. 8–9; and Conzen, *Immigrant Milwaukee,* pp. 112–13. As David Montgomery especially has demonstrated, such struggles over central aspects of capitalist prerogative and power grew in frequency in the post–Civil War era. This pattern alone suggests the superficiality of as-

sertions that nineteenth-century American workers "by and large . . . did not seriously question the legitimacy of the social order and their place within it," that they "aspired to improve their own position or that of their children" but not "to alter fundamentally the relative position of groups within the social order itself," that they were innocent of any "qualities of consciousness" that might set them apart from other groups in society. (M. B. Katz, M. J. Doucet, and M. J. Stern, *The Social Organization of Early Industrial Capitalism* [Cambridge, Mass.: Harvard University Press, 1982], p. 160; John Patrick Diggins, "Comrades and Citizens: New Mythologies in American Historiography," *American Historical Review* 90 [June 1985]: 625, 627. Cf. David Montgomery, *Workers' Control in America: Studies in the History of Work, Technology, and Labor Struggles* [Cambridge, Mass.: Cambridge University Press, 1979]; and Montgomery, *The Fall of the House of Labor: The Workplace, the State, and American Labor Activism, 1865–1925* [Cambridge: Cambridge University Press, 1987].)

25. Hirsch, *Roots of the American Working Class,* pp. 116–17; *Cincinnati Daily Enquirer,* December 11, 1853, March 17, 25, April 5, 1859; Ross, *Workers on the Edge,* pp. 151–59; Degler, "Labor," pp. 38, 80; *Sociale Republik,* June 19, 1858, April 2, 1859; Sorge, *Labor Movement,* p. 9; Ernst, *Immigrant Life in New York City,* pp. 120, 265n; Schlüter, *Die Anfänge,* p. 176; *New York Daily Tribune,* May 13, 1850; *Cincinnati Daily Commercial,* April 5, 1859; Morris, "Road to Trade Unionism," p. 106.

26. Degler, "Labor," p. 90; *Cincinnati Republikaner,* April 14, 1860; *Republik der Arbeiter,* September, 1850. For a provocative discussion of this subject, see Ira Katznelson, *City Trenchers: Urban Politics and the Patterning of Class in the United States* (New York: Pantheon, 1981), pp. 51–52.

27. *New York Daily Times,* April 18, 1853; *New York Herald,* April 22, 1853; *New York Daily Tribune,* March 23, May 13, 18, 23, 1850.

28. Heinzen and Sanne, "Biographical Notes," p. 34; Krueger, "Mathilda Franziska Anneke," pp. 164–66; Gavett, *Labor Movement in Milwaukee,* p. 7.

29. *New York Daily Tribune,* April 9, 1850.

30. *Republik der Arbeiter,* May 10, 1851, March 27, April 24, August 28, November 13, 1852; Heinzen and Sanne, "Biographical Notes," pp. 29, 34–35; *Die Reform,* June 1, September 4, 1853; *Sociale Republik,* January 29, 1859; *Cincinnati Republikaner,* May 14, 1860. The Williamsburg *Frauenverein* was led by Anna Schetzer-Traub, whose husband apparently presided over the *Arbeiterverein* (*Die Reform,* June 25, 1853).

31. *Sociale Republik,* June 19, 1858.

32. Laurie, *Working People of Philadelphia,* pp. 180–81; *New York Daily Tribune,* April 16, 22, 23, 26, May 14, 28, July 31, 1850; *Cincinnati Daily Enquirer,* April 16, 1853; *Chicago Daily Tribune,* December 7, 1857; Ernst, *Immigrant Life in New York City,* pp. 109–10; *Die Reform,* April 23, 1853.

33. *New York Daily Tribune,* April 12, 20, May 2, 6, 13, June 22, 1850; Ernst, *Immigrant Life in New York City,* p. 108; *Daily Democratic Press,* April

16, 12, 19, 26, May 14, 1853; *Die Reform*, April 16, 1853; *New York Daily Times*, April 13, 15, 1853, March 29, 1854; *Republik der Arbeiter*, May 7, 1853; *Cincinnati Daily Enquirer*, March 17, 25, April 1, 1859; *Sociale Republik*, April 2, 1859; Ross, *Workers on the Edge*, pp. 157–59.

34. Willich to Fritz Anneke, January 31, 1862, in Heinzen and Sanne, "Biographical Notes," Appendix to chapter 5, note 9; *Republik der Arbeiter*, May 17, 1853; *New York Daily Times*, April 13, 15, 1853; *New York Daily Tribune*, August 12, 1850; Ross, *Workers on the Edge*, p. 150.

35. *New York Daily Tribune*, April 23, 1850; Ware, *Industrial Worker*, pp. 31, 229–34.

36. *New York Daily Tribune*, April 17, 19, 23, 24, 25, 30, May 1, 6, 9, 12, 15, June 30, July 29, November 14, 1850; *New York Herald*, March 11, 15, 1850; Degler, "Labor," pp. 47, 73; *Republik der Arbeiter*, October, November, 1850; Schlüter, *Die Anfänge*, pp. 79–80.

37. *Republik der Arbeiter*, February 1850; *New York Daily Tribune*, April 11, 12, 15, 22, 26, 27, May 2, 6, 13, 23, June 8, 1850; *New York Herald*, April 12, 1850; Schlüter, *Die Anfänge*, pp. 79–80; Degler, "Labor," pp. 14, 25, 47.

38. Most centrally involved in founding the CVG were the upholsterers, cabinetmakers, bakers, shoemakers, and tailors—key strongholds of the immigrant craftworkers—as well as the turners, carvers, mechanics, and capmakers and furriers. *Republik der Arbeiter*, March, May, and August 1850; *New York Daily Tribune*, April 23, May 17, 1850; Schlüter, *Die Anfänge*, p. 131.

39. CVG delegates to the Congress included cabinetmaker J. G. Braubach and tailors Wilhelm Weitling, Jasper Beckmeier, and William Görge. *New York Daily Tribune*, May 24, June 7, July 2, 26, August 15, 1850; *Republik der Arbeiter*, March 1850.

40. *Republik der Arbeiter*, June, August-November 1850; Huch, "Die Anfänge der Arbeiterbewegung," pp. 45–46; Wittke, *Utopian Communist*, p. 192; Hirsch, *Roots of the American Working Class*, pp. 116–17.

41. *Republik der Arbeiter*, March, August 1850; *New York Daily Tribune*, April 23, June 10, July 25, August 12, 1850; *New Yorker Staats-Zeitung*, July 27, August 17, 1850.

42. *New York Daily Tribune*, June 10, July 25, 29, August 21, 1850; *New Yorker Staats-Zeitung*, July 27, 1850; *Republik der Arbeiter*, August and September, 1850.

43. *New York Herald*, July 23, 1850; *New York Daily Tribune*, July 25, 1850.

44. *New York Herald*, July 23, 26, 1850; *New York Daily Tribune*, July 29, 1850; Wilentz, *Chants Democratic*, p. 378.

45. *New York Herald*, July 25, 31, 1850; *Republik der Arbeiter*, September, 1850; *New Yorker Staats-Zeitung*, July 27, 1850.

46. *Republik der Arbeiter*, September 1850; *New Yorker Staats-Zeitung*, August 6, 7, 10, 1850; *New York Herald*, August 6, 7, 9, 1850; *New York*

Daily Tribune, August 6, 8, 1850; Wilentz, *Chants Democratic,* pp. 375–80; Degler, "Labor," pp. 80–81; Nadel, "Kleindeutschland," p. 265. The *Staats-Zeitung* asserted that "loafers" and "niggers" had sided with Wartz and the police in the street battle with strikers.

47. Accounts varied regarding the number arrested and the condition and fate of the wounded. Thirty-nine were eventually brought to trial. The high bail initially set kept most of the prisoners in jail through early September, when bail was reduced. Finally, in December the accused pled guilty to charges of "riotous assault and battery," and eight of them paid fines ranging from five to fifty dollars (for George Short). *New York Daily Tribune,* September 7, November 5, December 16, 1850.

48. *New York Daily Tribune,* July 25, 26, August 8, 1850; *New York Herald,* July 12, August 5, 7, 1850; *New Yorker Staats-Zeitung,* August 10, 17, 24, 1850.

49. *New York Daily Tribune,* July 26, 29, August 5, 12, 13, 14, 15, 21, 1850; *New York Herald,* August 5, 1850; *New Yorker Staats-Zeitung,* August 3, 1850; *Republik der Arbeiter,* September, 1850; *Belleviller Zeitung,* August 29, 1850; Huch, "Die Anfänge der Arbeiterbewegung," p. 47; Burgheim, *Cincinnati in Wort und Bild,* p. 159.

50. *New York Daily Tribune,* July 31, 1850; *New York Herald,* August 5, 1850.

51. *New York Daily Tribune,* August 14, 1850.

52. *New York Herald,* August 5, 1850; *New York Daily Tribune,* August 5, 1850.

53. *New York Herald,* August 5, 1850.

54. *New York Daily Tribune,* August 5, 1850; *New York Herald,* August 7, 1850.

55. *New York Herald,* July 25, August 6, 1850.

56. Mallon served on the Executive Committee of the English-speaking journeymen's society. *New York Herald,* August 5, 6, 7, 8, 1850; *New York Daily Tribune,* August 15, 1850.

57. *New York Herald,* August 1, 7, 9, 1850. See also the comments of English-speaking blacksmith leader Garret, quoted in the *New York Daily Tribune,* August 15, 1850.

58. *New York Herald,* July 31, August 1, 6, 9, 1850; *New York Daily Tribune,* July 25, August 5, 6, 15, 1850; *Republik der Arbeiter,* August and September 1850.

59. *New York Herald,* July 27, 1850.

60. *New York Herald,* August 5, 7, 1850.

61. *Republik der Arbeiter,* September 1850; Schlüter, *Die Anfänge,* p. 75; Wittke, *Utopian Communist,* pp. 144, 172; Gavett, *Labor Movement in Milwaukee,* p. 6; Conzen, *Immigrant Milwaukee,* p. 111; Commons, *History of Labor,* vol. I, p. 569; Ross, *Workers on the Edge,* p. 159.

62. *New York Daily Tribune,* August 5, 1850; *New York Herald,* August 5, 1850.

63. Specifically, the meeting called for limiting the size of individual land-holdings, freely distributing government-owned land to settlers, and protecting homesteads against forced sale arising from debt. *New York Daily Tribune,* August 5, 1850.

64. *New York Daily Tribune,* July 25, August 5, 12, 13, 14, 1850.

65. "Die feierliche Bestätigung und die Organisation der Arbeiter-Ver-brüderung der Vereinigten Staaten": *Republik der Arbeiter,* October 1850.

66. *Republik der Arbeiter,* October and November 1850; Wittke, *Utopian Communist,* p. 198–200; Schlüter, *Die Anfänge,* pp. 83–85.

67. *New Yorker Criminal Zeitung und Belletristisches Journal,* October 15, 1852; *Republik der Arbeiter,* May 31, December 20, 1851, July 31, September 11, 1852, September 10, December 7, 1853; Wittke, *Utopian Communist,* pp. 217–19.

68. Schlüter, *Die Anfänge,* pp. 132–33; Hirsch, *Roots of the American Working Class,* p. 116; Pierce, *History of Chicago,* vol. 2, p. 155; Commons, *History of Labor,* vol. 1, pp. 605–6; Ross, *Workers on the Edge,* pp. 148–49.

69. John R. Commons, Henry E. Hoagland, and their colleagues counted some four hundred strikes nationally in 1853–54. Commons, *History of Labor,* vol. 1, pp. 607n, 610.

70. *New York Daily Tribune,* December 15, 1849, June 4, August 6, 8, 12, 13, 14, 1850, April 12, 1853.

71. *New York Daily Tribune,* April 12, 1853.

72. Tailors attempted to launch a national union in 1853. *Die Reform,* April 30, 1853; *Cincinnati Daily Enquirer,* December 11, 1853; Commons, *History of Labor,* vol. 1, pp. 605–6, 610; Schlüter, *Die Anfänge,* p. 134.

73. *New York Daily Times,* February 16, 1853; *New York Herald,* February 18, 19, 1853; *Cincinnati Daily Enquirer,* March 17, 1853; *Republik der Arbeiter,* March 12, 19, 1853; *Die Reform,* May 7, 1853.

74. *Die Reform,* March 12, 1853; *New York Daily Times,* March 22, 25, April 2, 13, 15, 18, 1853; *New York Herald,* February 19, 1853; *Republik der Arbeiter,* March 12, 19, April 16, 23, 30, May 7, 1853; *New Yorker Staats-Zeitung,* April 16, 1853; *New York Daily Tribune,* May 3, September 1, 14, 1853.

75. *New York Daily Times,* April 2, 5, 7, 11, 12, 14, 15, 25, 29, 30, 1853; *New York Daily Tribune,* March 10, April 12, September 1, 14, 1853; *New Yorker Staats-Zeitung,* April 16, 1853; *New York Herald,* April 8, 1853; *Die Reform,* March 12, April 16, 23, 30, May 4, 7, June 11, 22, 25, 1853; *Republik der Arbeiter,* March 12, 19, April 16, 23, 30, May 7, 1853. On the organization of German shoemakers in Newark, see the *Newarker Zeitung,* reprinted in the *Newark Daily Advertiser,* April 6, 1853. The sweep and boldness of the wage movement soon cured the *Times* of its indulgent view of labor militancy. By mid-April, its columns were once again warning workers to seek redress only through "such measures as shall appeal to the sense of *justice* on the part of employers" (*New York Daily Times,* April 12, 1853).

76. *Die Reform,* April 23, 1853, May 4, 7, 1853; *Republik der Arbeiter,* April 16, 23, 1853; *New York Daily Times,* March 26, 1853; Gavett, *Labor*

Movement in Milwaukee, pp. 8–9; Hofmeister, *Germans of Chicago,* p. 116; *Daily Democratic Press,* April 16, 12, 19, 25, 26, May 5, 14, 1853; *Cincinnati Daily Enquirer,* March 17, April 16, 17, December 11, 1853; Ross, *Workers on the Edge,* pp. 143, 151–55; Commons, *History of Labor,* vol. 1, p. 607n.

77. *Die Reform,* March 26, July 13, 1853; *Republik der Arbeiter,* April 2, 16, 23, 1853; *Turn-Zeitung,* June 1, 1853; *New Yorker Staats-Zeitung,* March 18, 1853.

78. Schlüter, *Die Anfänge,* pp. 142–44; Obermann, *Joseph Weydemeyer: Ein Lebensbild,* p. 301; *Die Reform,* July 16, September 4, 1853.

79. *Die Reform,* March 26, July 23, 1853; *Turn-Zeitung,* November 15, 1852, December 1, 15, 1852. Here, Weydemeyer was evidently guided by conclusions that Marx and Engels had drawn from the 1848 experience and then outlined and circulated in their 1850 "Address of the Central Authority to the [Communist] League," Marx and Engels, *Collected Works,* vol. 10, pp. 277–87.

80. *Republik der Arbeiter,* January 1850; *New York Daily Tribune,* August 29, 1850; Wilentz, *Chants Democratic,* pp. 381–84; Amy Bridges, *A City in the Republic: Antebellum New York and the Origins of Machine Politics* (Cambridge, Mass.: Cambridge University Press, 1984), p. 115; Ernst, *Immigrant Life in New York City,* pp. 167, 170, 289n; Wittke, *Utopian Communist,* p. 158.

81. *New York Daily Tribune,* August 26, September 9, 1851; *Die Reform,* July 16, 1853; Obermann, *Joseph Weydemeyer: Ein Lebensbild,* p. 299.

82. *Republik der Arbeiter,* April 16, 23, May 7, 1853; *Die Reform,* March 26, April 16, May 4, 7, June 1, 22, 25, July 23, August 20, October 12, 26, December 7, 1853; Schlüter, *Die Anfänge,* p. 149.

83. Commenting on such phrases a half-century later, German-born socialist historian Hermann Schlüter wrote that "a good bit of petty-bourgeois water had been poured into the proletarian wine" (*"ein gut Teil kleinbürglichen Wassers in den proletarischen Wein geschüttet wurde"*) (Schlüter, *Die Anfänge,* pp. 136, 143). Obermann, *Joseph Weydemeyer: Ein Lebensbild,* pp. 299.

84. *Die Reform,* September 24, October 12, 1853; *Republik der Arbeiter,* December 7, 1853; Obermann, *Joseph Weydemeyer: Ein Lebensbild,* pp. 316–20; Ernst, *Immigrant Life in New York City,* pp. 118; Schlüter, *Die Anfänge,* p. 135. August Willich (whom Lloyd Easton perceptively ranked among Marx's "True Socialist" opponents) had begun his American career in alliance with Wilhelm Weitling, and he shared as much ideologically with Gustav Struve as with Joseph Weydemeyer. But even Willich was struck by the "straightwardly petty-bourgeois standpoint" (*"kleinbürgliche Stellung gerade"*) adopted by "most of the intelligent German workers," and he pointed to this as further proof that an independent national labor party remained a distant prospect (*Sociale Republik,* September 25, 1858. See also Easton, *Hegel's First American Followers,* pp. 169–70, 180–90).

85. Bridges, *City in the Republic,* p. 116; Koch, "Panic of 1857 and Its Effects in Ohio," pp. 168–70; Morris, "Road to Trade Unionism," pp. 100,

102; Ross, *Workers on the Edge,* p. 157; Pierce, *History of Chicago,* vol. 2, pp. 126, 156–57; *New York Herald,* January 8, 1855.

86. *New York Herald,* January 9, 1855.

87. *New York Herald,* January 8, 14, 16, 1855.

88. *Sociale Republik,* June 19, 1858; *New York Herald,* November 3, 6, 7, 10, 11, 13, 16, 1857; *New York Daily Tribune,* November 3, 6, 11, 12, 1857; Bridges, *City in the Republic,* p. 123; *Weekly Chicago Democrat,* November 14, 21, 1857; *Chicago Daily Tribune,* November 12, 16, 1857; Leah Hannah Feder, *Unemployment Relief in Periods of Depression* (New York: Russell Sage Foundation, 1936), pp. 31–35.

89. *Newark Daily Mercury,* November 10, 1857; *New York Herald,* November 6, 1857.

90. *Sociale Republik,* April 24, May 1, June 19, 26, August 28, September 11, December 11, 1858; January 15, February 2, March 12, April 2, 30, July 2, 23, 1859, April 28, 1860; *Cincinnati Republikaner,* March 16, 19, 20, 23, April 10, 14, May 16, 1860; *Newark Daily Advertiser,* March 29, 1859; *Der Arbeiter,* March 27, 1858; *Cincinnati Daily Enquirer,* March 25, 27, April 1, 9, 10, 1859.

91. *Sociale Republik,* April 24, October 2, 1858, January 29, March 12, 1859.

92. *Sociale Republik,* September 18, October 23, 30, 1858, April 16, 1859; Sorge, *Labor Movement,* p. 97.

Part III: Slavery and the People's Land
Introduction: The Challenge of Kansas-Nebraska

1. Interesting discussions of such parallels can be found in Shearer Davis Bowman's "Antebellum Planters and *Vormärz* Junkers in Comparative Perspective," *American Historical Review* 85 (1980): 779–808; and Peter Kolchin, *Unfree Labor: American Slavery and Russian Serfdom* (Cambridge, Mass.: Harvard University Press, 1987).

2. The *Louisville Daily Democrat,* March 4, 1854; the *Free West* (Chicago), May 18, 1854; Wagner, *Ein Achtundvierziger,* pp. 298–300; *State Gazette* (Trenton, N.J.), December 6, 1851.

3. *Hochwächter* (Cincinnati), November 26, 1851; Metzner, *American Turnerbund,* p. 13; Prahl, "The Turner," p. 100; Frederick Douglass, "Adopted Citizens and Slavery," *Douglass's Monthly* (August 1859); "Verhandlungen der Turner-Taglatzung zu Buffalo, vom 24. bis 27. September 1855," Sozialisticher Turnerbund von Nord-Amerika Papers, New York Public Library; Henry Metzner, "Satzungen des social. Turnerbundes in Nord-Amerika," *Jahrbücher der Deutsch-Amerikanischen Turnerei,* vol. 1, pp. 199–200; Büchele, *Land und Volk der Vereinigten Staaten,* p. 279. Büchele rendered the answer first in English as "No, Sir, he was a Dutchman," and then translated it into German as "Nein, er war ein Deutscher [a German]."

4. Sanderson, *Republican Landmarks,* pp. 220–21; *Belleviller Zeitung,* September 11, 1851; Bergquist, "Political Attitudes," pp. 131, 343; Ernest

Bruncken, "German Political Refugees in the United States during the Period from 1815–1860," *Deutsch-Amerikanische Geschichtsblätter* 4 (January 1904): 43; Schläger, *Sociale und politische Stellung*, p. 17; Wittke, *Against the Current*, p. 173; Prahl, "The Turner," p. 53.

5. *New York Daily Tribune*, August 26, September 9, 1851.

6. Wagner, *Ein Achtundvierziger*, pp. 229–440; Schläger, *Sociale und politische Stellung*, p. 18; Körner, *Memoirs*, vol. 1, p. 588; Schurz, *Reminiscences*, vol. 2, pp. 65–66; Reemelin, *Life*, pp. 46, 49–51, 105; *Belleviller Zeitung*, September 11, 1851; Baughin, "Nativism in Cincinnati," p. 90–92; Olson, "St. Louis Germans," pp. 121–22; William E. Gienapp, *The Origins of the Republican Party, 1852–1856* (New York: Oxford University Press, 1987), pp. 21–31; Stephen E. Maizlish, *The Triumph of Sectionalism: The Transformation of Ohio Politics, 1844–1856* (Kent: Kent State University Press, 1983), pp. 179–80; Jed Dannenbaum, *Drink and Disorder: Temperance Reform in Cincinnati from the Washingtonian Revival to the WCTU* (Urbana: University of Illinois Press, 1984), pp. 107–12; Tucker, "Political Leadership," pp. 104–35; Bergquist, "Political Attitudes," p. 342; Stephen L. Hansen, *The Making of the Third Party System: Voters and Parties in Illinois, 1850–1876* (Ann Arbor: UMI Research Press, 1980), p. 13; Conzen, *Immigrant Milwaukee*, pp. 194–202; Formisano, *Birth of Mass Political Parties*, pp. 182–85, 302; Walter D. Kamphoefner, "St. Louis Germans and the Republican Party, 1848–1860," *Mid-America* 57 (April 1975): 72–73.

7. *New Yorker Staats-Zeitung*, January 3, 1851; George M. Stephenson, *The Political History of the Public Lands from 1840 to 1862* (Boston: Richard G. Badger, 1917), pp. 113, 202–3; Johannsen, *Stephen A. Douglas*, pp. 318–19; Schlüter, *Die Anfänge*, pp. 40–41; Jean H. Baker, *Affairs of Party: The Political Culture of Northern Democrats in the Mid-Nineteenth Century* (Ithaca, N.Y.: Cornell University Press, 1983); Donald S. Spencer, *Louis Kossuth and Young America: A Study of Sectionalism and Foreign Policy, 1848–1852* (Columbia: University of Missouri Press, 1977), esp. pp. 11–47. The quoted reference to Pierce appeared in a notice placed in *Die Reform*, October 29, 1853, by the *Deutschamerikanischdemokratischer Bund* and signed by its chairman, the laborer-turned-cigarmaker Augustus Thum.

8. *Volks-Tribun*, November 21, 1846. Attempts to safeguard the living standards of free workers by restricting access to (and competition within) the free-labor market enjoyed support among the native-born, too. Among German-Americans, it drew additional strength from the still-lively guild tradition in the fatherland discussed in chapter 1 above.

9. Frederick J. Blue, *The Free Soilers: Third Party Politics, 1848–1854* (Urbana: University of Illinois Press, 1973), pp. 153–87, 232–68; David M. Potter, *The Impending Crisis: 1848–1861* (New York: Harper and Row, 1976), p. 114; Reemelin, *Life*, p. 98; Körner, *Memoires*, vol. 1, pp. 518, 545–49, 618; *Belleviller Zeitung*, April 25, August 8, 1850; *New Yorker Staats-Zeitung*, January 24, February 21, 1850; *Newark Daily Mercury*, June 3, 1853; *Congressional Globe*, 33rd Cong., 1st sess., p. 11; *Daily Pittsburgh Gazette*, January 28, 1854.

10. James Malin, "The Motives of Stephen A. Douglas in the Organization of the Nebraska Territory: A Letter Dated Dec. 17, 1853," *Kansas Historical Quarterly* 19 (November 1951): 352.

11. Potter, *Impending Crisis*, pp. 114, 154–67; Andrew W. Crandall, *The Early History of the Republican Party, 1854–1856* (Boston: Badger, 1930), pp. 18–19; Allen Nevins, *A House Dividing*, vol. 2, p. 301; Johannssen, *Stephen A. Douglas*, pp. 395–418, 426; Roy F. Nichols, "The Kansas-Nebraska Act: A Century of Historiography," *Mississippi Valley Historical Review* 43 (September 1956): 187–212.

12. *Congressional Globe*, 33rd Cong., 1st sess., pp. 281–82; Gienapp, *Origins*, pp. 71–73.

13. James Ford Rhodes, *History of the United States from the Compromise of 1850 to the McKinley-Bryan Campaign of 1896*, 8 vols. (1893; repr., Port Washington, N.Y.: Kennikat Press, 1967), vol. 1, p. 466; Nevins, *House Dividing*, vol. 2, p. 127; *Chicago Daily Tribune*, March 14, 1854; *New York Daily Tribune*, February 21, March 17, May 20, June 13, July 4, 1854—and, indeed, almost any edition throughout that spring and summer.

14. *Belleviller Zeitung*, March 30, 1854; *New York Daily Tribune*, February 28, 1854; Nevins, *House Dividing*, vol. 2, p. 128; Faust, *German Element*, vol. 2, p. 130. More than seventy years ago Frank Irving Herriott began the systematic investigation of this development in a series of articles, including "Senator Stephen A. Douglas and the Germans in 1854," *Illinois State Historical Society Transactions* (1912): 142–58; "The Germans of Chicago and Stephen A. Douglas in 1854," *Deutsch-Amerikanische Geschichtsblätter* 12 (1912); 381–404; "A Neglected Factor in the Anti-Slavery Triumph in Iowa in 1854," *Deutsch-Amerikanische Geschichtsblätter* 18–19 (1918–19): 174–352.

15. *Daily Pittsburgh Gazette*, February 20, 1854.

16. Chilton Williamson, *American Suffrage: From Property to Democracy, 1760–1860* (Princeton, N.J.: Princeton University Press, 1960), p. 277; Tucker, "Political Leadership," pp. 104–7; Conzen, *Immigrant Milwaukee*, pp. 195–96; *Chicago Daily Tribune*, October 30, 1858; Bergquist, "Political Attitudes," pp. 14, 24; W. Darrell Overdyke, *The Know-Nothing Party in the South* (Baton Rouge: Louisiana State University Press, 1950), pp. 18–19; Nevins, *Ordeal of the Union*, vol. 2, p. 128.

17. *Congressional Globe*, 33rd Cong., 1st sess., p. 1302, appendix, pp. 778–79.

18. George M. Stephenson, *A History of American Immigration, 1820–1924* (1926; repr., New York: Rusesell and Russell, 1964), pp. 96, 116–17, 122–24.

19. *Daily Pittsburgh Gazette*, February 24, March 1, 1854; the *Free West*, May 18, 1854; *Daily Cincinnati Gazette*, February 27, 1854; *New York Evening Post*, quoted in Herriott, "Douglas and the Germans," p. 11; *Buffalo Morning Express*, February 27, 1854; *Newark Daily Mercury*, March 11, 1854; *New York Daily Tribune*, February 28, 1854; *Daily Pittsburgh Gazette*, March

1, 1854; George Schneider, "Lincoln and the Anti-Know-Nothing Resolutions," *McLean County Historical Society* 3 (1900): 88; William Vocke, "The Germans and the German Press," *McLean County Historical Society* 3 (1900): 52–54.

20. Schlüter, *Die Anfänge,* pp. 213–14; Metzner, *History of the Turnerbund,* pp. 13–14; Prahl, "The Turner," p. 101.

21. Irving Katz, *August Belmont: A Political Biography* (New York: Columbia University Press, 1968), pp. 27, 43–44.

22. *New Yorker Staats-Zeitung,* June 22, July 1, 8, 18, 1848, February 21, 24, 1850, March 29, 1851, July 9, 1853; Robert Ernst, "The Economic Status of New York City Negroes, 1850–1863," *Negro History Bulletin* 12 (March 1949): 131.

Chapter 6. The Response in the East

1. Stephenson, *Political History of the Public Lands,* pp. 168–72.

2. *New York Daily Tribune,* February 17, 1854. On the Mechanics' Mutual, its origins and early evolution, see Wilentz, *Chants Democratic,* pp. 314, 346–49, 366–67, 375. Cigar-maker leader Louis Trong was also a prominent member.

3. *Caspar Meier and His Successors* (New York: Oelrichs and Co., 1898); Ernst, *Immigrant Life in New York City,* pp. 77–83, 91–5, 103, 214–17, 257n; Theodor Lemke, *Geschichte des Deutschthums von New York von 1848 bis auf die Gegenwart* (New York: Verlag von Theodor Lemke, 1891), pp. 11–17, 33–41, 86–90, 99–103, 106–12, 116–24; Reutnik, *Berümte deutsche Vorkämpfer,* pp. 134–44, 181–85, 417–21; Körner, *Das deutsche Element,* pp. 96–103, 112–14, 148–49; Griesinger, *Freiheit und Sclaverei unter dem Sternenbanner, oder Land und Leute in Amerika* (Stuttgart: A. Kroner, 1862), pp. 236–310; *New Yorker Staats-Zeitung,* April 22, 1848; Singer, *Steinway and Sons,* pp. 1–25; Ingermann, "Personal Experiences," p. 577; Lapham, "Germans of New York City," p. 207; Wust, *Guardian on the Hudson,* pp. 5, 20–21, 27, 29, 31; Eric Hirschler, *Jews from Germany in the United States* (New York: Farrar, Straus and Cudahy, 1955), pp. 61–62; Nadel, "Kleindeutschland," pp. 164n, 171.

4. Wust, *Guardian on the Hudson,* pp. 29–35; Eickhoff, *In der neuen Heimath,* pp. 9–46; Wittke, *German Language Press,* pp. 82–83; *New Yorker Staats-Zeitung,* May 10, 1854; Körner, *Das deutsche Element,* p. 105.

5. Wittke, *German Language Press,* pp. 77–85, 107, 170; Ernst, *Immigrant Life in New York City,* pp. 153–54; C. F. Huch, "Gottlieb Theodor Kellner," *Mitteilungen* 10 (1909): 26–31. Other papers with a similar bent failed to sustain themselves in this period.

6. *New York Daily Post,* February 16, 1854; *New York Daily Tribune,* February 23, 24, 1854. Control of the customhouse was a major patronage plum.

7. The following account of the February 23 Nebraska meeting is based largely on the following newspaper reports: *New Yorker Staats-Zeitung,* February 24, 1854; *New Yorker Demokrat,* reprinted in the *New York Evening*

Post of February 24, 1854, along with the *Post* reporter's own account; *New York Daily Tribune,* February 24; *New York Herald,* February 24, 1854.

8. *New York Herald,* March 4, 1854.

9. *New York Daily Times,* March 2, 1854; *Newark Daily Mercury,* March 3, 1854; *New York Evening Post,* March 2, 6, 1854.

10. The following account of the March 3 anti-Nebraska meeting is based on the following newspaper reports: *New Yorker Staats-Zeitung,* March 10, 1854; *New York Herald,* March 4, 1854; *New York Daily Times,* March 4, 1854; *New York Daily Tribune,* March 6 and 7, 1854; *New York Evening Post,* March 4 and 7, 1854.

11. *New Yorker Staats-Zeitung,* February 25, March 10, 1854; *New York Daily Tribune,* March 7, 1854; *Belleviller Zeitung,* March 16, 1854.

12. DeBow, *Statistical View of the United States, Seventh Census,* p. 399; Kennedy, *Population of the United States in 1860,* p. xxxii; Hirsch, *Roots of the American Working Class,* pp. 17–19, 25, 47; U.S. Census population schedules, manuscript returns, Essex County, N.J., seventh (1850) and eighth (1860) censuses, National Archives; Joseph Atkinson, *The History of Newark, New Jersey, Being a Narrative of Its Rise and Progress* (Newark: William B. Guild, 1878), pp. 186, 200; Urquhart, *History of Newark,* vol. 2, p. 867.

13. The account of this meeting is drawn from the following sources: Atkinson, *History of Newark,* p. 202–3, 207; *Newark Daily Advertiser,* September 28, 1854; Katzler, "Germans in Newark," pp. 1049, 1051, 1053, 1087, 1113–15; *Newark Daily Mercury,* April 16, 19, 20, 22, 23, 1852; David Lawrence Pierson, *Narratives of Newark* (Newark: Pierson Publishing Co., 1917), p. 277. After the Annekes departed Newark in 1858, Katzler apparently became editor of the *Newarker Zeitung.*

14. *Newark Daily Mercury,* August 14, 1857; Baker, *Lenau and Young Germany in America,* pp. 71–72.

15. In Germany, the first issue of Anneke's *Neue Kölnische Zeitung* emphasized its class partisanship, denouncing the hypocritical rich responsible for the misery of working people: "That these days the situation of the working people is very difficult is beyond question. No one will deny this, except perhaps the very same wealthy Moneybags, the so-called 'high society,' who have caused the workers' drudgery and who have minted our sweat into gold and silver for themselves."

To the aims of the Moneybags, the *Zeitung* would counterpose and defend the interests of the dependent classes. The editors declared: "The *Neue Kölnische Zeitung* . . . speaks for the working people. It will work diligently to educate and enlighten them and will strive to defend their interests and achievements in every way. The working people include all who toil all day in difficult conditions, stricken throughout life with sorrow and worry—including, for example, most artisans, particularly journeymen; servants; day laborers; factory workers; all small peasants; soldiers; clerks, etc." The *Zeitung* set itself the task of educating these social strata about their own interests, teaching them in particular "to distinguish friend from foe" so that they need "no longer allow others" (meaning the Frankfurt liberals) "to think and act for them" (*Neue Kölnische Zeitung*, September 10, 1848, in the Friedrich and Matthilde Anneke Papers, State Historical Society of Wisconsin, Madison).

16. Heinzen and Sanne, "Biographical Notes," passim; Schulte, *Fritz Anneke*, passim; Katzler, "Germans in Newark," p. 1050; Atkinson, *History of Newark*, p. 210; Noyes, *Organization and Revolution*, pp. 62–64, 258, 285, 268n. Fritz Anneke's commission in the *rheinpfaelzischen Volkswehr* is in the Anneke collection at the Wisconsin State Historical Society. While copies of the *Newarker Zeitung* have apparently not survived, the *Newark Daily Mercury* reprinted articles from the latter intermittently during the mid-1850s.

17. Edinger, "A Feminist Forty-Eighter," pp. 18–19; Wagner, *Mathilde Franziska Anneke*, pp. 35–87.

18. *Newark Daily Mercury*, April 26, June 3, November 8, 1853, May 26, June 19, 1854.

19. Reilly, "Rise and Growth of Manufactures," p. 901; Urquhart, *History of Newark*, vol. 2, p. 679; Atkinson, *History of Newark*, pp. 211–29; Pierson, *Narratives*, p. 283; *Newark Daily Eagle*, March 1, 1854.

20. *Newark Daily Mercury*, February 16, March 28, 1854.

21. *Newark Daily Mercury*, June 12, 1854.

22. Katzler, "Germans in Newark," pp. 1049, 1051, 1057; Atkinson, *History of Newark*, pp. 204–7.

23. The account of the March 9 meeting that follows is drawn from the *Newark Daily Eagle*, March 10, 1854, and the *New York Daily Tribune*, March 10, 1854.

24. The census data referred to in the text are presented in appendix table D. The inference that the chasm separating those claiming property valued at $200 or less from those with property worth $2,000 or more conforms to Susan Hirsch's general findings in Newark in these years as well as to Stuart Blumin's earlier research in contemporaneous Philadelphia. See Hirsch, *Roots of the American Working Class*, p. 83; and Blumin, "Mobility in A Nineteenth-Century American City: Philadelphia, 1820–1860" (Ph.D. diss., University of Pennsylvania, 1968), p. 60.

25. *Newark Daily Advertiser*, March 10, 1854; *Newark Daily Mercury*, March 10, 1854.

26. The following account of the April 3, 1854, "general" anti-Nebraska meeting draws on reports in the *Newark Daily Mercury*, March 16, 28, April 1, 3, 4, 5, 1854; *Newark Daily Advertiser*, April 1, 3, 4, 5, 1854; *Sentinel of Freedom*, April 11, 1854; *Newark Daily Eagle*, April 4, 1854.

27. Katzler, "Germans in Newark," p. 1056.

Chapter 7. The Response in the West

1. *Congressional Globe*, 31st Cong., 1st Sess., Appendix, p. 365.

2. Johannsen, *Stephen A. Douglas*, p. 165; *Daily Democratic Press*, March 17, 1854; Kennedy, *Population of the United States in 1860*, pp. xxix–xx.

3. Cist, *Cincinnati in 1859*, p. 164; Secretary of the Interior, *Statistics of the United States in 1860*, p. xviii; Goss, *Cincinnati*, vol. 2, p. 333; Ross, *Workers on the Edge*, pp. 26, 28–29; Abbott, "Divergent Development," pp. 129–34. The proportion of Germans in the population in 1840 and earlier represent educated guesses; hard figures for that era are not available. Some estimates of the German weight in the city's adult male population in 1840 range as high as 25 to 30 percent (Charles Cist, *Cincinnati in 1841: Early Annals and Future Prospects* [Cincinnati: author, 1841], pp. 38–39; Carl Wittke, "The Germans of Cincinnati," *Bulletin of the Historical and Philosophical Society of Ohio* 20 [January 1962]: 3; Goss, *Cincinnati*, vol. 1, p. 181). But the visiting Berlin historian Friedrich von Raumer believed that the German-born composed about 20 percent of greater Cincinnati's population as a whole in 1844, by which time the proportion was probably higher than in 1840 (Raumer, *America and the American People*, p. 360). Estimates of the size of the second-generation German-American population at mid-century are also unavoidably imprecise; only in 1870 did the census reports begin to include such data. But see parallel estimates of the size of Ohio's German stock in Roseboom, *Civil War Era*, p. 286n.

4. Elmer A. Riley, *The Development of Chicago and Vicinity as a Manufacturing Center prior to 1880* (London: Oxford University Press, 1970), p. 26; Abbott, "Divergent Development," p. 90; Everett Chamberlin, *Chicago and Its Suburbs* (Chicago: T. A. Hungerford and Co., 1874), p. 279; Andreas, *History of Chicago*, vol. 1, pp. 555–60, 567.

5. Louis P. Cain, "From Mud to Metropolis: Chicago before the Fire," *Research in Economic History* 10 (1986): 104–11; Cronon, "To Be the Central City," pp. 134–35; *Commerce, Railroads, and Manufactures of Chicago* (Chicago: Democratic Press, 1855), pp. 54–55; Andreas, *History of Chicago*, vol. 1, p. 571; Abbott, "Divergent Development," p. 90; *Sixth Annual Review of Chicago, 1857* (Chicago: Chicago Daily Press, 1858), pp. 30, 47.

6. *Commerce, Railroads, and Manufactures of Chicago*, pp. 54–55; Riley, *Development of Chicago*, p. 102; Andreas, *History of Chicago*, vol. 1, pp. 571, 568–69; *Chicago Daily Tribune*, December 4, 1852; Abbott, "Divergent Development," p. 124 and n; Pierce, *History of Chicago*, vol. 2, pp. 36–45.

7. Pierce, *History of Chicago*, vol. 2, p. 482; David W. Galenson, "Economic Opportunity on the Urban Frontier: Nativity, Work, and Wealth in Early Chicago" (unpublished paper, September 1990), table 3. I am indebted to Professor Galenson for permitting me to read and cite this paper—and to the late Herbert G. Gutman, who graciously supplied a breakdown of Chicago's occupational work force by nativity, compiled from the manuscript returns of the 1860 population census.

8. *Congressional Globe*, 31st Cong., 1st Sess., Appendix, p. 365.

9. Carl Vitz, "Martin Baum, Pioneer Cincinnati Entrepreneur," *Bulletin of the Historical and Philosophical Society of Ohio* 16 (1958): 215–39; Körner, *Deutsche Element*, pp. 177–80, 215–17; Goss, *Cincinnati*, vol. 2, pp. 9–12, 18; Reutnik, *Berühmte deutsche Vorkämpfer*, pp. 427–30; Ross, *Workers on*

the Edge, p. 78; Clark, "Cincinnati Coppersmiths," pp. 257–72; *Cincinnati Daily Commercial,* March 28, 1860; Donald C. Peirce, "Mitchell and Rammelsberg"; Cist, *Cincinnati in 1851,* pp. 203–4; Sikes, *Furniture Makers of Cincinnati,* pp. 196–98; Francis P. Weisenburger, *The Passing of the Frontier, 1825–1850* (Columbus: Ohio State Archaeological and Historical Society, 1941), p. 85.

10. Reemelin, *Life,* esp. pp. 12–13, 49–51, 82–83, 122–26; Körner, *Deutsche Element,* pp. 186–92; Reutnik, *Berühmte deutsche Vorkämpfer,* pp. 296–98; Goss, *Cincinnati,* vol. 2, pp. 10, 13–4.

11. The Henry Rödter Papers, Cincinnati Historical Society; Körner, *Deutsche Element,* pp. 182–86; Goss, *Cincinnati,* vol. 2, p. 13; Arndt and Olson, *German-American Newspapers,* p. 454.

12. Körner, *Deutsche Element,* pp. 192–94, 202–3; Goss, *Cincinnati,* vol. 1, pp. 441–42, 454; *Cincinnati Daily Enquirer,* July 13, 16, 1853.

13. Easton, *Hegel's First American Followers,* ch. 2; Körner, *Deutsche Element,* pp. 217–25; Goss, *Cincinnati,* vol. 2, p. 19.

14. Reemelin, *Life,* pp. 46–47; Goss, *Cincinnati,* vol. 2, p. 13; Körner, *Deutsche Element,* p. 185.

15. Reemelin, *Life,* p. 88; Baughin, "Nativism in Cincinnati," pp. 38–39, 84–95; Weisenburger, *Passing of the Frontier,* pp. 465–66; Körner, *Deutsche Element,* pp. 208–10; Burgheim, *Cincinnati in Wort und Bild,* pp. 86–87; Goss, *Cincinnati,* vol. 2, p. 15.

16. DeBow, *Statistical View of the United States, Seventh Census,* Appendix, p. 399; Kennedy, *Population of the United States in 1860,* p. xxxi; Ross, *Workers on the Edge,* pp. 94–140; Harsham, "Over-the-Rhine, 1860," p. 70; Walker, *Statistics of the Population in 1870,* p. 783; Bird, *Englishwoman in America,* p. 119.

17. Goss, *Cincinnati,* vol. 1, p. 181; *Volksblatt* (Cincinnati), October 2, 1853; Bird, *Englishwoman in America* p. 120.

18. *Daily Cincinnati Gazette,* March 24, 1854; *Turn-Zeitung,* April 15, 1854; Central Cincinnati Central Turner membership roster, Cincinnati Turner Collection, Cincinnati Historical Society; *Cincinnati Daily Enquirer,* January 11, 1854; Burgheim, *Cincinnati in Wort und Bild,* p. 151.

19. Burgheim, *Cincinnati in Wort und Bild,* p. 151; *Cincinnati Daily Enquirer,* March 28, 1854.

20. *Cincinnati Daily Enquirer,* March 28, 1854.

21. *New York Criminal-Zeitung und Belletristisches Journal,* December 30, 1853, January 6 and 13, 1854; *New Yorker Staats-Zeitung,* February 11, 1854; Wittke, "Germans of Cincinnati," p. 11; Billington, *The Protestant Crusade,* pp. 302–4; Rev. Alfred G. Stitch, "Political Nativism in Cincinnati, 1830–1860," *Records of the American Catholic Historical Society* 47 (September 1937): 268–69; William A. Baughin, "Bullets and Ballots: The Election Day Riots of 1855," *Bulletin of the Historical and Philosophical Society of Ohio* 21 (October 1963): 267–68.

22. The following account of the March 1853 protest against Bedini's visit draws heavily upon extensive newspaper coverage of the incident and its protracted legal and political aftermath. See the *Volksblatt* (Cincinnati), December 27, 29, 1853; *Cincinnati Daily Enquirer,* December 27, 29, 1853, January 4, 7, 10–19, 22, February 12, 1854; *Daily Cincinnati Gazette,* December 28–31, 1853, January 2, 6, 7, 9–21, February 21, 1854.

23. *Daily Cincinnati Gazette,* December 28, 1853; *Volksblatt* (Cincinnati), December 27, 1853.

24. *Daily Cincinnati Gazette,* December 28, 29, 1853; *Volksblatt* (Cincinnati), December 29, 1853; Burgheim, *Cincinnati in Wort und Bild,* p. 160.

25. *Cincinnati Daily Enquirer,* January 10–12, 1854; *Daily Cincinnati Gazette,* December 28, 1853.

26. *Daily Cincinnati Gazette,* December 28, 31, 1853, January 2, 6, 1854; *Cincinnati Daily Enquirer,* January 7, 1854; *Volksblatt* (Cincinnati), December 29, 1853.

27. *Wahrheits-Freund,* March 16, 1854; *Cincinnati Daily Enquirer,* January 3, 6, 1853; Moore, "A Tennessean Visits Cincinnati," p. 168; *New York Criminal-Zeitung und Belletristisches Journal,* December 30, 1853, January 6, 13, 1854; *Volksblatt* (Cincinnati), January 3, 1854; *Daily Cincinnati Gazette,* January 3, 6, 7, 1854.

28. Hassaurek lost his own case against city officials and the police in February. *Volksblatt* (Cincinnati), January 6, 7, 1854; *Cincinnati Daily Enquirer,* February 24, 1854; *Wahrheits-Freund,* April 13, 1854.

29. *Cincinnati Daily Enquirer,* February 28, 1854.

30. *Daily Cincinnati Gazette,* February 25, 27, 28, 1854; *Cincinnati Daily Enquirer,* March 3, 1854.

31. The *Gazette* of March 8 estimated that more than a thousand people braved the foul weather to attend the meeting. The *Enquirer* entangled itself in contradictions. Its March 8 edition reported that the meeting had been "very largely attended." The next day, it dubbed the meeting "a complete fizzle," insisting that "no more than six or seven hundred persons assembled, of whom, we are assured by a reliable authority, a considerable proportion were in favor of the bill, being drawn by curiosity alone." Though the *Enquirer*'s own account of the proceedings disproved this last assertion, the editor appeared undaunted. "Thousands who were at first inclined to be opponents of the measure are wheeling into its support," he insisted, adding confidently that "the anti-Nebraskaites are taken emphatically aback by the tide of public opinion which is setting in against them." The presence at the meeting of so prominent a Democrat as Charles Reemelin was no cause for concern or second thoughts, since Reemelin acted only because of "the failure of the party to confer upon him important offices."

32. By his own account, Reemelin had "cared nothing" about Ohio's notorious laws discriminating against free blacks and regarded Massachusetts's decision to send Charles Sumner to the U.S. Senate as New England's "throwing down the gauntlet . . . to the Southern States," proof "that Mas-

sachusetts, at least, did not want peace." The Compromise of 1850 had therefore come as a great relief to Reemelin, promising "an adjustment of difficulties engendered by false movements then going on in society about slavery." Reemelin, *Life*, pp. 87–88, 98, 123.

33. See the March 8, 1854, editions of both the *Gazette* and the *Enquirer*.

34. *Cincinnati Daily Enquirer*, March 23, 1854.

35. The following account of the March 24 Greenwood Hall meeting is drawn from the *Daily Cincinnati Gazette*, March 25, 1854; *Cincinnati Daily Enquirer*, March 25, 26, 1854.

36. *Cincinnati Daily Enquirer*, March 25, 1854.

37. *Cincinnati Daily Enquirer*, March 25, 1854.

38. *Turn-Zeitung*, April 15, 1854; *Cincinnati Daily Enquirer*, March 25, 26, 1854; *Daily Cincinnati Gazette*, March 24, 25, 1854.

39. *Cincinnati Daily Enquirer*, March 28, 1854.

40. *Cincinnati Daily Enquirer*, April 5, 1854.

41. *Daily Cincinnati Gazette*, February 27, 1854.

42. *Daily Cincinnati Gazette*, April 6, 1854.

43. *Cincinnati Daily Enquirer*, April 6, 7, 1854; *Daily Cincinnati Gazette*, April 7, 8, 1854. The *Columbian*'s estimate was cited in the *Enquirer* of April 8.

44. *Daily Cincinnati Gazette*, April 7, 1854; *Cincinnati Daily Enquirer*, April 8, 1854.

45. Johannsen, *Stephen A. Douglas*, p. 450; *Congressional Globe*, 33rd Cong., 1st sess., Appendix, pp. 338, 788.

46. Pierce, *History of Chicago*, vol. 2, pp. 195–97.

47. Bergquist, "Political Attitudes," pp. 134–35, 325–36; Körner, *Memoirs*, vol. 1, pp. 590–98.

48. Hofmeister, *Germans of Chicago*, p. 133; Pierce, *History of Chicago*, vol. 2, p. 219; I. D. Guyer, *History of Chicago: Its Commercial and Manufacturing Interests and Industry* (Chicago: Church, Goodman, and Cushing, 1862), p. 43; Andreas, *History of Chicago*, vol. 1, pp. 285, 410, 564, and vol. 2, p. 219; Bergquist, "Political Attitudes,"pp. 187–90, 251; *New Yorker Staats-Zeitung*, February 13, 1856. Republicans published the *National Demokrat*'s confidential founding documents, which stipulated "that said paper is to be printed and published at the office of the [pro-Douglas] *Chicago Times*, and its political character, spirit, and principles shall in all respects be in harmony, and accord with the *Chicago Times*" (*Weekly Chicago Democrat*, July 5, 1856).

49. *Daily Democratic Press*, February 20, 1854; Cole, *Era of the Civil War*, p. 123; Pierce, *History of Chicago*, vol. 2, p. 208. The original copy of this petition is in the Illinois State Archives. It contains fifteen separate sheets bearing a total of 765 signatures. Of these, 64 (about 8.5 percent of the total) are evidently non-German, though some may belong to immigrants who Anglicized their names to ease assimilation. A handwritten note accompanying the petitions indicates that they contain the signatures of "Henry Schultz [the first signatory] and 800 German voters of the County of Cook." The nu-

merical discrepancy may reflect an exaggeration on the part of the cover note's author or the subsequent loss of one or more sheets of signatures.

50. Occupations have been ascertained principally through the use of city directories. The greater ease with which non-German names have been linked to occupations reflects the directories' greater care in recording data about the native born—and, very likely, the greater incidence among immigrants of occupations deemed too lowly to merit systematic inclusion in the directories.

51. Körner, *Memoirs,* vol. 1, pp. 518, 545–59, 618; Bergquist, "Political Attitudes," pp. 88, 118–23, 140, 165–67, 315–16; Körner, *Deutsche Element,* chs. 12 and 13; Cole, *Era of the Civil War,* pp. 102–4; Tucker, "Political Leadership," pp. 72, 103, 107; Villard, *Memoirs,* vol. 1, pp. 32–33.

52. Bergquist, "Political Attitudes," pp. 118, 140; *Daily Democratic Press,* May 13, 1856; Körner, *Memoirs,* vol. 1, pp. 548–50, 617–18, vol. 2, pp. 1–3; *Belleviller Zeitung,* April 25, August 8, September 9, 1850.

53. *Belleviller Zeitung,* March 2, 1854; Tucker, pp. 152- 54.

54. Reutnik, *Berühmte deutsche Vorkämpfer,* pp. 432–35; Körner, *Deutsche Element,* pp. 279–81; Tucker, "Political Leadership," p. 141; J. H. A. Lacher, "Francis A. Hoffmann of Illinois and Hans Buschbauer of Wisconsin," *Wisconsin Magazine of History* 13 (1930): 328–43; Karl Kretzmann, "Francis Arnold Hoffmann," *Concordia Historical Institute Quarterly* 18 (1945): 38–51.

55. Schläger, *Sociale und politische Stellung,* pp. 6, 17; Baker, *Lenau and Young Germany in America,* pp. 71–73; Körner, *Memoirs,* vol. 1, p. 548; *Belleviller Zeitung,* March 16, 1854; Obermann, *Joseph Weydemeyer, Ein Lebensbild,* p. 313; Pierce, *History of Chicago,* vol. 2, pp. 167, 171- 72, 187.

56. Cunz, *Maryland Germans,* p. 275; Andreas, *History of Chicago,* vol. 1, p. 389. For Hielscher's role in the wartime *Chicagoer Arbeiterverein,* see ch. 10 below.

57. The following account of the March 17 Chicago anti-Nebraska meeting is drawn from the *Chicago Daily Journal,* March 17, 1854; the *Daily Democratic Press,* March 17, 1854; and the *Chicago Daily Tribune,* March 18, 1854.

58. The meeting's resolution appeared in the *Daily Democratic Press* of March 17, 1854, and the *Chicago Daily Tribune* of March 20, 1854.

59. *Chicago Daily Journal,* March 17, 1854.

60. Schläger's speech was quoted in the *Chicago Daily Journal,* March 17, 1854, and the *Chicago Daily Tribune,* March 22, 1854.

61. *Chicago Daily Tribune,* March 17, 18, 25, 1854; *Chicago Daily Journal,* March 17, 1820, 1854; *Daily Democratic Press,* March 17, 19, 20, 1854.

62. *Chicago Daily Tribune,* March 25, 1854.

63. Johannsen, *Stephen A. Douglas,* p. 451; Gerald M. Capers, *Stephen A. Douglas, Defender of the Union* (Boston: Little, Brown and Co., 1959), pp. 118–19; *Cleveland Plain Dealer,* March 18, 1854; letter in the *Daily Democratic Press,* March 20, 1854.

64. Adams spoke on April 19, 1854; Richard Brodhead of Pennsylvania returned to the incident on May 24 (*Congressional Globe,* 33rd Cong., 1st

sess., pp. 944–45, 1302; *New Yorker Criminal Zeitung und Belletristisches Journal,* December 15, 1854).

65. *Chicago Daily Journal,* March 17, 1854; *Daily Democratic Press,* March 20, 1854.

66. Pierce, *History of Chicago,* vol. 2, p. 207; *Daily Democratic Press,* March 17, 19, 20, 1854; *Chicago Daily Journal,* March 18, 20, 1854; *Daily Chicago Tribune,* March 17, 18, 1854; Bergquist, "Political Attitudes," p. 144.

67. Bergquist, "Political Attitudes," pp. 148–51. The resolutions of the Peoria conference appeared in *Der Demokrat* (Davenport, Iowa) of July 24, 1854, and are transcribed in the F. I. Herriott Papers, Iowa State Historical Department. See also two reports on the conference carried in the *Belleviller Zeitung,* April 6, 1854, and the *Deutscher Anzeiger* (Freeport), July 28, 1854. I am indebted to James M. Bergquist for bringing these reports to my attention.

68. *Chicago Daily Tribune,* March 7, 1854; Metzner, *American Turnerbund,* p. 18; *New Yorker Criminal Zeitung und Belletristisches Journal,* March 7, 1854; *Wahrheits-Freund* (Cincinnati), March 9, June 1, 1854; Arndt and Olson, *German Language Press,* p. 152. By 1860, Kansas contained more than four thousand German-born residents, who represented about 4 percent of the total population of 107,206 (*Eighth Census,* vol. 4, *Population,* p. xxix). No record of the *Kansas Zeitung* is available. Though Arndt and Olson suggest the paper was discontinued in 1859, the *New Yorker Demokrat* was reprinting news reports from the Kansas paper as late as October of 1860.

69. McPherson, *Battle Cry of Freedom,* pp. 145–69; James A. Rawley, *Race and Politics: "Bleeding Kansas" and the Coming of the Civil War* (New York: J. B. Lippincott, 1969), pp. 128–32; *Weekly Chicago Democrat,* June 14, 1856. The New York *Sociale Republik* began reporting on Kansas in its first issue (dated April 24, 1858) and returned frequently to that subject.

70. Henry Sherman may also have been killed later on. August Bondi, "With John Brown in Kansas," *Transactions of the Kansas State Historical Society* 8 (1903–4): 277–80 (which reprinted material from the *Herald* of Salina, Kansas, January and February, 1884); Morris U. Schappes, "August Bondi, Anti-Slavery Fighter," *Jewish Life* (November 1949), pp. 28–30; F. B. Sanborn, *The Life and Letters of John Brown* (1885; repr., New York: New American Library, 1969), pp. 230, 253–56, 271–72, 290–93, 296, 301, 331, 323; Stephen B. Oates, *To Purge this Land with Blood: A Biography of John Brown,* 2d ed. (Amherst: University of Massachusetts Press, 1984), pp. 98–99, 122–23, 136–37, 141, 147–57.

Chapter 8. "The Content of Freedom": Germans, Republicans, and Democrats

1. *Pittsburgh Post,* March 6, 1854; Eric Foner, *Free Soil,* p. 194; George H. Mayer, *The Republican Party, 1854–1966* (New York: Oxford University Press, 1967), pp. 28–29; Cole, *Era of the Civil War,* pp. 125–26; Gienapp, *Origins,* pp. 80–81, 108; Bergquist, "Political Activities," pp. 159–60.

2. Gienapp, *Origins*, pp. 413–48; Foner, *Free Soil*, pp. 129, 198; Paul Selby, "The Genesis of the Republican Party in Illinois," *Transactions of the Illinois State Historical Society* (1906): pp. 270–83; Don E. Fehrenbacher, *Prelude to Greatness: Lincoln in the 1850s* (Stanford, Calif.: Stanford University Press, 1973), pp. 39–47; Potter, *Impending Crisis*, pp. 247–59, 264n, 442n; Kirk H. Porter and Donald Bruce Johnson, eds., *National Party Platforms, 1840–1960* (Urbana: University of Illinois Press, 1961), pp. 27, 32–33.

3. Editorials from the *Newarker Zeitung* reprinted in the *Newark Daily Mercury*, June 3, 1853, May 26, June 12, 1854.

4. Obermann, *Joseph Weydemeyer: Ein Lebensbild*, pp. 335–40; *Sociale Republik*, September 25, 1858. See also Katznelson, *City Trenches*, chap. 3.

5. Chicago *Daily Democratic Press*, August 12, 1856; *Chicago Daily Tribune*, October 26, 1858; Huch, "Anschluss der Deutschen Philadelphias an die republikanische Partei im Jahre 1856," *Mitteilungen* 21 (1911): 16; *Daily Pittsburgh Gazette*, September 18, 1856; *Newark Daily Mercury*, August 19, 1856, October 30, 1860; *New York Daily Tribune*, August 22, October 8, 1856; *New Yorker Criminal Zeitung und Belletristisches Journal*, August 10, 1860; *Sociale Republik*, June 19, 1858; Müller, *Erinnerungen*, pp. 167–87; Formisano, *Birth of Mass Political Parties*, p. 304; Metzner, *American Turnerbund*, pp. 14–15; Wittke, *Refugees of Revolution*, pp. 206–7.

6. Obermann, *Joseph Weydemeyer: Ein Lebensbild*, p. 356; Wagner, *Ein Achtundvierziger*, pp. 300–301; *New York Daily Tribune*, August 22, October 27, 1856; *New Yorker Demokrat*, October 18, 1860.

7. Wittke, *German-Language Press*, p. 141; *Chicago Daily Tribune*, August 26, 1856, October 2, 19, 1858.

8. Huch, "Anschluss," pp. 10–16. Huch served as secretary at this meeting.

9. *Newark Daily Mercury*, June 24, 30, July 2, 3, 31, September 9, 1856, August 4, 1860; *New York Daily Tribune*, July 3, 1856.

10. Stein, "Through German Eyes," pp. 57–71; *Indianapolis Daily Journal*, May 1, 1856, March 5, 1858, February 21, 1860; Cunz, *Maryland Germans*, p. 273 and n.

11. Reutnik, *Berühmte deutsche Vorkämpfer*, pp. 343–44; Cunz, *Maryland Germans*, pp. 251, 260–61, 273, 305; Wittke, *Refugees of Revolution*, p. 268.

12. Cunz, *Maryland Germans*, p. 304; Wittke, *Refugees of Revolution*, p. 207.

13. *Cincinnati Republikaner*, March 22, 26, May 7, 18, and especially October 8, 1860; *Daily Pittsburgh Gazette*, October 13, 14, 1856; Chicago *Daily Democratic Press*, July 7, 30, October 20, 1856; *Chicago Daily Tribune*, October 26, 1858; *Newark Daily Mercury*, August 19, 1856; *New York Daily Tribune*, August 22, 1856; *New York Daily Times*, October 8, 1856; Müller, *Erinnerungen*, pp. 168–70; Philip S. Foner, *American Socialism and Black Americans* (Westport, Conn.: Greenwood Press, 1977), pp. 23–24; Wittke, *Refugees of Revolution*, p. 206.

14. *New York Daily Tribune,* October 29, 1856; Huch, "Anschluss," pp. 16–18; Wittke, *Refugees of Revolution,* p. 206.

15. "Deutscher Republikanische Kampflieder," *Mitteilungen* 2 (1906): 27–29; *New York Daily Tribune,* August 22, 1856.

16. The following account of the October 7, 1856, New York rally draws on reports in the *New Yorker Criminal Zeitung und Belletristisches Journal,* October 10, 1856, and the October 8, 1856, issues of the *New York Daily Tribune* and the *New York Daily Times,* October 8, 1856.

17. Foner, *Free Soil,* p. 38; Montgomery, *Beyond Equality,* p. 73.

18. *New York Herald,* January 16, 1856; *Newark Daily Mercury,* November 10, 11, 1857; *Sociale Republik,* April 24, 1858; *Cincinnati Daily Enquirer,* May 3, 1859; Obermann, *Joseph Weydemeyer: Ein Lebensbild,* p. 362; *Cincinnati Republikaner,* August 4, 1859, February 4, April 18, May 1, 14, 26, 1860.

19. On the fight over whether to soften the party's antislavery stance that took place on the floor of the 1860 Republican Convention, see Kenneth M. Stampp, "The Republican National Convention of 1860," in his *The Imperiled Union: Essays on the Background of the Civil War* (New York: Oxford University Press, 1981), pp. 152–54. See also Benjamin P. Thomas, *Abraham Lincoln: A Biography* (1952; repr., New York: Modern Library, 1968), 177–79; Foner, *Free Soil,* pp. 190, 198, 199–206, 218–19; and Sewell, *Ballots for Freedom,* pp. 305–6, 319, 344–60. By the end of 1859, even moderate Republican William Herndon was denouncing Republican congressional leaders for "grinding off the flesh from their knee caps, attempting . . . to convince the Southern men that we are *cowards*" (quoted in Sewell, *Ballot for Freedom,* p. 357; original emphasis).

20. *Cincinnati Republikaner,* May 18, 1860; Tucker, "Political Leadership," p. 194; Bondi, "With John Brown in Kansas," pp. 278, 285; *Sociale Republik,* April 24, 1858; *Indianapolis Daily Journal,* February 21, 1860. On the radicalizing role played by Germans in the formation of the St. Louis Republican party, see Kamphoefner, "St. Louis Germans," p. 88.

21. *Sociale Republik,* June 19, October 2, 1858, May 7, 1859; Katzler, "Germans in Newark," p. 1055; F. I. Herriott, "The Conference of German Republicans in the Deutsches Haus, Chicago, May 14–15, 1860," *Transactions of the Illinois State Historical Society* 35 (1928): 148; *Cincinnati Republikaner,* August 4, 13, 26, 1859, May 7, 1860; *Cincinnati Daily Enquirer,* May 3, 1859.

22. Sewell, *Ballots for Freedom,* pp. 265, 279–82, 312–13; Foner, *Free Soil,* 201–2; Kamphoefner, "St. Louis Germans," pp. 80–83.

23. Bondi, "With John Brown," p. 278; Cunz, *Maryland Germans,* pp. 304–5; Hildegard Binder Johnson, "German Forty-Eighters in Davenport," *Iowa Journal of History and Politics* 44 (January 1946): 45; Wittke, *Against the Current,* p. 175; *Sociale Republik,* October 29, all through November and December, 1859, and February 18, 1860.

24. *Chicago Daily Tribune,* December 2, 1859; Bruncken, "Wisconsin," pp. 207–8.

25. "Spectator" simply could not fathom "how Germans can bring their hatred of [the] Democracy so far as to ally themselves with the vilest of the African race" (*Cincinnati Daily Enquirer*, December 6, 1859). See also *Cincinnati Republikaner*, December 2, 3, 5, 1859; *Cincinnati Daily Commercial*, December 5, 1859. On Clark, see Lawrence Grossman, "In His Veins Coursed No Bootlicking Blood: The Career of Peter H. Clark, *Ohio History* 86 (Spring 1977): 79–95; Herbert G. Gutman, "Peter H. Clark: Pioneer Negro Socialist, 1877," *Journal of Negro Education* 34 (Fall 1965): 413–18. According to Conway, Willich also led a torchlight parade in Brown's memory through Cincinnati streets (Conway, *Autobiography*, vol. 1, p. 269). Members of the Boston *Turnverein* participated in a meeting called in Brown's honor a year later, on December 3, 1860. A hostile crowd forced the meeting to relocate from a free black sanctuary to a white church, where Turners joined black and white abolitionists to defend the gathering against further interruption (Wittke, *Against the Current*, pp. 175–76; Carlos Martyn, *Wendell Phillips* [New York: Funk and Wagnalls, 1890], pp. 303–4).

26. Tucker, "Political Leadership," p. 158; *New York Daily Times*, October 8, 1856; Wittke, *Refugees of Revolution*, p. 207; Huch, "Anschluss," pp. 10–12.

27. Körner, *Memoirs*, vol. 2, pp. 3–4; Bergquist, "Political Attitudes," pp. 156–60.

28. Letter from Browning to Lyman Trumbull, May 19, 1856, quoted in James Lee Sellers, "The Make-Up of the Early Republican Party," *Transactions of the Illinois State Historical Society* 37 (1930): 42; Foner, *Free Soil*, p. 205; Chicago *Daily Democratic Press*, May 24, 28, June 2, July 23, 30, August 28, 1856; *Chicago Daily Tribune*, August 26, 1856.

29. Tucker, "Political Leadership," p. 218; Formisano, *Birth of Mass Political Parties*, pp. 301 and n, 303.

30. Chicago *Daily Democratic Press*, June 6, 1856; Körner, *Memoirs*, vol. 2, pp. 77–78.

31. *Chicago Daily Tribune*, November 16, 1857; *Weekly Chicago Democrat*, November 21, 1857; Schläger, "Stellung," p. 301; Jay Monaghan, *The Man Who Elected Lincoln* (Indianapolis: Bobbs-Merrill, 1956), pp. 190, 214; Tucker, "Political Leadership," p. 249.

32. Schurz, *Reminiscences*, vol. 2, pp. 16, 69–70; Bergquist, "Political Activities," pp. 187–88; "Adopted Citizens and Slavery," *Douglass's Monthly*, August 1859.

33. "Belmont," reports his biographer, "as far as the record shows, never criticized slavery, either on moral or institutional grounds, throughout the entire antebellum era." Katz, *August Belmont*, pp. 43–44, 55–57, 60–61; *New York Herald*, January 3, 1860; *New York Daily Times*, November 3, 1860.

34. Körner, *Deutsche Element*, pp. 132, 226, 287; *New Yorker Demokrat*, October 29, 1860; *New York Daily Times*, November 1, 1860; Nadel, "Kleindeutschland," p. 247. Such phrases appeared almost daily in the *New Yorker Staats-Zeitung* during 1856. For an example of the role played by *Staats-*

Zeitung editors outside New York City, see the *Pittsburgh Post,* September 11, 20, 1856.

35. Wittke, *German-Language Press,* pp. 128–29, 139–40; *Wahrheits-Freund* of October 11, November 1, 1855, January 17, June 19, 1856, July 3, 10, June 28, 1860; Stein, "Through German Eyes," p. 60; *Weekly Chicago Democrat,* July 5, 1856; *Chicago Daily Tribune,* August 26, 1856, November 16, 1857; Morris Schappes, ed., *A Documentary History of the Jews in the United States, 1654–1875* (New York: Citadel Press, 1950), pp. 313, 648; Tucker, "Political Leadership," p. 178; Cunz, *Maryland Germans,* pp. 310–14.

36. Schurz, *Reminiscences,* vol. 2, pp. 69–70; *Newark Daily Mercury,* October 27, 1856. The files of the *Illinois Staats-Zeitung* for the 1850s have been lost, but its coverage of this event was reprinted in the Chicago *Daily Democratic Press* of March 18, 1856. See also the *Belleviller Zeitung,* March 18, 1856; *Weekly Chicago Democrat,* March 15, 29, 1856; and the *Chicago Daily Tribune,* March 10, 1856.

37. Wittke, *Refugees of Revolution,* pp. 62, 129, 209, 331; Wittke, *German Language Press,* p. 139; Katzler, "Germans of Newark," p. 1091; *Newark Daily Mercury,* June 24, 30, July 2, 31, August 19, September 9, October 4, 27, 1856, July 19, August 4, 23, October 22, 29, 1860; *Die Reform,* August 20, 1853; Huch, "Anschluss," pp. 21–22; Lesley Ann Kawaguchi, "The Making of Philadelphia's German-America: Ethnic Group and Community Development, 1830–1883" (Ph.D. diss., University of California, Los Angeles, 1983), pp. 376, 387–92; Conzen, *Immigrant Milwaukee,* pp. 196–97, 215–17; Bruncken, "Wisconsin," p. 201.

38. The Henry Rödter Papers, Cincinnati Historical Society; Körner, *Deutsche Element,* pp. 177–86, 205–6, 209–17; Goss, *Cincinnati,* vol. 2, pp. 9–13, 18; *Cincinnati Daily Enquirer,* October 9, 12, 1856; *Cincinnati Daily Commercial,* March 28, 1860.

39. Porter and Johnson, eds., *National Party Platforms,* p. 31; Reemelin, *Life,* pp. 155–56; Körner, *Deutsche Element,* pp. 190–91.

40. Bergquist, "Political Activities," pp. 190, 223–24, *Newark Daily Mercury,* August 11, 1860; Katzler, "Germans in Newark," p. 1050; Huch, "Kellner," p. 29; Huch, "Anschluss," pp. 13, 22; *Pittsburgh Post,* October 11, 1856.

41. *Der Arbeiter* ceased publication in May, and a new paper with a similar viewpoint—the *New Yorker Morgenzeitung*—was launched. See *Der Arbeiter,* March 27, 1858, April 3, 10, 17, 24, 1858, May 1, 8, 1858; *Sociale Republik,* May 1, 1858; Obermann, *Joseph Weydemeyer: Ein Lebensbild,* p. 348. Note that the *Arbeiter* gave the name of its editor as Benque, not "Banque" as Schlüter (and subsequent accounts based on Schlüter) have it.

Chapter 9. "The Spirit of 1848": Nationality, Class, and the Fight for Votes

1. "Democratic Party Platform of 1856," in Porter and Johnson, eds., *National Party Platforms,* pp. 23, 25.

2. "Democratic Party Platform of 1856," pp. 25–27; *New York Daily Times,* October 24, 1860; *Wahrheits-Freund,* June 19, 1856.

3. "Democratic Party Platform of 1856," p. 26; *Wahrheits-Freund,* July 10, 1856; *Weekly Chicago Democrat,* July 5, 1856; *Chicago Daily Tribune,* August 26, 1856, November 16, 1857; *New York Herald,* October 23, November 6, 1857; Degler, "Labor," pp. 184–93, 288–89; Bridges, *City in the Republic,* pp. 116–21. The Republican press of Newark responded to similar proposals in the same manner. See, for example, the *Newark Daily Mercury,* November 10, 11, 1857.

4. *Newark Daily Mercury,* November 9, 1860; *New Yorker Demokrat,* October 29, 31, 1860; *New York Daily Tribune,* November 1, 2, 1860.

5. *Der Arbeiter,* April 3, 1858; *New York Daily Tribune,* November 1–3, 1860.

6. *Cincinnati Daily Enquirer,* October 9, 10, 16, 1860; *Newark Daily Mercury,* November 1, 1860; *Newark Daily Advertiser,* November 11, 1860; *New Yorker Demokrat,* October 29, 31, 1860, November 5, 1860; Obermann, *Joseph Weydemeyer: Ein Lebensbild,* pp. 368–69.

7. *New York Daily Tribune,* October 8, 1856; *New York Daily Times,* October 8, 1856; *New Yorker Criminal Zeitung und Belletristisches Journal,* October 10, 1856; *New Yorker Demokrat,* October 31, November 5, 6, 14, 1860; *Belleviller Zeitung,* May 14, 1860; *Daily Pittsburgh Gazette,* September 18, 1856.

8. The following account of the October Democratic meeting draws on the *New Yorker Demokrat,* October 29, 31, 1860, and the *New York Daily Tribune,* November 1, 2, 1860.

9. The German Republicans claimed final victory, returning to the same hall in greater force later that night and holding another meeting of their own. *New Yorker Demokrat,* October 29, 31, 1860; *New York Daily Tribune,* November 1, 2, 1860.

10. *Pittsburgh Post,* October 6, 1856; *New York Daily Times,* October 24, 1860; *New York Herald,* October 24, 1860. On the roots of this outlook in the Democratic party, see George M. Fredrickson, *The Black Image in the White Mind: The Debate on Afro-American Character and Destiny, 1817–1914* (New York: Harper and Row, 1971), pp. 61–64; Baker, *Affairs of Party,* pp. 177–211.

11. *Belleviller Zeitung,* October 28, 1858; *New York Daily Times,* October 24, 1860; *New Yorker Staats-Zeitung,* March 12, 13, 1856; Bergquist, "Political Attitudes," pp. 155, 194; *Pittsburgh Post,* September 11, 1856; Huch, "Anschluss," pp. 25, 29; Conzen, *Immigrant Milwaukee,* p. 217; Bruncken, "Wisconsin," pp. 193–94, 215–17.

12. *Daily Pittsburgh Gazette,* November 11, 1856; Robert Fortenbaugh, "American Lutheran Synods and Slavery, 1830–1860," *Journal of Religion* 13 (1933): 72–79; Wittke, *We Who Built America,* p. 244; Cunz, *Maryland Germans,* p. 294n; Frederick C. Luebke, "The Immigrant Condition as a Factor Contributing to the Conservatism of the Lutheran Church—Missouri Synod," in his *Germans in the New World.*

13. Wittke, *German-Language Press,* p. 139; Peter Guilday, *The National Pastorals of the American Hierarchy (1792–1919)* (Westminster, Md.: Newman Press, 1954), p. 192; Rice, *American Catholic Opinion in the Slavery Controversy,* pp. 12, 76–79, 91, 157; *Wahrheits-Freund,* April 20, 1854, July 17, 31, 1856.

For a German Catholic perspective on the contest between Democrats and Republicans, see the *Wahrheits-Freund* of October 11, November 1, 1855, January 17, June 19, July 3, 10, 1856, June 28, 1860.

14. *Cincinnati Republikaner,* October 10, 1859.

15. See Foner, *Free Soil,* pp. 232–60; Holt, *Political Crisis,* pp. 176–81; Gienapp, "Nativism and the Creation of a Republican Majority in the North before the Civil War," *Journal of American History* 12 (December 1985): 529–59.

16. Julian, *Recollections,* p. 155; Johnson, "German Forty-Eighters in Davenport," p. 49; Gienapp, "Nativism," p. 544; Gienapp, *Origins,* pp. 121–22, 278–79; Holt, *Political Crisis,* p. 178.

17. Krem, "Trembles," pp. 197, 205–6; Gienapp, "Nativism," p. 538; Maizlish, *Triumph of Sectionalism,* pp. 216–17; Foner, *Free Soil,* pp. 197, 238, 242–55; Paul J. Kleppner, "Lincoln and the Immigrant Vote: A Case of Religious Polarization," in *Ethnic Voters and the Election of Lincoln,* ed. Frederick C. Luebke (Lincoln: University of Nebraska Press, 1973), p. 172; Kamphoefner, "St. Louis Germans," p. 88; Gienapp, "Nativism," p. 549.

18. *New York Daily Tribune,* January 22, 1856; Gienapp, "Nativism," 537, 540–42, 548–50; Seward quoted in Friedel, *Lieber,* pp. 299–300.

19. Herriott, "Deutsches Haus," pp. 122–24; Gienapp, *Origins,* pp. 405–6; *Newark Daily Mercury,* October 31, 1853; Gienapp, "Nativism," 539, 544; Holt, *Forging,* passim; *Daily Pittsburgh Gazette,* August 4, October 1, 2, 6, 1855.

20. Foner, *Free Soil,* pp. 250–53; Tucker, "Political Leadership," p. 215; Gienapp, "Nativism," p. 550.

21. Stein, "Through German Eyes," pp. 64–65; McPherson, *Battle Cry of Freedom,* pp. 140–41; Bruncken, "Wisconsin," p. 200; Stephenson, *History of American Immigration,* pp. 120–24; Stephenson, *Political History of the Public Lands,* pp. 151–57; Cole, *Irrepressible Conflict,* pp. 125, 145; *Congressional Globe,* 33rd Cong., 1st Sess., pp. 944–1048, 1302, 1703, 1706, 1808–9, Appendix p. 775; 2nd Sess., pp. 26, 447; 34th Cong., 1st Sess., 1409–14.

22. *New York Daily Times,* October 8, 1856; *New York Herald,* August 22, 1856; *Cincinnati Republikaner,* September 27, 1859, March 26, 1860. Similar arguments from Hecker appeared in the *Belleviller Zeitung,* August 12, 1856.

23. *New Yorker Demokrat,* November 1, 1860; *Cincinnati Republikaner,* October 1, 1858, September 27, 1859, March 26, 1860; *New Yorker Criminal Zeitung und Belletristisches Journal,* October 10, 31, 1856, November 9, 16, 1860; Stein, "Through German Eyes," pp. 64–70. Stein reproduces all quotations from Indianapolis's German press in their original form. Here as elsewhere, therefore, translations into English are solely my responsibility.

24. *Illinois Staats-Zeitung,* September 20, 1854, reprinted in the *Missouri Republican* (St. Louis), September 25, 1854.

25. *New York Daily Tribune,* August 22, October 8, 1856; *Cincinnati Republikaner,* March 26, October 8, 1860; *Indianapolis Daily Journal,* May 1, 1856; *New York Herald,* August 22, 1856; "Republican Party Platform of 1860," in *National Party Platforms,* p. 33; Wittke, *We Who Built America,* p. 249.

26. F. I. Herriott, "The Premises and Significance of Abraham Lincoln's Letter to Theodore Canissius," *Deutsch-Amerikanische Geschichstsblätter* 15 (1915): 181–254; Herriott, "The Germans of Iowa and the 'Two-Year Amendment' in Massachussets," *Deutsch-Amerikanische Geschichstsblätter* 13 (1913): 202–308; George Schneider, "Lincoln and the Anti-Know-Nothing Resolutions," *McLean County Historical Society Transactions* 3 (1900): 87–91; Körner, *Memoirs,* vol. 2, pp. 74–76; *Cincinnati Republikaner,* August 26, 1859.

27. Wittke, *Refugees of Revolution,* p. 212; *New Yorker Demokrat,* November 10, 1860; *Toledo Blade,* March 9, 1859, reprinted in *Cincinnati Daily Enquirer,* March 16, 1859; *Wahrheits-Freund,* July 3, 1856.

28. *New Yorker Criminal Zeitung und Belletristisches Journal,* July 11, September 26, 1856, October 17, 1860; *Sociale Republik,* September 4, 1858, January 1, April 2, 1859; *Cincinnati Republikaner,* September 27, 1859; *New York Daily Tribune,* August 22, 1856; *New York Herald,* August 22, 1856, October 14, 1858; *New York Daily Times,* October 14, 1858. Delegates from Cincinnati's German trade unions denounced the Massachusetts initiative as "yet another symptom of a general trend that conflicts with the principles and interests of the peoples of the republic" (*Cincinnati Republikaner,* August 13, 1859). For the Turner resolutions, see the "Verhandlungen der Turner-Taglatzung zu Buffalo," and Metzner, "Satzungen des social. Turnerbundes in Nord-Amerika," pp. 199–200, 269.

29. Bruncken, "Wisconsin," pp. 200–201; *Newarker Zeitung* editorial reprinted in the *Newark Daily Mercury,* June 19, 1854. Frederick Douglass, too, believed that antislavery German voters were being induced to cast their ballots for the Democracy by newspapers and political leaders who assured them "that the party is decidedly friendly to foreigners" while "the whole Republican party was one and the same with the Know-Nothing party, and if elevated to power would exercise it in such manner as to strip foreigners of all their political rights." In the meantime, "the slavery question . . . is cunningly treated as a secondary subordinate matter and thus kept in the background." "Thus startled and fancying that they felt the knife already at their throats, they walked straight into the trap set for them, and voted for Mr. Buchanan" in 1856 (*Douglass's Monthly,* August, 1859).

30. Bergquist, "Political Attitudes," pp. 280–83; *Sociale Republik,* October 2, 9, 23, 30, 1858; *Cincinnati Republikaner,* March 17, 1860; Obermann, *Joseph Weydemeyer: Ein Lebensbild,* p. 355–56; *New Yorker Criminal Zeitung und Belletristisches Journal,* October 22, 1858.

31. *Sociale Republik,* September 4, 1858, January 1, April 2, 1859; Katzler, "Germans in Newark," p. 1055; *Cincinnati Republikaner,* August 4, 1859, May 7, 1860; *Cincinnati Daily Enquirer,* May 3, 1859.

32. Foner, *Free Soil,* pp. 211–13, 271, 277; Sewell, *Ballots for Freedom,* pp. 343–65.

33. *Indianapolis Daily Journal,* February 21, 1860; Herriott, "Deutsches Haus," pp. 140–45; *Cincinnati Daily Commercial,* March 21, 1860. See also Schurz, *Speeches,* vol. 1, pp. 107, 111, 113; Körner, *Memoirs,* vol. 2, pp. 78–85; Cunz, *Maryland Germans,* pp. 299–300.

34. Herriott, "Deutsches Haus," pp. 118–19, 140–45; Bergquist, "Political Attitudes," pp. 283–85; *Cincinnati Republikaner,* March 17, 19, 20, 22, 26, 28, May 7, 1860; *Cincinnati Daily Commercial,* March 20, 22, 1860.

35. The most authoritative sources on the German meeting in Chicago are F. I. Herriott's "Conference in the Deutsches Haus" and James Berquist's "Forty-Eighters and the Republican Convention." See also Bergquist, "Political Attitudes," pp. 296–300; *Sociale Republik,* August 27, 1859, May 12, 1860; *Cincinnati Republikaner,* March 23, 1860; *Belleviller Zeitung,* May 17, 24, 1860; and Huch, "Anschluss," pp. 36–38.

36. Bergquist, "The Forty-Eighters and the Republican Convention," pp. 145–48; Bergquist, "Political Attitudes," pp. 280–83, 293–96; Herriott, "Deutsches Haus," p. 148; *Sociale Republik,* May 12, 1860; Obermann, *Joseph Weydemeyer: Ein Lebensbild,* pp. 363–64.

37. *Belleviller Zeitung,* May 7, 27, 1860; Herriott, "Deutsches Haus," pp. 188–89; Bergquist, "Forty-Eighters and the Republican Convention," pp. 149–53.

38. "Republican Party Platform of 1860," pp. 32–33.

39. Kamphoefner, "St. Louis Germans," p. 87; *Cincinnati Republikaner,* May 18, 21, 26, 1860; *Cincinnati Daily Commercial,* May 24, 1860.

40. *Cincinnati Republikaner,* May 19, 21, October 8, 1860; *Cincinnati Daily Commercial,* May 24, 1860; Easton, *Hegel's First American Followers,* pp. 89–90.

41. William E. Gienapp, "'Politics Seem to Enter into Everything': Political Culture in the North, 1840–1860," in *Essays on American Antebellum Politics, 1840–1860,* ed. Stephen E. Maizlish and John J. Kushma (College Station: Texas A&M University Press, 1982), pp. 15–69; Bergquist, "Political Activities," p. 327; Foner, *Free Soil,* p. 230; Frank G. Franklin, *The Legislative History of Naturalization in the United States: From the Revolutionary War to 1861* (1906; repr., New York: Augustus M. Kelley, 1971), pp. 278–300; Williamson, *American Suffrage,* pp. 276–77.

42. Obermann, *Joseph Weydemeyer: Ein Lebensbild,* p. 356–58, 369; *Cincinnati Republikaner,* May 18, 19, 21, 26, October 8, 1860; Thomas J. Kelso, "The German-American Vote in the Election of 1860: The Case of Indiana with Supporting Data from Ohio" (Ph.D. diss., Ball State University, 1967), pp. 120–22, 127–28, 172; George H. Daniels, "Immigrant Vote in the 1860 Election: The Case of Iowa," in *Ethnic Voters,* p. 120; Cunz, *Maryland Ger-*

mans pp. 285, 288; Andreas Dorpalen, "The German Element and the Issues of the Civil War," in *Ethnic Voters*, p. 73; Kleppner, *Third Electoral System*, pp. 73, 158; *Daily Pittsburgh Gazette*, November 11, 1856; Formisano, *Birth of Mass Political Parties*, pp. 183 and n, 298, 300–301; Gienapp, *Origins*, p. 538; Bruncken, "German Political Refugees," pp. 33, 40–42; Wittke, *We Who Built America*, pp. 225–27, 251; Krem, "Cleveland," p. 76; Holt, *Forging a Majority*, pp. 356–57, 368.

43. This conclusion is drawn by James M. Bergquist, "People and Politics in Transition: The Illinois Germans, 1850–60," in *Ethnic Voters*, p. 224; Kamphoefner, "St. Louis Germans," p. 88; and Kathleen Conzen, "Germans," in the *Harvard Encyclopedia of American Ethnic Groups*, ed. Stephan Thernstrom (Cambridge, Mass.: Harvard University Press, 1980), p. 421.

44. *Newark Daily Mercury*, November 11, 1856, November 2, 7, 1860. On ward composition, see Hirsch, *Roots of the American Working Class*, pp. 94–99.

45. Some German Republicans claimed still higher levels of support among their countrymen. *New York Daily Times*, November 7, 1856.

46. See the November 7, 1860, issue of the *New York Daily Tribune*, the *New York Daily Times*, and the *New York Herald*.

47. Joseph Schafer, "Who Elected Lincoln?" in *Ethnic Voters*, pp. 46–61; Bruncken, "Wisconsin," p. 205–6; Conzen, *Immigrant Milwaukee*, pp. 198, 201, 220–21.

48. *Daily Pittsburgh Gazette*, August 4, October 2, 9, 10, 1855, August 8, 1856; *Pittsburgh Post*, November 22, 1856; Huch, "Anschluss," p. 28; Holt, *Forging a Majority*, pp. 175–80, 216–17, 337, 355, 357, 366–67; Kleppner, "Lincoln and the Immigrant Vote," pp. 157–58.

49. E. Duane Elbert, "Southern Indiana Politics on the Eve of the Civil War, 1858–1861" (Ph.D. diss., Indiana University, 1967); Daniels, "The Case of Iowa," passim; Formisano, *Birth of Mass Political Parties*, pp. 182–84, 299–304; Gienapp, *Origins*, p. 425 and n; Herriott, "Deutsches Haus," p. 152.

50. Maizlish, *Triumph of Sectionalism*, pp. 223, 227; Dannenbaum, *Drink and Disorder*, p. 168; Gienapp, *Origins*, pp. 202–3, 425; Kelso, "The German-American Vote," passim; Krem, "Cleveland," pp. 73, 76; Wittke, *Refugees of Revolution*, p. 209.

51. *Cincinnati Daily Enquirer*, October 16, 17, 1856, November 8, 1860; *Daily Cincinnati Gazette*, November 6, 1856; Gienapp, *Origins*, pp. 425–26 and n; Dannenbaum, *Drink and Disorder*, pp. 170–71.

52. Hansen's computations show 73 percent of the state's Germans voting for Frémont and 69 percent for Lincoln (Stephen Hansen, *The Making of the Third Party System*, pp. 84, 99). See also Chicago *Daily Democratic Press*, March 3, 5, June 20, 1856; Bergquist, "Political Activities," pp. 345, 347–48; Hildegard Binder Johnson, "The Election of 1860 and the Germans in Minnestota," in *Ethnic Voters*, pp. 92–109.

53. Rather than support Buchanan, Heinrich Börnstein's *Anzeiger des Westens* endorsed the Fillmore slate "under protest" (Börnstein, "Under Pro-

test," *Missouri Historical Society Bulletin* 13 [October 1856], 23–29; Kamphoefner, "St. Louis Germans," pp. 75–76, 81).

54. Kenneth M. Stampp, *And the War Came: The North and the Secession Crisis, 1860–61* (Chicago: University of Chicago Press, 1964), pp. 123–58; Foner, *Business and Slavery,* pp. 235–38, 251–52; Körner, *Memoirs,* vol. 2, pp. 107–9; *Chicago Daily Tribune,* January 14, 1861; Müller, *Erinerrungen,* pp. 233–35; *New York Herald,* December 12, 1860.

55. *New York Herald,* January 1, 1861; Schlüter, *Lincoln, Labor, and Slavery,* pp. 130–37; Jonathan P. Grossman, *William Sylvis, Pioneer of American Labor: A Study of the Labor Movement during the Era of the Civil War* (1945; repr., Cincinnati: The Sylvis Society, 1986), pp. 45–47; James C. Sylvis, *The Life, Speeches, Labors and Essays of William H. Sylvis* (1872; repr., New York: Augustus Kelley, 1968), pp. 42–46; Philip Foner, *History,* vol. 1, pp. 302–3; Montgomery, *Beyond Equality,* p. 92.

56. Katz, *Belmont,* pp. 62, 64–65, 74–76, 83–89; Joel H. Silbey, *A Respectable Minority: The Democratic Party in the Civil War Era, 1860–1868* (New York: W. W. Norton and Co., 1977), pp. 63–64, 92–93, 113, 126; *New Yorker Criminal Zeitung und Belletristisches Journal,* April 26, 1861; *Illinois Staats-Zeitung,* January 24, 1861; Reemelin, *Life,* 159–60.

57. Schurz, *Speeches, Correspondence, and Political Papers,* vol. 1, pp. 165–78; Körner, *Memoirs,* vol. 2, pp. 107–9, 113; Huch, "Beteiligung," p. 48; *Illinois Staats-Zeitung,* January 8, 9, 19, 23, 24, 1861, February 19, 1861; *Chicago Daily Tribune,* January 9, 1861; Metzner, *American Turnerbund,* pp. 18–19; *New York Daily Tribune,* January 10, 1861.

58. *Daily Cincinnati Gazette,* February 13, 1861; *Cincinnati Daily Enquirer,* February 14, 1861; Daniel J. Ryan, *Lincoln and Ohio* (Columbus: Ohio State Archaeological and Historical Society, 1923), pp. 134–43.

59. Ryan, *Lincoln and Ohio,* p. 143; *Cincinnati Daily Enquirer,* February 14, 1861.

60. Friedrich Anneke, *Der zweite Freiheitskampf der Vereinigten Staaten von Nordamerika* (Frankfurt am Main: J. D. Sauerlander's Verlag, 1861).

61. Reemelin, *Life,* 159–60; Kapp, *Geschichte der Sklaverei* pp. xi–xii.

62. Estimates of the number of German troops serving the Union vary from 176,817 (Gould) to 200,000 (Lonn, Wiley) to 216,000 (Kaufmann, who alone included German-speaking soldiers from Austria, Switzerland, Poland, Hungary, and the Netherlands). Benjamin Apthorp Gould, *Investigations in the Military and Anthropological Statistics of American Soldiers* (New York: Hurd and Houghton, 1869), pp. 26–29; Ella Lonn, *Foreigners in the Union Army and Navy* (1951; repr., New York: Greenwood Press, 1969), pp. 52–53, 101–15, 146–47, 487–96, 576–79; Bell Irvin Wiley, *The Life of Billy Yank: The Common Soldier of the Union* (Baton Rouge: Louisiana State University Press, 1952), p. 307; *Jahrbucher der Deutsch-Amerikanischen Turnerei,* vol. 2, pp. 62–71, 81–82, 97–100, and vol. 3, pp. 141–44, 170; Metzner, *American Turnerbund,* pp. 20–22; Katzler, "Germans in Newark," pp. 1086–87 and n; Wittke, *Refugees of Revolution,* p. 25; Cunz, *Maryland Germans,* pp. 305–7.

63. On the Ninth Ohio, see Gustav Tafel's foreword in Constantine Grebner, *We Were the Ninth,* trans. Frederic Trautmann (1897; repr., Kent, Ohio: Kent State University Press, 1987), pp. 5–7; Carl Wittke, "The Ninth Ohio Volunteers: A Page from the Civil War Record of the German Turners of Ohio," *Ohio Archaeological and Historical Quarterly* 35 (April 1926): 402–17; Easton, *American Followers,* pp. 191–93; and Larry Koenig, "Cincinnati in the Civil War: Occupational Grouping of the Ohio Ninth Volunteer Infantry Regiment" (seminar paper, University of Cincinnati, June 1988). See also Lonn, *Foreigners in the Union Army and Navy,* pp. 94–115; Katzler, "Germans in Newark," pp. 1072–73, 1079, 1084, 1115n; *New York Herald,* June 14, 1861; *Illinois Staats-Zeitung,* April 20, 1861; Wagner, *Ein Achtundvierziger,* pp. 304–5; Pierce, *History of Chicago,* vol. 2, p. 256; Metzner, *American Turnerbund,* pp. 19–22; Tucker, "Political Leadership," p. 278.

64. "Der Geist von Achtundvierzig ist wieder erwacht" (*New Yorker Criminal Zeitung und Belletristisches Journal,* April 26, 1861.)

Chapter 10. "When Poor Men's Sons Must Sacrifice": The War and Beyond

1. Lonn, *Foreigners in the Union Army,* pp. 485–86n, 492, 512–13, 649–50; Wittke, "Ninth Ohio Volunteers," p. 415; *New York Daily Times,* November 4, 1863; Earl J. Hess, "The 12th Mo. Infantry: A Socio-Military Profile of A Union Regiment," *Missouri Historical Review* 76 (October 1981): 61.

2. Fritz Anneke to Matthilde Franziska Anneke, April 5, 1864, Anneke Papers; Schulte, *Fritz Anneke,* pp. 70–79; H. A. Rattermann, "General August Willich," *Der Deutsche Pionier* 9 (March 1878): 488–95; Earl J. Hess, "Sigel's Resignation: A Study in German Americanism and the Civil War," *Civil War History* 26 (March 1980): 12–13; *Illinois Staats-Zeitung,* February 20, August 1, 1862; Kevin J. Weddle, "Ethnic Discrimination in Minnesota Volunteer Regiments during the Civil War," *Civil War History* 35 (September 1989): 239–59.

3. In Chicago, for example, the *Turnverein* and *Arbeiterverein* organized benefits in behalf of the Hecker Regiment, while leaders of the local relief committee included Mrs. Julie Butz, Mrs. Elsie Schneider, Mrs. Emilie Brentano, Mrs. S. Gindele, and Mrs. A. Greenbaum. *Illinois Staats-Zeitung,* October 22, November 6, 1861, February 4, 1862, February 1, March 16, September 22, October 26, 1863, February 5, 1864; Nadel, "The Forty-Eighters and the Politics of Class in New York City," p. 60; and Katzler, "Germans in Newark," p. 1077.

4. *Illinois Staats-Zeitung,* July 31, August 1, 1862, February 27, 1863, January 6, 1864.

5. Robert P. Sharkey, *Money, Class, and Party: An Economic Study of the Civil War and Reconstruction* (Baltimore: Johns Hopkins University Press, 1959), pp. 144, 178–79; Phillip Shaw Paludan, *"A People's Contest": The Union and Civil War, 1861–1865* (New York: Harper and Row, 1988), pp.

182–83, 195–96; Schlüter, *Lincoln, Labor, and Slavery,* pp. 212–13, 215–20; Montgomery, *Beyond Equality,* pp. 98–101; *Illinois Staats-Zeitung,* June 10, July 22, 30, 1863, May 4, 1864.

6. August Belmont, *A Few Letters and Speeches of the Late Civil War* (New York: [Private Printer], [c. 1870]), p. 105; Katz, *August Belmont,* pp. 64–65, 74–76, 83–89, 139; Silbey, *A Respectable Minority,* pp. 63–64, 92–93, 113, 126, 130.

7. Iver Bernstein, *The New York City Draft Riots: Their Significance for American Society and Politics in the Age of the Civil War* (New York: Oxford University Press, 1990), pp. 17–42; *New Yorker Criminal Zeitung und Belletristisches Journal,* July 23, 31, 1863; Lapham, "Germans of New York City," pp. 211–12, 316; Bodger, "The Immigrant and the Union Army" (Ph.D. diss., Columbia University, 1951), p. 293; *The Diary of George Templeton Strong,* ed. Allan Nevins and Milton Halsey Thomas (New York: Macmillan, 1952), vol. 3, p. 343; Katzler, "The Germans in Newark," pp. 1074–75; *New York Daily Tribune,* July 15, 18, 1863.

8. *Illinois Staats-Zeitung,* November 9, 1861; *The Liberator* (Boston), September 4, 1863.

9. *Illinois Staats-Zeitung,* August 8, September 30, October 1, 1861. Similar opinions were expressed in meetings reported through late 1861 and well into 1862.

10. Halleck quoted in Hess, "Sigel's Resignation," pp. 12–13. *Chicago Tribune* coeditor J. L. Scripps enlisted the aid of George Schneider, by then ambassador to Denmark, in calming the German reaction (Scripps to Schneider, November 27, 1861, in the George Schneider Papers, Chicago Historical Society).

11. *Illinois Staats-Zeitung,* June 10, 13, November 4, 1862, January 13, July 22, 30, 1863. In 1862 an Illinois constitutional convention voted to exclude free blacks from the state; a subsequent referendum endorsed that decision (*Chicago Daily Tribune,* March 6, 1862; Cole, *Era of the Civil War,* p. 271).

12. Article in the *Chicago Times* reprinted in *Cincinnati Daily Enquirer,* March 31, 1864.

13. *Cincinnati Daily Enquirer,* April 2, 20, May 31, June 1, 1864; *Chicago Daily Tribune,* May 31, 1864; *Cleveland Plain Dealer,* March 31, April 2, 20, May 31, 1864; *Weekly Chicago Democrat,* May 31, June 1, 3, 1864; Katzler, "The Germans in Newark," p. 1076; Ruhl J. Bartlett, *John C. Frémont and the Republican Party* (1930; repr., New York: Da Capo Press, 1970), pp. 89–128; Wittke, *Against the Current,* pp. 189–93. The fullest and most recent political history of the German role in the Frémont campaign is Jörg Nagler, *Frémont contra Lincoln: Die deutsch-amerikanische Opposition in der Republikanischen Partei während des amerikanischen Bürgerkrieges* (Frankfurt: Peter Lang, 1984). A summary may be found in the same author's "The Lincoln-Frémont Debate and the Forty-Eighters," in *The German Forty-Eighters,* pp. 158–78.

14. Bartlett, *Frémont,* p. 112; Fritz Anneke to Matthilde Anneke, April 5, 1864, Anneke Papers; article in the Pittsburgh *Volksblatt* reprinted in the *Cincinnati Daily Enquirer,* July 2, 1864; Körner, *Memoirs,* vol. 2, pp. 410, 432.

15. McPherson, *Battle Cry of Freedom,* pp. 772–80, 803–6, 840 and n; Nagler, *Frémont contra Lincoln,* pp. 241–50; Bartlett, *Frémont,* pp. 109, 130–32. Frémont's rejection of massive land reform demonstrated a closer affinity on this score with the Republican party's middle-of-the-road majority than with the Radicals around George Julian and Thaddeus Stevens. See Eric Foner, "Thaddeus Stevens, Confiscation, and Reconstruction," in Foner, *Politics and Ideology,* pp. 128–149.

16. Katzler, "Germans in Newark," pp. 1078–79; Larry A. Greene, "The Emancipation Proclamation in New Jersey and the Paranoid Style," *New Jersey History* 91 (Summer 1973): 108–24; Metzner, *American Turnerbund,* pp. 24–25.

17. Fritz Anneke to Matthilde Anneke, February 19, 1864, Anneke Papers.

18. *Twelfth Census of the United States, Taken in the Year 1900,* vol. 7, *Manufactures,* pp. xlvii, lxxii; John A. Garraty, *The New Commonwealth, 1877–1890* (New York: Harper and Row, 1968), p. 97; North, *Growth and Welfare,* p. 28; David M. Gordon, Richard Edwards, and Michael Reich, *Segmented Work, Divided Workers: The Historical Transformation of Labor in the United States* (New York: Cambridge University Press, 1982), pp. 84–85, 100–127.

19. Charles Madison, *American Labor Leaders* (New York: Frederick Ungar, 1962), p. 41; *New York Daily Times,* February 22, 1869; *Illinois Staats-Zeitung,* December 15, 1871; Foner, *Reconstruction.*

20. Engels to Weydemeyer, August 7, 1851, in Marx and Engels, *Collected Works,* vol. 38, pp. 405–7; Schläger, *Sociale und politische Stellung,* pp. 18–21; Seeger, *Chicago: The Wonder City,* p. 344; John Higham, *Strangers in the Land: Patterns of American Nativism, 1860–1925* (1955; repr., New York: Atheneum, 1967), p. 196. On the conservatization of former radicals, see, for one example among many, Carl Wittke, "Friedrich Hassaurek: Cincinnati's Leading Forty-Eighter," *Ohio History Quarterly* 68 (January 1959): 12–13.

21. Fritz Anneke to Matthilde Anneke, July 21, 1870, Anneke Papers; Hans Trefousse, "The German-American Immigrants and the Newly Founded Reich," in *America and the Germans: An Assessment of a Three-Hundred-Year History,* ed. Frank Trommler and Joseph McVeigh (Philadelphia: University of Pennsylvania Press, 1985), vol. 1, pp. 160–75.

22. Kammen, *Socialism in German American Literature,* p. 62; Schlüter, *Die Anfänge,* p. 214; Metzner, *American Turnerbund,* pp. 22–30; Ralf Wagner, "Turner Societies and the Socialist Tradition," in *German Workers' Culture in the United States, 1850 to 1920,* ed. Hartmut Keil (Washington, D.C.: Smithsonian Institution Press, 1988), pp. 229–36; Keil and Jentz, eds., *German Workers in Chicago: A Documentary History,* p. 256.

23. Trefousse, *Carl Schurz,* pp. 189, 193, 208; Schurz, *Speeches,* vol. 2, pp. 437–38, vol. 3, pp. 89–90, and vol. 4, p. 509; Robert V. Bruce, *1877: Year of Violence* (1959; repr., Chicago: Quadrangle, 1977), pp. 65–66; Philip S. Foner, *The Great Labor Uprising of 1877* (New York: Monad Books, 1977), p. 212. The Liberal Republican movement of the early 1870s attracted many of the German-born liberals and democrats of the antebellum era. Jörg Nagler, "Deutschamerikaner und das Liberal Republican Movement 1872," *Amerikastudien* 33 (1988): 415–38.

24. Schurz, *Speeches,* vol. 5, p. 470.

25. Kathleen Neils Conzen, "German-Americans and the Invention of Ethnicity," in *America and the Germans,* vol. 1, pp. 131–47; Frank Trommler, "The Use of History in German-American Politics," in *America and the Germans,* vol. 1, pp. 287–93; Hartmut Keil, "German Immigrant Workers in Nineteenth-Century America: Working-Class Culture and Everyday Life in an Urban Industrial Setting," in *America and the Germans,* vol. 1, pp. 201–2.

26. Higham, *Strangers in the Land,* p. 219; Metzner, *American Turnerbund,* p. 7; Katzler, "The Germans in Newark," p. 1049; Albert B. Faust, *The German Element in the United States* (1909, 1927; repr., New York: Arno Press, 1969), vol. 2, pp. 186–87. References to "queer resolutions" appear in both Katzler and Faust. More recently, even the previous celebration of forty-eighter antislavery has come in for revision. "Their struggle against slavery was in the abstract," we are now told, because "forty-eighters . . . lived primarily in the North" and therefore "had no first-hand experience with the problem of slavery." Today, "documentary records of Southern plantations prove that out of simple self-interest Slave-owners treated their Slaves humanely and did not overwork them. . . . The most pitiful and tragic creatures were the white prostitutes of Southern States who had to cater to black slaves to make out a living. . . . In the school-integrations forced upon American cities by the Government no American city has shown such bloody resistance as the City of Boston, home of the anti-slavery movement. When by Federal Court Orders Blacks were forced upon Whites and Whites upon Blacks, the problem ceased to be abstract, so the reaction of Whites was like that of White Southerners." The above comes from an editorial note in *The German Language Press of the Americas,* ed. Karl J. R. Arndt and May E. Olson (Munich: K. G. Saur, 1980), vol. 3, p. 566.

27. Mencken is quoted in Hawgood, *Tragedy of German-America,* p. 42; Thomas Sowell, *Ethnic America: A History* (New York: Basic Books, 1981), pp. 51, 58–61.

28. *German-American Tricentennial (1683–1983) Newsletter,* Number 1 (n.d.).

29. The closest Professor Sowell comes is in his observation that "the Germans were organizers—whether of lodges, bowling clubs, labor unions, businesses, singing groups, orchestras, schools, theater groups, or churches" (Sowell, *Ethnic America,* p. 61).

30. The International's American membership in 1872 has been estimated at between three and five thousand. Samuel Gompers later recalled that the International had "dominated" the labor movement in New York City in this period. *Workingmen's Advocate* (Chicago), September 17, 1864, April 28, August 25, 1866; Sorge, *Labor Movement,* pp. 100, 109–13, 152–53, 198–99; Samuel Bernstein, *The First International in America* (New York: Augustus Kelley, 1965), p. 65; Morris Hillquit, *History of Socialism in the United States,* 5th ed. (1910; repr., New York: Dover Publications, 1971) p. 197; Gompers, *Seventy Years of Life and Labour,* pp. 26, 33, 47–49, 61–62, 71–72; Nadel, "Politics of Class," p. 57–58; Montgomery, *Beyond Equality,* pp. 162–76.

31. Key labor meetings, rallies, and confrontations took place at *Turnverein* halls, as in St. Louis and Chicago, and immigrants probably constituted 90 percent of the membership of the principal radical organization involved, the Workers Party of the United States. (They were mostly German). Bernstein, *First International,* pp. 284–96; Hillquit, *History of Socialism,* pp. 188–92; Carol Poore, "Whose Celebration? The Centennial of 1876 and German-American Socialist Culture," in *America and the Germans,* vol. 1, pp. 176–88; Bruce, *1877: Year of Violence,* pp. 129, 152–53, 159–61, 228, 260; *The Nation* 25 (August 2, 1877): 68–70.

32. Paul Avrich, *The Haymarket Tragedy* (Princeton, N.J.: Princeton University Press, 1984); Paul David, *The History of the Haymarket Affair: A Study in the American Social-Revolutionary and Labor Movements* (New York: Farrar and Rinehart, 1936). The Chicago *Times* and the *Daily Tribune,* both of May 5, 1886, are quoted in Harry Bernard, *The Eagle Forgotten: The Life of John Peter Altgeld* (New York: Bobbs-Merrill, 1962), pp. 132–33.

33. Foner, *History of the Labor Movement,* vol. 1, pp. 373–74.

34. The manifesto can be found in *Socialism in America: From the Shakers to the Third International,* ed. Albert Fried (Garden City, N.Y.: Doubleday, 1970), pp. 178–79.

35. Keil and Jentz, eds., *German Workers in Chicago: A Documentary History,* pp. 360–62; Philip S. Foner, ed., *We the Other People: Alternative Declarations of Independence by Labor Groups, Farmers, Woman's Rights Advocates, Socialists, and Blacks* (Urbana: University of Illinois Press, 1976), pp. 99–104; Philip S. Foner, ed., *The Autobiographies of the Haymarket Martyrs* (New York: Humanities Press, 1969), pp. 70–71, 85, 165–66.

36. Schlüter, *Lincoln, Labor, and Slavery,* p. 70.

Selected Bibliography:
Primary Sources

Archives and Manuscript Collections

Anneke, Friedrich and Mathilde. Papers. State Historical Society of Wisconsin, Madison.

Brentano, Lorenz. Papers. Chicago Historical Society.

Chicago Foreign Language Press Survey. University of Chicago Libraries.

Cincinnati Turnverein Papers. Cincinnati Historical Society.

Dick, Johann Georg. Papers. Cincinnati Historical Society.

Hamilton County Incorporation Records. Recorder's Office. Hamilton County Courthouse, Cincinnati.

Herriott, Frank Irving. Papers. Iowa State Historical Department, Des Moines.

Illinois State Archives, Springfield.

International Workingmen's Association Papers. State Historical Society of Wisconsin, Madison.

Legislative Archives Division. National Archives.

Puchta, George. Collection. Hamilton County Public Library, Cincinnati.

Rödter, Henry. Papers. Cincinnati Historical Society.

Schmidt, Ernst. Papers. Chicago Historical Society.

Schneider, George. Papers. Chicago Historical Society.

Schmitt, Peter. Papers. Cincinnati Historical Society.

Scholer, Gustav. Papers. New York Public Library.

Sozialistischer Turnerbund von Nord-Amerika. Papers. New York Public Library.

U.S. Census. Population Schedules. Essex County, N.J. Seventh (1850) and eighth (1860) censuses. National Archives (microfilm).

Periodicals

Der Arbeiter (New York)
Belleviller Zeitung
Buffalo Morning Express
Chicago Daily Journal
Chicago Daily Tribune
Cincinnati Daily Commercial
Cincinnati Daily Enquirer
Cincinnati Republikaner
Cleveland Plain Dealer
Congressional Globe (Washington, D.C.)
Daily Cincinnati Gazette
Daily Democratic Press (Chicago)
Daily Pittsburgh Gazette
Free West (Chicago)
Hochwächter (Cincinnati)
Hunt's Merchant's Magazine
Illinois Staats-Zeitung (Chicago)
Indianapolis Daily Journal
The Liberator (Boston)
Louisville Daily Democrat
Missouri Republican (St. Louis)
Newark Daily Advertiser
Newark Daily Eagle
Newark Daily Mercury

New Yorker Criminal-Zeitung und Belletristisches Journal
New Yorker Demokrat
New Yorker Staats-Zeitung
New York Daily Times
New York Daily Tribune
New York Evening Post
New York Herald
Nonpareil (Cincinnati)
North American Review
Pittsburgh Post
Die Reform (New York)
Republik der Arbeiter (New York)
Sentinel of Freedom (Newark)
Sociale Republik (New York)
State Gazette (Trenton, N.J.)
Turn-Zeitung (New York, Philadelphia, Cincinnati, Baltimore)
Volksblatt (Cincinnati)
Volks-Tribun (New York)
Wahrheits-Freund (Cincinnati)
Weekly Chicago Democrat
Workingmen's Advocate (Chicago)
Young America (New York)

Government Publications

U.S. House of Representatives, Committee on Foreign Affairs. *Report on Foreign Criminals and Paupers* (Report No. 359), 34th Cong., 1st sess. Washington, D.C.: Government Printing Office, 1856.

Report of the Committee of the Senate upon the Relations between Labor and Capital, and Testimony Taken by the Committee. Washington, D.C.: Government Printing Office, 1885.

Publications of the Seventh Census

DeBow, J. D. B. *Statistical View of the United States, Compendium of the Seventh Census.* Washington, D.C.: Beverley Tucker, 1854.

Kennedy, Jos. C. G. *Abstract of the Statistics of Manufactures of the Seventh Census.* Washington, D.C.: Government Printing Office, 1858.

The Seventh Census: Report of the Superintendant of the Census. Washington, D.C.: Robert Armstrong, 1853.

Publications of the Eighth Census

Kennedy, Joseph C. G. *Population of the United States in 1860; Compiled from the Original Returns of the Eighth Census.* Washington, D.C.: Government Printing Office, 1864.

Secretary of the Interior. *Manufactures of the United States in 1860.* Washington, D.C.: Government Printing Office, 1865.

Secretary of the Interior. *Statistics of the United States, (Including Mortality, Property, &c.), in 1860; Compiled from the Original Returns and Being the Final Exhibit of the Eighth Census.* Washington, D.C.: Government Printing Office, 1866.

Publications of the Ninth Census

Walker, Francis A. *Statistics of the Population of the United States in 1870.* Washington, D.C.: Government Printing Office, 1872.

Publications of the Twelfth Census

Twelfth Census of the United States, Taken in the Year 1900. Washington, D.C.: United States Census Office, 1902.

Other Works by Contemporaries

Books and Pamphlets

Abbott, Edith, ed. *Historical Aspects of the Immigration Problem.* Chicago: University of Chicago Press, 1926.

Anneke, Friedrich. *Der zweite Freiheitskampf der Vereinigten Staaten von Nordamerika.* Frankfurt am Main: J. D. Sauerlander's Verlag, 1861.

Annual Review of the Commerce, Manufactures, Public and Private Improvements of Chicago for the Year 1854. Chicago: Daily Democratic Press, 1854.

Banfield, Thomas C. *Industry of the Rhine.* 2 vols. London: Charles Knight and Co., 1846.

Basler, Roy P., ed. *The Collected Works of Abraham Lincoln.* 8 vols. New Brunswick, N.J.: Rutgers University Press, 1953.

Becker, M. J. *The Germans of 1849 in America.* Mt. Vernon, Ohio: Republican Printing House, 1887.

Bird, Isabella Lucy. *The Englishwoman in America.* 1856; repr., Madison: University of Wisconsin Press, 1966.

Born, Stephan. *Erinnerungen eines Achtundvierzigers, mit dem Bildnis dem Verfassers.* 3d ed. Leipzig: Verlag von Georg Heinrich Meyer, 1898.

Büchele, Karl. *Land und Volk der Vereinigten Staaten von Nord-Amerika.* Stuttgart: Hallberger'sche Verlagshandlung, 1855.

Burgheim, Max. *Cincinnati in Wort und Bild: Nach authentischen bearbeitet und zusammengestellt.* Cincinnati: Burgheim Publishing Co., 1891.

Busch, Moritz. *Travels between the Hudson and the Mississippi, 1851–1852.* Trans. and ed. Norman H. Binger. Lexington: University Press of Kentucky, 1971.

Busey, Samuel S. *Immigration: Its Evils and Consequences*. New York: De Witt and Davenport, 1856.

Cist, Charles. *Cincinnati in 1841: Early Annals and Future Prospects*. Cincinnati: author, 1841.

———. *Sketches and Statistics of Cincinnati in 1851*. Cincinnati: Wm. H. Moore and Co., 1851.

———. *Sketches and Statistics of Cincinnati in 1859*. Cincinnati: author, 1859.

Commerce, Railroads, and Manufactures of Chicago. Chicago: Democratic Press, 1855.

Conway, Moncure Daniel. *Autobiography, Memories and Experiences*. 2 vols. New York: Houghton, Mifflin and Co., 1904.

Duden, Gottfried. *Report on a Journey to the Western States of North America and a Stay of Several Years along the Missouri (during the Years 1824, '25, '26, 1827)*. Columbia: University of Missouri Press, 1980.

Eickhoff, Anton, ed. *In der neuen Heimath: Geschichtliche Mittheilungen über die deutschen Einwanderer in allen Theilen der Union*. New York: E. Steiger and Co., 1884.

Eighth Annual Review of the Trade and Commerce of the City of Chicago, for the Year 1859. Chicago: Chicago Daily Press and Tribune, 1860.

Eighty Years' Progress of the United States, from the Revolutionary War to the Great Rebellion: Showing the Various Channels of Industry through which the People of the United States Have Arisen from a British Colony to their Present National Importance. New York: New National Publishing House, 1864.

Fifth Annual Review of the Commerce, Manufactures, and the Public and Private Improvements of Chicago, for the Year 1856. Chicago: Daily Democratic Press, 1857.

Fourth Annual Review of the Commerce, Railroads, and Manufactures of Chicago, for the Year 1855. Chicago: Daily Democratic Press, 1856.

Foner, Philip S., ed. *The Autobiographies of the Haymarket Martyrs*. New York: Humanities Press, 1969.

———, ed. *The Life and Writings of Frederick Douglass*. 5 vols. New York: International Publishers, 1950–75.

Freedley, Edwin T. *Philadelphia and Its Manufactures: A Hand-Book Exhibiting the Development, Variety, and Statistics of the Manufacturing Industry of Philadelphia in 1857*. Philadelphia: Edwin Young, 1858.

Fried, Albert, ed. *Socialism in America, from the Shakers to the Third International*. Garden City, N.Y.: Doubleday, 1970.

Gerth, Hans, ed. *The First International: Minutes of the Hague Congress of 1872 with Related Documents*. Madison: University of Wisconsin Press, 1958.

Geschichtliche Mittheilungen über der Deutschen Freien Gemeinden von Nord-Amerika. Philadelphia: Deutschen Freien Gemeinden von Philadelphia, 1877.

Gompers, Samuel. *Seventy Years of Life and Labour: An Autobiography*. 1925; repr., New York: Augustus M. Kelley, 1967.

Grebing, Helga, ed. *Arbeiterbewegung: Sozialer Protest und Kollective Interressenvertretung bis 1914*. München: Deutscher Taschenbuch Verlag, 1985.

Grebner, Constantine. *We Were the Ninth*. Trans. Frederic Trautmann. 1897; repr., Kent, Ohio: Kent State University Press, 1987.

Griesinger, Theodor. *Freiheit und Sclaverei unter dem Sternenbanner, oder Land und Leute in Amerika*. Stuttgart: A. Kroner, 1862.

———. *Lebende Bilder aus Amerika in humoristischen Schilderungen*. Cincinnati: Max Weil and Co., 1861.

Grund, Francis. *The Americans in their Moral, Social, and Political Relations*. 1837; repr., New York: Johnson Reprint Corp., 1968

Hodgskin, T. *Travels in the North of Germany: Describing the Present State of the Social and Political Institutions, the Agriculture, Manufactures, Commerce, Education, Arts and Manners in that Country, Particularly in the Kingdom of Hanover*. 2 vols. Edinburgh: Archibald Constable and Co., 1820.

Howitt, William. *The Rural and Domestic Life of Germany: with Characteristic Sketches of its Cities and Scenery, Collected in a General Tour, and during a Residence in the Country in the Years 1840, 41 and 42*. Philadelphia: Carey and Hart, 1843.

Jantke, Carl, and Hilger, Dietrich, eds. *Die Eigentumslosen: Der deutsche Pauperismus und die Emancipationskrise in Darstellungen und Deutungen der zeitgenössischen Literatur*. München: Verlag Karl Alber Freiburg, 1965.

Julian, George W. *Political Recollections*. 1884; repr., Westport, Ct.: Greenwood Press, 1970.

Kapp, Friedrich. *Geschichte der Sklaverei in den Vereinigten Staaten von Amerika*. Hamburg: Otto Meisner, 1861.

Keil, Hartmut, and Jentz, John B., eds. *German Workers in Chicago: A Documentary History of Working-Class Culture from 1850 to World War I*. Urbana: University of Illinois Press, 1988.

Körner, Gustav. *Das deutsche Element in den Vereinigten Staaten von Nordamerika, 1818–1848*. Cincinnati: Verlag von A. E. Wilde and Co., 1880.

———. *The Memoirs of Gustave Koerner, 1809–1896*. Ed. Thomas I. McCormack. 2 vols. Cedar Rapids: Torch Press, 1909.

Kriege, Hermann. *Die Väter unserer Republik in ihrem Leben und Wirken*. New York: Verlag von J. Uhl, 1847.

Laurens, J. Wayne. *The Crisis: or, The Enemies of America Unmasked*. Philadelphia: G. D. Miller, 1855.

Lemke, Theodor. *Geschichte des Detschthums von New York von 1848 bis auf die Gegenwart*. New York: Theodor Lemke, 1891.

Loomis, Rev. Samuel Lane. *Modern Cities and Their Religious Problems*. New York: Baker and Taylor, 1887.

Meusch, Hans, ed. *Die Handwerkerbewegung von 1848/49: Vorgeschichte, Verlauf, Inhalt, Ergebnisse*. Eschwege: Gildverlag Hans-Gerhard Dobler, 1949.

Müller, Jakob. *Aus den Erinerungen eines Achtundvierzigers: Skizzen aud der deutsch-amerikanischen Sturm- und Drang-Periode der 50er Jahre*. Cleveland: Rudolph Schmidt Printing Company, 1896.

Nevins, Allan, ed., *The Diary of Philip Hone, 1828–1851*. 2 vols. 1927; repr., New York: Kraus Reprint Co., 1969.

Nevins, Allan, and Thomas, Milton Halsey, eds. *The Diary of George Templeton Strong.* New York: Macmillan, 1952.

Penny, Virginia. *How Women Can Make Money, Married or Single.* Philadelphia: McKinney and Martin, 1870.

Perry, Thomas Sergeant, ed. *The Life and Letters of Francis Lieber.* Boston: James R. Osgood and Co., 1882.

Pösche, Theodore, and Göpp, Charles. *The New Rome; or, The United States of the World.* New York: G. P. Putnam and Co., 1853.

Pollard, S. and Holmes, C., eds. *Documents of European Economic History.* 3 vols. London: Edward Arnold, 1968.

Porter, Kirk H., and Johnson, Donald Bruce, eds. *National Party Platforms, 1840–1960.* Urbana: University of Illinois Press, 1961.

von Raumer, Frederick. *America and the American People,* trans. William W. Turner. New York: J. and H. G. Langley, 1846.

Reemelin, Karl. *Life of Charles Reemelin, in German: Carl Gustav Rümelin, From 1814–1892.* Cincinnati: Weier and Daiker, 1892.

Rosenberg, Nathan, ed. *The American System of Manufactures.* Edinburgh: Edinburgh University Press, 1969.

Sanborn, F. B., ed. *The Life and Letters of John Brown, Liberator of Kansas, and Martyr of Virginia.* 1885; repr., New York: New American Library, 1969.

Sanderson, John P. *Republican Landmarks: The Views and Opinions of American Statesmen on Foreign Immigration.* Philadelphia: J. B. Lippincott and Co., 1856.

Schaff, Philip. *America: A Sketch of Its Political, Social, and Religious Character,* ed. Perry Miller. 1855; repr., Cambridge, Mass.: Harvard University Press, 1961.

Schappes, Morris, ed. *A Documentary History of the Jews in the United States, 1654–1875.* New York: Citadel Press, 1950.

Schläger, Eduard. *Die sociale und politische Stellung der Deutschen in den Vereinigten Staaten: Ein Beitrag zu der Geschichte des Deutsch-Amerikanerthums der letzten 25 Jahre.* Berlin: Puttkamer and Mühlbrecht, 1874.

Schurz, Carl. *The Reminiscences of Carl Schurz.* 2 vols. New York: Doubleday, Page and Co., 1909.

———. *Speeches, Correspondence, and Political Papers,* ed. Frederic Bancroft. 6 vols. 1913; repr., New York: Greenwood Publishing Co., 1969.

Sixth Annual Review of the Commmerce, Manufactures and the Public and Private Improvements of Chicago for the Year 1857. Chicago: Chicago Daily Press, 1858.

Sorge, Friedrich. *The Labor Movement in the United States,* ed. B. Chamberlin and P. Foner. Westport, Conn.: Greenwood Press, 1977.

Stanton, Elizabeth Cady; Anthony, Susan B.; and Gage, Matilda Josilyn, eds. *The History of Woman Suffrage.* New York: Fowler and Wells, 1881.

James C. Sylvis. *The Life, Speeches, Labors and Essays of William H. Sylvis.* 1872; repr., New York: Augustus Kelley, 1968.

de Tocqueville, Alexis. *Democracy in America,* ed. Phillips Bradley. 2 vols. 1835, 1840; repr., New York: Alfred A. Knopf, 1945.

Twelfth Annual Review of the Trade and Commerce of the City of Chicago, for the Year 1860. Chicago: Chicago Daily Tribune, 1861.

Villard, Henry. *Memoirs of Henry Villard, Journalist and Financier, 1835–1900.* 2 vols. Cambridge: Houghton, Mifflin and Co., 1904.

Wagner, Phillip. *Ein Achtundvierziger. Erlebtes und Gedachtes.* Brooklyn, N.Y.: Verlag von Johannes Wagner, 1882.

Whitney, Thomas R. *A Defence of the American Policy, as Opposed to the Encroachments of Foreign Influence, and Especially to the Interference of the Papcy in the Political Interests and Affairs of the United States.* New York: Dewitt and Davenport, [1856].

Wolff, Adolf. *Berliner Revolutionschronik: Darstellung der Berliner Bewegung im Jahre 1848 in politischer, sozialer und literarischer Beziehung,* ed. C. Gompertz. 1848; repr., one-volume ed. Berlin: Ferd. Dummlers Verlagsbuchhandlung, 1898.

Articles

Bondi, August. "With John Brown in Kansas." *Transactions of the Kansas State Historical Society* 8 (1903–1904): 275–89.

Engels, Friedrich. "On the History of the Communist League." In Karl Marx and Friedrich Engels, *Selected Works,* vol. 2, pp. 238–57. Moscow: Progress Publishers, 1962.

Friesen, Gerhard K. "A Letter from M. F. Anneke: A Forgotten German-American Pioneer in Women's Rights." *Journal of German-American Studies* 12 (1977): 34–46.

Huch, C. F. "Die Anfänge der Arbeiterbewegung unter den Deutschamerikanern." *Mitteilungen des Deutschen Pionier-Vereins von Philadelphia* 17 (1910): 39–52.

———. "Anschluss der Deutschen Philadelphias an die republikanische Partei im Jahre 1856." *Mitteilungen des Deutschen Pionier-Vereins von Philadelphia* 21 (1911): 1–48.

———. "Der Befreiungs-Verein." *Mitteilungen des Deutschen Pionier-Vereins von Philadelphia* 17 (1910): 34–37.

———. "Die Deutschamerikaner und die deutsche Revolution." *Mitteilungen des Deutschen Pionier-Vereins von Philadelphia* 17 (1910): 25–33.

———. "Die Deutschen in Philadelphia ums Jahre 1847." *Mitteilungen des Deutschen Pionier-Vereins von Philadelphia.* 17 (1910): 13–52.

———. "Die ersten Jahre der Philadelphia Turngemeinde." *Mitteilungen des Deutschen Pionier-Vereins von Philadelphia* 26 (1912): 29–36.

———. "Die freireligiöse Bewegung unter den Deutschamerikanern." *Mitteilungen des Deutschen Pionier-Vereins von Philadelphia* 11 (1909): 1–33.

———. "Gottlieb Theodor Kellner." *Mitteilungen des Deutschen Pionier-Vereins von Philadelphia* 10 (1909): 26–31.

———. "Der patriotische Verein." *Mitteilungen des Deutschen Pionier-Vereins von Philadelphia* 17 (1910): 21–25.

———. "Revolutionsvereine und Anleihen." *Mitteilungen des Deutschen Pionier-Vereins von Philadelphia* 18 (1910): 1–19.

———. "Der Sozialistische Turnerbund." *Mitteilungen des Deutschen Pionier-Vereins von Philadelphia* 26 (1912): 1–15.

Ingerman, Elizabeth, ed. "Personal Experiences of an Old New York Cabinetmaker." *Antiques* 84 (November 1963): 576–80.

von Katzler, William. "The Germans in Newark." In F. J. Urquhart, *A History of the City of Newark, New Jersey,* pp. 1057–87. New York: Lewis Historical Publishing Co., 1913.

Koester, Leonard, ed. "Early Cincinnati and the Turners: From Mrs. Karl Tafel's Autobiography." *Historical and Philosophical Society of Ohio Bulletin* 6 (October 1948): 18–22.

"Letters of the Right Reverend John Martin Henni and the Reverend Anthony Urbanek." *Wisconsin Magazine of History* (1926): 66–94.

Marx, Karl, and Engels, Friedrich. "Address of the Central Authority to the [Communist] League." In Marx and Engels, *Collected Works,* vol. 10, 277–87.

Rattermann, Heinrich. "Friedrich Hassaurek." *Der Deutsche Pionier* 17 (1885): 3–20.

———. "General August Willich." *Der Deutsche Pionier* 9 (February, March 1878): 439–45, 488–95.

———. "Kritik des Wheelinger Congress von 1852." *Der Deutsche Pionier* 8 (July 1876): 155–59.

Schläger, Eduard. "Das Freidenkerthum in den Vereinigten Staaten." *Internationale Monatsschrift* 1 (January 1882): 51–70.

———. "Der Wheelinger Congress im September 1852." *Der Deutsche Pionier* 8 (June 1876): 90–97.

Schneider, George. "Lincoln and the Anti-Know-Nothing Resolutions." *McLean County Historical Society Transactions* 3 (1900): 87–91.

Vocke, William. "The Germans and the German Press." *McLean County Historical Society* 3 (1900): 45–58.

Wollenweber, L. A. "Aus den Aufzeichnungen von L. A. Wollenweber über seine Erlebnisse in Amerika, namentliche in Philadelphia." *Mitteilungen des Deutschen Pionier-Vereins von Philadelphia* 13 (1909): 1–32.

———. "Aus meinem Leben." *Mitteilungen des Deutschen Pionier-Vereins von Philadelphia* 14 (1910): 1–28.

Index

Abendzeitung (newspaper), 161
Abolitionism. *See* Slavery
Adams, Stephen, 206, 241–42
Age of Reason (Paine), 93
Agrarian laborers: background of, 19–20; decline of, 56, 58, 61; and estate division, 36; feudalism of, 20–21, 36; growth of, 55, 76; Howitt on, 19–20; and intelligentsia, 45; Menzel on, 58; mortgages of, 36; and nobility, 36; poverty of, 22; taxation of, 36. *See also* Peasants
Ahrens, Heinrich, 84, 105, 115
Albinger, Ludwig, 116
Alcoholic beverages. *See* Temperance laws
Allen, Richard V., 268
Allgemeine Arbeiterbund, 137, 138, 231
Allgemeine Arbeiterbund von Nord-Amerika, 144; on John Brown, 222; on class structure, 89; on Fugitive Slave Law, 221; on immigrants, 145; members of, 125, 137, 145; on political parties, 245; purposes of, 125, 144–45; on slavery, 221
Allgemeine Arbeiterverbrüderung, 43, 45, 137
Allgemeiner deutscher Arbeiterkongress (ADA), 43–44
American and Foreign Antislavery Society, 156
American (Know-Nothing) party, 239, 244

Amerikanische Arbeiterbund: and M. Anneke, 124–25; background of, 140; decline of, 142; growth of, 142; on Kansas-Nebraska Act, 164, 165, 166, 214, 215; members of, 141–42; and panic of 1854–55, 142; on Franklin Pierce, 151; and protective associations, 141–42; purposes of, 140–41, 142, 214; and *Sozialistischer Turnerbund*, 142; and Joseph Weydemeyer, 124–25, 140–41, 142
Amerikanischer Revolutionsbund für Europa, 85, 86
Amerikanischer Turnerbund, 265, 267
Anneke, Fritz: and M. Anneke, 103; on army, 41; background of, 171; on Civil War, 255, 262–63; in Cologne Workers Association, 171; in Communist League, 171; and demonstrations, 144; on education, 41; on freedom of speech, press, and association, 41; on Frémont, 219; and Greiner, 173; on Kansas-Nebraska Act, 173, 176, 214; on Lincoln, 261; and New York Communist Club, 100; in Newark, 171; as newspaper editor, 171; on political parties, 152, 171–72, 214, 216, 228, 245, 250, 253; on public employment, 220; on slavery, 214, 245; on Sunday laws, 90; on

temperance laws, 90, 245; on voting, 41; on wages, 41; on Wilhelm I, 265; on work hours, 41
Anneke, Mathilde Giesler, 103, 124–25, 171
Anti-Semitism, 35
"Appeal of the Independent Democrats" (Chase et al.), 153–54
Apprentices: and *Allgemeiner deutscher Arbeiterkongress,* 44; articles of, 42; characteristics of, 23–24, 30; growth of, 30; in guilds, 24; and journeymen, 123; and masters, 123; as radical democrats, 46; riots by, 36; and solidarity, 123; women as, 123
Arbeiter-Verbrüderung, 43, 45, 137
Arbeitervereine: and *Allgemeine Arbeiterbund von Nord-Amerika,* 144; and Bedini, 189; in Civil War, 258, 260; class structure of, 114; on conscription, 258; on Emancipation Proclamation, 260; on Frémont, 261; on Lincoln, 261; on martial law, 259; on mechanics' lien law, 220; members of, 114, 115, 116, 124, 187, 204; newspapers on, 255; on political parties, 244, 245–46; on slavery, 260; and solidarity, 131. *See also* Cooperative associations; *Frauenvereine*
Aristocracy, 25, 36, 47
Arnold, Franz: in *Arbeitervereine,* 115; background of, 102; on *Centralkommission der vereinigten Gewerbe,* 127; on cooperative associations, 117; on political parties, 151, 216; on socialism, 102; in trade unions, 115; in *Turnvereine,* 91
Artisanry, Save Yourself! (Kinkel), 45
Artisans. *See* Craftworkers
Artisans' Congress, 42, 43, 44
Association der Social-Reformer, 105, 106, 144
Astor, John Jacob, 113, 160
Austria, 46
Aycoberry, Pierre, 29

Bakers. *See* Food preparers

Baltimore, Maryland: *Centralkommission der vereinigten Gewerbe* in, 128; cooperative associations in, 117; demonstrations in, 144; *Freimännervereine* in, 96, 116; International Workingmen's Association in, 269; political parties in, 217; *Schneidervereine* in, 131; strikes in, 128, 139; trade unions in, 113; *Turnvereine* in, 91, 222, 256
Baltimore *Correspondent* (newspaper), 228
Baltimore *Wecker* (newspaper), 217, 228
Bamberger, Leopold, 227
Banfield, Thomas C., 28, 29
Banks, Nathaniel, 246
Banks and credit institutions, 43, 220
Barr, William V., 135
Barrelmakers, 63, 77
Bassi, Ugo, 188
Bates, Edward, 246
Baum, Martin, 183
Bayard, James A., 155
Bayrhoffer, Karl Theodor, 50
Beard, Charles and Mary R., 8
Bechmeier, Jasper, 114, 129
Beck, Karl, 93, 114
Becker, August, 161, 217
Bedini, Gaetano, 188–91
Beer gardens, 59–60
Bell, John, 107, 229, 230
Belleviller Zeitung (newspaper), 202
Belmont, August, 157, 160, 227, 254, 259
Benevolent societies, 62, 95, 114, 128. *See also* Cooperative associations
Benjamin, Jacob, 208
Benque, William, 230, 231
Bergquist, James M., 247, 253
Berlin, Ira, 3–4
Berlin, Germany: craftworkers in, 29, 30; factories in, 28; journeymen in, 30; nominal masters in, 32; population of, 27–28, 63; riots in, 35–36
Berlin artisan association, 50
Berlin Workers' Congress, 50
Bernstein, Iver, 259
Berthoff, Rowland, 3

Bierwirth, Leopold, 85, 160
Bildungsverein für Arbeiter, 40, 41
Bird, Isabella Lucy, 5, 186
Bismarck, Otto von, 264–65, 266
Blacks. *See* Free blacks; Slavery
Blacksmiths. *See* Metalworkers
Blankenheim, Johann, 114
Blum, Robert, 50, 105, 171
Bomhart (or Bornhard; tailor), 132–33, 136, 236–37
Bondi, August, 208–9, 220–21, 222
Bootmakers. *See* Shoemakers
Born, Stephan, 32, 39, 40–41, 43, 45
Bottcher, Friedrich, 96
Boudine, Charles A., 74
Bradley, Joseph P., 179
Brady, William V., 83–84
Braubach, John G., 115
Breckinridge, John C., 230
Brewers. *See* Food preparers
Brodhead, Richard, 155
Brooklyn, New York, 91, 113, 142
Brown, John, 8, 208, 209, 222–26, 248
Browning, Orville H., 224
Brownson, Orestes, 98
Buchanan, James, 214, 220, 227, 228, 229
Büchele, Karl, 54, 61, 82, 150
Buffalo, New York: cooperative associations in, 117, 136; immigrants in, 2, 64; International Workingmen's Association in, 269; strikes in, 128; trade unions in, 113
Buffalo *Demokrat* (newspaper), 228
Buffalo *Weltbürger* (newspaper), 185
Burbridge, Stephen, 259
Busch, Moritz: on Heinzen, 112; on immigrants, 65, 66; on Kinkel, 84, 87; on religion, 95
Buschmann, Carl, 114, 133
Busey, Samuel C., 108
Business organizations. *See* Protective associations
Butchers. *See* Food preparers
Butler, Andrew P., 241
Butz, Caspar, 116, 216, 222, 247, 248

Cable workers. *See* Metalworkers
Calvinists, 47. *See also* Protestants

Cameron, Simon, 241
Camphausen, Ludolf, 36, 41, 42
Canals, 26, 43, 55
Cap workers. *See* Clothing workers
Capitalism, 39, 43, 88
Carpenters. *See* Construction workers
Caspar, Johann, 54
Cass, Lewis, 152
Catholic church: charitable and relief societies of, 95; Cincinnati platform on, 187; conservatism of, 46–47, 95, 98; Douglas on, 238; and Enlightenment, 47; and evangelicals, 98; and *Freimännervereine,* 191; on Kossuth, 98; and liberals, 98; and political parties, 238, 239, 240, 250; and Protestants, 47, 98–99; and radical democrats, 98; and religious disaffection, 48, 95; on revolutions, 94; schools of, 98–99; on slavery, 238–39; on *Sozialistischer Turnerbund,* 95; A. Stephens on, 239. *See also Deutschkatholiken;* Jesuits
Centralization of industries: atypical nature of, 28–29; and clothing workers, 71, 120; and furniture makers, 73, 75; and shoemakers, 69, 70
Centralkommission der vereinigten Gewerbe (Central Commission of United Trades; CVG): background of, 127–28; and cooperative associations, 135; growth of, 128, 131; members of, 127–28; and New York City Industrial Congress, 128, 133, 134; newspapers on, 129; on police brutality, 136; rally by, 134; and solidarity, 131, 134; on wages, 136; and Weitling, 127, 135, 137; on work hours, 136
Charitable and relief societies, 62, 95, 114, 128. *See also* Cooperative associations
Charivari, 169
Chase, Salmon P., 196, 240, 252
Chicago, Illinois: *Arbeitervereine* in, 114, 125, 258, 260, 261; *Association der Social-Reformer* in, 105; clothing workers in, 72–73; and

Compromise of 1850, 200; craft organizations in, 126; craftworkers in, 183; demonstrations and riots in, 90, 144; Douglas in, 200; and Fugitive Slave Law, 200; furniture makers in, 76; growth of, 182; immigrants in, 2, 58, 64, 182–83; and Kansas-Nebraska Act, 200–207; leatherworkers in, 78; and Lincoln, 253; newspapers on, 65, 81; political parties in, 150, 228, 248–49, 252–53; shoemakers in, 70; strikes in, 140; temperance laws in, 90; trade unions in, 113; *Turnvereine* in, 91, 216, 255, 256; unemployment in, 81; unskilled workers in, 183

Chicago Daily Journal (newspaper), 206

Chicago Daily Press (newspaper), 81

Chicago Daily Tribune (newspaper), 65, 226, 269–70

Chicago *Free West* (newspaper), 156

Chicago German Society, 112

Chicago *National Demokrat* (newspaper), 228

Chicago *Stimme des Volkes* (newspaper), 249

Chicago Times (newspaper), 269

Child labor, 62, 79, 141

Church-state separation, 49

Cigarmakers: and child labor, 79; cooperative associations of, 40; and division of labor, 79; and entrepreneurs, 79; growth of, 63; and industrialization, 79; journeymen as, 38, 79; professionals as, 79; and size of factories, 79; and solidarity, 123, 124; in *Turnvereine*, 93; and urbanization, 79; wages of, 79; women as, 79

Cincinnati, Ohio: *Arbeitervereine* in, 114, 132, 186, 189; *Association der Social-Reformer* in, 105; Bedini in, 188; and Brown, 223–24; Catholics in, 188–91; and Chase, 252; clothing workers in, 71, 72, 73; cooperative associations in, 116, 117, 136; craft organizations in, 126; craftworkers in, 186; demonstrations and riots in, 144,

188–91; *Freimännervereine* in, 96–97, 150, 186, 190–91; and Frémont, 252; furniture makers in, 75–76; General Trades Union in, 140; growth of, 181–82; Hecker in, 91; immigrants in, 2, 58, 63, 64, 182, 183–84, 186; International Workingmen's Association in, 269; and Kansas-Nebraska Act, 191–99; Kinkel in, 91; Kossuth in, 91; leatherworkers in, 78–79; and Lincoln, 252, 255; political parties in, 246–47, 252; as "Queen City of the West," 181; *Schneidervereine* in, 132; shoemakers in, 70; strikes in, 128, 140; trade unions in, 113, 140, 246; *Turnvereine* in, 91, 186, 189, 216, 246, 256; unemployment in, 81; unskilled workers in, 186; wagonmakers in, 77

Cincinnati Daily Enquirer (newspaper): on *Arbeitervereine*, 255; on Civil War, 257; on Fugitive Slave Law, 197; on immigrants, 188; on Kansas-Nebraska Act, 191–92, 193–94, 199; on political parties, 252; on slavery, 193–94, 197

Cincinnati *Demokratisches Tageblatt* (newspaper), 157, 185

Cincinnati *Hochwächter* (newspaper), 97, 216

Cincinnati platform, 187–88

Cincinnati *Republikaner* (newspaper), 125, 220, 246–47, 249

Cincinnati *Volksblatt* (newspaper), 97, 111, 184, 185

Cincinnati *Volksfreund* (newspaper), 228

Cincinnati *Wahrheits-Freund* (newspaper), 94, 228, 234, 238–39

Cist, Charles, 70, 71, 75, 184

Citizenship. *See* Naturalization

Clancy, George, 135

Clark, Peter A., 223

Class consciousness and class structure: *Allgemeine Arbeiterbund von Nord-Amerika* on, 89; of *Arbeitervereine*, 114; background of, 3; Born on, 39; composition of, 23, 60–64; and cooperative associations, 135; defined, 122; effects of, 3; Higham on, 1–2; and immigrants, 3, 10; International Workingmen's Association on, 270; and Kansas-Nebraska Act, 173–75, 176–78, 191, 194, 197–99, 201, 275; and manufacturers, 61; and masters, 42; and merchants, 61; newspapers on, 226, 263–64; and politicians and political parties, 62, 225–26; and professionals, 62, 79; and solidarity, 122; and *Turnvereine*, 93, 265; and unskilled workers, 62; and urbanization, 60–61; Weydemeyer on, 141, 215; Willich on, 215; and working class, 122

Clayton, John M., 155–56

Cleveland, Ohio: cooperative associations in, 117, 136; free blacks in, 149; *Freimännervereine* in, 96; immigrants in, 2; political parties in, 252; strikes in, 128, 140; trade unions in, 113; *Turnvereine* in, 91

Cleveland *Germania* (newspaper), 228

Cleveland Plain Dealer (newspaper), 206

Clothing workers: background of, 71; and boycotts, 134; and centralization, 71, 120; in cooperative associations, 40, 117; Freedley on, 73; growth of, 62, 63, 71; and industrialization, 73, 120; and journeymen, 38; and masters, 24; newspapers on, 73; and nominal masters, 32; and size of factories, 72; and solidarity, 131; and "Southern work" employers, 134; strikes by, 117, 120, 128–35; in trade unions, 114; in *Turnvereine*, 93; wages of, 72, 73, 134; women as, 71, 72, 73; work hours of, 72, 73, 120. *See also* Shoemakers

Cloth printers. *See* Textile workers

Cluer, John, 105

Cluss, Adolphus, 100, 115

Coachmakers, 27, 76–77

Coal miners. *See* Miners

Cologne, Germany, 27, 29, 30, 32, 41

Cologne Workers Association, 37, 171

Columbian (newspaper), 199

Columbus *Westbote* (newspaper), 86, 157, 229

Commerford, John, 136, 159

Communist League, 38–39, 40, 41–42, 100, 171

Communist Manifesto (Marx and Engels), 38

Communists: and craftworkers, 39; historical interpretation by, 100; and industrialization, 101; Kriege on, 105; newspapers on, 109; Willich as, 102

Compromise of 1850: and Chicago, 200; Dietz on, 167; and Douglas, 200; Körner on, 152, 202; newspapers on, 152; political parties on, 233; purposes of, 152; Reemelin on, 152, 193, 195

Confectioners. *See* Food preparers

Conscription, 258, 259

"Consensus" interpretation, 268

Constitutional monarchy, 37

Construction workers, 29, 40, 63, 64, 119

Contractors, 22

Conway, Moncure Daniel, 223

Cook, Isaac, 200

Cooperative associations: and *Allgemeine Arbeiterbund*, 137, 138; Arnold on, 117; background of, 116; Born on, 40–41; and *Centralkommission der vereinigten Gewerbe*, 135; and class consciousness, 135; and Committee of Thirteen, 135; decline of, 119, 138; members of, 40–41, 116, 117, 138; newspapers on, 135; Proudhon on, 40; purposes of, 116, 117–18; Schiff on, 118; Weitling on, 40, 117–19, 135, 137. *See also* *Arbeitervereine;* Charitable and relief societies; Protective associations

Coopers, 63, 77

Cordwainers. *See* Shoemakers

Cottage industry workers, 22–23, 24, 26, 40

Cotton goods workers. *See* Textile workers

Craft guilds. *See* Guilds

Craftworkers: and Artisans' Congress, 42; Bird on, 186; and capitalism, 39; and *Centralkommission der*

vereinigten Gewerbe, 127–28;
characteristics of, 65–66, 67; on
Civil War, 256; and communism,
39; in Communist League, 39; and
cooperative associations, 40, 117;
decline of, 71; as *Deutschkatholiken,*
49; and division of labor, 67; and
economic development, 67–68;
employees of, 64–65; Engels on,
40; and factories, 28–29; growth of,
20, 22, 23, 26, 29, 30–31, 32; as
immigrants, 7–8, 17; and
industrialization, 29, 67–68; and
intelligentsia, 45, 63; on Kansas-
Nebraska Act, 191, 201; as
Lichtfreunde, 49; on Lincoln, 250;
newspapers on, 66; on political
parties, 234–37; as radical
democrats, 46; and religion, 10; and
Revolutions-Vereine, 85; riots by, 35,
36, 37, 46; on secession, 254; on
slavery, 10, 216; strikes by, 127; on
Sunday laws, 89–90; on temperance
laws, 89–90; in *Turnvereine,* 93;
types of, 23, 62; unemployment of,
35; urbanization of, 26; wages of,
22, 33, 63–64, 66–67; and
Weitling, 50; women as, 124. *See
also specific types of craftworkers*
Crate, Henry, 134
Credit institutions and banks, 43, 220
Crittenden, John J., 253–54
Crux, Charles, 115
Cuba, 157, 230
Cutlery workers, 29

Dabney, Robert, 106
Daily Cincinnati Gazette (newspaper),
97, 156, 189, 192, 198
Daily Democratic Press (newspaper),
206–7
Davenport *Demokrat* (newspaper), 157
Dawley, Alan, 69
Democratic Congress, 45
Democratic party: F. Anneke on, 228,
250; Bamberger on, 227; and
"Barnburner" faction, 152; Belmont
on, 227; on Compromise of 1850,
233; and craftworkers, 234–37;
Douglass on, 226–27; and elite,

160; Fickler on, 229; and Free Soil
party, 152; and "fusion," 227, 235;
Hecker on, 242, 243; and Hellmuth,
200, 230; Höffer on, 229;
Hoffmann on, 203, 205, 213;
Hollinger on, 230; on homestead
laws, 151, 241; Hübschmann on,
229; on immigrants, 233–34, 237,
241, 242; and Irish-Americans, 200,
226, 237, 251; on Kansas-Nebraska
Act, 155–56, 157, 158, 193–94,
198, 199, 204, 213, 233, 234, 241;
Kapp on, 242, 243; Kellner on,
230; H. Kiersted on, 229; Kobbe
on, 227; and Körner, 200; Kriege
on, 151; Laible on, 229; on land
reform, 151; merchants on, 228; on
monopolies, 151, 234; Morwitz on,
229; on naturalization, 241–42;
newspapers on, 227, 228, 229, 252;
Ottendorfer on, 227; and panic of
1857, 234, 235; Pelz on, 236; on
popular sovereignty, 233; religious
groups on, 238, 250, 252; Rödter
on, 229; Rosenthal on, 230; rural
voters on, 250, 252; and G.
Schneider, 200; Schurz on, 226,
228; on secession, 253; on slavery,
2, 233, 234, 236, 237–38, 242,
259; Struve on, 242; on Sunday
laws, 151; on temperance laws, 151;
United German Democratic Central
Committee of, 161; unskilled
workers on, 250; urban voters on,
250; W. Wagner on, 230; Willich
on, 223; and Zotz, 200
Demokratischer Verein, 41
Demonstrations, 143–44. *See also specific
headings*
Dengler (capmaker), 132
Deph, H., 114
Depression of 1873, 269
Dericus, Lewis, 99
Detroit, Michigan: *Arbeitervereine* in,
116; cooperative associations in,
117; immigrants in, 2; International
Workingmen's Association in, 269;
political parties in, 252; trade unions
in, 113; *Turnvereine* in, 216
Detroit Free Press (newspaper), 252

Detroit *Michigan Demokrat*
(newspaper), 228
Deutsch-Amerikaner (magazine), 203
Deutsche Frauenzeitung (newspaper),
124, 171
Deutsche demokratische Verein, 186, 197
*Deutsche Handwerker- und
Gewerbekongress*, 42, 43, 44
Deutscher Kirchenfreund (newspaper), 94
Deutschkatholiken, 48, 49, 50. *See also*
Catholic church
Devyr, Thomas, 105
Dietz, George, 166–67, 229
Diversey, Michael, 200–201, 228
Division of labor, 28, 67, 75, 78, 79
Doberrer, Michael, 97
Dodd, William E., 9
Domschke, Bernhard, 203
Douai, Adolph, 161, 216, 217, 247
Douglas, Stephen A.: Belmont on, 227;
and Buchanan, 220, 227, 228;
burning in effigy of, 206–7; in
Chicago, 200; on Compromise of
1850, 200; and Cook, 200; and
Diversey, 200, 228; Greenbaum on,
228; and Hellmuth, 200; Hoffmann
on, 203, 205; on immigrants, 238;
on Kansas-Nebraska Act, 152–53,
199–200, 220; and Körner, 200,
202; and Milwaukee, 251;
newspapers on, 200, 228; political
campaigns of, 220, 227; political
parties on, 220; on popular
sovereignty, 168; Reemelin on, 230;
on religious groups, 238; and G.
Schneider, 200, 207; on slavery,
152, 183; on western United States,
181, 183; and Zotz, 200
Douglass, Frederick, 8, 9, 150, 226–27
Dred Scott case, 221, 248
Dulon, Rudolf, 96
Dürlam, H., 115

Education and schools: *Allgemeine
Arbeiterbund* on, 137; *Allgemeine
Arbeiterbund von Nord-Amerika* on,
145; *Amerikanische Arbeiterbund* on,
141; F. Anneke on, 41; Cincinnati
platform on, 187; Gottschalk on,
41; Louisville platform on, 103;

Peoria conference on, 207; and trade
unions, 113; types of, 24, 98–99;
Willich on, 41
Eggerlin, Karl, 190
1848 Revolution, 6–8, 83–84, 86–87,
115–16, 221
Eiselen, J. A., 91
Elections and voting: *Allgemeine
Arbeiterbund* on, 137; and
Allgemeiner deutscher Arbeiterkongress,
43; F. Anneke on, 41; Bayard on,
155; Brodhead on, 155; Cincinnati
platform on, 187, 188; and
Frankfurt Assembly, 44; Gottschalk
on, 41; and immigrants, 241, 249;
Kansas-Nebraska Act on, 155; and
naturalization, 249; political parties
on, 151, 241; and Two-Year
Amendment, 241; Willich on, 41
Emancipation Proclamation, 260–61.
See also Slavery
Emigrants. *See* Immigrants
Engels, Friedrich, 39, 40, 103, 264
Engineers, 26–27
Enlightenment, 47, 48, 50, 99, 103–4
Entrepreneurs, 61–62, 63, 65, 66, 79
Esenbeck, Christian Nees von, 43, 45,
50
Esselen, Christian, 90–91, 115, 244–
45, 253
Esslingen, Germany, 41
Estate system, 21, 36
Ethnic America (Sowell), 268
Ethnic identity, 83
Evangelical Lutheran Synod, 94, 238.
See also Lutherans
Evangelicals, 98
Evangelische Kirchen-Zeitung
(newspaper), 50
Evans, George Henry, 104, 105, 136,
151
Expatriates. *See* Immigrants

Faber, Eberhard, 160
Factory workers: and *Allgemeiner
deutscher Arbeiterkongress*, 44; and
craftworkers, 28–29; growth of, 29;
and industrialization, 69; and
nominal masters, 33; riots by, 35;
and size of factories, 28; types of,

27, 28–29, 69, 71, 75; and *Verlag* sector workers, 26
Fathers of Our Republic, The (Kriege), 106
Feldner, G., 151
Feuerbach, Ludwig, 49, 105
Fickler, Joseph, 229
Fillmore, Millard, 246
Financiers, 61
Fisch, J. P., 97
Fischer, Adolph, 271
Foner, Eric, 8, 219, 221–22
Food preparers: cooperative associations of, 40; and coopers, 77; growth of, 27, 62, 63, 64; newspapers on, 80; strikes by, 119; unemployment of, 80; wages of, 64, 80; work hours of, 80
Ford, Francis Clay, 3
Försch, Johan A.: as activist, 84; and demonstrations, 143; on Frémont, 219; on Kansas-Nebraska Act, 162, 163, 164, 167–68; on land reform, 143; as minister, 96; on monopolies, 164; and political parties, 151, 216; on popular sovereignty, 168; on public employment, 220; on revolutions, 168–69; on slavery, 167–68; and solidarity, 131; in trade unions, 115
Fort Sumter, 255
Foundry workers. *See* Metalworkers
Frankfurt Assembly, 37, 44–45, 85–86
Frankfurt workers' club, 37–38
Franklin, Benjamin, 106
Frankoni, Louis, 114, 130, 137
Frauenvereine, 125. *See also Arbeitervereine*
Free blacks, 149–50, 158, 265–66. *See also* Slavery
Free Soil party, 150–52, 157, 200. *See also* German Free Soil party
Freedley, Edwin T., 73
Freien Gemeinden, 48, 96
Freiligrath, Ferdinand, 103
Freimännervereine: and Bedini riot, 190–91; characteristics of, 96; defined, 96; on Fugitive Slave Law, 150; on land reform, 105; members of, 96, 97, 99, 116, 203; on

political parties, 244; and religious groups, 99, 191; on Sunday laws, 99; on temperance laws, 99
Frémont, John C.: and American party, 239, 244; F. Anneke on, 219; *Arbeitervereine* on, 261; and Cincinnati, 252; and Emancipation Proclamation, 260; Försch on, 219; and Illinois, 253; and Lincoln, 260; and Newark, 251; newspapers on, 218, 242, 244; presidential campaign of, 213, 214, 220, 261–62; Rödel on, 219; on slavery, 260
French Revolution, 5
Friedlien, George, 97
Friedrich Wilhelm IV (king of Prussia), 36, 41, 42, 47
Fries (tailor), 132
Fries, George, 194–95
Fröbel, Julius, 45, 216
Fugitive Slave Law: *Allgemeine Arbeiterbund von Nord-Amerika* on, 221; Bates on, 246; Breckinridge on, 230; and Chicago, 200; Crittenden on, 253; Foner on, 221–22; *Freimännervereine* on, 150; intelligentsia on, 158; Louisville platform on, 150; newspapers on, 197; Pennington on, 177; political parties on, 151, 221, 247, 248; radical democrats on, 196, 221–22. *See also* Slavery
Furniture makers, 27, 63, 64, 73, 74–76

Gagern, Heinrich von, 36–37
Gams, Kaspar, 114, 140, 187, 192, 196
Garment workers. *See* Clothing workers
Gebhard, Frederick, 160
Gemeinschaft freier Menschen, 96
Gerlach, Ludwig von, 48
German Democratic Association, 186, 197
German Element in the United States, The (Faust), 267
German-American Tricentennial Commission, 268
German-Americans: adjustment to United States of, 83; characteristics of, 6, 7, 9, 126; community

institutions of, 83; discrimination against, 83; ethnicity of, 10, 83; influence of, 4; and Irish-Americans, 122; religious beliefs of, 10; solidarity of, 83; wages of, 83. *See also* Immigrants; *specific headings*
Germania Club, 228
Gerwig, Adolf, 192
Gewerbefreiheit, 33
Gibbs, D. J., 208
Gidlitz, Marc, 160
Gilchrist, Robert, 254
Godkin, E. L., 269
Gollmer, Hugo, 92
Gompers, Samuel, 269
Göpp, Charles, 87, 110
Gottschalk, Andreas, 41, 42
Greeley, Horace, 240, 246
Greenbaum, Heinrich, 228
Gregory VI (pope), 46–47
Greiner, Ludwig, 173, 175, 176, 217
Grund, Francis, 56
Gudath, A., 114
Guilds: and *Allgemeiner deutscher Arbeiterkongress*, 44; and Artisans' Congress, 44; Banfield on, 29; decline of, 33; growth of, 21, 42; members of, 24, 29, 33, 42; and solidarity, 123
Gutman, Herbert, 3–4

Haas, A., 114
Hagen, Ernest, 74
Hale, John P., 203
Halleck, Henry, 260
Hallgarten, Charles, 160
Handicraft workers. *See* Craftworkers
Handlin, Oscar, 1
Handschuh, J. Andrew, 114, 129, 159
Hansemann, David, 36, 37
Hansen, Marcus Lee, 6
Hansen, Stephen, 253
Harnessmakers, 62, 77–79
Hartmann, Joseph, 162, 163, 166, 216
Hassaurek, Friedrich: in *Arbeitervereine*, 187; background of, 97; and Bedini riot, 190, 191; in *Freimännervereine*, 97; on Kansas-Nebraska Act, 196; and Reemelin, 229; on strikes, 140; on wages, 140

Hat and cap workers. *See* Clothing workers
Havemeyer, William F., 160
Hawgood, John A., 9
Haymarket affair, 269–70
Hecker, Friedrich: characteristics of, 6–7, 46, 50; in Cincinnati, 91; on economics, 45; Hilgard on, 87; Körner on, 224–25; on political parties, 218, 219, 242, 243; on slavery, 219, 236, 242
Heinisch, Rochus, 109, 173, 180
Heinzen, Karl: as activist, 84; on Brown, 222; Busch on, 112; and Douai, 161; on economics, 45; influence of, 112; and Körner, 112; on political parties, 150, 216, 247; on slavery, 149; in *Turnvereine*, 91
Hellmuth, Karl, 105, 150, 200, 230
Helmuth (cabinetmaker), 121
Hempel, Johann, 114
Hengstenberg, E. W., 47
Hesing, Anton C., 265
Hielscher, Theodor: in *Arbeitervereine*, 116, 204; and 1848 Revolution, 115–16, 221; in *Freimannervereine*, 116, 203; and Friedrich Wilhelm IV, 36; and newspapers, 116, 203; on political parties, 217, 221, 246; in *Turnvereine*, 91, 116, 203
Higham, John, 1–2, 267
Hilgard, Theodor, 87
Hillgärtner, George, 203
Hobsbawm, Eric J., 6
Höffer, Frank, 229
Hoffmann, Francis A.: background of, 202–3; on Douglas, 203, 205; on Kansas-Nebraska Act, 202, 203, 204, 205; on political parties, 203, 205, 213, 224, 225; on slavery, 203, 205
Höhn, H., 115
Hollinger, Conrad, 230
Homestead laws: background of, 159; Mechanics' Mutual Protectives on, 159; political parties on, 151, 241, 247, 248; trade unions on, 246; *Turnvereine* on, 246. *See also* Land reform
Housepainters, 93

Housing, 69–70, 143
Howitt, William, 19–20, 48
Hübschmann, Francis, 229
Hundertpfund, Jacob, 109
Hunt's Merchant's Magazine, 61, 72

Ill, Fridolin, 173, 176, 217
Illinois, 58, 96, 181, 253
Illinois Staats-Zeitung (newspaper), 66,
203, 242–43, 264, 265
Immigrants: causes of, 2–3, 34, 53–55,
84, 104; and ethnicity, 10; growth
of, 2, 3, 4–5, 6, 7–8, 15, 26, 34,
54, 57–58, 263; importance of, 1;
money carried abroad by, 19, 20,
58; newspapers on, 4, 65, 66, 188,
192, 206, 240–41, 242, 244;
political parties on, 233–34. *See also*
German-Americans; Irish-Americans;
specific headings
Independent Democrats, 160
Indianapolis *Freie Presse* (newspaper),
106–7, 116, 203, 242
Indianapolis *Indiana Volksblatt*
(newspaper), 87, 228
Industrialization, 19–20, 28–29; and
cigarmakers, 79; and clothing
workers, 73, 120; and communists,
101; and coopers, 77; and
craftworkers, 29, 67–68; and factory
workers, 69; and furniture makers,
73, 74, 75; growth of, 2, 19, 20,
26–28, 29, 263; and leatherworkers,
77–78; New York Communist Club
on, 100; newspapers on, 263; and
Rammelsberg, 184; and shoemakers,
69; and textile workers, 28; and
Vormärz, 26–28; Weydemeyer on,
100
Insurance, 43, 113
Intelligentsia: and agrarian workers, 45;
and craftworkers, 45, 63; as
Deutschkatholiken, 49; and
economics, 45; as entrepreneurs, 63;
on free blacks, 158; on Fugitive
Slave Law, 158; influence of, 36–
37; on Kansas-Nebraska Act, 158;
as *Lichtfreunde*, 49; members of, 45,
184; on slavery, 158; in trade
unions, 115

International Workingmen's Association,
269, 270
Irish-Americans, 122. *See also*
Immigrants; *specific headings*
Ironworkers. *See* Metalworkers

Jackson, Andrew, 101
Jackson, J. P., 179
Jacob, William, 25–26
Jacobi, Abraham, 100, 115
Jacobi, Fritz, 100, 216
Jefferson Club, 222
Jesuits, 187. *See also* Catholic church
Jewelers, 27, 93
Jews, 48, 94. *See also* Anti-Semitism
Job mobility, 24
Johnson, Andrew, 262
Johnson, Hildegard Binder, 6–7
Jonassohn, Louis, 115
Jones, M. A., 1, 57
Journeymen: and *Allgemeiner deutscher
Arbeiterkongress*, 43, 44; and
apprentices, 123; in Artisans'
Congress, 42; in Berlin artisan
association, 50; and capitalism, 43;
characteristics of, 23–24, 30, 31; as
cigarmakers, 38, 79; as clothing
workers, 38; and Enlightenment, 50;
growth of, 30; in guilds, 24; Kocka
on, 42–43; mandatory travel by, 42,
44; marriages of, 42; and masters,
31, 38, 43, 122; newspapers on,
118; as radical democrats, 46; riots
by, 36; strikes by, 38, 39–40; in
trade unions, 38; wages of, 31, 32,
39; work hours of, 31, 39; and
work-book system, 42, 44
Journeymen's associations. *See* Protective
associations
Journeymen's Congress, 43–44
Judd, Norman, 226
Julian, George, 240
Junkers, 24–25, 47

Kaiser, Charles, 151, 208
Kaiser, Christian, 88
Kamm, Friedrich, 100
Kansas-Nebraska Act: amendment to,
155–56; American and Foreign
Antislavery Society on, 156;

Amerikanische Arbeiterbund on, 164,
165, 166, 214, 215; F. Anneke on,
173, 176, 214; Bayard on, 155;
Benjamin on, 208; Bondi on, 208,
220–21; Bradley on, 179; Brodhead
on, 155; Brown on, 208; Buchanan
on, 220, 227, 228; and Chicago,
200–207; and Cincinnati, 191–99;
and class structure, 173–75, 176–
78, 191, 194, 197–99, 201, 275;
Clayton on, 155–56; clergy on, 157;
craftworkers on, 191, 201; Dietz on,
166–67; Douglas on, 152–53, 199–
200, 220; Försch on, 162, 163,
164, 167–68; G. Fries on, 194–95;
Gams on, 192, 196; Gerwig on,
192; Greiner on, 173, 175, 176,
217; Hartmann on, 162, 163, 166;
Hassaurek on, 196; Heinisch on,
173, 180; Hellmuth on, 230;
Hoffmann on, 202, 203, 204, 205;
Ill on, 173, 176; and immigrants,
155; intelligentsia on, 158; Irish-
Americans on, 215; J. P. Jackson on,
179; Charles Kaiser on, 208;
Kaufmann on, 167; Kellner on, 164,
167; H. Kiersted on, 196, 229;
Körner on, 201–2; Kossuth on,
170; Laible on, 229; on land
reform, 151, 154–55, 159, 164;
Lehlbach on, 173, 175; merchants
on, 157; Meyerhofer on, 164;
Molitor on, 195, 196; and New
York City, 160–69; and Newark,
169–80; newspapers on, 156, 157,
161, 162, 164, 165, 169, 172, 173,
177, 191–92, 193–94, 198, 199,
202, 216, 229; Pennington on, 177,
179; Peoria conference on, 207;
Pierce on, 153, 166, 176, 208;
Poinier on, 177; political parties on,
155–56, 157, 158, 193–94, 198,
199, 204, 213, 233, 234, 241, 248;
and popular sovereignty, 153, 155;
Pugh on, 199; purposes of, 152–53;
ratification of, 153, 207, 214;
Reemelin on, 193, 195, 196; Renau
on, 192; E. Richter on, 162, 163,
164, 165–66; Roos on, 173, 175,
176; Rosenstein on, 167; Eduard

Schläger on, 203, 204; Schöffner
on, 173, 175, 176; Sherman
brothers on, 208; on slavery, 151,
153, 154–55, 159, 164;
Sozialistischer Turnerbund on, 163,
165; Stallo on, 196; Thum on, 164;
Turnvereine on, 208; Vecchioni on,
167; on voting, 155; Walker on,
192–93; Ward on, 177;
Weydemeyer on, 164; Wiener on,
208; Wiest on, 196
Kansas-Zeitung (newspaper), 208
Kapp, Friedrich: on Civil War, 256; on
immigrants, 7; as newspaper editor,
161; on political parties, 216, 218–
19, 242, 243; on slavery, 218, 242
Kasperi, H., 115
Kauffmann, Sigismund, 91, 167
Kellner, Gottlieb, 115, 161, 164, 167,
230
Kellogg, William, 253
Kersten, Joachim, 114, 260
Keyser, John H., 136
Kiersted, Hezekiah, 183–84, 190, 196,
229
Kiersted, Jeremiah, 183
Kinkel, Gottfried: as activist, 50; and
M. Anneke, 103; Busch on, 84, 87;
characteristics of, 84; in Cincinnati,
91; on economics, 45; and Schurz,
110, 265
Klein, Frederick, 132
Klein, Henry, 115
Knapp, Frederick W., 115
Know-Nothing party. *See* American
(Know-Nothing) party
Kobbe, William A., 227
Koch, Eduard Ignaz, 96
Kocka, Jürgen, 42–43
Komp, Albert, 100
Kopp, Wilhelm, 216, 247
Kornblüth, Jacob, 183
Körner, Gustav: background of, 202;
on Brown, 225; on Compromise of
1850, 152, 202; and Douglas, 200,
202; on economic liberalism, 108;
on 1848 Revolution, 84; and
Frankfurt Assembly, 85–86; on
Hecker, 224–25; and Heinzen, 112;
as Illinois lieutenant governor, 224;

on Kansas-Nebraska Act, 201–2;
and Lincoln, 224–25, 262; and
newspapers, 202; on political parties,
200, 224, 225, 248; on radical
democrats, 87, 108; and Eduard
Schläger, 203; on secession, 254; on
slavery, 201–2
Kossuth, Lajos, 87–88, 91, 98, 155,
170
Kreismann, Hermann, 111, 225–26,
248
Kreitler, Hermann, 216
Kreitler, John, 115
Kriege, Hermann, 45, 84, 105, 113,
151–52
Kroll, August, 95–96
Kruer, A., 85

Labor courts, 145
Labor unions. *See* Trade unions
Laborers. *See* Unskilled workers
Laible, John, 229
Land reform: *Allgemeine Arbeiterbund*
on, 137; *Allgemeine Arbeiterbund
von Nord-Amerika* on, 145;
Amerikanische Arbeiterbund on, 141;
causes of, 104; Chase on, 196;
Cincinnati platform on, 188;
Commerford on, 136; Dabney on,
106; demonstrations about, 143;
effects of, 104; and elite, 24; Evans
on, 104, 136, 151; Försch on, 143;
and *Freimännervereine*, 105; German
Democratic Association on, 197;
Göpp on, 110; and immigrants,
104; Independent Democrats on,
160; Kansas-Nebraska Act on, 151,
154–55, 159, 164; Keyser on, 136;
Kriege on, 105, 151; and Louisville
platform, 105–6; Mechanics' Mutual
Protectives on, 159–60; and
National Reform Association, 104–
5; political parties on, 151, 220,
246; T. Pösche on, 110; purposes
of, 24; Ryckman on, 136; trade
unions on, 104, 105, 220; and
Turnvereine, 105; Vale on, 136;
Weydemeyer on, 141; and
workingmen's movements, 104. *See
also* Homestead laws

Landowners, 17, 49
Laurens, J. Wayne, 108
League of the Just, 105
Leatherworkers, 62, 77–79
Lehlbach, Friedrich August: on Kansas-
Nebraska Act, 173, 175; and
Kossuth, 170; as minister, 95, 96,
170; on political parties, 217; and
rationalism, 95, 96
Leipzig, Germany, 27, 29, 30, 46
Lewis and Hanford Company, 72
Lewis, Garthwaite and Company, 235
Lexow, Rudolf and Friedrich, 161
Liberals, 37, 45, 98, 106–13, 160–61
Lichtfreunde, 48–49, 50. *See also*
Protestants
Lieber, Francis, 84, 87, 109, 111
Liebrich, T. Conrad, 115, 216
Lievre, Eugen, 116, 151
Lincoln, Abraham: F. Anneke on, 261;
Arbeitervereine on, 261; Belmont on,
259; and Chicago, 253; and
Cincinnati, 252, 255; on Civil War,
8; craftworkers on, 250; and
Emancipation Proclamation, 260,
261; and Frémont, 260; and Illinois,
253; on immigrants, 248; and Irish-
Americans, 251; and Körner, 224–
25, 262; and Missouri, 253; on
naturalization, 249; and New Jersey,
250, 251; and New York City, 251;
newspapers on, 217, 248–49;
Oberkline on, 255; Ottendorfer on,
259; on political parties, 224;
presidential campaigns of, 214, 248,
262; radical democrats on, 250;
Reemelin on, 230; on slavery, 8,
248, 259, 260; and *Turnvereine*,
255; and Wisconsin, 251
Lindauer, Gottfried, 115
Locksmiths. *See* Metalworkers
Longshore workers, 113
Loomis, Samuel Lane, 3
Louisville *Anzeiger* (newspaper), 228
Louisville platform, 102–4, 105–6,
108, 149–50
Lowe, John, 134
Lutheraner, Der (newspaper), 94
Lutherans, 47, 252. *See also* Missouri
Synod; Protestants

Maas, Benjamin, 131
McClellan, George, 259
Machinists, 26–27, 36, 93
McPherson, James M., 8
Maffey, L. A., 115
Mahlke, C. Ludwig, 115, 216
Mallon, Edward, 134
Manufacturers, 56, 60–61, 93
Marx, Karl, 100, 103, 140
Marxists, 99, 101, 142
Märzgefallenen, 36, 37
Masons. *See* Construction workers
Masters: and *Allgemeiner deutscher Arbeiterkongress*, 32, 33, 43, 44; and apprentices, 123; in Artisans' Congress, 42; characteristics of, 23, 24, 30, 31; and class structure, 42; and clothing workers, 24; and cottage industry workers, 24; growth of, 23, 30, 32; and guilds, 24, 42; and journeymen, 31, 38, 43, 122; and merchants, 24; as radical democrats, 46; riots by, 36; and shoemakers, 24; and textile workers, 24; types of, 32
Mechanics, 27
Mechanics' lien law, 136, 141, 187, 220
Mechanics' Mutual Protectives, 159–60
Meier, Caspar, 160
Meier, J. Matthew, 74
Meininger, Charles, 97
Mencken, H. L., 267–68
Menzel, Gottfried, 54–55, 58, 66
Merchants: Büchele on, 61; characteristics of, 23; and class structure, 61; as *Deutschkatholiken*, 49; growth of, 22, 60–61; as immigrants, 17; on Kansas-Nebraska Act, 157; as *Lichtfreunde*, 49; and masters, 24; on political parties, 228; in *Turnvereine*, 93; wages of, 61
Metalworkers: and *Allgemeiner deutscher Arbeiterkongress*, 43; Banfield on, 29; decline of, 76; growth of, 27, 29, 62, 63, 76; and pig iron used, 21; and size of factories, 29, 76; strikes by, 119
Metternich, Klemens von, 35

Meyerhofer, Wilhelm, 164
Middle class, 36–37. *See also* Class consciousness and class structure
Milde (archbishop of Vienna), 94
Millenialism, 50
Milwaukee, Wisconsin: *Association der Social-Reformer* in, 105; clothing workers in, 72–73; cooperative associations in, 117, 135–36; and Douglas, 251; furniture makers in, 76; immigrants in, 2, 58, 64; leatherworkers in, 78; and Lincoln, 251; political parties in, 251; shoemakers in, 70; strikes in, 140; trade unions in, 113; *Turnvereine* in, 256
Milwaukee *Banner und Volksfreund* (newspaper), 228
Milwaukee *Seebote* (newspaper), 228, 238
Miners, 21, 26, 27, 29, 43
Mirari vos (Gregory VI), 47
Missouri Compromise, 153, 213
Missouri Synod, 94, 238. *See also* Lutherans
Mitchell, Robert, 75, 76, 184
Molitor, Stephan: background of, 185; and *Deutsche demokratische Verein*, 186; as intellectual, 184; on Kansas-Nebraska Act, 195, 196; as newspaper editor, 185; on political parties, 224
Monopolies, 101, 151, 164, 234
Montgomery, David, 219
Moor, August, 229
Morwitz, Edward, 229
Münch, Friedrich, 223–24
Mutual benefit societies, 62, 95, 114, 128. *See also* Cooperative associations
Myer, Sebastien, 183

National Demokrat (newspaper), 200, 254
National Era (magazine), 153
National Labor Union (NLU), 269, 270
National Reform Association, 104–5
Nativism. *See* American (Know-

Nothing) party; Immigrants; *specific headings*

Naturalization: *Allgemeine Arbeiterbund* on, 137; *Amerikanische Arbeiterbund* on, 141; Lincoln on, 249; political parties on, 241–42, 246, 248; time involved in, 155, 249; trade unions on, 246; *Turnvereine* on, 246; and voting, 249

Neebe, Oscar, 271

Neu England Zeitung (newspaper), 150, 203

Neue Kölnische Zeitung (newspaper), 171

Neue Zeit (newspaper), 103

Neumann, Gustav A., 161, 227

New York *Abend-Zeitung* (newspaper), 216

New York *Arbeiter* (newspaper), 230–31, 235

New York Association for Improving the Condition of the Poor, 62, 63, 65

New York City: *Amerikanische Arbeiterbund* in, 142; *Arbeitervereine* in, 124, 245–46; *Association der Social-Reformer* in, 105; clothing workers in, 63, 71–72, 117; cooperative associations in, 116, 117; craft organizations in, 126; craftworkers in, 63; demonstrations and riots in, 144, 259; elite in, 160; *Freimännervereine* in, 96; furniture makers in, 63, 64, 74, 76; immigrants in, 2, 58, 63; International Workingmen's Association in, 269; and Kansas-Nebraska Act, 160–69; and Lincoln, 251; lynchings in, 259; political parties in, 216, 236–37, 240, 246, 247, 251; shoemakers in, 63–64, 68, 69, 70; *Sozialistischer Turnerbund* in, 92–93, 256; strikes in, 117, 126–27, 128–35, 139; trade unions in, 113, 269; *Turnvereine* in, 91, 93, 245–46, 256; unemployment in, 80

New York City Industrial Congress, 115, 118, 128, 133, 134

New York Communist Club, 99, 100, 145

New York Daily Times (newspaper): on Civil War, 257; on class structure, 263–64; on immigrants, 65; on industrialization, 263; on Kansas-Nebraska Act, 165; on political parties, 251; on popular sovereignty, 220; on slavery, 220; on strikes, 139; on wages, 80, 139

New York Daily Tribune (newspaper): on *Centralkommission der vereinigten Gewerbe*, 129; on clothing workers, 73; on craftworkers, 66; on food preparers, 80; on immigrants, 4; on Kansas-Nebraska Act, 156, 161, 173; on protective associations, 127; on shoemakers, 68, 69; on slavery, 161; on "Southern work" employers, 129; on *Sozialistischer Turnerbund*, 163

New York Evening Post (newspaper), 156, 165

New York German Society, 105, 112–13, 160

New York Herald (newspaper), 143–44, 165

New York *Katholische Kirchenzeitung* (newspaper), 95

New York *Sociale Republik* (newspaper), 125, 220, 221, 244

New York State, 58, 90, 240

New York *Volks-Tribun* (newspaper), 123, 152

New Yorker Criminal-Zeitung und Belletristisches Journal (newspaper), 161, 216, 244

New Yorker Demokrat (newspaper): background of, 161; editors of, 161, 216; on Kansas-Nebraska Act, 162, 164, 216; on Lincoln, 248–49; on political parties, 216; on temperance laws, 90

New Yorker Staats-Zeitung (newspaper): on communism, 109; competitors of, 161; on Compromise of 1850, 152; conservatism of, 109; on economic liberalism, 108–9; on 1848 Revolution, 83, 86, 87; and elite, 160; influence of, 160–61; on Kansas-Nebraska Act, 157, 162, 165, 169; and liberals, 160–61;

owners and editors of, 109, 160–61, 164, 185; on political parties, 157, 227, 229; on radical democrats, 86, 108–9, 161; on "red republicanism," 109; on slavery, 157–58, 164; on socialism, 109; on strikes, 158; on Wilmot Proviso, 157

Newark, New Jersey: F. and M. Anneke in, 171; *Arbeitervereine* in, 115, 124; *Association der Social-Reformer* in, 105; clothing workers in, 72–73; cooperative associations in, 116, 117; craftworkers in, 170; demonstrations and riots in, 144, 259; and Frémont, 251; immigrants in, 58, 64, 169–70; International Workingmen's Association in, 269; and Kansas-Nebraska Act, 169–80; Kossuth in, 170; leatherworkers in, 79; and Lincoln, 251; political parties in, 216–17, 246, 247, 250–51; *Schneidervereine* in, 131; shoemakers in, 70; and slavery, 172, 179–80; strikes in, 128; trade unions in, 113, 246; *Turnvereine* in, 91, 93, 216, 246, 256

Newark Daily Advertiser (newspaper), 107

Newark *Daily Eagle* (newspaper), 173

Newark Daily Mercury (newspaper), 144, 156, 172, 240–41, 251

Newark *Sentinel of Freedom* (newspaper), 107

Newarker Zeitung (newspaper), 171–72, 214

Nobility, 25, 36, 47

North American Review (magazine), 61, 112

Oberkline, Friedrich, 247, 255, 256

Ottendorfer, Oswald, 109, 227, 259

Pacific Railroad, 188

Paine, Thomas, 93, 106, 223

Painters, 93

Palmer, R. R., 5

Panic of 1847–48, 33

Panic of 1854–55, 80, 119, 142, 143, 215

Panic of 1857, 119, 143, 215, 234, 235

Parker, Cortland, 179

Peasants: and estate system, 36; feudal dues of, 36; growth of, 22; as immigrants, 17; Jacob on, 25–26; and Junkers, 24–25; mortgages of, 36; and Napoleonic Wars, 24; and nobility, 25, 36; and potato blight, 33; taxation of, 36; types of, 22; as unskilled workers, 22, 62; and *Vormärz*, 24; wages of, 22; in working class, 22. *See also* Agrarian population

Pelz, Victor, 114, 235, 236

Pennington, William, 172, 177, 179

Peoria conference, 207

Peoria *Illinois Banner* (newspaper), 157

Peyer, Johannes, 115

Philadelphia, Pennsylvania: *Arbeitervereine* in, 125; *Association der Social-Reformer* in, 105; *Centralkommission der vereinigten Gewerbe* in, 128; cooperative associations in, 116, 117; demonstrations in, 144; *Freimännervereine* in, 96; furniture makers in, 75; immigrants in, 58, 64; International Workingmen's Association in, 269; political parties in, 216; *Schneidervereine* in, 131; shoemakers in, 70; strikes in, 128, 139; trade unions in, 113; *Turnvereine* in, 91, 216, 256; unemployment in, 80, 81; wagonmakers in, 77

Philadelphia *Freie Presse* (newspaper), 87

Philadelphia Trades Convention, 125

Phillips, Wendell, 8

Pierce, Franklin: *Amerikanische Arbeiterbund* on, 151; and immigrants, 151; on Kansas-Nebraska Act, 153, 166, 176, 208; newspapers on, 203; as president, 152; on slavery, 152, 166

Pietists, 47

Pittsburg Republikaner (newspaper), 109

Pittsburgh, Pennsylvania: *Arbeitervereine* in, 120, 125; cooperative associations in, 116, 117; immigrants in, 64; International

Workingmen's Association in, 269; Kossuth in, 87–88; political parties in, 251–52; strikes in, 128, 139–40; trade unions in, 113; *Turnvereine* in, 91, 216

Pittsburgh Gazette (newspaper), 251

Pittsburgh Post (newspaper), 251

Pius IX (pope), 47

Plasterers. *See* Construction workers

Poinier, Horace J., 177

Poland, 46–47

Poor houses, 188

Poppenhausen, Carl, 160

Popular sovereignty, 153, 155, 168, 220, 233

Pösche, Theodore, 87, 110, 224

Potato blight, 33

Price, Ben, 116

Printers and typesetters: and *freie Gemeinden*, 96; journeymen as, 38, 39–40; strikes by, 32, 38, 39–40; in *Turnvereine*, 93; women as, 124

Professionals, 17, 62, 79, 115

Prohibition laws. *See* Temperance laws

Proletarierbund, 100

Protective associations: and *Amerikanische Arbeiterbund*, 141–42; decline of, 143; growth of, 119, 122, 127, 138; members of, 114, 142, 151; and New York City Industrial Congress, 128; newspapers on, 127; and political parties, 151; and solidarity, 131, 138. *See also* Cooperative associations; Trade unions

Protestantische Zeitblätter (newspaper), 96

Protestants: asceticism of, 97; and Catholics, 47, 98–99; conservatism of, 95, 238; and Enlightenment, 47; and Junkers, 47; and nobility, 47; on political parties, 238, 250; Radowitz on, 47–48; and rationalism, 47; and religious disaffection, 48, 95; A. Stephens on, 239. *See also Lichtfreunde;* Lutherans

Proudhon, Pierre-Joseph, 40

Public employment projects, 143, 220, 234

Puchta family, 65

Pugh, George, 199

Purcell, John Baptist, 189, 190

Putting-out workers, 20, 23, 26, 29

Pyne, James, 105

Rader, Maximilian, 85

Radical democrats: in Civil War, 6; decline of, 264; defined, 6; Foner on, 221–22; and Franklin, 106; and *Freimännervereine*, 96; on Fugitive Slave Law, 196, 221–22; and immigrants, 107; and A. Jackson, 101; Körner on, 87, 108; Lieber on, 87; on Lincoln, 250; members of, 46; and monopolies, 101; newspapers on, 86, 87, 108–9, 161; and Paine, 106; and religious groups, 98; and *Revolutions-Vereine*, 85; on slavery, 149, 196, 259; as socialists, 101; and *Turnvereine*, 91; and Washington, 107

Radowitz, Joseph Maria von, 47–48

Railroads, 21, 26, 43, 55, 188

Rammelsberg, Frederick, 75, 76, 111–12, 121–22, 184

Rapp, Wilhelm, 91, 92, 217

Rationalism, 47, 48, 94, 95, 96

Raumer, Frederick von, 55

Reagan, Ronald, 268

Reconstruction, 262, 265–66

"Red republicanism," 109, 142

Reemelin, Charles: background of, 184; on Bell, 230; on Breckinridge, 230; on Civil War, 255–56; on Compromise of 1850, 152, 193, 195; on Douglas, 230; on 1848 Revolution, 87; and German Society, 185; and Hassaurek, 229; on Kansas-Nebraska Act, 193, 195, 196; on Lincoln, 230; on political parties, 229–30; on secession, 254; on slavery, 193, 195, 229; on trade unions, 111

Reform, Die (newspaper), 161

Reformed church, 47. *See also* Protestants

Relief societies, 62, 95, 114, 128. *See also* Cooperative associations

Religious disaffection, 48. *See also specific headings*

Renau, William, 187, 192
Republican party: F. Anneke on, 216,
245, 250, 253; *Arbeitervereine* on,
244, 245–46; Arnold on, 216;
background of, 158; Becker on,
217; Belmont on, 227; Bergquist
on, 247; Bornhard on, 236–37; on
Brown, 222, 248; Browning on,
224; Butz on, 216, 247; and class
structure, 225–26; Douai on, 216,
247; on Douglas, 220; on Dred
Scott case, 248; on Emancipation
Proclamation, 261; Esselen on, 253;
Foner on, 219; Försch on, 216;
Freimännervereine on, 244; Fröbel
on, 216; on Fugitive Slave Law,
221, 247, 248; Greiner on, 217;
Hartmann on, 216; Hecker on, 218,
219; Heinzen on, 216, 247;
Hielscher on, 217, 221, 246;
Hoffmann on, 224, 225; on
homestead laws, 247, 248; Ill on,
217; on immigrants, 239, 240–41,
243, 245–46, 248, 250, 251, 252,
253; F. Jacobi on, 216; on Kansas-
Nebraska Act, 158, 213, 248; Kapp
on, 216, 218–19, 243; and Know-
Nothing party, 239, 240, 252–53;
Kopp on, 216, 247; Körner on,
224, 225, 248; Kreismann on, 225–
26, 248; H. Kreitler on, 216; on
land reform, 220, 246; Lehlbach on,
217; Liebrich on, 216; Lincoln on,
224; Mahlke on, 216; on Missouri
Compromise, 213; Molitor on, 224;
Montgomery on, 219; Münch on,
223–24; on naturalization, 246,
248; newspapers on, 216, 220, 221,
227, 238, 239, 249, 251, 252; Pelz
on, 236; Pösche on, 224; Rapp on,
217; Reemelin on, 229–30; and
religious groups, 238, 239, 240,
250; Schäfer on, 216; Eduard
Schläger on, 216; W. Schlüter on,
216; Schmitt on, 216; Schnauffer
on, 217; G. Schneider on, 216;
Schünemann-Pott on, 216; Schurz
on, 226, 265; on secession, 248,
253, 254; Seidensticker on, 224; on
slavery, 2, 213–14, 217, 220, 221,
222, 239, 242, 245, 246, 247, 248,
250, 253, 259–60, 262; D. Smith
on, 9; *Socialer Arbeiterverein* on, 221;
Stallo on, 224; Struve on, 219; on
Sunday laws, 240, 243, 250, 252,
253; on tariffs, 220, 246, 247, 248;
on temperance laws, 239–40, 243,
245, 252; Trumbull on, 224;
Turnvereine on, 216, 225, 244,
245–46; on Two-Year Amendment,
244; and urban voters, 253; on
voting, 241; P. Wagner on, 216;
Weydemeyer on, 248; and working
class, 250
Republik der Arbeiter (newspaper), 118,
124, 135, 161
Revolutions-Vereine, 84–85, 86
Richter, Erhard: as activist, 116; on
Kansas-Nebraska Act, 162, 163,
164, 165–66; on political parties,
151
Richter, Heinrich, 115
Robert Blum Society, 171
Rödel, Peter, 89, 115, 143, 219, 220
Rödter, Heinrich, 184–85, 186, 229
Ronge, Johannes, 50
Roos, Leonhard, 171, 173, 175, 176
Rosecrans, William S., 259
Rosenstein (liberal), 167
Rosenthal, Wilhelm, 115, 230
Rotteck, Karl von, 19
Rumpler, George, 95
Ryckman, Lewis B., 136

Sabbatarian laws. *See* Sunday laws
Saddlemakers, 62, 77–79
St. Louis, Missouri: *Association der
Social-Reformer* in, 105;
*Centralkommission der vereinigten
Gewerbe* in, 128; cooperative
associations in, 116, 117;
Freimännervereine in, 96; immigrants
in, 2, 63, 64; International
Workingmen's Association in, 269;
Schneidervereine in, 132; strikes in,
128; trade unions in, 113;
Turnvereine in, 91; unemployment
in, 81
St. Louis *Anzeiger des Westens*
(newspaper), 248

Sanderson, John P., 107, 108
Sauer (carpenter), 132, 133
Schäfer, G., 216
Schaff, Philip, 94, 95, 112
Schiff, Charles, 118
Schläger, Eduard: on
  "Americanization," 264; on Brown,
  222; on Kansas-Nebraska Act, 203,
  204; and Körner, 203; in National
  Labor Union, 269, 270; as
  newspaper editor, 115, 203; on
  political parties, 216; at Wheeling
  conference, 203
Schlüter, Hermann, 271
Schlüter, Wilhelm, 166, 216
Schmidt, Ernst, 115
Schmitt, Nikolaus, 96, 216
Schnauffer, Carl Heinrich, 217
Schneider, George, 156, 200, 203, 207,
  216
Schneider, Joseph, 37
Schneidervereine, 131–32
Schöffner, Emil, 170, 173, 175, 176
Schreinervereine, 127
Schroder, M., 114
Schultz, A., 115
Schünnemann-Pott, Friedrich, 216
Schurz, Carl: on army, 266; on
  Bismarck, 266; conservatism of, 265,
  266; on constitutional monarchy,
  37; on economic liberalism, 110,
  265; on free blacks, 265–66; on
  French Revolution, 5; and Godkin,
  269; on immigrants, 53, 82, 90,
  266, 268; and Kinkel, 110, 265; on
  political parties, 226, 228, 265; on
  Reconstruction, 265–66; on
  secession, 254; as secretary of the
  interior, 266; wealth of, 90; on
  work hours, 266
Schwab, Gustav, 160
Schwenck, Nikolaus, 66, 81, 89
Secession, 248, 253–55
Seeman, H., 137
Seidensticker, George, 224
Seiler, Sebastian, 100, 145
Seligman brothers, 160
Serfs, 24–25
Seward, William, 240
Shalk, Adolph and Herman, 229

Sherman, "Dutch Bill" and "Dutch
  Henry," 208–9
Shoemakers: and centralization, 69, 70;
  Cist on, 70; in cooperative
  associations, 40, 117; Dawley on,
  69; in factories, 69, 71; growth of,
  62, 63–64, 68, 69, 70; housing of,
  69–70; and industrialization, 69;
  and masters, 24; newspapers on, 68,
  69; and nominal masters, 32; and
  size of factories, 69, 71; and
  solidarity, 132; in trade unions,
  114–15; unemployment of, 68–69;
  wages of, 69, 70; women as, 70, 71;
  Young on, 70. *See also* Clothing
  workers
Short, George, 130
Sigel, Franz, 91
Skilled workers. *See* Craftworkers
Slavery: *Allgemeine Arbeiterbund von
  Nord-Amerika* on, 221; F. Anneke
  on, 214, 245; *Arbeitervereine* on,
  260; Belmont on, 227; Bondi on,
  208–9; Breckinridge on, 230;
  Brodhead on, 155; Brown on, 8;
  Buchanan on, 227, 228; Büchele on,
  150; Cass on, 152; Cincinnati
  platform on, 188; craftworkers on,
  10, 216; Crittenden on, 253; Douai
  on, 217; Douglas on, 152, 183;
  Douglass on, 8; Dred Scott case on,
  221; Esselen on, 244–45; Evans on,
  151; Försch on, 167–68; Frémont
  on, 260; Fries on, 194–95; Hecker
  on, 219, 236, 242; Heinzen on,
  149; Hoffmann on, 203, 205;
  immigrants on, 9; intelligentsia on,
  158; J. P. Jackson on, 179; Kansas-
  Nebraska Act on, 151, 153, 154–
  55, 159, 164; Kapp on, 218, 242;
  Kellner on, 167; Körner on, 201–2;
  Kriege on, 151–52; Lincoln on, 8,
  248, 259, 260; Louisville platform
  on, 149, 150; Marxists on, 101; and
  Missouri Compromise, 153; and
  Newark, 172, 179–80; newspapers
  on, 152, 156, 157–58, 161, 164,
  172, 193–94, 197, 203, 220, 222,
  228, 231, 238–39, 242, 244; Parker
  on, 179; Pennington on, 172;

Peoria conference on, 207; Phillips on, 8; Pierce on, 152, 166; political parties on, 2, 150, 151, 213–14, 217, 220, 221, 222, 233, 234, 236, 237–38, 239, 242, 245, 246, 247, 248, 250, 253, 259–60, 262; radical democrats on, 149, 196, 259; Reemelin on, 193, 195, 229; religious groups on, 238–39; Rosenstein on, 167; G. Schneider on, 156; *Socialer Arbeiterverein* on, 221; *Sozialistischer Turnerbund* on, 150, 157, 163; A. Stephens on, 239; Struve on, 217, 219, 242; Sylvis on, 254; trade unions on, 246; *Turnvereine* on, 246; Vocke on, 156; Willich on, 223; and working class, 9. *See also* Emancipation Proclamation; Free blacks; Fugitive Slave Law

Smith, Adam, 39

Smith, Donnal V., 9

Social classes. *See* Class consciousness and class structure

Socialer Arbeiterverein, 221

Socialism, 5, 101–2, 109, 270–71

Sorge, Friedrich A., 4–5, 100, 269

Sozialistischer Turnerbund: and *Amerikanische Arbeiterbund*, 142; background of, 91; characteristics of, 93; convention of, 150; growth of, 91–92; on Kansas-Nebraska Act, 163, 165; members of, 91–93; newspapers on, 95, 163; on political parties, 150; purposes of, 91; religious groups on, 95; on slavery, 150, 157, 163; on socialism, 101–2; and solidarity, 131

Spies, August, 271

Stallo, Johann, 184, 185, 196, 224

Stampp, Kenneth, 253

Steam engines, 26, 27, 28

Steamboats, 55

Steffen, F., 115, 137

Steffens, Edward, 97, 190–91

Steinway, Henry, 160

Stephens, Alexander, 239

Stephens, Uriah, 254

Stoppelbein, Philip, 115

Strauss, David, 49

Strikes: causes of, 119, 120–21, 126–27, 129, 138, 139, 140; characteristics of, 120; growth of, 38, 119–20, 138–42, 144, 269; newspapers on, 118, 139, 158; and solidarity, 139–40. *See also specific headings*

Struve, Gustav: as activist, 46, 50; and *Allgemeine Arbeiterbund von Nord-Amerika*, 125, 145; on economics, 45; as newspaper editor, 161; on political parties, 219, 242; on religion, 93; on slavery, 217, 219, 242; and *Sozialistischer Turnerbund*, 91, 93; and *Turnvereine*, 91

Suffrage. *See* Elections and voting

Sunday laws: *Allgemeine Arbeiterbund* on, 137; *Allgemeine Arbeiterbund von Nord-Amerika* on, 145; *Amerikanische Arbeiterbund* on, 141; F. Anneke on, 90; Cincinnati platform on, 187, 188; craftworkers on, 89–90; *Freimännervereine* on, 99; growth of, 98; Heinisch on, 109; Hundertpfund on, 109; political parties on, 151, 240, 243, 250, 252, 253; purposes of, 98; trade unions on, 246; *Turnvereine* on, 246

Syllabus Errorum (Pius IX), 47

Sylvis, William, 254, 263

Tailors. *See* Clothing workers

Tanners, 62, 77–79

Tariffs, 43, 220, 246, 247, 248

Taverns, 59–60

Taxation: of agrarian workers, 36; *Allgemeine Arbeiterbund von Nord-Amerika* on, 145; and *Allgemeiner deutscher Arbeiterkongress*, 43; and elite, 24; of nominal masters, 32, 33; of peasants, 36; purposes of, 24

Taylor, George Rogers, 62

Temperance laws: *Allgemeine Arbeiterbund von Nord-Amerika* on, 145; *Amerikanische Arbeiterbund* on, 141; F. Anneke on, 90, 245; craftworkers on, 89–90; enforcement of, 90; *Freimännervereine* on, 99; growth of, 98; Heinisch on, 109;

Hundertpfund on, 109; newspapers on, 90; political parties on, 151, 239–40, 243, 245, 252; purposes of, 98; *Turnvereine* on, 244

Textile workers: cooperative associations of, 40; growth of, 21, 26, 27, 28, 29; and industrialization, 28; and masters, 24; and nominal masters, 32; strikes by, 119; and *Vormärz*, 26

Thirteenth Amendment, 262. *See also* Slavery

Thompson, E. P., 6

Thum, Augustus, 115, 164

Toaspern, Hermann, 115, 151

Tocqueville, Alexis de, 56, 97–98

Trade unions: on banks, 220; and Benque, 230; Chicago German Society on, 112; and Civil War, 258; decline of, 143, 215; and education, 113; growth of, 113, 127, 144, 215, 258, 269; and Haymarket affair, 269; on homestead laws, 246; and insurance, 113; on land reform, 104, 105, 220; and leisure activities, 113; Lieber on, 111; members of, 4–5, 32, 38, 101, 114–16, 124, 235; on naturalization, 246; New York German Society on, 113; newspapers on, 127; and panic of 1854–55, 143, 215; and panic of 1857, 143, 215; on political parties, 246; Rammelsberg on, 111–12, 121–22; Reemelin on, 111; Rosecrans on, 259; Schaff on, 112; on slavery, 246; and solidarity, 125, 142; on Sunday laws, 246; suppression of, 258–59; types of, 113–14; Weitling on, 114, 124, 136–37; on work hours, 269. *See also* Protective associations; *specific trade unions*

Trumbull, Lyman, 224

Turnvereine: background of, 91; on Bates, 246; on Brown, 222; characteristics of, 91, 93–94; in Civil War, 256, 258; and class structure, 93, 265; on homestead laws, 246; on A. Johnson, 262; on Kansas-Nebraska Act, 208; on land reform, 105; and Lincoln, 255;

members of, 91, 92, 93–94, 114, 116, 203, 271; name change of, 265; nationalism of, 91; on naturalization, 246; and Paine, 93; on political parties, 91, 94, 216, 225, 244, 245–46; purposes of, 91; rationalism of, 94; on Reconstruction, 262; on secession, 255; on slavery, 246; on Sunday laws, 246; on temperance laws, 244. *See also specific Turnvereine*

Turn-Zeitung (newspaper), 161, 217, 218, 222

Twentieth (United Turner Rifles) Regiment, 256

Two-Year Amendment, 241, 244

Typesetters. *See* Printers and typesetters

Uhl, Jakob, 84

Uhlich, Leberecht, 49, 50

Unions. *See* Trade unions

Union-shop agreements, 121–22

United German Democratic Central Committee, 161

United States: economy of, 55, 81–82; as model for new Germany, 85–86; occupations in, 273–75; population of, 55–56; size of, 55; wages in, 275. *See also specific headings*

United Trade and Laborers' Organization of Allegheny County, 125

Unskilled workers: and charitable and relief societies, 62; and class structure, 62; growth of, 26, 62; peasants as, 22, 62; on political parties, 250; strikes by, 139; types of, 62, 77, 78; urbanization of, 26; women as, 62

Urbanek, Anthony, 94–95

Urbanization: and beer gardens, wine gardens, and taverns, 59; of cigarmakers, 79; and class structure, 60–61; of craftworkers, 26; growth of, 26, 57, 58, 59, 263; of unskilled workers, 26

Vale, Gilbert, 136

Van Buren, Martin, 152

Vecchioni, August, 115, 167

Verein freier Männer, 96
Verein freier Menschen, 217
Verein für geistige Aufklärung und sociale Reform, 96
Vereinigte Protektivunion der Schneider, 128–29, 134
Verlag sector workers, 20, 23, 26, 29
Vocke, William, 156
Vogel, George, 115
Volk, Das (newspaper), 41
Volksbund für die alte und neue Welt, 86, 171
Voting. *See* Elections and voting

Wagner, Jakob, 114
Wagner, Philip, 203, 216
Wagner, Wilhelm, 230
Wagonmakers, 27, 76–77
Walker (attorney), 192–93
Walker, George, 97
Wallis, George, 63
Walther, C. F. W., 94
Ward, Marcus L., 177
Wartz, Frederick, 130–31
Weavers. *See* Textile workers
Weed, Thurlow, 240
Weekly Chicago Democrat (newspaper), 208
"Weihnachts riot," 188–91
Weil, Henry, 160
Weitling, Wilhelm: and *Allgemeine Arbeiterbund von Nord-Amerika,* 137; and M. Anneke, 124; and *Centralkommission der vereinigten Gewerbe,* 127, 135, 137; and cooperative associations, 40, 117–19, 135, 137; and craftworkers, 50; and Lievre, 116; and millenialism, 50; as newspaper editor, 161; on political parties, 141; and Seiler, 100; on solidarity, 122; on strikes, 118–19; and trade unions, 114, 124, 136–37; on women's rights, 124; and Workers' Brotherhood, 137
Weydemeyer, Joseph: and *Amerikanische Arbeiterbund,* 124–25, 140–41, 142; on class consciousness and class structure, 141, 215; and Engels, 264; on industrialization, 100; on

Kansas-Nebraska Act, 164; on land reform, 141; and Marx, 140; in New York Communist Club, 100; as newspaper publisher, 161; on political parties, 215, 248; in trade unions, 115; on working class, 100–101, 102
Wheeling conference, 86, 176, 203
Whigs, 2, 213
White-collar workers, 93
Whitney, Thomas R., 5, 108, 112
Wichern, Johann Hinrich, 49
Wiener, Theodore, 208
Wiest, Gottlieb F., 115, 187, 196
Wilhelm I (king of Prussia and German emperor), 264–65
Willich, August: on army, 41; on Brown, 223; in Civil War, 256; on class structure, 215; as communist, 102; on education, 41; on freedom of speech, press, and association, 41; on immigrants, 126; imprisonment of, 42; in New York Communist Club, 100; on political parties, 215, 223; on slavery, 223; in *Turnvereine,* 91; on voting, 41; on wages, 41; on work hours, 41
Wilmot Proviso, 157, 167
Windmüller, Jakob, 84, 162
Wire workers. *See* Metalworkers
Wislicenus, G. A., 48–49, 50
Wittke, Carl, 7, 189
Wolff, Wilhelm, 100
Women and women's rights: *Allgemeine Arbeiterbund von Nord-Amerika* on, 125, 145; and M. Anneke, 103, 124; as apprentices, 123; as cigarmakers, 79; as clothing workers, 71, 72, 73; as craftworkers, 124; as *Deutschkatholiken,* 48; discrimination against, 123–24, 125; in *Frauenvereine,* 125; as *Lichtfreunde,* 48; and Louisville platform, 103; newspapers on, 123, 124, 125; as rationalists, 48; as shoemakers, 70, 71; in trade unions, 124; as typesetters, 124; as unskilled workers, 62; wages of, 70, 73; and Weitling, 124
Wood, Fernando, 234

Woodworkers, 29, 62
Woolen goods workers. *See* Textile
  workers
Work-book system, 42, 44
Workers' Brotherhood, 137
Workers' clubs, 37, 38. *See also specific
  workers' clubs*
Workingmen's movements, 104

World War I, 267

Yarn workers. *See* Textile workers
Young, Edward, 70

Ziegler, David, 183
Zotz, Alois, 200

A Note on the Author

Bruce Levine is a member of the history department at the University of Cincinnati and the former director of research and writing for the American Social History Project at the City University of New York. He has also taught at Columbia University and Wayne State University. His other publications include *Half Slave and Half Free: The Roots of Civil War* (1992) and the first volume of *Who Built America? Working People and the Nation's Economy, Politics, Culture and Society* (1989), of which he is the principal author.

Books in the Series
The Working Class in American History

Worker City, Company Town:
Iron and Cotton-Worker Protest in Troy
and Cohoes, New York, 1855–84
Daniel J. Walkowitz

Life, Work, and Rebellion in the Coal Fields:
The Southern West Virginia Miners, 1880–1922
David Alan Corbin

Women and American Socialism, 1870–1920
Mari Jo Buhle

Lives of Their Own:
Blacks, Italians, and Poles in Pittsburgh, 1900–1960
John Bodnar, Roger Simon, and Michael P. Weber

Working-Class America:
Essays on Labor, Community, and American Society
Edited by Michael H. Frisch and Daniel J. Walkowitz

Eugene V. Debs: Citizen and Socialist
Nick Salvatore

American Labor and Immigration History, 1877–1920s:
Recent European Research
Edited by Dirk Hoerder

Workingmen's Democracy:
The Knights of Labor and American Politics
Leon Fink

The Electrical Workers:
A History of Labor at General Electric
and Westinghouse, 1923–60
Ronald W. Schatz

The Mechanics of Baltimore:
Workers and Politics in the Age of Revolution, 1763–1812
Charles G. Steffen

The Practice of Solidarity:
American Hat Finishers in the Nineteenth Century
David Bensman

The Labor History Reader
Edited by Daniel J. Leab

Solidarity and Fragmentation:
Working People and Class Consciousness in Detroit, 1875–1900
Richard Oestreicher

Counter Cultures:
Saleswomen, Managers, and Customers
in American Department Stores, 1890–1940
Susan Porter Benson

The New England Working Class and the New Labor History
Edited by Herbert G. Gutman and Donald H. Bell

Labor Leaders in America
Edited by Melvyn Dubofsky and Warren Van Tine

Barons of Labor:
The San Francisco Building Trades
and Union Power in the Progressive Era
Michael Kazin

Gender at Work:
The Dynamics of Job Segregation by Sex during World War II
Ruth Milkman

Once a Cigar Maker:
Men, Women, and Work Culture in American
Cigar Factories, 1900–1919
Patricia A. Cooper

A Generation of Boomers:
The Pattern of Railroad Labor Conflict
in Nineteenth-Century America
Shelton Stromquist

Work and Community in the Jungle:
Chicago's Packinghouse Workers, 1894–1922
James R. Barrett

Workers, Managers, and Welfare Capitalism: The Shoeworkers
and Tanners of Endicott Johnson, 1890–1950
Gerald Zahavi

Men, Women, and Work: Class, Gender, and Protest
in the New England Shoe Industry, 1780–1910
Mary Blewett

Workers on the Waterfront:
Seamen, Longshoremen, and Unionism in the 1930s
Bruce Nelson

German Workers in Chicago:
A Documentary History of Working-Class Culture
from 1850 to World War I
Edited by Hartmut Keil and John B. Jentz

On the Line:
Essays in the History of Auto Work
Edited by Nelson Lichtenstein and Stephen Meyer III

Upheaval in the Quiet Zone:
A History of Hospital Workers' Union, Local 1199
Leon Fink and Brian Greenberg

Labor's Flaming Youth:
Telephone Operators and Worker Militancy, 1878–1923
Stephen H. Norwood

Another Civil War:
Labor, Capital, and the State
in the Anthracite Regions of Pennsylvania,
1840–68
Grace Palladino

Coal, Class, and Color:
Blacks in Southern West Virginia, 1915–32
Joe William Trotter, Jr.

For Democracy, Workers, and God:
Labor Song-Poems and Labor Protest, 1865–95
Clark D. Halker

Dishing It Out: Waitresses and Their
Unions in the Twentieth Century
Dorothy Sue Cobble

Working Women of Collar City: Gender, Class,
and Community in Troy, 1864–86
Carole Turbin

The Spirit of 1848:
German Immigrants, Labor Conflict, and the Coming
of the Civil War
Bruce Levine